ANTITRUST LAW

AND

ECONOMICS

IN A NUTSHELL

FOURTH EDITION

By

ERNEST GELLHORN
Attorney—Jones, Day, Reavis & Pogue
former T. Munford Boyd Professor of Law,
University of Virginia; Dean, Case Western
Reserve University

WILLIAM E. KOVACIC
Professor of Law
George Mason University School of Law
and Of Counsel Bryan Cave

WEST GROUP
A THOMSON COMPANY

ST. PAUL, MINN.
1994

Nutshell Series, In a Nutshell, the Nutshell Logo and the West Group symbol are registered trademarks used herein under license.

COPYRIGHT © 1976, 1981, 1986 WEST PUBLISHING CO.
COPYRIGHT © 1994 By WEST PUBLISHING CO.

> 610 Opperman Drive
> P.O. Box 64526
> St. Paul, MN 55164–0526
> 1–800–328–9352

All rights reserved
Printed in the United States of America

Library of Congress Cataloging-in-Publication Data

Gellhorn, Ernest.
  Antitrust law and economics in a nutshell / by Ernest Gellhorn, William E. Kovacic. — 4th ed.
     p.   cm. — (Nutshell series)
  Includes index.
  ISBN 0–314–02683–5
  1. Antitrust law—United States.   2. Antitrust law—Economic aspects—United States.   I. Kovacic, William E.   II. Title. III. Series
KF1652.G44   1994
343.73 ' 0721—dc20
[347.303721]   94–20209
                                                  CIP

ISBN 0–314–02683–5

TEXT IS PRINTED ON 10% POST CONSUMER RECYCLED PAPER

5th Reprint — 2001

PREFACE

The fourth edition of this text continues to pursue the goal that guided its predecessors–to provide a basic understanding of the legal and economic principles that govern modern antitrust practice. As with earlier editions, we seek to give students and practitioners a reliable guide to the antitrust landscape they will confront in the coming years. A brief tour through recent antitrust history indicates that the tasks of defining the existing equilibrium of antitrust doctrine and predicting its future location remain elusive and difficult.

The past few decades present striking contrasts in doctrine and enforcement policy. This era embraces two notably dissimilar periods of analysis. In 1962, the Supreme Court decided Brown Shoe Co. v. United States (1962), which held that a merger between two firms accounting for five percent of total industry output violated the principal antimerger provision of the antitrust laws. In doing so, the Court laid the foundation for an antitrust jurisprudence that often subordinated economic efficiency to the decentralization of social, political, and economic power. In the ten years between *Brown Shoe* and United States v. Topco Associates, Inc. (1972), which forbade an allocation of territories adopted as part of the operation of a joint purchasing cooperative, the Court adopted a hostile view of mergers and vertical contractual restrictions and used brightline, per se tests expansively to prohibit questioned conduct. This trend crested in United States v. Arnold, Schwinn & Co. (1967), where the Court ruled that nonprice vertical restraints were per se illegal. Relying mainly on antiquated concepts of title applied in property or sales law, *Schwinn* concluded that vertical market division agreements "are so obviously destructive of competition that their mere existence is enough" to warrant condemnation.

But the contesting forces in antitrust are never at rest. Thus, it was only a few years later, in United States v. General Dynamics Corp. (1974) (rejecting challenge to horizontal merger predicated on the parties' combined share of historical output) that the tide of robust interventionism began to ebb, followed shortly in Brunswick Corp. v. Pueblo Bowl-O-Mat, Inc. (1977) and Continental T.V., Inc. v. GTE Sylvania (1977) by a massive sea change. In its holding and outlook, *Sylvania* quickly became the most important case in the post-World War II era. *Sylvania* repudiated *Schwinn's* rule of per se illegality for nonprice vertical restraints and abandoned the indifference or hostility to efficiency that marked many Warren Court antitrust decisions. In subjecting nonprice restraints to rule of reason analysis, *Sylvania* gave decisive effect to transaction cost theories that emphasized the efficiency gains from vertical contractual restrictions. Although it did not discard other analytical tools, *Sylvania* gave primacy to economic analysis—particularly price theory—in formulating and applying antitrust rules.

If *Sylvania* is antitrust's modern Everest, then *Brunswick* is its K2—overshadowed by a more conspicuous neighbor, but barely less impressive a landmark. In a powerful doctrinal and symbolic departure from *Brown Shoe's* egalitarian antitrust philosophy, *Brunswick* provided the much-quoted declaration that the antitrust laws "were enacted for the 'protection of competition, not competitors.'"[1] By this aphorism, the Court encumbered private antitrust litigants with the formidable requirement that they prove "antitrust injury" and discarded the view that the demise of individual firms necessarily harmed the competitive process.

1. *Brunswick* quoted the phrase "competition, not competitors" from the Court's *Brown Shoe* merger decision. As discussed in Chapter 2 below, this language appears twice in *Brown Shoe*. In the first instance, the phrase is unqualified; in the second, the Court added that the Clayton Act's antimerger provision sought to preserve small business as an end in itself. *Brunswick* invoked the first, unqualified mention of the phrase—a choice that bespoke a retreat from the social and political decentralization goal embodied in the second reference.

PREFACE

In the spirit of *Sylvania* and *Brunswick*, most (but not all) of the Court's subsequent decisions have narrowed antitrust's reach. Occasionally the Court has accomplished this result by adopting more permissive liability standards. See, e.g., Northwest Wholesale Stationers, Inc. v. Pacific Stationery & Printing Co. (1985) (narrowing the circumstances in which group refusals to deal can be summarily condemned). More frequently, retrenchment has occurred through the strengthening of evidentiary, injury, and standing requirements that antitrust plaintiffs must satisfy. See, e.g., Monsanto Co. v. Spray-Rite Corp. (1984) (ruling that proof of a sequence consisting of complaints from retailers to a manufacturer followed by the manufacturer's termination of a disfavored retailer fails, without more, to establish a vertical agreement to maintain resale prices). Some Warren–era precedents (such as *Schwinn*) have collapsed, yet many others remain standing, even though they rest on dubious analysis and afford protection only to private litigants who first satisfy daunting antitrust injury and standing requirements.

When the previous edition of this text appeared in 1986, the more permissive philosophy embodied in *Sylvania* and *Brunswick* had deeply influenced the federal antitrust enforcement agencies and the courts. During Ronald Reagan's presidency, the Department of Justice and the Federal Trade Commission adopted a rigorously-focused efficiency orientation and used their resources almost exclusively to prosecute horizontal output restrictions and large horizontal mergers. By 1986, efficiency-based analysis had gained broad acceptance in the federal courts. With rare exceptions such as Aspen Skiing Co. v. Aspen Highlands Skiing Corp. (1985) (condemning a monopolist's unjustified refusal to continue to deal with a rival), Supreme Court decisions continued to erode the legacy of *Brown Shoe* and its progeny by retreating from reliance on per se standards and bolstering evidentiary and procedural biases against intervention. In Matsushita Electrical Industrial Co. v. Zenith Radio Corp. (1986), the Court endorsed a district court's summary dismissal of allegations that a collection of Japanese television manufacturers had engaged in a twenty-year long conspiracy to price their products below cost in the United States and drive American electronics equipment manufacturers out of business. In the Court's strongest testament to nonintervention in the 1980s, *Matsushita* treated predatory pricing claims skeptically and encouraged recourse to summary judgment to dismiss claims that rested on ambiguous circumstantial evidence or lacked "economic rationality." From academia, the theory of contestable markets (which posited the sufficiency of competition in markets occupied by a single firm so long as entry and exit conditions permitted hit-and-run attacks by other companies) had expanded the circumstances in which courts and enforcement officials would regard even highly concentrated markets as susceptible to entry and thus subject to effective competitive discipline.

The permissive philosophy of *Sylvania* and *Brunswick* remains powerful, but a continued narrowing of antitrust doctrine and policy is less certain today than it was in 1986. Intervening developments have complicated the picture in several ways. First, numerous commentators have challenged the view (implicit in *Sylvania* and *Brunswick*) that antitrust's central (if not exclusive) appropriate aim is to enhance economic efficiency.[2] These views have been accepted in lower court decisions such as McGahee v. Northern Propane Gas Co. (1988) (reversing dismissal of predatory pricing allegations) which embrace a multidimensional goals structure reminiscent of *Brown Shoe*. Non-efficiency concerns are not a dominant theme of modern antitrust jurisprudence, but they remain a potentially important undercurrent in many litigated disputes.

Second, there is an expanding economics literature which suggests that efficiency concerns, properly evaluated,

---

2. See John J. Flynn, *The Reagan Administration's Antitrust Policy, "Original Intent" and the Legislative History of the Sherman Act*, 33 Antitrust Bull. 259 (1988) (discussing non-efficiency goals literature).

dictate tighter antitrust controls on conduct such as vertical restraints, leveraging, and dominant firm pricing, product development, and investment conduct.[3] The redirection of antitrust liability standards accomplished by *Sylvania* and later cases had followed substantially from judicial acceptance of "Chicago School" perspectives reflected in treatises such as Robert Bork's *Antitrust Paradox* (1978) and Richard Posner's *Antitrust Law* (1976). Since the late 1970s, many researchers have reexamined Chicago School orthodoxy and, using tools such as game theory and information economics, have sought to disprove assumptions underpinning Chicago's austere enforcement prescriptions. Several recent judicial decisions show signs of heeding the pro-enforcement implications of this literature, and the history of antitrust policy suggests that future significant instances of absorption are likely.

The possibilities for a reassessment of Chicago precepts are most evident in Eastman Kodak Co. v. Image Technical Services, Inc. (1992). In *Kodak*, the Supreme Court sustained the Ninth Circuit's reversal of summary judgment against claims that a manufacturer of copiers unlawfully had tied the sale of service for its machines to the sale of replacement parts. The Court rejected Kodak's argument that its lack of market power in copiers precluded substantial competitive harm, as purchasers could account for service policies when bargaining with rival suppliers of original equipment. After warning about the dangers of relying on economic theory as a substitute for examining "actual market realities," the Court cited various economic authorities for the view that Kodak could inflict competitive harm by exploiting imperfections in the ability of some purchasers to obtain and act on information relating to lifecycle service costs. *Kodak* indicates doubts about giving decisive effect to

3. See, e.g., Janusz A. Ordover & Garth Saloner, *Predation, Monopolization, and Antitrust*, in 1 Handbook of Industrial Organization 537 (Richard Schmalensee & Robert D. Willig eds. 1989) (discussing economic literature favoring closer scrutiny of single-firm behavior).

economic theory in a limited factual framework, and it suggests how "post-Chicago" economics may lead courts to sustain theories of competitive harm that the Chicago School disregarded.

Third, public enforcement officials at the federal and state levels have embraced antitrust programs that surpass the Reagan Administration's restrictive antitrust agenda. In the late 1980s, state governments attacked mergers and distribution practices that the Reagan antitrust agencies deemed benign or procompetitive. Such efforts received powerful support from the Supreme Court in California v. American Stores Co. (1990), which upheld the ability of state governments to obtain divestiture to remedy antitrust violations such as illegal mergers. In April 1992, the Bush Administration issued enforcement guidelines that seek to overcome recent, judicially-imposed limits on merger enforcement and to apply the U.S. antitrust laws extraterritorially on grounds other than the consumer welfare standard that animated Reagan-era policy. And the Clinton Administration is striving to expand enforcement beyond frontiers established by the Bush antitrust enforcement agencies.

Fourth, in decisions such as Federal Trade Commission v. Superior Court Trial Lawyers Ass'n (1990), the Supreme Court occasionally has strayed from a path that foreshadowed abandonment of the sharp historical dichotomy between rule of reason and per se offenses.[4] The Court reversed a court of appeals ruling that applied a rule of reason standard to an agreement by a group of attorneys to refuse to accept cases involving indigent criminal defendants unless the District of Columbia government increased the fees for such cases. Unlike several earlier cases since the late 1970s, *Superior Court Trial Lawyers* emphatically reasserted the dichotomy between per se and reasonable-

---

4. See also Palmer v. BRG, Inc. (1990) (citing, without elaboration, *Topco* for the proposition that agreements between competitors to allocate sales territories are illegal per se).

ness inquiries and displayed little recognition that the boundary between the two forms of analysis is often indistinct.

Finally, the Supreme Court in recent years largely has avoided wrestling with substantive liability rules and has focused mainly on evidentiary and procedural requirements. This has undermined, but not extinguished, the ability of private litigants to invoke expansive precedents from the 1960s and early 1970s. Much criticized (but not overruled) decisions such as United States v. Von's Grocery Co. (1966) (forbidding a merger between two grocery chains accounting for 7.5 percent of retail grocery sales in metropolitan Los Angeles) remain fair game for litigants to cite as bases for applying broad liability standards.[5]

Collectively, these developments present important challenges to or qualifications of the comparatively narrow enforcement approaches dictated by *Sylvania*, *Brunswick*, and their progeny. Thus, antitrust today remains in transition. Amid the recent evolution of legal doctrine, public enforcement perspectives, and academic commentary, the principal task of this volume remains the same: to provide a critical examination of antitrust law. Although the basic approach of previous editions has been preserved, developments in recent years have dictated some changes in coverage and emphasis.

The fourth edition's exposition of antitrust's legal framework gives increased attention to the expanded role of evidentiary standards and procedural screens in determining litigation outcomes, and to the tension between per se tests and reasonableness standards. This edition also treats recent revisions of public enforcement guidelines for mergers and addresses their relationship to existing case law. Fuller coverage of immunity-related doctrines also appears,

---

5. In Hospital Corp. of Am. v. FTC (1986), Judge Richard Posner examined the Supreme Court's horizontal merger jurisprudence (including *Von's Grocery*) since the early 1960s and observed that "[n]one of these decisions has been overruled."

as the Supreme Court has devoted unusual energy in recent years to examining the antitrust significance of government intervention (and attempts to solicit such intervention) in the economy. To indicate how recent case law and commentary are likely to affect the future equilibrium of antitrust doctrine, current trends in law and policy are placed in their historical context.

The fourth edition continues its predecessors' focus on economics in introducing the antitrust newcomer to the law's framework and operation. In using economic analysis to illuminate antitrust case law, we frequently have made simplifying assumptions and excluded technical justifications. Admittedly, neither is irrelevant, and this text can only serve as a beginning. The notion that economic analysis should play an integral role in devising and applying antitrust legal standards is no longer remarkable. So pervasive is economic analysis is antitrust adjudication and policymaking that familiarity with basic industrial organization concepts is indispensable. Current debate deals less with the appropriate role for economic analysis than with the choice among rival economic models for evaluating business conduct. This text does not espouse exotic new economic ideas or theories; instead, it focuses on generally accepted economic doctrine and applies widely accepted concepts to antitrust. Where significant differing or emerging views appear in thoughtful antitrust cases or commentary, we have sought to present those positions with clarifying observations. Our goal is to acquaint the reader with economic ideas that now have wide currency in the courts and enforcement agencies or promise to have a major impact in the coming years.

The ongoing reformulation and refinement of legal theories and economic hypotheses place progressively greater demands on the antitrust student and practitioner. More than ever, mastery of antitrust demands the skills of the legal technician, the economist, the historian, and the political scientist. The ambiguity and uncertain direction of spe-

PREFACE

cific doctrines pose vexing analytical challenges, but they stem from economic, political, and social adjustments that give antitrust continuing relevance and intellectual vitality. Indeed, attempts to define antitrust's core principles and distill its critical insights proceed with unequalled urgency today.

For most of this century, antitrust mainly has been the parochial concern of the United States and a handful of countries in Western Europe. Competition policy now commands a much broader audience. Although shaped somewhat differently, antitrust plays a key role in the European Community. Canada has given antitrust an expanded role, and Japan has begun more serious enforcement efforts in response to intense U.S. political pressure. The discrediting of central planning has inspired many nations in Africa, Asia, Eastern Europe, Latin America, South America, and the former Soviet Union to create antitrust systems to facilitate the adjustment to a marked-based economy. For the student and practitioner, the effort to analyze antitrust law and economics today yields more than insight into the economies of a few western nations. Increasingly it offers a valuable tool for understanding how a growing number of developed and developing nations will expand the role of market rivalry as the foundation for economic organization and growth through the end of this century and well into the next.

ERNEST GELLHORN
WILLIAM E. KOVACIC

Washington, D.C.
May 1994

*

OUTLINE

TABLE OF CASES

References are to Pages

A

TABLE OF CASES

B

C

D

E

F

G

H

I

J

K

L

M

N

O

P

Q

R

S

T

U

X

Y

Z

ANTITRUST LAW
AND
ECONOMICS
IN A NUTSHELL

*

CHAPTER I

RESTRAINTS OF TRADE
AT COMMON LAW

The antitrust laws seek to control the exercise of private economic power by preventing monopoly, punishing cartels, and otherwise protecting competition. Examining the origins of the antitrust laws helps to understand and interpret them. Their historical lineage extends from common law actions which limited restraints of trade and, to some extent, sought to proscribe monopoly power and middleman profits. Many proponents of the Sherman Act viewed the measure as a federal enactment of common law prohibitions against restraints of trade. See Martin J. Sklar, *The Corporate Reconstruction of American Capitalism, 1890–1916,* at 105–17 (1988). Thus, Senator John Sherman, the statute's namesake, said Congress was setting forth "the rule of the common law which prevails in England and in this country." 20 Cong. Rec. 1167 (1889). The Act's very terminology drew extensively from the common law's vocabulary.

In seeking to "federalize" the common law of trade restraints, the Sherman Act's authors intended to incorporate those strands of the common law that banned anticompetitive arrangements such as price-fixing cartels. During congressional deliberation on the Act, Senator Sherman discussed several illustrative common law cases that condemned cartels and similar trade restraints. 21 Cong. Rec. 2457–59 (1890). This and other descriptions of relevant case law in the legislative debates indicate that the statute's

1

proponents perceived the common law to embody a preference for competition and hostility toward cartels and other anticompetitive tactics. See William Letwin, *Law and Economic Policy in America: The Evolution of the Sherman Antitrust Act* 85–99 (1965): Thomas C. Arthur, *Farewell to the Sea of Doubt: Jettisoning the Constitutional Sherman Act,* 74 Cal. L. Rev. 263, 279–80 (1986).

Senator Sherman and his colleagues suggested that common law cases had provided well-defined, integrated conduct standards. Historians today regard this view as an unsupportable simplification. In the late nineteenth century, the common law of trade restraints was turbulent and unclear, particularly concerning whether "naked" trade restraints should be condemned automatically once their existence was proven, or should be evaluated by reasonableness tests. See James May, *Antitrust in the Formative Era: Political and Economic Theory in Constitutional and Antitrust Analysis,* 50 Ohio St. L.J. 258, 311–31 (1989).

Before 1890, English and American common law courts used two basic approaches to examine trade restraints. Some decisions permitted restrictive covenants in a contract when such covenants were limited in time and space and reasonably related to the contract's central purpose—such as a five-year limit on the seller of a bakery not to compete with the buyer who purchased the seller's good will (i.e., his going business value) as well as his bakeshop. Other cases took a more permissive view and even upheld unlimited territorial divisions. For example, an agreement by three luggage manufacturers to divide their sales territories so that each could sell his goods without competition from the others in his assigned territory was enforceable because it left the trade open to any third party. See Wickens v. Evans (1829).

Thus, it is neither instructive nor accurate to reconcile all cases or to force the common law preceding the Sherman Act into any single mold. See Michael J. Trebilcock, *The Common Law of Restraint of Trade: A Legal and Economic Analysis* (1986). Nevertheless, a review of some leading common law rulings and of the conflicting interests they sought to reconcile is useful because it illuminates a central feature of the antitrust statutes. By anchoring the Sherman Act in a dynamic body of legal principles, Congress insured that the new antitrust statute would have an evolutionary character. Future interpretations of the statute would undergo recurring adjustment by the same changing currents of politics and economics that had shaped the common law before 1890. See Herbert Hovenkamp, *The Sherman Act and the Classical Theory of Competition*, 74 Iowa L. Rev. 1019 (1989).

Common law landmarks also offer a valuable perspective on judicial antitrust analysis. Common law precedents influenced early antitrust decisions, and recent antitrust opinions continue to use common law cases to define doctrine. See Business Electronics Corp. v. Sharp Electronics Corp. (1988); National Soc'y of Prof. Engineers v. United States (1978). The "rule of reason," first applied in 1711, remains the basic standard for deciding close antitrust cases. (Its meaning has changed over time and is still changing.) Ancient property law rules against restraints on alienation continue to govern resale price maintenance. Whether such precedent deserves so much honor, however, is unclear.

A. CONTRACTS IN RESTRAINT OF TRADE

A complex system of guilds regulated relations among master, journeyman, and apprentice in feudal England.

Periods of service, wages, and prices were defined, usually by custom or statute. Occasionally a master would seek to extend the usual term by preventing his servant from becoming a full-fledged master at his term's end or by otherwise protecting himself from competition. Although it is unclear whether John Dyer was a journeyman, apprentice, or master [1] in the first known case, Dyer's Case (1414), the court angrily denied an attempted collection on a bond for John Dyer's breach of his agreement not to "use his art of a dyer's craft within the town ... for half a year." Not only was the condition restraining the dyer void as against the common law, but the court said it would have fined or imprisoned the plaintiff had he been in court. It seems, then, that the common law of trade restraints originated not with notions of competition and protection of the free market, but rather in support of "fair" commercial activity and of crumbling guild customs.

Later cases reflected the conflict more clearly. Courts approved contracts with restrictive trade covenants for the same reasons they upheld other contracts which were freely formed and supported by consideration. Enforcement enhanced property values, increased trade, and satisfied the parties' expectations. And courts were not arbiters of how owners could dispose of their property. Yet courts also were disinclined to validate agreements barring the promisor from using his skills and earning a living. Nor did they want to deny the public the advantages of competition. Nonetheless, until the eighteenth century, freedom of contract generally held sway; courts were not suited to deter-

1. It is possible that the defendant promised not to compete as a master in connection with the sale of his business (and hence was victimized after "having just met with great loss," as Lord Parker assumed three centuries later), but the restraint's short duration suggests that he was oppressed by an over-reaching master.

mine the adequacy or fairness of a contract's terms. But then a solicitude for wage earners and a philosophic acceptance of the need to assure that a free market in fact existed (coincidental with the industrial revolution) slowly became dominant themes.

The clash between these competing principles first came to a head in the now celebrated case of Mitchel v. Reynolds (1711), where the plaintiff leased a bakeshop for five years on condition that the assignor of the lease (also a baker) would not practice his baker's art in the parish during the lease term. The purchaser of the lease was buying not only the use of the bakeshop but also the trade that went with it, and he would not acquire the lease if the seller could readily destroy its value to him. Hence he demanded and received the defendant's restrictive promise. But when sued on his bond, the defendant presented, in essence, the argument that prevailed in *Dyer's Case*: namely, because he had served his time as an apprentice and had been admitted to the guild, no private person lawfully could prevent him from working his trade. Not only did the court reject this plea, but Lord Parker's opinion also systematically classified all restraints of trade and set forth doctrinal principles (still applied) to distinguish good restraints from bad.

Lord Parker's basic distinction was between general (invalid) and particular (valid) restraints. General restraints were condemned because their aim is to limit competition. Viewed as a Mephistophelean pact (general restraints are "of no benefit to either party, and only oppressive"), the court justified its rule: the person agreeing not to use his trade had to be protected from himself. The public was entitled to intercede in the bargain before he became a welfare charge or deprived the public of the benefits of his competitive labors. Moreover, not all particular restraints were valid. They had to be supported by "good consideration" (which explained why the contract in *Dyer's Case* was void). These "partial" or "ancillary" restraints, as they became known, were upheld if limited in time and restricted to a geographical place. *Mitchel* originated the "rule of reason"—was the restraint reasonable?—which will become a familiar term throughout this text.

Whether a trade restraint was ancillary depended on whether the covenant was subordinate to the transaction's main lawful purpose, or was the object of the contract and therefore a "naked covenant not to compete." As later decisions explained, the interests of the parties and the public were to be protected. The courts, therefore, inquired: For what *purpose* was the restraint imposed? What was the agreement's *effect*? (Could the promisor readily practice his trade elsewhere—and could the public receive the benefit of his competition somewhere?) Not surprisingly, restrictive covenants in employment contracts were scrutinized more closely than covenants connected to a sale of a business. As courts became more sophisticated they also asked whether the lawful objective could be obtained in some less restrictive way. (Was it necessary to bind an employee's right to his trade in order to protect business secrets?)

As the philosophy of laissez faire grew more firmly entrenched, exceptions to the rule of reason developed. Courts first suggested that the parties themselves could best judge what was reasonable, a doctrine familiar to students of contract law (and the peppercorn theory of consideration). It followed, then, that courts could presume that the terms were reasonable and not against the public interest; this presumption became conclusive when courts refused to admit contrary evidence of market conditions. Ultimately the exceptions engulfed the rule, at least in England, where price-fixing agreements often withstood challenge by victims of such arrangements, and the House of Lords went so far as to uphold a worldwide covenant not to compete. Compare Nordenfelt v. Maxim Nordenfelt Guns & Ammunition Co. (1894) (enforcing ancillary restraint that barred seller of an arms-manufacturing business from competing with the purchaser anywhere in the world for 25 years) with Mogul Steamship Co. v. McGregor Gow & Co. (1891) (refusing to ban agreement by loose combination of steamship companies to set predatory prices and destroy a rival, but ruling that the agreement would be void at common law as contrary to "public policy" and unenforceable among the parties to it); see also Tony Freyer, *Regulating Big Business—Antitrust in Great Britain and America 1880–1990,* at 121–32 (1992); Donald Dewey, *The Common Law Background of Antitrust Policy,* 41 Va. L. Rev. 759 (1955).

The "common law" was somewhat less receptive to trade restraints in the United States. One line of decisions banned price-fixing agreements and other anticompetitive arrangements when the challenged restraint affected an article of "prime necessity." See Richardson v. Buhl (1889). A related branch of rulings dispensed with the distinction between essential and non-essential items and prohibited naked trade restraints dealing with commodities and services other than matters of prime necessity. See Hoffman v. Brooks (1884). Nonetheless, in the 1870s and 1880s, counselors also could identify many state court decisions that mirrored the permissive approaches that English jurists had embraced for evaluating ancillary and nonancillary restrictions, alike. See Leslie v. Lorillard (1888); Skrainka v. Scharringhausen (1880). By 1890, the American common law was beset by a tension between cases that viewed cartels tolerantly (by assessing their reasonableness—particularly their capacity to preclude new entry into the market) and those which condemned cartels outright as naked restraints.

In 1898, then-Circuit Judge William Howard Taft wrote the Sixth Circuit's opinion in United States v. Addyston Pipe & Steel Co. (1898) and forever changed judicial perceptions about the common law's treatment of trade restraints. Taft found that American common law decisions had distinguished between ancillary and nonancillary restraints. Apart from reasonable ancillary restraints, he concluded that the common law had condemned all other restraints of trade: "Where the sole object of both parties in making the contract … is merely to restrain competition, and enhance or maintain prices, it would seem that there was nothing to justify or excuse the restraint, that it would necessarily have a tendency to monopoly, and therefore would be void." Taft asserted that, contrary to English experience, the weight of American authority declined to apply a reasonableness test to price-fixing, concerted refusals to deal, territorial divisions, or similarly restrictive agreements, whether or not they otherwise could be labelled ancillary. Though doubtful as a historical restatement,[2] Taft's formulation influenced subsequent judicial efforts to interpret the Sherman Act in light of the "common law" that Congress meant to embody in the new federal antitrust statute.

As this discussion indicates, the concept of restraint of trade (and what is reasonable or unreasonable) is neither an absolute nor an unvarying standard. Every commercial

2. Taft slighted American common law cases in which courts measured price-fixing and other directly restrictive covenants by a rule of reason. Taft "chose his common law cases carefully … and imposed on them his own ideas. What emerged was not the restatement it pretended to be so much as a new structure." R. Bork, *Antitrust Paradox*, at 27; see also Mark F. Grady, *Toward a Positive Economic Theory of Antitrust*, 30 Econ. Inquiry 225, 227–29 (1992).

promise that curbs the promisor's future dealings—for example, by reserving business to the promisee and excluding others—"restrains trade." II E. Allan Farnsworth, *Farnsworth on Contracts* 17 (1990). But it would be a *reductio ad absurdum* to conclude that agreements essential to create trade also illegally restrained trade. Yet some bargains may preclude a great deal of trade or competition, and their suppression of competition (and cost to society) may outweigh any possible benefit. The important policy question, therefore, is not whether the restraint is ancillary, but rather whether its anticompetitive tendencies are outweighed by its capacity to increase society's wealth (for example, by protecting existing property rights).

A routine sales transaction illustrates the issue. Suppose that A agrees to supply goods to B (thus satisfying B's needs for these goods for one week). Even as a simple one-shot sales transaction, the agreement excludes A's competitors, C and others, from making the same sale to B during this week. This "cost," however, is readily accepted as a necessary counterpart to the benefits of A's sale to B. However, what if B agrees to buy from A not just a one-week supply but all of B's requirements of these goods for the next 20 years? This elongated agreement effectively removes B's needs from the demand market as far as C and other competitors of A are concerned. Few sellers can wait 20 years for the next sale. And where B is the dominant or sole current buyer of the commodity which A and C (and others) sell, the agreement inevitably restrains trade, and possibly does so unreasonably.

The point is that the line between ordinary business transactions and agreements deemed to be restraints of trade is elusive and unmarked. Frequently one merges into the other. At the extremes the rule is readily seen and applied. Thus a seller's covenant not to compete with his purchaser for a limited time in a narrowly defined commu- nity in connection with the sale of a business and its highly personalized goodwill is generally upheld. Without it, the seller of a small business frequently would be unable to obtain a favorable (or possibly any) price for his business. Or the restraint's effect may be *de minimis* and of no public interest. At the other end of the spectrum, agreements that fix the price at which all sellers of the commodity sell their product, or divide sales territories so that each seller has an exclusive area free of competition in that territory, seem clearly to restrain trade—and unreasonably. The difficulty, of course, is that many (perhaps most) agree- ments fall between these poles, and courts have had to draw the line somewhere.

The rule of reason, then, is essentially a rule of construc- tion.

B. MONOPOLY AND CONSPIRACY

The common law also addressed monopolistic practices. Some monopolies were privileged, others illegal. Grants of monopoly explicitly sanctioned by courts, custom, or Parlia- ment were not questioned. Thus courts recognized limited patents for inventors, approved customary monopolies held by towns and guilds, and acquiesced in Parliamentary grants. Eventually all other monopolies were held to be void.

This development can be traced to the now famous Case of Monopolies (Darcy v. Allein) (1602). Queen Elizabeth I appears to have granted Darcy, her groom, the sole right to import playing cards into England. When Allein, a London haberdasher, made and sold some playing cards, Darcy challenged this infringement of his monopoly. The Court

of King's Bench, however, unanimously held the monopoly
void and dismissed the suit. "Letters patent" from the
Crown encroached on the privileges and freedoms of her
subjects to engage in trade. The ruling was justified on
several grounds: monopoly harms actual and potential competitors, denies others the opportunity to practice a trade,
and injures the public through higher prices and poorer
quality. Since the Crown could, of course, intentionally do
no wrong, the court rationalized its position by saying that
the Queen had been deceived in making the grant.

The Court's position was further vindicated when Parliament enacted the Statute of Monopolies of 1624 (21 Jac. 1,
c. 3) voiding "all" monopolies (with the several exceptions
already noted). Before reading this result too broadly, one
should note that the legislation stemmed less from a preference for competition than from a constitutional objection to
the Crown's assumption of power to grant monopolies and
to the arbitrary basis on which they were given.[3] Whatever
the reason (and the rapid erosion of the mercantile system
probably contributed as much as anything), the common
law courts became increasingly hostile to monopolies.
Nineteenth century legislation furthered this trend and
abolished the legal basis of most monopolies.

Common law decisions of the colonial courts embraced
this antipathy toward quasi-public monopolies. Opposition
to all grants of monopolistic privilege lacking explicit legislative sanction became an established American tradition,
although few reported cases actually faced the issue. This
antimonopoly view usually was expressed in state constitu-
tions and statutes. See Henry R. Seager & Charles A.

3. A few years after Darcy's playing card monopoly was judged void,
the very same monopoly was given—by Parliament—under the Statute of
Monopolies to the Company of Card Players. The more things change, the
more they stay the same.

Gulick, *Trust and Corporation Problems* 341–43 (1929). Yet neither the English nor American common law actually ruled that private monopoly (i.e., garnered by competitive effort or agreement) was illegal, except in dicta.

However, the common law doctrine of conspiracy condemned combinations to gain any unlawful objective, even if accomplished by otherwise lawful acts. (To compound the confusion, the common law conspiracy doctrine also reached "unlawful" means used to accomplish otherwise proper objectives.) In this context, unlawful covered anything obviously contrary to public policy including, possibly, monopoly. The doctrine never gained wide currency in commercial competition, although it was once applied vigorously in this country against labor unions. Otherwise it usually appeared only as a further basis for rejecting an agreement already banned as an unreasonable trade restraint. By statute some states barred corporate combinations designed to eliminate competition.

Finally, various market interference offenses were indictable under common law and also by statute. They sought to prevent middlemen from cornering markets or otherwise raising prices. They reflected the view, not completely abandoned in antitrust law today, that middlemen performed no useful function. These offenses, which had such quaint names as "forestalling" (buying goods before they reached the general market) and "regrating" (buying with the intent to resell in the same market) [4] never achieved significance in the United States.

The common law often provided (and still affords) a defense to enforcement of contracts with "oppressive"

---

4. Related offenses included "engrossing" (buying in bulk with the goal of raising the price), "forbearing" (like forestalling but with intent to sell at a higher price), and—best of all—"badgering" (buying corn victuals in one place and reselling them elsewhere at a profit).

terms. As a public policy tool, it was severely limited. Restrictive covenants were tested only when one party sought to enforce them against another who, in turn, was willing to contest the covenant. Then the court could declare the covenant void and unenforceable if it did not meet the reasonableness test. But the common law rule did not bar others from working under or observing such agreements; their acceptance depended on the parties' satisfaction with the bargain rather than competitive norms. Nor did the common law reach noncontractual restraints, such as a trust or holding company—or the acquisition of market power through means such as mergers or selective price cutting. Although supported by notions of the free market and the desire to encourage competition, the common law doctrines were at most only a short step in that direction.

C. CONCLUSION

Congress passed the Sherman Act at a time of dynamic change in the views of common law courts about the appropriate standard for evaluating restraints of trade. In 1890, two models of common law analysis vied for the approval of American judges. One model assessed naked restraints and ancillary restraints alike with a rule of reason and asked whether the challenged conduct could create a monopoly by precluding other merchants from entering the market and competing for sales. This view emphasized the freedom of individuals to make contracts and assumed that, without coercive limits on new entry, the market's self-correcting tendencies would protect consumers from exploitation. The second model divided trade restrictions into two categories, evaluating ancillary restrictions with a rule of reason and treating cartels as inherently unreasonable and subject to condemnation without regard to market circumstances, including entry conditions. This view perceived greater danger in direct restraints of trade, despite their private, voluntary nature.

The Sherman Act's proponents and Judge Taft in *Addyston Pipe* selectively examined the competing models of common law analysis and embraced the latter. In doing so, they supplied the fundamental analytical framework that antitrust has used for over a century. The Sherman Act and Taft's creative restatement of the common law embodied an emerging vision of the competitive process that distrusted unadorned private trade restraints and displayed confidence in the ability of public institutions such as courts and government enforcement agencies to identify and correct privately imposed impediments to competition. See William H. Page, *Ideological Conflict and the Origins of Antitrust Policy,* 66 Tulane L. Rev. 1 (1991). By outlawing certain private restraints and providing an affirmative means for intervention by public agencies and aggrieved private parties, the Sherman Act went well beyond the common law's mere refusal to enforce restrictive agreements against their participants. At the same time, it established that conduct standards would evolve much as they had under the common law until 1890—through case by case adjudication subject to changes in economic learning and shifts in perceptions about the relative ability of public institutions and private rivalry to erode the effects of market imperfections.

CHAPTER II

THE ANTITRUST STATUTES

The common law's inability to reach certain anticompetitive behavior and rising concern over abuses by corporate giants in the late Nineteenth Century spawned legislation curbing the power of the railroads and "trusts." Congress' first responses—the Interstate Commerce Act of 1887 and the Sherman Antitrust Act of 1890—did not allay public discontent. Continuing abuses and undulating business cycles, coupled with disappointing judicial interpretations of the new antitrust act, created further pressures until the antitrust issue dominated the Presidential election of 1912 and led to the adoption, in 1914, of the Clayton and Federal Trade Commission Acts.

A. THE DEMAND FOR REGULATION

In the eyes of many common law courts, the market place protected the public as long as the legal right to trade—primarily, freedom to enter and compete—was guaranteed. This safeguard's inadequacy first became apparent as railroads were believed to have abused their privileged position. Capital requirements of railroad construction precluded competitive service to sparsely settled territories. Nor was the right to build railroads freely available (even with eminent domain authority) in densely populated areas. Without competition, railroad rates and service seemed beset by discrimination among shippers and localities, traffic and earning pools, and secret rebates to powerful shippers or buyers. Railroads also appeared to boost rates where they had monopolies and to use the resulting profits unfairly to cut prices on competitive routes. See Herbert Hovenkamp, *Regulatory Conflict in the Gilded Age: Federalism and the Railroad Problem,* 97 Yale L. J. 1017 (1988).

Several states responded by forming regulatory agencies to oversee rates and service. When the constitutionality of such measures was challenged, the Supreme Court held that railroads were businesses "affected with a public interest" subject to state regulation. Munn v. Illinois (1876). But state jurisdiction was limited and constitutionally ineffective for interstate commerce. As a result, Congress created the Interstate Commerce Commission (ICC) in 1887 and charged the ICC with assuring just and reasonable rates and barring undue discrimination. It sought, in other words, to substitute government regulation for the temper of competitive markets.

If the railroads' trade abuses first illuminated the common law's inadequacy, its limits were exposed more forcefully by the tactics of the Standard Oil Company and other "trusts" [1] controlling many major industries—including fuel oil, sugar, cotton and linseed oil, lead, and whiskey. Lawsuits attacked the trusts from several angles. The primary challenge was that the participating companies had acted ultra vires (beyond their charters) by forming trust arrangements. See People *ex rel.* Peabody v. Chicago Gas Trust Co. (1889). A second argument was that trust practices constituted unreasonable trade restraints and created

1. Standard's attorneys created the trust from the theory of stockholders' voting trusts. By this device, owners of stock in several companies transferred their securities to a set of trustees and received certificates entitling them to a share of the pooled earnings of the jointly managed firms. The trust label soon was applied to all suspect business combinations. See Morton J. Horwitz, *The Transformation of American Law 1870–1960,* at 80–85 (1992).

unlawful monopolies. However, these attacks took time, were costly, and did not always prevail.

The trusts' opponents assailed them on several policy grounds. Foremost was the concern that fewer and fewer enterprises were dominating more and more business each year. The transportation and communications revolution after the Civil War linked once insular geographic areas into unified markets, enabling low-cost producers to capture sales in regions previously served by local firms alone. Investors and financial institutions obtained better information about investment opportunities, causing capital to flow more rapidly to new and growing firms. See Robert H. Wiebe, *The Search for Order 1877–1920,* at 11–75 (1967).

To many Americans, the resulting industrial upheaval endangered democratic institutions and threatened intolerable social and political corporate hegemony. In 1887, legal scholar Frederic Jesup Stimson warned that "American ingenuity has invented a legal machine which may swallow a hundred corporations or a hundred thousand individuals; and then, with all the corporate irresponsibility, their united power be stored, like a dynamo, in portable compass, and wielded by one or two men. Not even amenable to the restraints of corporation law, these 'trusts' may realize the Satanic ambition,—infinite and irresponsible power free of check or conscience." Frederic J. Stimson, *"Trusts",* 1 Harv. L. Rev. 132, 132 (1887).

A second basis for challenging the trusts dealt with their methods for subduing rivals. Predatory tactics such as below-cost pricing and business espionage often seemed to spur consolidation. The public thought the trusts gained power with coercive threats of "sell or be ruined," and their record showed that they had the means and the will to execute the threats.[2] Such tactics outraged small firms and the agrarian West, spurring the formation of the Populist Party. See Samuel P. Hays, *The Response to Industrialism 1885–1914,* at 27–32 (1957).

A third and related objection involved the trusts' use of outrageous methods to achieve unreasonable ends beyond destroying competitors. Investors were defrauded by watered stocks; workers were discarded as worn out tools by indiscriminate and harsh plant closings; liberty was endangered by bribery of public officials; civil peace and property were threatened by arson; and fair competition was disturbed by bogus companies and harassing lawsuits. Frequent depressions or severe business cycles and scandalous financial transactions, invariably involving trusts or railroads, further shocked the public and sapped its confidence in unregulated markets. The atmosphere is hard to recapture. The public was naive, and the trusts were ruthless. See Robert Higgs, *Crisis and Leviathan* 77–82 (1987).

Not surprisingly, the trusts had few defenders. The public clamored for action: it wanted the law to destroy the trusts' power. By 1888 both major parties had received the message, and their platforms contained strongly worded antimonopoly planks. See Hans B. Thorelli, *The Federal*

---

2. To obtain its fuel oil monopoly, Standard Oil would first drive the price of kerosene to a penny or two per gallon in isolated markets, well below cost. After forcing all competitors to sell or close down, Standard would raise the price far above the previous market level and extort monopoly profits. Distant observers have read the record differently. Compare John S. McGee, *Predatory Price Cutting: The Standard Oil (N.J.) Case,* 1 J.L. & Econ. 137 (1958) (finding little evidence in the Standard Oil trial record that Standard attained monopoly power through predatory pricing) with F.M Scherer & David Ross, *Industrial Market Structure and Economic Performance* 388–91 (3d ed. 1990) (finding that McGee underestimated the usefulness of predatory pricing to enable Standard to reduce the cost of buying out rivals). Whatever the actual facts, they were perceived at the time as described in the text.

Antitrust Policy 149–51, 157–59 (1955). Though the public's mandate was clear, it was not specific. Little thought had focused on how to constrain the trusts without destroying business and jobs at the same time.

Professional economists and academics expert in corporate law generally thought prohibiting the massive enterprises to be futile, needless, or counterproductive, mainly because the trusts were "natural" and desirable results of competition—else why would they have occurred and flourished in the first place? This benign view of industrial concentration emerges in the correspondence of Justice Oliver Wendell Holmes, Jr. with Lord Pollock in the early 1900s. Holmes complained that "the Sherman Act is a humbug based on economic ignorance and incompetence." Holmes disdained trust critics who slighted "the originality, the courage, the insight shown by the great masters of combinations" and who insisted that such entrepreneurs "can be summed up as tricksters." Holmes deemed the organizational skill of the trusts' managers to be at least as important as "the more obvious contributions of professional inventors and the like." [3] For this and other reasons, most economists shared the view of Richard T. Ely, who declared "[i]f there is any serious student of our economic life who believes that anything substantial has been gained by all the laws passed against trusts ... this authority has yet to be heard from." Richard T. Ely, *Monopolies and Trusts* 243 (1900).

Proponents of antimonopoly measures favored a different tack and took direction from the common law. Generally

---

3. 1 Holmes–Pollack Letters 141, 163 (Mark D. Howe ed. 1941). See also Alfred D. Chandler, Jr., *The Visible Hand: The Managerial Revolution in American Business* (1977) (explaining the trusts' emergence as the result of the search for an optimal corporate structure for attaining scale economies and lower unit costs).

they recommended statutes to prohibit monopolies and other combinations to which the common law only denied enforcement. This view drew support from a small set of academics who favored banning conduct, such as local price discrimination, that was believed to create and sustain monopoly power. See F.M. Scherer, *Efficiency, Fairness, and the Early Contributions of Economists to the Antitrust Debate*, 29 Washburn L.J. 243 (1989). Their work meshed with the view of many lawyers, judges, and legislators that most monopolies were not "natural" evolutionary phenomena, but instead were "unnatural" intrusions upon the economy and could stand only with "artificial" buttresses such as publicly imposed tariffs or private contrivances such as cartel agreements. See James May, *Antitrust Practice and Procedure in the Formative Era: The Constitutional and Conceptual Reach of State Antitrust Law, 1880–1918*, 135 U. Pa. L. Rev. 495, at 563–71 (1987).

As the Twentieth Century approached, Congress found a common ground between these conflicting visions of the trusts. It built a statute along common law principles, barring excesses such as combinations in restraint of trade and monopolizing activity. At the same time, it sought to permit fair competition and healthy combinations.

B. THE SHERMAN ACT
1. THE STATUTE

Like many legislative watersheds, the debates and events surrounding the passage of the Sherman Act contain something for everyone. To generations of observers, the Sherman Act's legislative record has supplied a wishing well into which one can peer to glimpse evidence that supports preferred policies. Despite substantial ambiguity and contentious modern debate about the origins of the American antitrust laws, some features of the formative era assist in understanding the Sherman Act and subsequent case developments.

Senator Sherman assured his colleagues that the statute "does not announce a new principle of law, but applies old and well recognized principles of the common law." 21 Cong.Rec. 2456 (1890). Yet many of the common law's dimensions were hazy, and the 51st Congress may not have grasped the diversity and instability of existing common law solutions to restraint of trade issues in 1890. To define and apply critical concepts such as "restraint of trade" and "monopolize" in specific cases, courts would be required to consider the goals that Congress intended to achieve. The legislative record contains many declarations favoring free enterprise and unrestricted competition. From such statements, Judge Robert Bork has concluded that "[t]he legislative history of the Sherman Act ... displays the clear and exclusive policy intention of promoting consumer welfare"—which he defines as the improvement of allocative efficiency. R. Bork, *The Antitrust Paradox,* at 61. Other commentators dispute Bork's efficiency thesis and discern other congressional aims of equal or greater significance. These include preserving opportunities for firms and individuals to compete, see Eleanor M. Fox, *The Modernization of Antitrust: A New Equilibrium,* 66 Cornell L. Rev. 1140 (1981); preventing unfair redistributions of wealth from consumers to producers, see Robert H. Lande, *Wealth Transfers as the Original and Primary Concern of Antitrust: The Efficiency Interpretation Challenged,* 34 Hastings L.J. 65 (1982); and sustaining the vitality of democratic institutions, see David Millon, *The Sherman Act and the Balance of Power,* 61 S. Cal. L. Rev. 1219 (1988). Still other scholars reject Bork's view that "public interest" goals spawned the Sherman Act; instead, they argue that the Act is best understood as the product of private interest rent-seeking—mainly, efforts by small merchants and farmers to shift wealth from large manufacturers to themselves. See Thomas J. DiLorenzo, *The Origins of Antitrust: An Interest Group Perspective,* 5 Int'l Rev. L. & Econ. 73 (1985); Thomas W. Hazlett, *The Legislative History of the Sherman Act Re-examined,* 30 Econ. Inquiry 263 (1992).

Modern research about the Sherman Act's aims often assumes that the 51st Congress espoused many potentially conflicting goals without indicating how courts should make tradeoffs among competing goals. However, as James May has shown, to assume that Congress consciously embraced inconsistent aims misconceives the intellectual framework that molded the Sherman Act. Professor May finds that Congress in 1890 saw no need for "tradeoffs," for it thought its aims to be consistent and mutually reinforcing. J. May, *Antitrust in the Formative Era,* 50 Ohio St. L.J. at 391–94. Congress believed it could attain its varied objectives without collisions among them.

Notwithstanding disputes about the Sherman Act's intended aims, Congress made a clear, momentous choice about implementing its competition policy commands. The statute did not specify prohibited conduct in detail. Rather, Congress gave federal courts a new jurisdiction: federal judges were to create a common law of federal antitrust within the general aim of—but apparently not confined by—the prior common law.

The major substantive provisions of most antitrust laws are few and brief. The Sherman Antitrust Act of 1890, 15 U.S.C.A. §§ 1–7, is no exception. Its two main sections are:

§ 1: Every contract, combination in the form of trust or otherwise, or conspiracy, in restraint of trade or commerce among the several States, or with foreign nations, is declared to be illegal [and is a felony punishable by fine and/or imprisonment]....

§ 2: Every person who shall monopolize, or attempt to monopolize, or combine or conspire with any other person or persons, to monopolize any part of the trade or commerce among the several States, or with foreign nations, shall be deemed guilty of a felony [and is similarly punishable]....

Note how the basic thrust of the two sections differs. Section 1 requires collective action. One person cannot contract, combine, or conspire by herself. Section 2, on the other hand, applies chiefly to unilateral conduct: "every person who ...:" Consequently Section 1 case law often is concerned with finding an agreement, unlike Section 2 disputes, where the prime concern is a structural condition (monopoly).

Section 1 addresses improperly restrictive agreements while Section 2 examines the creation or misuse of monopoly power through wrongfully exclusionary means. Both sections seek the same end—to curtail practices yielding market control—but Section 2's reach is generally limited by a threshold finding of monopoly power. Section 2 does not forbid "monopoly" per se, but instead bars "monopolization" and attempts to monopolize. Thus, Section 2 cases focus not on the fact of monopoly alone, but rather on how a monopoly has been gained or sustained. The crucial interpretative challenge posed by the Sherman Act is to define the specific forms of collective and unilateral conduct that pose unacceptable competitive dangers.

Finally, the statute proscribes (thou shall not) rather than prescribes (thou shall) conduct; it does not authorize positive administrative regulation of business conduct. Yet the Sherman Act moved well past the common law's mere refusal to enforce offensive contracts. Its most important addition to the existing legal regime was to authorize public bodies and private parties to enforce the statute. To this end, the Act supplies powerful remedies: trade restraints and monopolization are punishable as crimes; equity's broad powers are available to enjoin specific behavior and otherwise service antitrust policy; and treble damages and attorneys fees are available for aggrieved claimants. Thus, the legal risks of illegal restraints and monopolistic acts are significant, especially when contrasted with the common law where there was only a remote chance that questioned acts would be challenged as unenforceable. Despite this stringency, the statute defines the boundary between permissible and illegal conduct vaguely.

In sum, the Sherman Act's primary effect when compared to the common law was to enable government agencies and private parties to enforce prohibitions against trade restraints and monopolization. Final responsibility for defining the Sherman Act's broad commands lay with the courts, which were not limited to common law decisions in performing that task.

2. EARLY INTERPRETATIONS

Early judicial reaction to the Sherman Act was extreme. The Supreme Court first emasculated the Act's coverage by an unrealistically narrow reading and then applied the Act so rigidly as to render it unworkable unless broad exceptions were allowed. Finally the Court adopted a flexible "rule of reason," reading the statute as condemning only unreasonable conduct. But a clear standard was not provided. Thus, even this reading was widely criticized as being too hospitable to anticompetitive conduct on the one hand, or as allowing excessive judicial discretion to rule the economy on the other.

Not until 1895 did the Supreme Court first interpret the Sherman Act. The decision foreshadowed future difficulties. In United States v. E.C. Knight Co. (1895), the Court refused to apply the statute to the sugar trust, which controlled over 98 percent of the country's sugar refining capacity. The Court held that the law ignored restraints affecting merely the manufacture of commodities, noting that "[c]ommerce succeeds to manufacture, and is not a part of it." Because the trust's refining capacity was concentrated in Pennsylvania, the government had not proven a *direct* restraint on interstate commerce within the Sherman Act's jurisdiction. If followed, *E.C. Knight* would have interred the Act, at least for manufacturing monopolies.[4]

Another way to destroy legislation is to stifle its capacity to adjust to practical necessities. Whether this was the original judicial design, the Supreme Court's early reading of Section 1 threatened to have this effect. In a series of closely divided opinions, beginning with United States v. Trans–Missouri Freight Ass'n (1897), the Court forbade price-fixing agreements and territorial divisions because Section 1 condemned "every" trade restraint, without exception. Later cases quickly softened this absolute position in dicta, first limiting condemnation to "direct" and "immediate" restraints with no aim to promote the legitimate business of either participant (Hopkins v. United States (1898)), and then concluding that restraints lawful at common law (or some of them) fell outside the category of

4. *E.C. Knight* was overruled in Mandeville Island Farms v. American Crystal Sugar Co. (1948). Sherman Act claimants still must show that challenged conduct is in or affects interstate commerce, but subsequent decisions have severely attenuated this requirement. See Chapter 13.

restraints banned by the Sherman Act. United States v. Joint Traffic Ass'n (1898).

This doctrinal dispute had little effect on popular support for antitrust enforcement. Antimonopoly agitation ebbed after 1890, and for a time the public accepted quixotic judicial approaches and executive indifference.[5] All this changed when Theodore Roosevelt became President—and even more so during the term of his successor (William Howard Taft). Amid great public excitement generated by Roosevelt, the Supreme Court in Northern Securities Co. v. United States (1904) ruled that holding companies were not exempt from the Sherman Act and that an arrangement placing two competing railroads under one entity (in fact, a profit-pooling agreement) illegally restrained trade.

Fueled by the successful challenge to the trust building efforts of financiers James J. Hill and J.P. Morgan, and sparked by the President's tempestuous reaction to his new Justice's (Oliver Wendell Holmes, Jr.) dissent,[6] the public reacted sharply to the Court's opinion in Standard Oil Co. v. United States (1911). The decision ordered that the oil trust be dissolved into 33 companies, but the Court also ruled that the Sherman Act outlawed only restraints whose character or effect were unreasonably anticompetitive.

5. President Cleveland's Justice Department welcomed the outcome in the the failed sugar trust prosecution. Soon after *E.C. Knight* was decided, Attorney General Richard Olney wrote to a friend: "You will have observed that the government has been defeated in the Supreme Court on the trust question. I always supposed it would be and have taken the responsibility of not prosecuting under a law I believe to be no good . . . ." Alan Nevins, *Grover Cleveland: A Study in Courage* 671 (1932).

6. Holmes' dissent shattered his once cordial relationship with Roosevelt. As Max Lerner recounts, "Roosevelt was furious. 'I could carve out of a banana,'" he is reported (perhaps apocryphally) to have cried, "'a justice with more backbone than that.'" *The Mind and Faith of Justice Holmes,* xxxiii (Max Lerner ed. 1943). Lerner, however, omits Holmes' supposed rejoinder: "Some banana! Some backbone!"

Some critics worried that conservative federal judges would quickly render the Act insignificant again; others feared a return to lackluster enforcement by the Justice Department. Business leaders contended that if the Sherman Act now prohibited only unreasonable restraints, businesses should be advised in advance about which restraints were lawful and which were not. During the 1912 Presidential campaign, public debate again focused on the role of government in the economy—including antitrust legislation. After the victory of Woodrow Wilson's "New Freedom," Congress created the Federal Trade Commission and enacted the Clayton Act. With the Sherman Act, these enactments set in place the essential framework of the federal antitrust laws.

C. THE CLAYTON AND FEDERAL
TRADE COMMISSION ACTS

Woodrow Wilson won the 1912 election, but most of the opposition's arguments became law. Wilson believed that effective antitrust enforcement required specification of unlawful business practices. The "rule of reason" denied businesses guidance and gave courts excessive discretion to emasculate the law through interpretation. Wilson therefore proposed supplementing the Sherman Act with legislation enumerating illegal acts precisely (in what became the Clayton Act) and providing criminal sanctions to ensure compliance. See Woodrow Wilson, *The New Freedom* 172 (1913).

Wilson also urged the creation of an administrative agency, an interstate trade commission, to promote fair competition by investigating and publicizing (but not otherwise prosecuting) trade abuses as well as by advising business about the legality of specific practices. Wilson assailed his chief adversary (Theodore Roosevelt) for proposing a federal commission with power to investigate any business activity and to set maximum prices for goods produced by monopolists. "If the government is to tell big business men how to run their business," Wilson warned, "then don't you see that big business men have to get closer to the government even than they are now? Don't you see that they must capture the government, in order not to be restrained too much by it?" W. Wilson, *New Freedom*, 201–02.

As his proposals traveled through Congress, Wilson became persuaded by Louis Brandeis (his closest adviser on antitrust and not yet a Supreme Court justice) that his preferred mix of specific prohibitions and criminal penalties was ill-conceived. Detailing prohibited practices might be somewhat effective, but only if criminal penalties were not assessed. Otherwise courts probably would construe the new law narrowly; and, in any case, Congress was unwilling to endorse criminal penalties unless the trade abuse was universally condemned (and therefore already reachable by the Sherman Act). Another pitfall of clarity was that it might in practice invite ingenious (and successful) efforts at evasion by business. In this vein, the Conference Committee Report on the Clayton Act and the FTC Act warned that "[i]t is impossible to frame definitions which embrace all unfair practices. There is no limit to human inventiveness in this field...." H.R. Rep. No. 1142, 63rd Cong., 2d Sess. 18 (1914). A growing consensus, therefore, favored a general condemnation of undesirable trade practices, especially for its capacity to respond flexibly to changing conditions and business techniques. Owing to growing concern over judicial hostility to antitrust enforcement, it was decided that an administrative agency also should be entrusted with enforcement responsibilities.

1. THE CLAYTON ACT

The Clayton Act of 1914, 15 U.S.C.A. §§ 12–27, declared four practices illegal but not criminal: price discrimination—selling a product at different prices to similarly situated buyers (§ 2); tying and exclusive dealing contracts—sales on condition that the buyer stop dealing with the seller's competitors (§ 3); corporate mergers—acquisitions of competing companies (§ 7); and interlocking directorates—common board members among competing companies (§ 8). Each prohibition was qualified (under somewhat different tests) by the general condition that the specified practice was illegal only "where the effect ... may be substantially to lessen competition" or "tend to create a monopoly in any line of commerce." Never a paragon of clarity, Section 2, dealing with price discrimination, was rewritten (but not improved) by the Robinson–Patman Act of 1936; its text is now a model of statutory obfuscation. Jurisdictional holes in Section 7, the antimerger law, were patched and its prohibitions were expanded by the Celler–Kefauver Act of 1950.

2. THE FEDERAL TRADE COMMISSION ACT

Section 5 of the FTC Act of 1914 (as amended in 1938 and 1975) provides that "unfair methods of competition in or affecting commerce, and unfair or deceptive acts or practices in or affecting commerce are hereby declared unlawful." 15 U.S.C.A. § 45. The Act provides no criminal penalties and limits the FTC to issuing prospective decrees. With the Justice Department, the FTC shares enforcement of the Clayton Act. (The Justice Department cannot enforce the FTC Act.) The Commission also can attack Sherman Act violations because courts have ruled that Section 5's ban upon unfair methods of competition includes Sherman Act offenses. FTC v. Cement Institute (1948); Neil W. Averitt, *The Meaning of 'Unfair Methods of Competition' in Section 5 of the Federal Trade Commission Act,* 21 B.C. L. Rev. 227, 239–40 (1980).

In creating an administrative agency with antitrust authority, Congress sought to ensure greater fidelity to its own competition policy goals. This choice stemmed mainly from the Supreme Court's *Standard Oil* decision in 1911, which ruled that the Sherman Act's ban upon "every" contract in restraint of trade proscribed only unreasonable trade restraints. Many legislators feared that a judiciary predisposed to distrust government intervention in the economy routinely would apply the rule of reason to exculpate business defendants. Although some legislators believed the rule of reason standard to be deficient in substance, Congress' chief aim was to vest adjudicatory power in a body more responsive to its own preferences.

D. INSTITUTIONAL IMPLICATIONS

The form and substance of the antitrust statutes have important institutional implications that help explain how antitrust doctrine and enforcement policy have developed over time and will change in the future.

1. OPENENDED SUBSTANTIVE COMMANDS

Congress cast many provisions of the antitrust statutes in broad terms and thereby gave federal judges a pivotal role in defining the statutes' prohibitions. In Sugar Institute v. United States (1936), the Supreme Court emphasized the breadth of judicial authority under the antitrust laws: "We have said that the Sherman Anti–Trust Act, as a charter of freedom, has a generality and adaptability comparable to that found to be desirable in constitutional provisions. It does not go into detailed definitions." Cf. Thomas C. Arthur, *Workable Antitrust Law: The Statutory Approach to Antitrust,* 62 Tulane L. Rev. 1163, 1171–75 (1988) (arguing that decisions such as *Sugar Institute* exaggerate the Sherman Act's delegation of interpretative power to federal judges). No scheme of federal economic regulation grants judges comparable discretion to determine litigation outcomes through their interpretations of legislative commands.

How judges exercise their discretion depends heavily on their policy preferences, training, and experience. In 1911, before he became Attorney General and an Associate Justice of the Supreme Court, James C. McReynolds said that "no one can tell with certainty" what factors would shape the judiciary's interpretation of the Sherman Act, but added that "much depends on the economic views entertained by the Judges." Alexander M. Bickel & Benno C. Schmidt, Jr., 9 *History of the Supreme Court of the United States* 166 (1984). Next to persuading Congress to amend the antitrust laws, a president's surest means for leaving a lasting imprint on antitrust policy is the power to choose federal judges. See William E. Kovacic, *Reagan's Judicial Appointees and Antitrust in the 1990s,* 60 Ford. L. Rev. 49 (1991).

2. THE CHOICE OF GOALS

In exercising their discretion under the antitrust statutes, judges must decide which criteria will guide their choice among competing analytical approaches. In a formative statement of this point, Judge Bork observes that "[a]ntitrust policy cannot be made rational until we are able to give a firm answer to one question: What is the point of the law—what are its goals? Everything else follows from the answer we give. Is the antitrust judge to be guided by one value or by several? If by several, how is he to decide cases where a conflict in values arises? Only when the issue of goals has been settled is it possible to frame a coherent body of substantive rules." R. Bork, *Antitrust Paradox*, at 50.

Bork's answer to this question–that the legislative history of the Sherman Act and the other antitrust statutes demonstrates an overriding aim to increase consumer welfare by enhancing allocative efficiency–has inspired a heated debate about the aims of antitrust.[7] As noted above, many commentators have disputed this view and proposed other goal structures. As a group, Bork's critics have shown that Congress conceived the antitrust system to embrace objectives reaching beyond the attainment of allocative efficiency.

Many historians object to how Bork and some of his critics have scanned the historical record in search of "an immediately usable historical past." Daniel R. Ernst, *The New Antitrust History*, 35 N.Y.L.Sch. L. Rev. 879, 885 (1990). These historians find that legal scholars tend to rest their modern policy prescriptions on studies that brush aside significant ambiguities in the historical record surrounding antitrust's formative era. By doing so, they neglect the possibility that Congress pursued no single aim in the Sherman Act, but acted from a "powerful, widely shared vision of a natural, rights-based political and economic order that simultaneously tended to ensure opportunity, efficiency, prosperity, justice, harmony, and freedom." J. May, *Antitrust in the Formative Era*, 50 Ohio St. L.J. at 391.

7. Cf. Andrew I. Gavil, *Antitrust Casebooks: Ideology or Pedagogy?*, 66 N.Y.U. L. Rev. 189 (1991) (discussing how views of antitrust's goals influence editorial choices by antitrust casebook authors).

Congress in 1890 may have seen no need to make trade-offs among an array of goals, but subsequent experience and developments in economic theory have undermined important factual assumptions that shaped original legislative expectations about the harmonious attainment of varied economic, political, and social ends. It is now evident that achieving certain of the original goals sometimes will come at the expense of others. (For example, large scale production and distribution may reduce costs but also eliminate competitive opportunities for small firms.) It also seems unlikely that antitrust specialists will devise a contemporary enforcement approach that gives full effect to an original intent that foresaw no conflict in the simultaneous pursuit of a host of economic, social, and political aims. Consequently, future adjudication and enforcement practice probably will be guided less by understandings of original intent and more by modern views of what constitutes sound policy. Judicial receptivity to a suggested goals structure is likely to depend heavily on its administrability. Despite its questionable statement of original intent, Judge Bork's efficiency prescription offers federal judges the attractive quality of apparent simplicity in application. Commentators proposing multi-dimensional goals structures generally have not provided judges an assuring method for ranking efficiency and nonefficiency goals and resolving possible conflicts among them.

The goals debate is not a mere academic concern. Modern Supreme Court antitrust decisions show that judicial views about antitrust's proper aims influence doctrine. In Brown Shoe Co. v. United States (1962), the Supreme Court for the first time interpreted the 1950 Cellar–Kefauver Amendment, which extended the Clayton Act's original antimerger provision to cover acquisitions of assets. Midway through the Court's opinion, Chief Justice Earl Warren observed that "[t]aken as a whole, the legislative history [of the 1950 Amendment] illuminates congressional concern with the protection of *competition*, not *competitors*, and its desire to restrain mergers only to the extent that such combinations may tend to lessen competition." *Brown Shoe* (emphasis in original). At the opinion's end, Chief Justice Warren concluded that the amended statute forbade Brown Shoe's purchase of Kinney, which yielded a post-acquisition market share of five percent of shoe retailing:

> Of course, some of the results of large integrated or chain operations are beneficial to consumers. Their expansion is not rendered unlawful by the mere fact that small independent stores may be adversely affected. It is competition, not competitors, which the Act protects. But we cannot fail to recognize Congress' desire to promote competition through the protection of viable, small, locally owned businesses. Congress appreciated that occasional higher costs and prices might result from the maintenance of fragmented industries and markets. It resolved these competing considerations in favor of decentralization. We must give effect to that decision.

Fifteen years later, in Brunswick Corp. v. Pueblo Bowl–O–Mat, Inc. (1977), the Court reviewed a bowling alley operator's challenge to Brunswick's acquisition of the assets of one of the plaintiff's bankrupt competitors. The plaintiff asserted that its profits would have increased had Brunswick not purchased the failing rival. A unanimous Court rejected the claim, holding that the plaintiff failed to prove "*antitrust* injury, which is to say injury of the type the antitrust laws were designed to prevent and that flows from that which makes defendants' acts unlawful." *Brunswick* (emphasis in original). Justice Thurgood Marshall's opinion for the Court said "[t]he antitrust laws ... were enacted for 'the protection of *competition*, not *competitors*.'"

Here Justice Marshall quoted the first of *Brown Shoe's* two
admonitions about antitrust's concern for "competition, not
competitors." Significantly, he did not cite the latter passage in which Chief Justice Warren repeated the "competition, not competitors" aphorism, but condemned the merger to vindicate Congress' desire to protect small firms. In
Brunswick, the Court studied the Janus-like features of
Brown Shoe and ignored the face of business egalitarian-
ism.

Since *Brunswick* courts have embraced an efficiency orientation more often than judicial decisions of the Warren
Era. Many cases cite Judge Bork for the view that Congress designed the Sherman Act as a "consumer welfare
prescription." See, e.g., Reiter v. Sonotone Corp. (1979)
(legislative debates "suggest that Congress designed the
Sherman Act as a 'consumer welfare prescription'" [citing
R. Bork, *Antitrust Paradox,* at 66]). Although a "consumer welfare" standard is consistent with an efficiency perspective, no court has retraced and endorsed the logic by
which Judge Bork equates "consumer welfare" with a singleminded concern with allocative efficiency. Nor have
courts that have adopted a "consumer welfare" standard
indicated that such a formula excludes consideration of
other goals. See William E. Kovacic, *The Antitrust Paradox
Revisited: Robert Bork and the Transformation of Modern
Antitrust Policy,* 36 Wayne L. Rev. 1413, 1446–51 (1990).

Although mainstream judicial antitrust analysis today
reflects a goals hierarchy dominated by efficiency, this
pattern is not universal. Populist solicitude for small entrepreneurs and the dispersion of economic and political
power remains an important impulse in the antitrust system. See Atlantic Richfield Co. v. USA Petroleum Co.
(1990) (Stevens, J., dissenting); *McGahee* (1988). Until the
Supreme Court precludes reliance on other goals, judges

sometimes will permit nonefficiency arguments to trump efficiency concerns.

Even if the Supreme Court declines to resolve the goals issue, efficiency probably will remain paramount in antitrust litigation for the foreseeable future. This has less to do with original legislative intent or concerns about administrability than with the courts' awareness of global economic conditions. Since World War II, decisions such as *Brown Shoe* (1962) have emphasized non-efficiency goals when American firms were preeminent. See Phillip Areeda, *Antitrust Law as Industrial Policy,* in Antitrust, Innovation, and Competitiveness 29, 34–35 (Thomas M. Jorde & David J. Teece eds. 1992). The ascent of Western Europe and Japan in the 1970s as potent economic rivals to the United States created strong political pressure to reexamine national policies, including antitrust, that affect the competitive position of American firms. Today it is more difficult for courts to discount efficiency and vindicate other aims as American companies struggle against formidable foreign competitors.

3.   PERMEABILITY OF THE ADJUDICATION PROCESS

Congress provided a highly decentralized mechanism for adjudicating antitrust disputes. Thirteen courts of appeals, 94 district courts, and the FTC share power to decide cases and interpret the statutes' broad commands. New ideas can (and do) enter the antitrust system on a small scale. A well-reasoned opinion by one federal judge can establish a new theory or conduct standard as an acceptable basis for decision. The Supreme Court hears few antitrust cases, and genuine analytical differences among the lower federal courts are common. Dispersed adjudicatory power gives litigants many paths through which to inject preferred theories into the antitrust system.

Decentralization also results from Congress' decision to confer antitrust standing on many entities, including two federal agencies, state governments, private companies, and consumers. No single gatekeeper controls access to the courts or decides what ideas may be asserted to support antitrust claims. Decentralized prosecution means that one entity's rejection of certain theories does not bar others from using those theories. For example, in the 1980s, state governments impeded the Reagan Administration's efforts to retrench public enforcement policy concerning distribution restraints and mergers by bringing cases that the Reagan antitrust agencies disfavored. See Chapter 13.

The antitrust system's permeability influences the direction of antitrust doctrine and analysis over time. The openness of the adjudication process means that today's orthodoxy will face periodic challenges by rival theories that may become prevailing analytical approaches. Because the system is susceptible to new ideas, changing political and economic conditions, coupled with ferment in economic learning, impart instability to existing doctrine and analysis. See William E. Kovacic, *The Influence of Economics on Antitrust Law,* 30 Econ. Inquiry 294 (1992). To predict future litigation outcomes accurately not only requires mastery of existing standards and analytical techniques but also appreciation for the power of new theories and changing political trends to alter judicial decisionmaking.

4. COEXISTENCE WITH OTHER ECONOMIC REGULATORY SCHEMES AND THEORIES OF ECONOMIC ORGANIZATION

Since 1890, U.S. antitrust policy has depended fundamentally on how dearly the country has valued competition over rival systems of economic organization. The antitrust laws embody a social preference for the primacy of market forces and limited government supervision of the economy. These measures, however, are neither the sole nor final expressions of national economic policy. The antitrust laws coexist with many other statutes and policies that either stress more intrusive government efforts to guide economic activity or exempt various industries from the competition rules applying to business generally.

Antitrust's economic policy role has varied dramatically over time as a function of three opposing forces. One force is the cooperative or planning vision of business–government relations, which urges that competitors be allowed to coordinate production and product development activities under the guidance of public agencies. In 1914, Walter Lippmann's formative indictment of antitrust barriers to cooperation attacked "the antitrust people" for their efforts at "breaking up the beginning of a collective organization, thwarting the possibility of cooperation, and insisting upon submitting industry to the wasteful, the planless scramble of little profiteers." In a scathing assessment of the antitrust laws, Lippmann said that "[h]ow much they have perverted the constructive genius of this country it is impossible to imagine." Walter Lippmann, *Drift and Mastery* 78–79 (1914: Prentice–Hall Edition, 1961). Charles Van Hise, an economist and major figure in economic policy debates in the early Twentieth Century, likewise argued that "[i]f we isolate ourselves and insist upon the subdivision of industry below the highest economic efficiency and do not allow cooperation, we shall be defeated in the world's markets." Charles R. Van Hise, *Concentration and Control: A Solution of the Trust Problem in the United States* 277–78 (1912).

From the end of World War I until the late 1930s, the ascent of cooperation and planning theories severely diminished antitrust enforcement. In the 1920s, the Justice Department and the FTC concentrated more on promoting "fair" competition, particularly through trade associations and other "sentinels" of fair business conduct, than on wiping out restrictive practices and attacking monopoly power. In the first half of the 1930s, U.S. economic policy emphasized industry-wide coordination of output and pricing under the aegis of government-sponsored cartels. Only by the decade's end, after the collapse of the New Deal's National Recovery Administration and the appointment of Thurman Arnold to head the Justice Department's Antitrust Division did antitrust emerge from the "era of neglect." Richard Hofstadter, *What Happened to the Antitrust Movement?*, in The Paranoid Style in American Politics and Other Essays 193 (1965); see also Ellis W. Hawley, *The New Deal and the Problem of Monopoly* (1966).

Since the late 1930s, except for a hiatus during World War II, significant antitrust enforcement generally has been a serious force affecting business practices and the organization of American industry. During the post-war era, however, some commentators who otherwise favor government intervention to promote economic growth have argued that antitrust is counterproductive. See, e.g., Lester C. Thurow, *Head to Head: The Coming Economic Battle Among Japan, Europe, and America* 29–35, 286 (1992). Their view emerges today in debates about the proper role of government in promoting the development of specific industries and in facilitating cooperation among rival firms. A number of subjects addressed later in this text, including the treatment of horizontal restraints and joint ventures (see Chapters 5 and 6), reflect concessions to the view that antitrust has unduly impeded collaboration among competitors.

A second constraining force on antitrust has been the successful efforts of firms to enlist the government's help to suppress competitors. Privately imposed trade restraints tend to decay over time, mainly because firms eventually defect from anticompetitive agreements in search of private gain. By contrast, publicly imposed trade restraints are more durable due to the state's superior ability to block new entry and enforce compliance with output restrictions. Efforts to impose public restraints on private rivalry have led courts to devise doctrines, treated in Chapter 13 as the state action and *Noerr* doctrines, to reconcile antitrust's competition mandate with conflicting policies that protect attempts (and successful efforts) by private economic actors to persuade government bodies to curtail rivalry.

A third constraining force consists of modern commentary that doubts the antitrust system's capacity to distinguish effectively between procompetitive and anticompetitive conduct and warns of antitrust's potential to reduce consumer welfare. See Fred S. McChesney, *Be True to Your School: Conflicting Chicago Approaches to Antitrust and Regulation,* 10 Cato J. 775 (1991). Some observers emphasize inherent limits on the ability of government agencies and courts to understand the purpose and effect of business practices. See George Bittlingmayer, *Decreasing Average Cost and the Addyston Pipe Case,* 25 J.L. & Econ. 201 (1985); Harold Demsetz, *How Many Cheers for Antitrust's 100 Years?,* 30 Econ. Inquiry 207 (1992). Others stress the antitrust system's susceptibility to rent-seeking by firms that use antitrust suits to handicap rivals, see William J. Baumol & Janusz A. Ordover, *Use of Antitrust to Subvert Competition*, 28 J.L. & Econ. 247 (1985); Michael E. DeBow, *The Social Costs of Populist Antitrust: A Public Choice Perspective*, 14 Harv. J.L. & Pub. Pol'y 205 (1991), or by public officials who face weak incentives to make policy choices that maximize taxpayer interests. See William F. Shughart, III, *Antitrust Policy and Interest Group Politics* 82–120 (1990). This perspective has not exerted the influence of the two forces mentioned above, but it has inspired a reexamination of the widely-assumed public interest rationales for antitrust. See *The Causes and Consequences of Antitrust: A Public Choice Perspective* (Fred S. McChesney & William F. Shughart, III, eds. 1994).

5. SUMMARY

The antitrust system's institutional traits ensure that existing doctrine and policy will remain subject to continuing pressures that adjust enforcement approaches and judicial analysis over time. Since 1977, antitrust has moved considerably toward accepting a relatively conservative efficiency orientation. This perspective has been, and will continue to be, criticized by those who prefer a different goals hierarchy and by those who believe that efficiency, properly conceived, dictates more expansive enforcement. The antitrust system's decentralized character ensures that competing views will press upon enforcement officials and federal judges. Thus, the chapters that follow seek to offer both a static snapshot of existing doctrine and a dynamic view of likely future developments.

CHAPTER III

ANTITRUST ECONOMICS (IN A NUTSHELL)

Antitrust promotes competition out of the belief that competition presses producers to satisfy consumer wants at the lowest price while using the fewest resources. Producer rivalry lets consumers bid for goods and services, thus matching their desires with society's opportunity costs.

In economic terms, competition maximizes consumer welfare by increasing both allocative efficiency (making what consumers want as shown by their willingness to pay) and productive efficiency (producing goods or services at the lowest cost thus using the fewest resources), and by encouraging progressiveness (rewarding innovation). Competition maximizes society's total wealth but does not necessarily result in optimal income distribution. By emphasizing competition, current antitrust policy focuses mainly on maximizing the size of society's economic pie. How that pie is distributed is left mainly for other forces to decide (i.e., the market or other legislation).[1]

In seeking to foster competition, antitrust relies on the "market" system (free enterprise) to decide what shall be

1. Scholars dispute how antitrust would change if wealth distribution effects guided judicial and enforcement agency decisions. Compare Robert H. Lande, *Chicago's False Foundation: Wealth Transfers (Not Just Efficiency) Should Guide Antitrust,* 58 Antitrust L.J. 631, 641–44 (1989) (major adjustments likely in analysis of mergers and price discrimination) with Terry Calvani, *Rectangles & Triangles: A Response to Mr. Lande,* 58 Antitrust L.J. 657 (1989) (anticipating minimal change).

produced, how resources shall be allocated in the production process, and to whom goods will be distributed. The market system relies on consumers to decide (by their willingness or refusal to buy) what and how much shall be produced, and on competition among producers to determine (by making the appropriate quality product at the lowest price) who will manufacture it.

Yet the economic case for free markets does not imply that the market always will function properly when confronted by efforts to substitute private rule (e.g., competitor agreements to fix prices above the competitive price) for the more or less automatic adjustment mechanisms that competition provides. The antitrust laws are a legislative acknowledgment that markets display varying degrees of rivalry, and that some markets are not competitive. Antitrust tries to assure that the gap between the ideal of competition and the reality of some forms of private rule does not grow dangerously wide.

Choices other than reliance on competition to protect consumer welfare are possible. Before the development of an industrial society (particularly in feudal times), status or tradition governed production, resource allocation, and distribution. Today, central planning—which substitutes government control for free market exchange—makes these economic decisions in some sectors of our economy and in some areas of the world. However, even a system of central control must wrestle with the same questions of who produces and consumes what goods. The shift to market systems in many formerly communist or socialist states reflects the realization that, despite their flaws, markets resolve these questions more effectively than central planning. Indeed, in many countries, the transition to a market system has included the enactment of antitrust laws. See Clive S. Gray & Anthony A. Davis, *Competition*

Policy in Developing Countries Undergoing Structural Adjustment, 38 Antitrust Bull. 425 (1993).

For lawyers aspiring to practice skillfully in fields of law that concern the market system, a basic familiarity with economics is indispensable. Recognition of this principle is as old as the Sherman Act itself. In the late 1890s, Justice Holmes observed that "[f]or the rational study of the law the black letter man may be the man of the present, but the man of the future is the man of statistics and the master of economics." Oliver Wendell Holmes, Jr., *The Path of the Law,* 10 Harv. L. Rev. 457, 469 (1897). Nearly twenty years later, Louis Brandeis, who was Holmes' friend and colleague on the Supreme Court, told a bar association group that training for legal practice should include the "study of economics and sociology and politics which embody the facts and present the problems of the day." To punctuate his point, Brandeis quoted a scholar who said "[o]ne can hardly escape from the conclusion that a lawyer who has not studied economics and sociology is very apt to become a public enemy." Louis D. Brandeis, *The Living Law,* in The Curse of Bigness 316, 325 (Osmond K. Frankel ed. 1934).

These admonitions apply with special force in antitrust. Because antitrust cases involve economic issues, the disputes that set trends and establish primary principles revolve significantly around the perceived economic effect of business conduct. Today, microeconomics (or "price theory")—the study of how individual economic units (the consumer, firm, and industry) behave—falls squarely within the antitrust lawyer's province. Hiring expert economic consultants or witnesses will not discharge the lawyer's responsibility. Competence in antitrust requires a working knowledge of traditional economic concepts of competition, monopoly, monopolistic competition, and oligopoly, as well as a grasp of newer theories dealing with information, transaction costs, game theory, and contestable markets. These theories serve as starting points for policy analysis. Their main value is their ability to help clarify thought and to bring a conceptual basis to untidy areas of the law.

This Chapter focuses on basic economic principles relevant to antitrust policy. It is not a substitute for the study of economics. Rather, the emphasis here is on the central core. This is not to say that the core's content is frozen in time. Economics is a dynamic discipline with rival schools of thought. Over time, the forming and testing of hypotheses spur the discovery, refinement, and displacement of analytical models. Even where economists agree on core principles, disputes often arise over applications of specific theories and interpretations of empirical data. This text strives to describe general areas of agreement, to note major areas of dispute, and to identify emerging theories and applications that may influence courts and enforcement agencies in the next few years.

A. SOME BASIC EXPLANATIONS AND BEHAVIORAL ASSUMPTIONS

1. THE DEMAND SCHEDULE

When economists refer to "demand" or "the demand function," they are identifying a *demand schedule*—a statement of the different quantities of a good or service that a consumer would buy at each of several different (alternative) price levels. Because the amount of an item that a person will purchase cannot be determined without also considering its price, demand cannot be identified as a set, specific quantity. Rather, the demand for a product consists of a *range* of alternative quantities. The relationship between the various possible prices and the quantities demanded at each price constitutes the demand schedule.

The demand schedule or demand curve for any good can also be illustrated on a simple, two-dimensional price/quantity graph as follows in Figure 1:

FIGURE 1: DEMAND CURVE

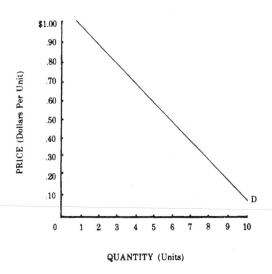

QUANTITY (Units)

Notice that the demand curve slopes downward, reflecting the law of diminishing value. Simply stated, this rule holds that the more one has of any good, the lower the (personal substitution) value it possesses for her. The value a consumer will attach to successive units of a commodity diminishes as her total consumption of that commodity increases (the consumption of all other commodities being held constant). For example, even the most ice cream-addicted child will experience diminishing marginal utility after her fifth chocolate soda in the same afternoon.

Notice as well that the reverse is also true, namely, the higher the relative price for the good, the lower its rate of consumption. This simple statement, that one will seek to buy less of an economic good as the price is raised (or more as its price is lowered), is an economic postulate central to understanding basic price theory and to our analysis of antitrust. It can be stated many ways: technically—the quantity demanded varies inversely with price; graphically—the demand curve is negatively or downwardly sloped; popularly—the more you have the less you want. It matters not whether one remembers this fundamental law of demand on the basis that the demand curve for all commodities is negatively sloped, that the rate of consumption increases as price falls, or that the more sodas one drinks in an afternoon the less one will pay for another, as long as the central point is understood.

Observed behavior substantiates the basic theorem; it is a law of demand because it describes a general truth about consumers' desires and about market behavior.[2] For example, since the early 1970s, consumers have radically modified long-established automobile purchasing habits and boosted consumption of smaller, more fuel efficient vehicles because of increased gasoline prices and other pressures. A price decline increases the rate of consumption because more of the item will be consumed in current uses, because

2. Sometimes consumer behavior is said to defy this proposition. *Giffen's Paradox* posits that consumers will buy more of some goods where the relative price of such goods rises. Common theoretical illustrations include situations where the good is sought for speculation; demand is for prestige items; price is believed to indicate higher quality; or the income effect for the buyer of purchasing *inferior* (as opposed to *normal*) goods overcomes the loss of satisfaction from substituting a lower quality good for a good of higher quality. For explanations of why these examples further support (or do not disprove) the theory, see Richard G. Lipsey, Peter O. Steiner, Douglas D. Purvis & Paul N. Courant, *Economics* 133–36 (9th ed. 1990).

new uses will develop (which were valued at too low a level
to have justified paying the former, higher rate), and because new users will appear from among consumers whose
marginal utilities or incomes were too low. The reverse, of
course, holds true for the case of higher prices. All of these
factors explain why a change in the price of a commodity
alters the amount demanded.

2. PROFIT–MAXIMIZING BEHAVIOR BY FIRMS

Economic theory generally assumes that each business
has one primary goal—to make as much money (more
particularly, profit—the amount by which revenues exceed
costs) as possible. That is, every firm seeks to maximize its
profits. It follows, then, that the firm's ultimate aims will
not be influenced by who manages the firm or the type of
firm involved; the imperative to generate profits ordinarily
pervades all firms, corporate giants or small proprietor-
ships, alike.[3] Business managers may not maximize profits
consciously, but competition among firms drives them to
act as if they did. Firms fail or prosper depending on how
successfully they approximate this result.

Not all firms are equally assiduous in seeking to maximize their owners' (shareholders') wealth. The simple profit
maximization model assumes that the costs to shareholders
of monitoring managers and implementing incentives to
perform efficiently are negligible. Where such costs in fact
are significant, managers might emphasize goals other than
profit maximization (e.g., paying themselves extravagant
salaries) or might tolerate excessive organizational slack.
See Jean Tirole, *The Theory of Industrial Organization* 35–

3. Various other factors (e.g., restraints on corporate control) may
distort how the firm achieves this end. In forming public policy that
governs firm conduct, it is necessary first to understand the firm's basic
aim and operation where such conditions are not controlling.

41 (1988). Yet managerial discretion resulting from weaknesses in monitoring and incentive schemes is not unbounded. Managerial compensation can be tied to firm performance, managerial skill can be measured by comparing the firm's performance to that of its rivals, and the market for corporate control confronts the slothful manager with the possibility that others will buy her firm and install new management. See Bengt R. Holmstrom & Jean Tirole, *The Theory of the Firm,* in 1 Handbook of Industrial Organization 61, 86–106 (Richard Schmalensee & Robert D. Willig eds. 1989). As F.M. Scherer and David Ross conclude, "the profit maximization assumption at least provides a good first approximation in describing business behavior. Deviations, both intended and inadvertent, undoubtedly exist in abundance, but they are kept within more or less narrow bounds by competitive pressures, the self-interest of stock-owning managers, and the threat of managerial displacement by outside shareholders or takeovers." F.M. Scherer & D. Ross, *Industrial Market Structure and Economic Performance,* at 52. As a rough rule of thumb, the more competitive the market, the less significant will be departures from profit-maximizing conduct.

Profit maximization theory supports further predictions about firm behavior. In making production decisions, the firm will adhere to the principle of substitution—that for a given set of technical possibilities, efficient (profit-maximizing) production will substitute cheaper factors (of labor, land, or capital) for more expensive ones. Which factors are "cheaper" depends on their ability to produce the same output. It also follows that a firm will tend to change production methods with shifts in the relative prices of inputs. Therefore, if labor costs increase relatively (or if material costs drop), a firm will become capital intensive, and vice versa. The theory of the firm *suggests* that, to maximize profits, the firm will seek to organize its factors of production efficiently and put its resources to their most valuable (highest valued) use. It only suggests this result, however. Where the market is competitive, market pressures will force this result over time.

Efficient production generally means that a firm will seek the lowest possible costs for a particular rate of output. A profit-maximizing firm will increase production when the additional revenue exceeds the additional costs. That is, the firm will expand its output as long as the marginal, or last, unit adds more to revenues than it does to costs— namely, as long as the marginal revenue exceeds or equals marginal cost.[4] If the firm finds that greater production increases profit, it will expand output; if greater production decreases profit, output will be reduced. This rule of profit-maximizing behavior is readily illustrated as follows in Figure 2:

4. As used here (and by economists), "cost" must include a normal, competitive return on investment sufficient to attract capital into the industry.

FIGURE 2: PROFIT MAXIMIZATION BY A FIRM [5]

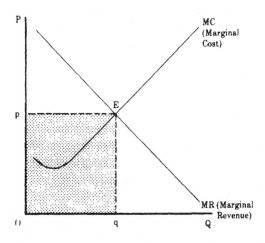

Thus, if it is profitable for a firm to produce at all, it will expand output whenever marginal revenue (*MR*) exceeds marginal cost (*MC*) and keep expanding output until marginal revenue equals marginal cost (or the intersection of *MC* and *MR* at equilibrium point *E*).[6] As explained further below, the profit-maximizing price for this hypothetical firm in a competitive market is *p* which equates with output *q* (and generates total revenues reflected by the shaded square bounded by the lines drawn between points *p–E–q–O*, assuming a single price). Again, this explanation merely sets forth what common sense suggests. As a firm increases production, costs will first decline (the hook on *MC*), but

5. In this and subsequent figures, "P" on the vertical line stands for "price (per unit)," and "Q" on horizontal line stands for "quantity (units)."

6. This simplified analysis stops short of exploring long-run versus short-run factors which would require consideration of fixed and variable costs, average and total costs, and long- and short-run variations. Though not pursued here, examination of these additional factors confirms the basic principles.

as the firm's output reaches and then passes its most efficient production level, marginal costs will increase. And when these incremental per unit costs exceed the amount received for the last item produced, the firm will cease raising its production.

B. BASIC ECONOMIC MODELS

Economic theory traditionally concludes that the structure of an industry affects its behavior and, ultimately, its performance. Though merely theoretical constructs, structural economic models yield predictions about likely firm and market behavior. These models are analytic tools, however, and they do not completely explain real world markets. The brief description below is designed to *introduce* beginning antitrust students and practitioners to core economic concepts that are critical in antitrust. Actual markets reside between the polar extremes of perfect competition and monopoly and are affected by many forces. Nevertheless, understanding these models is important because they assist in discerning how markets operate, in interpreting judicial antitrust decisions (which often rely on these and related economic concepts), and in evaluating antitrust enforcement.

1. PERFECT COMPETITION

Perfect competition describes a market where consumer interests are controlling. Producers respond to consumer tastes by producing what buyers want and, in competition with each other, at the lowest price. The market is efficient in the sense that no rearrangement of production or distribution will improve the position of any consumer or seller (without making someone else worse off). Societal wealth is maximized because resources are put to their highest valued use and output is optimal.

The following conditions, which suggest the existence of perfect competition, are also useful in predicting whether competitive behavior is likely in a market:

(1) There are many buyers and sellers.

(2) The quantity of the market's products bought by any buyer or sold by any seller is so small relative to the total quantity traded that changes in these quantities leave market prices unaffected.

(3) The product is homogeneous; no buyer has a reason to prefer a particular seller and vice versa.

(4) All buyers and sellers have perfect information about market prices and the nature of the goods sold.

(5) There is complete freedom of entry into and exit out of the market.

Brief analysis explains why these market conditions are conducive to competition. With many sellers, no one producer can charge more for her product than the cost (including a reasonable investment return) of making and selling it. If a higher price were charged, the buyer simply would turn to the seller's competitors. Easy entry and exit are important because they make investment attractive: a company that is frozen in a market and cannot be sold is less attractive; and easy entry limits the ability of firms in the market to produce less and raise prices individually or collectively.

An example illustrates the workings of a perfectly competitive market. In a mythical industry producing a standardized product known as a widget, there are 100 well-informed sellers and 500 well-informed buyers. No individual seller (or buyer) can affect the price of a widget, as each has a trivial part of the market. Except as the market is changing (to reflect changing costs, consumer tastes, etc.), the price will be uniform. Since the product is homogeneous, buyers will shift purchases to sellers offering the best prices and services. This pressure forces sellers to improve their product and services while also providing lower relative prices. See also Herbert Hovenkamp, *Economics and Federal Antitrust Law* 1–14 (1985).

Graphically, the situation confronting any particular seller may be represented as follows in Figure 3:

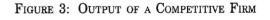

FIGURE 3: OUTPUT OF A COMPETITIVE FIRM

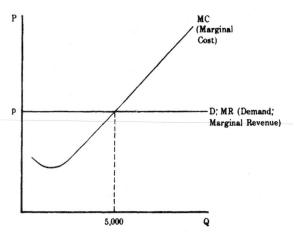

The *individual* seller faces a level, *horizontal,* or *infinitely elastic demand curve* since 99 other firms sell widgets that are perfect substitutes for her widget.[7] The seller takes whatever price the market sets and is therefore often called a price-taker. Regardless of the amount of her

7. The widget *industry* faces a *downwardly sloping demand curve* similar to that shown in Figure 1; however, because each firm sells such a small fraction of the amount demanded, the demand curve facing each seller seems virtually horizontal.

output that she puts on the market, the price will be *p*. Thus, if she raises her price above *p*, her sales will drop to zero. Nor does she have an incentive to charge less than the market price because all that she can produce can be sold at the prevailing price.

The output of a price-taking seller is determined by her costs. Since a price-taker can sell all, or as little, as she wants at the market price, her marginal revenue curve—the revenue she receives from the last unit sold—is identical to the demand curve; with a horizontal individual demand curve, each unit sold by the seller adds the same amount to her revenue. But as the seller increases her sales, the marginal costs of production will rise, as she tries to squeeze extra output from a limited facility, pays overtime, buys raw materials from a greater distance, etc.[8] This is reflected in the rising nature of the marginal cost curve in Figure 3, supra. The firm may alter its costs only by changing the size of its production run. As indicated earlier, the individual seller will operate where her marginal cost equals marginal revenue, here at 5,000 units, as this is the point at which profits are maximized.

So far we have described only the operation of one firm in a perfectly competitive market. The industry as a whole is the sum of its parts. Total output will be determined by what consumers will pay (the demand curve) at that price. Price is set by the cost of producing that output by the lowest-cost producers of that amount. If costs rise, so will price (but output will fall) as long as everything else remains the same—and vice versa. To illustrate the aggrega-

8. The theory of perfect competition also requires that costs eventually rise. Continually decreasing costs would lead a firm to increase output until it produced the entire industry output, in contrast to conditions encountered by most firms. This situation often is described as natural monopoly. See infra pp. 70–71.

tion of all firms in the widget industry, an additional graph
(Figure 4) is useful:

FIGURE 4: OUTPUT OF A COMPETITIVE INDUSTRY

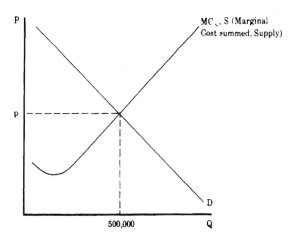

The *industry* marginal cost curve represents the sum of
individual cost functions; it is also the industry supply
schedule. The industry demand curve is *downwardly sloping* as there is no perfect substitute for widgets. The
individual firms' demand curves were flat, indicating infinite price elasticity of demand (greater responsiveness of
the amount demanded to a change in price), because the
widgets of the other 99 firms were a perfect substitute.
However, as there is no perfect substitute for widgets, the
industry demand curve will reflect some inelasticity. Thus,
a decrease in the price of widgets (e.g., due to new cost-
cutting technology) will increase the quantity demanded;
an increase in the industry price (e.g., due to a cartel
controlling a factor of production) will cause a decrease in
the quantity demanded.

Perfect competition yields favorable results for consumers because resources are used and distributed efficiently. The demand curve facing the industry represents a social ranking of wants, that is, the amount consumers are willing to pay for a widget as compared to an alternative expenditure. The marginal cost curve expresses the cost in resources to society of producing another widget. Under such a system, products are produced until the value of the next unit would not be justified in the eyes of any available consumer. The economy is productively efficient as factors of production are employed where their value is the greatest. And the economy is allocatively efficient as products are produced in the quantity consumers want.

The essential points bear repetition so they are not missed. In a perfectly competitive market, the individual firm is merely a quantity adjuster. All firms sell at marginal cost and earn only a normal return on investment. Each firm takes price as set by the market; no firm can affect the price by adjusting output or adjust output by raising or lowering price. Each firm strives to maximize profits by adjusting its output (either increasing or decreasing the quantity sold) until its marginal cost equals the prevailing market price. Here the consumer is sovereign. Firms in a competitive market respond to (rather than dictate) changes in market prices. Finally, the free-market system coerces efficiency from individual firms, and no firm realizes monopoly profits.

The theory of perfect competition is important even though it precisely describes few, if any, markets. Its insights illuminate how a competitive market works and the benefits it can confer. It also provides a standard for measuring market performance. The conditions of perfect competition (of many sellers/buyers, small market shares, product homogeneity, perfect information, and easy entry and exit) are similarly useful in suggesting where competitive behavior is likely. On the other hand, the absence of these conditions does not necessarily prevent a market from behaving competitively. As experience in several industries (e.g., the production of commercial airliners) shows, intense competition can occur even as markets become highly concentrated. In other words, these conditions neither define perfect competition nor are a priori present where competitive rivalry is inevitable or likely.

2. MONOPOLY

In general terms, private monopoly is the other side of the theoretical coin of perfect competition. A seller with monopoly power restricts her output in order to raise her price and maximize her profits. Not only does this transfer wealth from consumers to producers, but it also reduces output and may relieve the producer of pressure to innovate or otherwise be efficient.

Monopoly markets are often described by three structural and functional factors, namely:

(1) One seller occupies the entire market.

(2) The seller's product is unique (i.e., there are no close substitutes to which consumers can turn).

(3) Substantial barriers bar entry by other firms into the industry, and exit is difficult.

Note again that the existence of some of these conditions is useful only in predicting where monopoly pricing and output restrictions are likely since these results may not in fact occur and since markets with much different conditions also may exhibit monopoly practices. In other words, these conditions by themselves do not determine whether monopoly effects will exist.[9]

Perhaps the most distinctive feature of a monopoly (or imperfectly competitive) market is the existence of barriers to entry. Without such constraints, other firms are likely to enter and take sales away if the monopolist seeks to raise price or lower quality from the competitive norm. The most potent entry barriers often are legal constraints that effectively bar other firms from serving specific markets (e.g., air quality restrictions that prevent construction of new plants in a geographic area) or grant exclusive property rights to inventors of new products or production processes for which there are no close substitutes (e.g., patents for certain drugs). Other entry barriers include essential raw materials or distribution channels that make entry unlikely because of a relative cost disadvantage facing those currently outside the market. As discussed in Chapter 4, defining what constitutes an entry barrier is a controversial matter in deciding antitrust cases and in setting government enforcement policy.

By definition, monopoly describes the situation where one seller produces the output of an entire industry or market—and the *downwardly sloping* industry demand curve is ipso facto identical to that seller's demand curve. If all widget producers in our discussion of perfect competition had merged into one firm, it would be in such a monopoly position.

Because she faces the downwardly sloping market demand curve rather than the competitive firm's flat demand

---

9. In practice, economists and lawyers often define monopoly simply in terms of effects. That is, they suspect a market is monopolized if a firm consistently makes supranormal profits, if its costs exceed costs attainable at the most efficient scale of production, if selling expenditures are excessive, or technological progress is inadequate. Such effects flow from the existence or use of monopoly power.

curve, the monopolist does not maximize her profits at the competitive output of 500,000 units. The reason is simple. For the competitive seller marginal revenue is the same at all output levels, and always equals the market price. How much she produces has no impact on price and is determined by the shape of her marginal cost curve. The monopolist, on the other hand, finds marginal revenue always less than price because her demand curve slopes downward. If only a single price is charged, every expansion of output requires a price reduction (reducing her average revenue); therefore, the last unit sold produces less revenue than the preceding sale. A monopolist who cannot discriminate in her prices among customers and who expands output will have to accept a lower price, not just on the additional units but on all units sold. The monopolist can obtain additional sales only by lowering the price charged on her entire output.

As a result, the monopolist faces a choice on production and price: either sell at a higher price (with fewer unit sales) or sell at a lower price (with greater unit sales). In making this choice, the monopolist will maximize profits at less than the competitive output level—namely, where marginal revenue equals marginal cost. Thus, contrary to the competitive result, the monopolist will maximize profits by restricting output and setting price above marginal cost.

The description of the monopoly market can also be understood by reference to the market demand curve which was plotted above in Figure 1. Viewing that curve as the market demand for widgets, the monopolist has the same curve for her firm's demand. Knowing this demand, she can determine the price which would maximize her profits by determining her marginal revenue (i.e., the revenue earned from each additional widget sold). The seller can determine her total revenue from each price, then the marginal revenue for each additional unit sold, and finally, assuming that she could manufacture widgets at a cost of ten cents each, the profit from each additional unit sold:

TABLE 1—DEMAND SCHEDULE, MARGINAL
REVENUE AND ECONOMIC PROFIT

Price	Amount Demanded	Total Revenue	Marginal Revenue	Marginal Cost	Total Cost	Economic Profit
$1.00	1	$1.00	$1.00	$.10	$ .10	$ .90
.90	2	1.80	+ .80	.10	.20	1.60
.80	3	2.40	+ .60	.10	.30	2.10
.70	4	2.80	+ .40	.10	.40	2.40
.60	5	3.00	+ .20	.10	.50	2.50
.50	6	3.00	0	.10	.60	2.40
.40	7	2.80	− .20	.10	.70	2.10
.30	8	2.40	− .40	.10	.80	1.60
.20	9	1.80	− .60	.10	.90	.90
.10	10	1.00	− .80	.10	1.00	0

As this table shows, the seller's most profitable position is to sell five units at $.60. At this point her economic profit is $2.50, a return on investment that she cannot improve. That is, she maximizes her profits at a price of $.60 because there would be no additional profit from selling an additional unit.

Another way to see why the monopolist exercises her pricing/output option in this way is to draw a graph (Figure 5) of the monopolist's demand (or average revenue) and marginal revenue curves:

FIGURE 5: PRICING BY A MONOPOLIST[10]

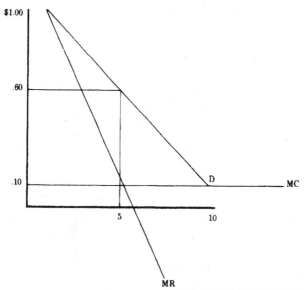

As stated earlier, the marginal revenue line is always less than price because the monopolist has to lower her price on *all* units in order to sell an extra (last, or marginal) unit.[11]

10. Actually, the monopolist would like to increase output slightly since her profit-maximizing position is where marginal revenue and marginal cost intersect. See Figure 6 below. This could be achieved if widgets were sold in partial units (and price were set at less than 10 cent intervals). For simplicity, this illustration rounds these figures.

11. For a technical explanation of why the MR curve slopes downward if the demand curve is a downwardly sloping straight line, and why it is twice as steep, see R. Lipsey et al., *Economics,* at 246–49, 950.

To describe a more realistic picture of the situation facing the monopolist, then, one need only alter Figure 5 to show an increasing marginal cost curve. Both the competitive industry (as shown in Figure 4 above) and the monopolist generally face increasing marginal costs because an increase in production will raise unit costs. This is shown by the price/quantity graph in Figure 6:

FIGURE 6: PROFIT-MAXIMIZING MONOPOLIST

(INCREASING MARGINAL COST)

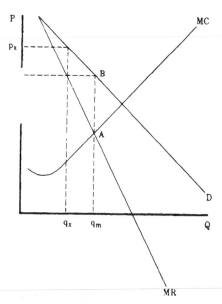

The monopolist maximizes her profit by producing an output quantity where her marginal revenue equals marginal cost (Point A, Figure 6; q_m will be drawn in, vertically, where MR intersects MC) and by charging whatever price her demand curve reveals is necessary to sell that output (Point B, Figure 6).[12] Stated more simply, the profit-maximizing monopolist, facing a downward sloping demand curve, will increase her output only as long as her profits increase.[13] The monopolist's total net revenue no longer

12. The monopolist's output will equal that amount revealed where the marginal revenue curve (MR) and the marginal cost line (MC) intersect. The output q_m will be sold at price p_m.

13. This discussion assumes that the monopolist's profit is her total revenue less her marginal cost. In fact, the monopolist's profit is determined by her average total cost curve. All we know when marginal cost increases when marginal cost (*MC*) exceeds marginal revenue (*MR*) for a unit because, by definition, the cost of producing and selling this last unit of sales then exceeds the revenue garnered by that sale. That is, it is sold at a loss. And to maximize her profit, the monopolist sets the price (p_m) at which the market demand curve intersects this quantity (q_m). If, for example, she sets price above this level, at say p_x, consumers would buy only quantity q_x. While unit price (p_x) and profit per unit would be higher, total profits would fall. Similarly, if prices were set below this level and quantity were unchanged, she would not be charging "all the market could bear." Remember, profits are *always* maximized by selling the quantity indicated where marginal costs equal marginal revenue.

Note that the theory of monopoly describes a seller who is insulated from the loss of customers by sellers of other identical or substitute products. However, all products face some substitutes for the services they provide, so that total monopoly power never exists. Monopoly power is a matter of degree and not an absolute; it is not the complete counterpart to perfect competition.

Before closing this section, we note the existence of another market structure in which a single firm can distort the efficient allocation of resources. Unlike monopoly, which involves a market occupied by a single seller, the condition of *monopsony* exists when there is a single purchaser for a good or service. The most common illustrations involve labor markets in which one entity is the sole employer for a specific group of workers. For example, a sports league may be the only purchaser of the services of players who participate in the sport. A monopsonist im-

equals marginal revenue is that the monopolist does better at this output level than at any other output, not that her operation is particularly profitable.

pedes efficient resource allocation by setting lower prices for the affected input and using fewer resources than it would in a competitive market featuring many buyers. See Roger D. Blair & Jeffrey L. Harrison, *Monopsony: Antitrust Law and Economics* 36–61 (1993).

3. COMPETITION AND MONOPOLY COMPARED

Compared to perfect competition, the primary effects of monopoly are reduced output, higher prices, and a transfer of income from consumers to producers. In short, should a perfectly competitive industry become monopolized, and all cost curves remain unaffected, price will rise (from p_c to p_m, Figure 7) and quantity produced will fall (from q_c to q_m, Figure 7). This is readily seen in Figure 7, which overlays the price/quantity graphs for the two industries on one another:

FIGURE 7: MONOPOLIZING A COMPETITIVE INDUSTRY [14]

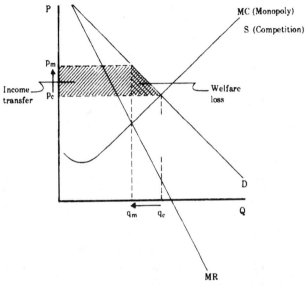

For example, when the industry is competitive, price will be at p_c and output at q_c. Should the industry become monopolized, output would be reduced to q_m and price raised to p_m. Monopoly pricing and production decisions also will cause a transfer of income from consumers to producers which, if costs remain unchanged, will be reflected in increased profits for the monopolist as generally illustrated by the diagonally-lined rectangle.[15]

Monopoly pricing also leads to what is known as a deadweight welfare loss, illustrated by the cross-hatched triangular area in Figure 7. It represents the loss in value to consumers who at the competitive price would buy the

14. This figure duplicates onto one graph Figures 4 and 6 supra.

15. This simplified description does not distinguish between average and marginal costs. Including average cost would alter the rectangle's size and shape, but it would not dispute the basic point that income is being transferred from consumers to producers. See F.M. Scherer & D. Ross, *Industrial Market Structure and Economic Performance*, at 679–81.

product, but who at the monopoly price are deflected to "inferior" substitutes. The fact that the monopolist's price exceeds her marginal cost in this region indicates that the value of the product to consumers who no longer buy it exceeds society's cost of producing it. This loss to some customers is not recouped by the monopolist (or anyone else), for the monopolist obtains no revenue from output that she does not produce. Society is poorer because resources in the economy could be used more productively in the industry restricting output than in the industry making the inferior substitute in which they are actually used. The area of the deadweight loss indicates society's welfare loss due to monopolistic resource misallocation.

The precise magnitude of the deadweight loss is uncertain and disputed. In 1954 Arnold Harberger found the deadweight loss to be relatively trivial and, by implication, a thin reed on which to rest a far-reaching antimonopoly policy. Arnold Harberger, *Monopoly and Resource Allocation,* 44 Am. Econ. Rev. 77 (1954). Subsequent studies have been inconclusive, finding evidence that sustains and refutes Harberger's analysis. See Roger D. Blair & David L. Kaserman, *Antitrust Economics* 38 (1985). After trying to correct for possible methodological biases that shaped Harberger's results, Professors Scherer and Ross have concluded that the deadweight welfare loss from monopolistic resource misallocation in the United States "lies somewhere between 0.5 and 2 percent of gross national product." F.M. Scherer & D. Ross, *Industrial Market Structure and Economic Performance,* at 667.[16]

The ill-effects of monopoly extend beyond wealth distribution distortions and deadweight allocative efficiency loss-

16. According to the theory of the "second best," the deadweight loss may be overstated. See F.M. Scherer & D. Ross, *Industrial Market Structure and Economic Performance,* at 33–38.

es. The lure of enjoying supranormal profits can induce firms to invest resources in socially unproductive activity that may yield market power. See Richard A. Posner, *The Social Cost of Monopoly and Regulation,* 83 J. Pol. Econ. 807 (1975). For example, a firm might spend heavily for the services of lawyers and lobbyists to persuade government authorities to impose import quotas that bar foreign rivals from expanding operations in the U.S. market. Although their exact dimensions are unmeasurable, the opportunity costs of rent-seeking behavior are believed to constitute a significant social cost of monopoly. Judge Richard Posner observes that the diagonally-lined rectangle in Figure 7 roughly approximates the cost resulting from competition among firms to become a monopolist. Thus, the area of this rectangle may also represent a resource cost to society. See R. Posner, *Antitrust Law,* at 11–13.

Another cost attributed to monopoly is a greater managerial tolerance for waste and inefficiency. See Harvey Leibenstein, *Beyond Economic Man* (1980). As suggested earlier in this Chapter, the absence of the competitive discipline imposed by other sellers can magnify flaws in the mechanisms by which shareholders monitor the performance of business managers, thus enabling those managers to pursue goals other than profit maximization. Shirking by managers can yield higher costs that lead marginal cost to equal marginal revenue at an output even smaller than an efficient monopolist would produce; this causes further resource misallocation.

While most emphasis is placed on the undesirable features of monopoly in comparison with competition, especially with respect to allocative and productive efficiency, monopoly is not universally condemned. Monopoly sometimes is said to be necessary to generate profits that support risky but valuable inventive activity. See Joseph A. Schumpeter,

Capitalism, Socialism and Democracy 81–110 (1950). Other observers dispute this hypothesis and argue that policies designed to stimulate rivalry (e.g., by discouraging mergers and horizontal alliances involving industry leaders) inspire superior efforts to innovate by driving firms to develop new or improved products. See Michael E. Porter, *The Competitive Advantage of Nations* 662–64 (1990). Extensive theoretical and empirical efforts to test these competing views have failed to establish strong links between alternative market structures and levels of technological progress. See Wesley M. Cohen & Richard C. Levin, *Empirical Studies of Innovation and Market Structure,* in 1 Handbook of Industrial Organization 1060 (Richard Schmalensee & Robert D. Willig eds. 1989).

Monopoly also can result inexorably in some industries from efforts to realize economies of scale and scope. In what is known as a "natural monopoly," a single firm's average costs decline with output, meaning that it is always less costly for the one firm to produce any level of output rather than subdivide production among two or more firms. See Michael A. Crew & Paul R. Kleindorfer, *The Economics of Public Utility Regulation* 4–9 (1986); Sanford V. Berg & John Tschirhart, *Natural Monopoly Regulation: Principles and Practice* 21–52 (1988). The natural monopolist also may realize important economies of scope where it is possible for one firm to produce two products more cheaply than two or more firms could. · It should be noted, however, that by definition a monopoly profit is an unnecessary payment to a firm; it would have produced the same goods even at a competitive price. Government bodies use a variety of regulatory controls and incentive schemes to prevent natural monopolists from charging prices above competitive levels. See Ronald R. Braeutigam, *Optimal Policies for Natural Monopolies,* in 1 Handbook of Industrial Organization 1290 (Richard Schmalensee & Robert D. Willig eds. 1989); Jean–Jacques Laffont & Jean Tirole, *A Theory of Incentives in Procurement and Regulation* (1993).

4. MONOPOLISTIC COMPETITION

Originated in the 1930s by Edward Chamberlin, the theory of monopolistic competition seeks to reconcile the contending forces of perfect competition and monopoly, yet it is not necessarily the middle ground between the two. Monopolistic competition is said to exist if a market has the following traits:

(1) There are many buyers and sellers, all of which are small.

(2) All buyers and sellers have perfect information about the prices in the market and the nature of the goods sold.

(3) There is complete freedom of entry into and exit out of the market.

(4) The sellers' products are heterogeneous; from the buyer's perspective, each seller's product differs at least somewhat from every other seller's product.

The fourth characteristic is crucial—each producer sells a somewhat differentiated, but substitutable, product. There are many sellers, yet each seller's product is distinct and distinguishable by brand or other means of identification from those sold by others in the industry. See B. Curtis Eaton & Richard G. Lipsey, *Product Differentiation*, in 1 Handbook of Industrial Organization 725 (Richard Schmalensee & Robert D. Willig eds. 1989). This contrasts with both competitive and monopolistic retailing where distinctive product packaging, advertising, and similar selling techniques are absent because they would not increase either price or output in the case of competition or demand in the case of monopoly.

Monopolistic competition theory often conceives of products as being arrayed spatially in a continuum according to consumer preferences. In locational models of consumer choice, the competitive significance of any product brand depends on the size of gaps that separate it from other brands that consumers regard as substitutes. In making purchasing decisions, the consumer hunts for brands that occupy the segment of the product space that satisfies her tastes. As she scans the product space for beverages, a cola drinker probably perceives Coke and Pepsi to be fairly close neighbors. By contrast, the same consumer might detect greater spatial gaps between cola drinks and carbonated lemon/lime drinks, flavored seltzers, or reconstituted fruit juices. See Dennis W. Carlton & Jeffrey M. Perloff, *Modern Industrial Organization* 332–42 (1990).[17]

Where an industry has many sellers with differentiated products, monopolistic competition theory predicts that sellers will emphasize *nonprice competition,* namely in advertising, product quality, and sales techniques, rather than price competition. It also forecasts that industry members will realize normal, competitive returns on investment since firms in the market "compete" by increasing selling costs and entry is possible; prices, on the other hand, will reflect monopoly conditions because price will embody these "extra" selling costs, output will be less than with pure competition, and average costs will be higher.

17. As discussed in Chapter 4, locational models that evaluate competition in differentiated product industries sometimes serve to define relevant markets in antitrust analysis. See Jonathan B. Baker & Timothy F. Bresnahan, *The Gains from Merger or Collusion in Product–Differentiated Industries,* 33 J. Indus. Econ. 427 (1985).

Commonly cited illustrations of this theory involve the retailing sector and consumer goods industries such as breakfast cereals, cigarettes, deodorants, proprietary drugs (e.g., aspirin), household bleach, and soft drinks. In each instance, several firms sell virtually identical products or services that are separately identified in the buyer's mind. Firms seem to gain sales mainly from advertising and other forms of nonprice competition. Monopolistic competition resembles monopoly in that sellers face negatively sloped demand curves for their somewhat unique products. It also presents aspects of competition, however, in that firms face many actual or potential competitors, and earn normal profits.

Where elements of both competition and monopoly exist, sellers can price their products above competitive levels because brand differentiation gives them a degree of monopoly power. Other similar products are not complete substitutes either because of physical differences or special features such as trademarks, distinctive styles, or advertising. On the other hand, sellers are not in the same position as monopolists because close substitutes exist for their products. For example, other antifreeze is recognized by consumers as an adequate replacement for Prestone, even though the latter has established (in this case, primarily by advertising) a strong consumer preference. Thus it is asserted that competitive pressures from close substitutes force sellers of branded products to respond with more advertising, product distinctions, or similar costly efforts that dissipate monopoly profits. Consequently, firms in monopolistic competition do not get the rewards of monopoly (their return on investment is similar to what firms earn in competitive industries), yet output and prices continue at a monopoly level. It seems, in other words, the worst of all possible worlds.

The theory of monopolistic competition is an important step in understanding monopolistic behavior. In particular, it shows how monopolistic elements in an industry can lead to production at a point where output is restricted and costs exceed those of the most efficient scale, even though the industry firms only earn a "normal" return. As a description of actual behavior, however, the theory is largely inadequate. It unrealistically assumes that all firms in an industry have identical cost and demand curves. Also, it rests upon scant empirical evidence. Moreover, monopolistic competition can, in theory, provide substantial consumer benefits. Real and imagined product differences may benefit consumers through greater product variety. Selling expenses by firms in such industries may reduce buyer search costs. These benefits may surpass the costs of either less efficient production or image advertising, thereby in fact improving consumer welfare. Finally, there are alternative—but not necessarily mutually exclusive—explanations for non-price competition. The most prominent is the theory of oligopoly, namely that sellers tacitly coordinate prices in order to earn supranormal profits. In this circumstance, product differentiation can provide an avenue for competitive activity.

5. OLIGOPOLY

Of even greater significance in antitrust than the monopolistic competition model is the theory of oligopoly. Its basic postulate that where the market contains only a *few sellers,* all sellers recognize that they are largely interdependent. Therefore, each seller accounts for its rivals' reactions when setting output and prices. This means that oligopolists will not drop prices to increase market share because they expect that any gains will be cancelled immediately when rival sellers retaliate with similar price cuts.

As a consequence, oligopoly sellers focus on coordination and anticipation. Competition occurs indirectly—by disguised price cuts (through improved quality, credit terms, delivery service, or secret selective price reductions) and nonprice competition such as product differentiation, advertising, and sales promotions. Such competition is limited, however, lest it invite retaliation or increase average total costs (which would deny the oligopolist supranormal profits). In monopolistic competition, by contrast, rivalry forces profits to normal levels because there are many sellers, each seeking to increase her market share at her rivals' expense; hence effective interfirm coordination is impossible.

The primary theoretical difference, then, between oligopoly on the one hand, and competition and monopoly (and even monopolistic competition) on the other hand, is that in oligopoly markets price and output decisions are made while anticipating the reactions of one's rivals. Neither the competitive firm nor the monopolist considers the reactions of others; the competitive seller has no impact on her rivals, and the monopolist has no close rivals. On the other hand, coordination among oligopolists is unlikely to be perfect; cost curves may differ, and more efficient firms have a strong incentive to engage in disguised price cutting to capture additional sales at or above their marginal cost but below the "market" price. Oligopoly theory does not assume that output and pricing decisions in oligopoly are identical to those in monopoly; rather, each is expected to be somewhere between predicted competitive and monopoly levels.

Both oligopolists and monopolists are affected by the actions of other firms. The oligopolist's price strategy is determined not only by her costs but also by her estimate of her rivals' pricing strategies. The monopolist's prices are determined by her costs and the price of substitute goods which, in turn, sets her demand curve. The difference between the two, then, is that the actions of rival firms both affect the oligopolist and are affected by her; the situation is circular, and the moves and countermoves of each oligopolist can be hard to predict.

Important features of oligopoly analysis can be seen in the following simple illustration: assume that three firms, Able, Baker, and Charlie, are the only sellers of widgets. If they could coordinate their output and pricing decisions, they would raise price above a competitive level and earn monopoly profits. To do so, however, requires some understanding that no firm will undercut another firm's price increase, or the advantage will be lost for all. Yet each firm's "best" pricing/output decision cannot be defined in advance without some understanding of what rivals will do. That is, Able's best (profit-maximizing) policy depends on how much Baker and Charlie produce and the price they set for their products. And, by the same analysis, neither Baker nor Charlie can know what to do until they know what Able's policy will be—or what the other will do. This is not the end of the matter, however. For now each firm also must anticipate what its rivals expect it to do. This process of guessing and outguessing one's rivals, of course, can go on and on, and for this reason oligopoly marketing strategy is often called a guessing game.

Left to their own devices, Able, Baker, and Charlie probably would eliminate most of the guesswork by forming a cartel (or to use the turn of the century term, a "trust") and collectively acting as a monopolist. However, as discussed in Chapter 5, antitrust doctrine treats such attempts at formal coordination as unlawful per se and frequently subjects such conduct to criminal prosecution under Section 1 of the Sherman Act. Even without direct evidence proving coordination on output or pricing, firms can be attacked successfully with circumstantial proof that establishes a "tacit" agreement. The question, therefore, arises: can firms achieve similar ends without express or tacit agreements prohibited by the antitrust laws? Can oligopolists use other strategies to achieve (or approximate) the results that forbidden coordination would yield?

For much of this century, economists have struggled to develop a theory that satisfactorily describes and predicts oligopoly market outcomes. From the 1950s through the mid–1970s, researchers emphasized efforts to observe the performance of firms in oligopoly markets and to measure the results. This approach was pioneered by Joe Bain who studied the profit rates of 42 industries for the years 1936–40 and found that where the eight largest firms controlled 70 percent or more of the market, average profits were considerably higher than in less concentrated markets. Joe S. Bain, *Relation of Profit Rate to Industry Concentration: American Manufacturing, 1936–40,* 65 Q. J. Econ. 293 (1951). Bain's survey suggested that oligopolistic (i.e., highly concentrated) industries acted interdependently to restrict output and raise prices above average cost and thus to earn supranormal returns. Many later studies confirmed Bain's basic findings. See Leonard Weiss, *The Concentration–Profits Relationship and Antitrust,* in Industrial Concentration: The New Learning *188 (Harvey J. Goldschmid, H. Michael Mann & J. Fred Weston eds. 1974).*

The work of Bain and other scholars indicating a strong, positive relationship between concentration and profitability gave considerable support to the "structuralist" school of antitrust, which argued that an industry's structure largely determined its conduct and performance. See James W. Meehan, Jr. & Robert J. Larner, *The Structural School, Its Critics, and Its Progeny: An Assessment,* in Economics and

Antitrust Policy 179 (Robert J. Larner & James W. Meehan, Jr. eds. 1989). Relying on structuralist models, many commentators urged broad antitrust efforts to deconcentrate American industry, including legislation to restructure monopolies and oligopolies. See Carl Kaysen & Donald F. Turner, *Antitrust Policy: An Economic and Legal Analysis* 110–19, 261–66 (1959): *White House Task Force Report on Antitrust Policy (Neal Commission),* reprinted in 21 Antitrust L. & Econ. Rev. 11, 65–76 (1968–69).

In the 1960s and early 1970s, scholars associated with the "Chicago School" of antitrust raised forceful arguments that Bain's work and subsequent studies were flawed and that deconcentration proposals were misguided. Critics focused on technical defects in studies correlating concentration with profits and questioned the persistence of any such correlation over time. Even accepting the statistical correlations as accurate reflections of industry profits, some scholars explained such results by the hypothesis that firms of superior efficiency generally will expand their market shares. Increasing concentration in an otherwise open market, then, could simply be the result of competitive efficiency with the "winners" in the market struggle gaining a larger proportion of sales. See Harold Demsetz, *Two Systems of Belief About Monopoly,* in Industrial Concentration: The New Learning 164 (Harvey J. Goldschmid, H. Michael Mann & J. Fred Weston eds. 1974).

Although the relationship between oligopoly market structure and economic performance remains a subject of study and debate, the structure-conduct-performance model on which many suggested policies (including deconcentration) toward oligopolies rested in the 1960s and 1970s has lost much of its influence as an antitrust policymaking tool. Nonetheless, as discussed in Chapter 9, the structuralist model continues to affect antitrust, particularly in judicial opinions and in government enforcement guidelines that govern mergers involving direct competitors. Merger policy builds on the assumption that firms are more likely to restrict output through formal coordination or noncoordinated interdependent behavior as the number of significant players in an industry drops. Under existing merger doctrine, antitrust scrutiny is more acute in oligopoly markets as concentration increases. Thus, merger policy has inherited and retained the structuralist model's skepticism toward increases in concentration in oligopoly industries.

This does not mean, however, that modern merger analysis relies only on concentration data. Courts and enforcement agencies also consider market characteristics other than concentration that make it easier for oligopolists to cooperate through express or tacit collusion. Industries marked by product homogeneity, frequent sales, similar cost structures among firms, and high entry barriers are more prone to collusion and more likely to approximate the performance of a collective monopoly. See Alexis Jacquemin & Margaret E. Slade, *Cartels, Collusion, and Horizontal Mergers,* in 1 Handbook of Industrial Organization 415 (Richard Schmalensee & Robert D. Willig eds. 1989).

Beyond studying the effect of market structure on firm profits, economists have sought to develop models that explain the behavior of *noncooperative* oligopolies: markets featuring a small number of firms that act independently (i.e., they do not coordinate their conduct through formal agreements such as cartel arrangements) but nonetheless recognize that the actions of other industry participants can affect their profits. Economic models have attempted to identify possible alternative courses of action and to rationalize how an oligopolist seeking to maximize profits would react to the behavior and possible strategies of its rivals.

For most of this century, the basic tools for analyzing noncooperative oligopoly behavior were *conjectural variation models* that originated mainly in the Nineteenth Century work of Antoine Augustin Cournot and Joseph Bertrand. In these models each firm forms a hypothesis about how its adversary will respond to a change in its own behavior. See D. Carlton & J. Perloff, *Modern Industrial Organization,* at 258–80. The hypothesis is known as a *conjecture*, and the firm's prediction of its rival's likely reaction is a *conjectural variation.* Based on its conjectural variations, each firm makes pricing and output choices to maximize its profits. In the basic Cournot model, each firm hypothesizes that if it changes its level of output, other firms will continue to produce at their existing levels of output. In essence, Cournot-based analysis "predicts a tendency for price to fall toward marginal cost as the number of sellers rises (that is, less concentrated industries are more likely to have prices near the competitive level)." F.M. Scherer & D. Ross, *Industrial Market Structure and Economic Performance,* at 208. The Cournot model and the other leading conjectural variations models (Bertrand and Stackelberg) work best when used in *single-period* settings. They assume that firms face each other in a single competitive episode and do not adjust their behavior according to how rivals actually change prices and output over time. This simplifying assumption facilitates explanation and empirical testing, but it is criticized for failing to capture the likely moves and countermoves of rivals.

Modern economic research has attempted to overcome the limits of static, single-period models. For roughly the past decade, game theory—the study of "rational" (optimizing) strategy in small group situations where the rivals are mutually dependent—has provided the principal means for economists to examine strategic interactions among rival oligopolists. See Carl Shapiro, *Theories of Oligopoly Behavior,* in 1 Handbook of Industrial Organization 330 (Richard Schmalensee & Robert D. Willig eds. 1989). Game theory uses sophisticated mathematical techniques to identify alternative courses of action facing oligopolist sellers and to predict how their competitive interactions will unfold over time.

An oligopoly readily lends itself to study as a game. Oligopolists are players in a contest whose outcome depends on each player's ability to anticipate its opponents' moves, to assess its own capabilities, and to develop effective strategies for blunting or forestalling rivals. Game theoretic models typically assume that firms participate in *repeated games,* confronting one another in a series of encounters; each firm observes its rivals' conduct in the previous encounter and adjusts its own behavior for the next episode. Compared to most conjectural variations models (where rivalry occurs in one episode), this *multiperiod* dimension more truly replicates many markets in which firms know that their conduct today is likely to influence their competitors' behavior tomorrow.

Although it captures phenomena that elude single-period models, game theory has its own limitations for oligopoly analysis. Among other difficulties, many game theory models fail to produce a unique equilibrium and instead present an infinite number of potential equilibria, or no equilibrium at all. See David M. Kreps, *Game Theory and Economic Modelling* 91–132 (1990). Nonetheless, game theory is beginning to affect antitrust analysis of oligopoly industries. Perhaps most important, game theory is providing a richer understanding of how firms signal their desire to cooperate with rivals, demonstrate their intent and ability to punish disfavored conduct, monitor their rivals' acts, and detect deviations from preferred behavior.

C. CURRENT DEVELOPMENTS

The search for new approaches to explain oligopoly behavior is but one front on which modern research has extended microeconomic theory and its application to industrial organization problems. See Jonathan B. Baker, *Recent Developments in Economics That Challenge Chicago School Views,* 58 Antitrust L.J. 645 (1989). Described below are several other trends in modern economic research that are influencing antitrust analysis.

Oligopoly issues are one part of a larger antitrust research agenda for game theorists. See Eric Rasmussen, *Games and Information: An Introduction to Game Theory* (1989); Drew Fudenberg & Jean Tirole, *Noncooperative Game Theory for Industrial Organization: An Introduction and Overview,* in 1 Handbook of Industrial Organization 259 (Richard Schmalensee & Robert D. Willig eds. 1989). Another line of inquiry shows how incumbent firms can exploit superior information about their costs and market conditions to chasten or exclude competitors. Debate over the application of *asymmetric information* models focuses upon whether the results of such research can be translated into testable hypotheses from which standards of business conduct might be derived. Some commentators concede the need for further work to derive operational criteria but anticipate that such criteria will be forthcoming. See Carl Shapiro, *The Theory of Business Strategy,* 20 Rand J. Econ. 125 (1989). Others are considerably less sanguine about this possibility. See Franklin M. Fisher, *Games Economists Play: A Noncooperative View,* 20 Rand J. Econ. 113 (1989).

Business strategy and information theory figure prominently in two other areas of study dealing with exclusionary conduct. One branch of analysis addresses the use of nonpricing strategies to exclude rivals by, among other means, denying them access to essential inputs or distribution channels (sometimes called "raising rivals' costs") or by making preemptive investment decisions that discourage other firms from entering specific markets or expanding capacity. See ABA Antitrust Section: Monograph No. 18, *Nonprice Predation Under Section 2 of the Sherman Act* (1991). Another field of study seeks to show how producers can exploit information asymmetries to impose welfare-reducing tying arrangements and other restrictions on specific classes of consumers. See Steven C. Salop, *Exclusionary Vertical Restraints Law: Has Economics Mattered?,* 83 Am. Econ. Rev. 168 (1993). In Eastman Kodak Co. v. Image Technical Services, Inc. (1992), which affirmed a reversal of summary judgment against the plaintiff's tying and attempted monopolization claims, the Supreme Court relied on this line of research to support its conclusion that information imperfections could reduce the ability of durable equipment users to protect themselves from overreaching by original equipment suppliers in the aftermarket for parts and service.

Many developments described above tend to dictate closer scrutiny of business conduct. However, not all recent industrial organization research implies the need for more restrictive enforcement. One line of inquiry that has discouraged recourse to expansive antitrust standards is transaction cost economics—the study of how organizational structure and contractual design affect the cost of organizing activity within the firm, and between firms and external parties such as suppliers, distributors, and consumers. See Oliver E. Williamson, *Transaction Cost Economics,* in 1 Handbook of Industrial Organization 135 (Richard Schmalensee & Robert D. Willig eds. 1989). Transaction cost research has identified efficiency reasons for which firms use various forms of internal organization and has underscored the importance of contractual techniques in curbing opportunistic behavior that, if left unchecked, undermines business arrangements that increase efficiency. By showing that the main purpose of many forms of economic organization—for example, joint ventures, vertical integration, and restrictive distribution contracts—often is to reduce costs, transaction cost scholars have spurred a reevaluation of antitrust doctrines that have treated such arrangements with hostility. See Paul L. Joskow, *The Role of Transaction Cost Economics in Antitrust and Public Utility Regulatory Policies,* 7 J. L. Econ. & Org. 53, 55–66 (1991). The Supreme Court has applied these concepts in holding that industry participants may organize and cooperate where collaboration is likely to make production more efficient. See, e.g., Broadcast Music, Inc. v. Columbia Broadcasting System, Inc. (1979).

The second development concerns the behavior and performance of firms in markets for which entry and exit are costless and unimpeded. In a *perfectly contestable market,* firms are constantly vulnerable to hit and run entry and exit and therefore are induced to perform efficiently and charge competitive prices. For markets to be perfectly contestable, firms need not be be small and numerous, nor is it essential that they produce homogenous goods. See William J. Baumol, John C. Panzar & Robert D. Willig, *Contestable Markets and the Theory of Industry Structure* (Revised Edition 1988). Where the vital assumption of frictionless entry and exit holds true, even the largest firm cannot raise prices much above a competitive level without risking a substantial loss of sales at the hands of a new entrant. Few, if any, industries are perfectly contestable, but contestability theory suggests that markets containing a small number of large firms may be highly contestable and highly competitive. This theory has led courts and enforcement agencies to give greater weight to entry conditions in determining the legality of exclusionary practices and mergers. See, e.g., United States v. Waste Management, Inc. (1984) (merger with almost 50 percent market share did not violate antitrust law because entry barriers were very low).

Transactions cost economics and contestability theory have undermined the presumption that any deviation from the model of perfect competition is anticompetitive and harmful. These theories have encouraged a greater recognition that effective competition can take place in a variety of market structures and can derive strength from numerous firm organizational forms and contracting approaches.

D. CONCLUSION

This introduction to basic economic concepts and to several primary and emerging theories is relevant to a study of antitrust because such ideas suggest how antitrust policy can help maximize consumer welfare by controlling the misuse of private economic power. Antitrust enforcement requires an understanding of the competitive market system, how it operates, its limitations, and why it is worth preserving. From this foundation, particular antitrust policies can be assessed by considering whether business practices deviate from the competitive norm, or by measuring the costs and benefits of specific enforcement actions.

However, just as it is essential to understand the economic theory of antitrust, it is important to realize the theory's limitations. One apparent shortcoming is its inability to explain—absent reprehensible behavior—substantial and persistent monopoly in a market capable of supporting many firms. The assertion that superior efficiency is at the core of persistent monopoly does not adequately explain why the cost of a monopoly's superior factors of production or management is not bid up over time, thus dissipating the monopoly profit. Similarly, the contrary assertion that barriers to entry permit persistent monopoly effectively sidesteps the issue. A barrier to entry is an obstacle that affects some firms and entrants but not others; if a given obstacle affects all firms and entrants in the same fashion, it is simply a condition affecting the rate of entry. Absent reprehensible behavior or legal barriers (such as patents), it is difficult to see how an entrant's costs would persistently exceed those of existing firms.

Economic theory also has had difficulty explaining the behavior of oligopolistic and monopolistically competitive industries. Yet game theorists recently have made major contributions to the theoretical tools for analyzing behavior in these industry settings. These theoretical developments in turn have provided a basis for scholars to conduct more sophisticated empirical research, including industry case studies. See Timothy J. Bresnahan, *Empirical Studies of Industries with Market Power,* in 1 Handbook of Industrial Organization Economics 1011 (Richard Schmalensee & Robert D. Willig eds. 1989). Much work remains to be done, however, to translate the insights of game theory into operational antitrust standards. See Robert H. Porter, *A Review Essay on Handbook of Industrial Organization,* 29 J. Econ. Lit. 553, 571 (1991). Where the efficient market organization remains difficult to perceive, some assumptions and normative judgments may be useful in bridging the gap left by incomplete theory and uncertain empirical evidence.

For the coming years, the outcome of two ongoing debates likely will determine how economics affects antitrust. The first deals with the appropriate role of economics in antitrust analysis. As described in Chapter 2, many commentators argue that the antitrust laws are designed to serve social and political objectives beyond economic efficiency. Where such factors confirm economic goals, these additional arguments further support antitrust efforts to foster economic efficiency. Where they conflict with efficiency, however, the soundness of this approach and the tradeoffs involved must be carefully assessed. For example, should the exercise of monopoly power be condemned even though that power was acquired solely by competitive efforts which are otherwise applauded? To condemn monopoly in this circumstance may discourage vigorous competitive effort by large firms nearing monopoly size.

As this indicates, economics is not the end of the analysis. To be sure, an understanding of the economic impact of a challenged business practice often will suggest the appropriate judicial response. But not all—or, perhaps more accurately, not many—outcomes in antitrust cases can be explained by so rigorous an analysis. The history of antitrust is often as important to predicting enforcement choices and adjudication outcomes as the most lucid economic understanding, and non-efficiency concerns have exerted a powerful influence on antitrust in various periods since 1890. However, since the mid–1970s, courts and enforcement officials generally have agreed that rational antitrust policy should not pursue social and political aims (e.g., preserving opportunities for small firms to compete) when vindicating such values would undermine economic efficiency. Given the administrability difficulties associated with trading efficiency off against other goals, especially in times of acute global economic rivalry, we expect this trend to continue, even though occasional departures are sure to occur.

The second debate concerns the choice among contending economic models of analysis. Economic ideas have informed antitrust policy continually since 1890, yet the use of economic analysis in antitrust has not followed a straight path. During the 1960's, when the antitrust laws were applied expansively, real market divergences from the model of perfect competition were viewed suspiciously and often were subject to prosecution. Enforcement agencies and courts frequently presumed that if the market was imperfect it could not be competitive. Seeing room for improvement, these institutions showed little inhibition to intervene.

In the 1960s and 1970s, Chicago School antitrust scholars explained how many market structures and practices that antitrust treated with hostility could be beneficial. Chicago School theorists favored an antitrust policy that consisted of "little other than prosecuting plain vanilla cartels and mergers to monopoly." Frank H. Easterbrook, *Workable Antitrust Policy,* 84 Mich. L. Rev. 1696, 1701 (1986). These views attained strong footholds in judicial opinions in the 1970s and, with some modifications, became the preeminent basis for judicial decisionmaking and federal enforcement policy in the 1980s.

Current debate about antitrust policy deals less with whether economics is central to antitrust (most concede that it is) and more with which economic ideas offer the soundest analytical framework. Since the late 1970s, industrial organization research has focused chiefly on the related fields of game theory and strategic behavior. In general, the policy implications of this research support more expansive antitrust intervention than Chicago School advocates endorse. As this brief chronology suggests, changes in antitrust doctrine usually lag behind the formation of a consensus among economists about the appropriate content of liability standards. See W. Kovacic, *Influence of Economics on Antitrust Law,* at 297–301. Has the time come for game theory and other branches of "post-Chicago" economics to displace major aspects of Chicago School analysis and generate a more expansive antitrust policy?

At least four considerations suggest that courts will absorb the game theoretic literature slowly. First, a greater consensus still needs to develop on the analytical basis, accuracy (in prediction), and utility of game theory for most antitrust applications. Second, most judges will be chastened by the mathematical orientation and daunting complexity of modern microeconomics, and few will feel comfortable without extensive analysis and restatement by legal scholars. See Alvin K. Klevorick, *The Current State of the Law and Economics of Predatory Pricing*, 83 Am. Econ. Rev. 162 (1993). Third, if judges are to use the new analytical approaches widely, scholars and practitioners must provide relatively simple, administrable standards that can be applied in the typical courtroom setting of incomplete facts, disputed interpretations, and limited judicial economic training. (For example, a great attraction of structural analysis was that it devised relatively easy-to-apply standards based on concentration data.) Finally, applying game theory to antitrust disputes will pose significant informational demands that courts may be reluctant to compel litigants to satisfy. Not only may judges doubt their (or a jury's) ability to interpret such information properly, but the time needed to collect and assimilate the data may mean that the industry in question changes significantly between the date the complaint is filed and a decision on liability is rendered.

Thus, for the coming few years, we anticipate that Chicago School efficiency precepts will continue to provide the principal starting point of analysis for most public enforcement policy and judicial decisionmaking. The rate of absorption of competing economic views will depend upon how quickly commentators distill the teachings of game theory or other new economic models into administrable, operational enforcement principles and liability standards. Thus, the student of antitrust in the 1990s must comprehend the comparatively permissive economic models on which current doctrine and policy rest, but with an appreciation for how alternative economic models could alter the views of judges and enforcement officials about where antitrust's center of gravity should lie.

CHAPTER IV

THE MONOPOLY PROBLEM

Finley Peter Dunne was neither a lawyer nor an economist, but he still knew something about antitrust. Through the fictional Mr. Dooley, this turn-of-the-century political cartoonist seized upon a fundamental ambivalence in the Sherman Act and its treatment of corporate gigantism. "Th' trusts," said Mr. Dooley, restating the views of Theodore Roosevelt, "are heejous monsthers built up be th' enlightened intherprise iv th' men that have done so much to advance progress in our beloved country ... On wan hand I wud stamp thim undher fut; on th' other hand not so fast." W. Letwin, *Law and Economic Policy in America*, at 205.

The ambivalence Mr. Dooley attributed to Theodore Roosevelt and other trust-busters in the early 1900s runs deep through the history of efforts to apply Section 2 of the Sherman Act and its ban against attempted monopolization and monopolization. The American experience with antitrust since 1890 has been "complicated by the American habit of both respecting the accomplishments of bigness and fearing the political and economic consequences of increasing concentration of economic power." Marver H. Bernstein, *Regulating Business by Independent Commission* 222 (1955).

The tension between competing visions of monopoly power has left an indelible imprint on judicial interpretations of Section 2 of the Sherman Act. The conflict sometimes is evident in the pages of a single judicial decision. In United States v. Aluminum Co. of America (1945) (*Alcoa*), Alcoa was found to have illegally monopolized the production of aluminum ingot. In his opinion for the court, Judge Learned Hand offered a famous synthesis of the dangers of monopoly: "Many people believe that possession of unchallenged economic power deadens initiative, discourages thrift and depresses energy; that immunity from competition is a narcotic, and rivalry is a stimulant, to industrial progress; that the spur of constant stress is necessary to counteract an inevitable disposition to let well enough alone."

As Judge Hand suggests, monopoly power is feared both because of its consequences and its potential for abuse. Restriction of output raises prices and transfers income from customers to producers, and the prospect of obtaining supranormal profits can induce socially wasteful efforts to attain monopoly power. The restriction of output, moreover, may indicate that the monopolist has used its power to exclude rivals from the market by means other than superior performance in the form of better products, prices, and service. Thus, the use of certain tactics to obtain or preserve a substantial market advantage is condemned.

But the existence of monopoly power cannot, and should not, be attributed automatically (or even ordinarily) to trade practices whose benefits for consumers are slight and whose adoption is pointless except to exclude rivals from the market. The ultimate reward of monopoly—namely, above normal profits—is in essence what every vigorous competitor seeks. Competition's imperative to surpass rivals can drive firms to devise products, processes, and methods of organization of such singular distinction that they yield monopoly power. Judge Hand ultimately found that Alcoa had not attained its aluminum monopoly innocently, but he cautioned that "[a] single producer may be the survivor out of a group of active companies, merely by virtue of his superior skill, foresight, and industry.... The successful competitor, having been urged to compete, must not be turned upon when he wins."

Other considerations also discourage an automatic assumption that a restricted output and higher price necessarily stem from predatory conduct. They may be the rational acts of a profit-maximizing firm possessing market (i.e., a degree of monopoly) power. It is a general and wise rule of law that conduct defined as illegal (especially if subject to criminal sanctions, as in the Sherman Act) be limited to *avoidable* acts. Moreover, monopoly profits can signal the attractiveness of entry and elicit new sources of supply that break down monopoly power and restore competition. Since legal constraints cannot be directly enforced effectively or accurately against all market participants, it is often desirable that market forces be allowed to self-correct market abuses. Unless monopolists are permitted to charge monopoly prices, such corrections cannot occur.

Since the mid-1940s, courts have applied a largely unchanged standard in trying to define the bounds of acceptable dominant firm conduct. To engage in illegal monopolization, the defendant must possess monopoly power in a relevant market and must have used improperly exclusionary acts to gain or protect that power. See Eastman Kodak Co. v. Image Technical Services, Inc. (1992) (*Kodak*); United States v. Grinnell Corp. (1966) (*Grinnell*). The significance of this test has hinged on how courts have interpreted its two operative terms: what constitutes substantial monopoly power, and what behavior should be deemed improperly exclusionary?

A. MONOPOLY POWER

Without market power, actual or probable, there is little reason to be concerned with the acts of a single firm under the antitrust laws. Consequently, one of the two elements in the Section 2 offense of monopolization is "the possession of monopoly power." *Kodak*. A firm without market power cannot impose its choices on competitors or customers. Such a firm takes the market price; it has no ability to charge more than its rivals, and no reason to sell for less.

In economic terms, market power is the ability profitably to raise prices above the competitive level for a sustained period of time.[1] This sweeping definition is too broad to be useful in antitrust, however. Departures from the perfectly competitive market model are common, indicating that countless firms have at least some quantum of market power. Therefore, the first issue for monopolization analysis is to determine what degree of market power is so significant that its exercise warrants scrutiny and control. See Benjamin Klein, *Market Power in Antitrust: Economic Analysis After Kodak*, 3 Supreme Ct. Econ. Rev. 43, 71–85 (1993). Applying Section 2 to attack all instances and uses of market power would be unwise and administratively hopeless. No business could operate without fear of subsequent examination in a criminal prosecution or a civil suit, including private treble damage actions. Thus, antitrust controls for single-firm behavior usually address significant market power. On the other hand, a narrow definition of market power could eviscerate the Sherman Act. The issue

1. A firm's market power is reflected in the slope and shape of the demand curve it faces. The more steeply (negatively) sloped or inelastic the demand curve, the greater the firm's market power. See Figure 1, p. 46 supra; see also William M. Landes & Richard A. Posner, *Market Power in Antitrust Cases*, 94 Harv. L. Rev. 937 (1981).

is important and should not be passed over lightly despite its complexity.

The Sherman Act gives courts little direction for deciding when a firm is a monopolist for antitrust purposes. Section 2 ("Every person who shall monopolize ... any part of the trade or commerce") makes no mention of market power and provides no guidance for delineating markets, measuring market power, or determining what minimal aggregation constitutes monopoly power under the Act. Such questions are vital in antitrust litigation. Defining a relevant market and evaluating the defendant's power within that market are critical exercises in Section 2 cases, in challenges to mergers, and, increasingly, in disputes involving agreements in restraint of trade.

For the most part, courts in Section 2 cases have focused less on the measurement of monopoly power and more on the uses and abuses of monopoly power. This tendency has been criticized in the past by commentators who would dispense with a painstaking search for evidence of abusive conduct and instead would apply a "no-fault" monopolization approach to disperse persistent monopoly power unattributable to superior performance. See 3 Phillip Areeda & Donald F. Turner, Antitrust Law ¶¶ 614–23 (1978). Legislative proposals to establish a "no-fault" standard stirred debate among academics and policymakers in the 1960s and 1970s, but no measure ever neared enactment. See William E. Kovacic, *Failed Expectations: The Troubled Past and Uncertain Future of the Sherman Act as a Tool for Deconcentration*, 74 Iowa L.Rev. 1105, 1136–39 (1989).

Three different approaches could be used to measure market power: performance, rivalry, and structure. The first identifies how much a firm's actual performance deviates from the competitive norm. This usually involves determining how much a firm's prices depart from its marginal cost, or the amount that a firm's net profits exceed the industry average (if that average reflects similar risks in a competitive industry). Performance tests based upon accounting profits or markups suffer from many difficulties. See Kenneth G. Elzinga, *Unmasking Monopoly: Four Types of Economic Evidence,* in Economics and Antitrust Policy 11 (Robert J. Larner & James W. Meehan, Jr. eds. 1989). Marginal costs are difficult to estimate, and profit data may not reflect actual market power where a firm fails to maximize profits. Moreover, the reliability of cost data can vary greatly according to the firm's choice of accounting conventions.

The rivalry test studies the sensitivity of the firm's sales or output to changes in its rivals' sales and prices and to adjustments in buyer behavior. Economists have developed three principal econometric techniques for measuring market power: estimating residual demand to assess how much a firm could raise prices by cutting output after accounting for the demand responses of buyers and the supply responses of competitors; calculating industry demand elasticities to assess whether firms can exploit the inability of buyers to substitute other goods by raising price above cost; and observing pricing behavior to determine whether industry pricing patterns suggest a general equilibrium of supracompetitive pricing punctuated by occasional price wars, which are followed by a return to prevailing high price levels. These empirical methods put a premium on collecting and accurately interpreting large amounts of data that may be unattainable (or available only at great cost) in most cases. However, the continuing refinement of such techniques may increase their use in the future. See Jonathan B. Baker & Timothy F. Bresnahan, *Empirical Methods of*

Identifying and Measuring Market Power, 61 Antitrust L.J. 3 (1992).

The third and most widely used method is the structural approach, which essentially involves counting the number of firms in a market and comparing each firm's share of market activity (usually sales or output). Market shares are then used as surrogates for market power, and it is inferred that a firm with a major share of the market has monopoly power. Such inferences can be seriously misleading where ease of entry into the market would deny an incumbent the ability to raise prices by curbing output, or where product differentiation obscures the full range of products that constrain a firm's ability to charge more for its own goods. See Robert Pitofsky, *New Definitions of Relevant Market and the Assault on Antitrust*, 90 Colum. L. Rev. 1805, 1810–13 (1990). Proper application of structural tests requires careful consideration of various market conditions, including entry barriers and product differentiation.

In sum, market power measurement is an inexact and often misunderstood process. In a monopolization case, the product and geographic markets usually are first defined. Next the defendant's sales are compared with those of rival sellers. Then this market share is used as a rough index of the defendant's market power, along with ease and likelihood of entry, availability of secondhand goods or other acceptable (but nonequivalent) substitutes, and similar factors which indicate whether the defendant has the ability to raise prices and reduce output.

We previously considered the concept of "market" in the sense of identifying the general conditions under which sellers and buyers exchange goods. We now use the term in another sense: to define the boundaries that identify groups of sellers of goods. This requires a delineation of the product and geographic lines within which specific groups of goods, buyers, and sellers interact to establish price and output. While antitrust (and economic) analysis press toward identifying links in the chain of available alternatives—to draw lines and identify markets—such distinctions are inevitably somewhat artificial; they result from having to base decisions on imperfect data. The process of inclusion and exclusion is a matter of degree, and hence the basis of frequent disagreement. The aim is to select the set of alternatives (e.g., those available to buyers) and transactions that are sufficiently interrelated so that further subdivision is unsupportable. The goal is easy to state; the execution is often difficult.

1. PRODUCT MARKET

To define the product market in which the seller operates, one seeks to locate all substitutes available to buyers of the seller's product. The definition process asks whether the seller's product competes with other products, and whether these products limit her ability to raise price. Too narrow a definition will exclude genuine substitutes and overstate the defendant's ability to affect price and output; if nonsubstitutes are included, the defendant's market share (and inferentially her market power) will be understated because some of the included products will hardly affect her power to set prices.

Determining whether various products are sufficiently close substitutes to be included within a market often poses a difficult empirical question. Obviously corn is not a close substitute for virgin aluminum, but what of scrap aluminum? For many uses, aluminum fabricators favor scrap. Other illustrations further demonstrate the problem. For example, does the sole manufacturer of cellophane directly compete with producers of saran wrap, wax paper, or aluminum foil, or does the cellophane firm have a monopoly of a distinctive product? Is tea a good substitute for carbonated beverages? If tea and Coke are included within the same market, then what of coffee, milk, or water?

Notice the importance of such line drawing in determining the market power of a seller of carbonated beverages. The seller of Coke may have only one rival soft drink seller (Pepsi) and consequently have apparent power to set a supracompetitive price for Coke. But if the seller also faces dozens of rivals in the larger beverage market, she may have little power to control the price of beverages—and perhaps even of Coke if users would transfer their loyalties as soon as price changes. Depending on the product market selection, the Coke seller's market share will fluctuate widely.

The *Cellophane* case is not only the leading case outlining the dimensions of product market analysis, but it also illustrates how judicially developed criteria are applied—and sometimes misapplied. In United States v. E.I. du Pont de Nemours & Co. (1956) (*Cellophane*), the primary question was the product market in which du Pont's market power should be measured. While the ultimate issue was whether du Pont had monopolized the cellophane market in violation of Section 2, the government had the burden of proving that du Pont possessed a high degree of market power. The government relied on du Pont's production of almost 75 percent of the cellophane sold in the United States as showing, at least prima facie, du Pont's monopoly power. It also argued that other flexible wrapping materials were not sufficiently competitive to limit du Pont's control of the cellophane market price. Du Pont countered that cellophane was not a separate product market since it competed directly and closely with flexible packaging materials such as aluminum foil, wax paper, saran wrap, and polyethylene. With these goods included in the product market, du Pont's market share fell to under 20 percent—well below the minimum monopolization threshold of 65 percent or more established in earlier cases. Note, du Pont did not deny that cellophane was distinctive; rather it contended that since cellophane faced severe competitive pressure from substitute flexible wrapping materials, the firm could not exclude competitors and its power over price was correspondingly limited.

The government proposed that before other products could be included in the cellophane product market, they must be largely fungible and sell at close to the price of cellophane. The Supreme Court rejected this narrow measure of physical and price identity, however, since the producers of many patented or branded products would be monopolies under such a definition and would be subjected to Section 2 scrutiny. Instead it called for "an appraisal of the 'cross-elasticity' of demand in the trade" to determine whether the "commodities [are] reasonably interchangeable by consumers for the same purposes." Reasonable interchangeability, the Court said, has three components: "[the product] market is composed of products that have reasonable interchangeability for the purposes for which they are produced—*price, use* and *qualities* considered" (emphasis added).

Applying the quality test—that is, determining whether the physical attributes of cellophane and other flexible wrappings were sufficiently similar—the Court was persuaded that cellophane generally had no qualities desired by consumers which a number of other products did not possess. Du Pont sold 80 percent of its cellophane for packaging in the food industry. Commercially suitable packaging material for fresh vegetables, for example, must be transparent so that consumers can examine the quality of the produce, must have low permeability to gases so that surrounding odors will not contaminate the enclosed produce, and must have low moisture permeability so that produce freshness will be retained. Many flexible wrapping products other than cellophane (specifically, pliofilm, plain glassine, and saran) have these qualities. Therefore, including other flexible wrappings with cellophane appeared reasonable.[2]

The functional interchangeability test—whether buyers could shift back and forth from cellophane to other flexible wrappings—also supported du Pont's contention that cellophane belonged in a broader product market. Despite cellophane's advantages of transparency and strength, it faced competition in each of its uses. The government did not challenge du Pont's statistics showing that cellophane controlled less than half of any use (except cigarettes which were not argued to be a separate market) and that buyers frequently shifted their product loyalties.

The two tests of reasonable interchangeability—quality and end-use—are essentially subjective, and the Court's conclusions are not without support. Less persuasive, however, was the Court's examination of price movements and responsiveness to indicate whether cellophane belonged in the larger flexible wrapping market. This test measures the cross-elasticity of demand between products by looking mainly at how sales of one product respond to price changes in the other. The logic for this criterion was clearly explained: "If a slight decrease in the price of cellophane causes a considerable number of customers of other flexible

---

2. This line was not perfect. Aluminum foil is opaque and could not serve as an alternative material for packaging fresh produce, yet it was included in the larger product market.

wrappings to switch to cellophane, it would be an indication that a high cross-elasticity of demand exists between them; that the products compete in the same market." In other words, if a buyer of cellophane will shift her purchases to wax paper in response to an increase in the price of cellophane, this price responsiveness indicates that wax paper competes with cellophane and that both belong to the same product market. In holding that other flexible wrappings competed with cellophane, the Court relied on the finding that some price-sensitive buyers shifted their purchases in response to price changes, and that for other users, who were not so sensitive, packaging constituted an insignificant part of their product's price.

In focusing on substitute products the Court was considering direct competition from other products. Equally important in evaluating monopoly power is whether firms making other products could switch to producing cellophane and did so whenever du Pont tried to raise its cellophane price. Competition from production (elasticity of supply or "supply substitution") can be as effective as that of consumption (i.e., substitute products). In *Cellophane,* patents and other entry barriers insulated du Pont from such competitive inroads by other producers.

The Supreme Court's analysis of cellophane's demand elasticity was flawed. Buyer price responsiveness to changes in cellophane prices establishes that other flexiwrap products are close substitutes (and that du Pont lacked monopoly power) only if competitive prices were in fact being charged for cellophane. But if du Pont already was charging a monopoly price for cellophane, the high cross-elasticity for cellophane may have signified only that du Pont could not have raised its price still further without a substantial sales loss. See Donald F. Turner, *Antitrust Policy and the Cellophane Case,* 70 Harv. L. Rev. 281, 308–

10 (1956). In what is now termed the "*Cellophane* fallacy," the Supreme Court failed to consider that a finding of high demand cross-elasticity may mean only that the firm already has exercised monopoly power by raising price to the profit-maximizing point. Thus, the concept of demand cross-elasticity helps establish whether two products are close substitutes only when both are sold at competitive prices. In *Cellophane* the high cross-elasticity was a misleading measure of the relevant product market for determining whether du Pont had monopoly power.[3] It may, however, be a useful measure of market power (and of a separate product market) where price is shown to be close to cost. The Court's reliance on evidence of high cross-elasticity of demand to determine the product market would have been correct if two cellophane producers in a competitive market had sought to merge and the question was whether the merged cellophane company would now have monopoly power (see Chapter 9).

In later applications of *Cellophane's* test of reasonable interchangeability, the Court relied only on the elements of quality and end-use. In United States v. Grinnell Corp. (1966), the government charged Grinnell with monopolizing the supply of accredited central station protective services (CSPS), an alarm system designed to warn of possible hazards from burglary, fire, and flooding. In finding that CSPS constituted a distinct product, the Court excluded other fire and burglar alarm systems such as watchmen and local alarm systems from the product market because they were less reliable and thus less desirable to customers. The Court purported to follow *Cellophane's* methodology, but

---

3. The record indicated that du Pont had realized a supranormal rate of return (averaging 31 percent before taxes) on its cellophane investment during the period in question. *Cellophane* (Warren, C.J., dissenting). Moreover, there were no reasonable substitutes for cellophane in the cigarette market.

did not examine price responsiveness. As Justice Fortas' dissent pointed out, the Court overlooked evidence that users had switched between CSPS and substitute warning systems depending on changes in relative prices. *Grinnell* (Fortas, J., dissenting).

Litigation from the 1970s and early 1980s involving IBM's conduct in the computer industry further illustrates product market definition problems that can arise. There IBM had dominated the production of central processing units (CPUs) and other hardware such as peripheral equipment. Several firms, including Telex, entered the peripheral field by copying IBM's equipment and by selling it below IBM's price. When IBM countered by reducing its prices and by introducing design changes—with the result that Telex began losing customers and then money—Telex sued. *Telex Corp. v. International Business Machines Corp.* (1973). The immediate issue was the product market.

The District Court limited that the market to peripherals that could be plugged into IBM machines (i.e., IBM plug-compatible peripheral equipment) because IBM's own products defined the market in which it competed. This gave IBM a monopoly because it held a commanding share of placements of peripheral equipment compatible with its own mainframes. However, this analysis overstates IBM's market share and relative market power at any one time. As the developer of its computers and peripheral equipment, IBM necessarily began with a monopoly position. By including only IBM compatible peripherals in the denominator of the equation and all IBM-controlled peripheral installations in the numerator, even substantial peripheral sales by IBM competitors would not markedly change IBM's share for many years.

The Tenth Circuit reversed the district court's finding of liability, mainly because the court had exaggerated IBM's position in the peripherals market by slighting supply substitution. The court of appeals expanded the defined market (and denominator) to *all* peripherals, including those not compatible with IBM computers, emphasizing that (a) makers of peripherals compatible with non–IBM CPUs could shift production to IBM–compatible peripherals at low cost, and (b) CPU and peripherals makers could install inexpensive interfaces that would permit a CPU to accommodate peripherals not originally designed to be compatible with it.

The district court's market definition/market power analysis also did not consider possible changes over time in new placements of peripherals. To measure IBM's power in the peripheral market more precisely, one would examine IBM's annual share of new installations among IBM plug-compatible units as well as among all hardware units. Net new orders or installations would reflect more accurately the current relative market power of IBM and its rivals. Assume that IBM had sold 1,000 units when the first imitator appeared. It then has 100 percent of the market (and is a monopolist). But suppose the new entrant is highly successful and captures 75 of the 100 new IBM plug-compatible peripheral installations sold the next year. If the market is defined as all installations—new or old—the new competitor has only 75 of 1,100 total units or 6.8 percent. On the other hand, if the market consists of new installations, the new firm has 75 of 100 units and its market share is 75 percent. Neither figure completely indicates IBM's position, but success in making new installations may afford a more reliable measure of IBM's current market power.

2. GEOGRAPHIC MARKET

After wrestling with product market complexities, one might expect the determination of geographic markets would be relatively easy. Sometimes it is. Where products are sold nationwide and transportation costs are insignificant, courts frequently define the geographic market as the entire nation. Or where a firm and its rivals sell their product only in a limited geographic area and their customers have no ready access to an outside source of supply, the general rule has been to define the geographic market as that particular area and to include only the sales made within that market. See, e.g., Union Leader Corp. v. Newspapers of New England, Inc. (1960).

Where the seller's geographic market is less certain, however, attention is paid not only to actual sales patterns but also to price relationships and movements in different areas. A close correlation among prices and price movements, especially when supported by sales interchanges, will be a strong indication that a geographic market has been identified. Conversely, significant price differences and uncorrelated price changes may suggest that more than one geographic market exists, even where some sales interchanges occur. Transportation barriers are another principal basis for separating geographic markets. In sum, the relevant geographic market in antitrust analysis is that "section of the country" where a firm can increase its price without attracting new sellers or without losing many customers to alternative suppliers outside that area.

Applying these criteria in drawing geographic market boundaries does not necessarily assure accuracy. As with product markets, looking to current sales and buying practices can be either over- or under-inclusive. If the market is not monopolized, relying on actual sales ignores "fringe" suppliers whose presence "keeps" the market price at competitive levels—that is, they would ship into the geographic area if the price rose. On the other hand, if the market is monopolized (and price exceeds marginal cost), the monopoly price may attract sellers from distant areas who otherwise would not have entered because of higher transportation and selling costs. The sales figures within the geographic market would include sales of firms located there only because the market is monopolized. Consequently, geographic market definitions in monopoly cases tend to understate market shares where the market price reaches monopoly levels and to overstate a defendant's market power (shares) where it faces competitive rivals. Thus, geographic market-drawing tests that rely on actual sales patterns may give erroneous results. However, this difficulty is probably better resolved by adjusting the weight given or reliance placed on market shares rather than in determining geographic market boundaries.

Another geographic market problem is that markets can be identified from either the supply or demand viewpoint. Consider, for example, a typical purchase of a new car in Peoria. To the individual buyer the alternative sources of supply are the various automobile dealerships in Peoria. To auto manufacturers who sell cars in Peoria, however, the transaction (and possible price) takes on quite a different aspect. Their rivalry with other producers competing for the consumer's new car dollars is nationwide or, for certain vehicles, worldwide. Note the significance of our answer. If the relevant geographic market is Peoria, market shares for the car manufacturer may differ markedly from their national or international figures. And the issue cannot be decided in the abstract. The answer, if there be one, depends on the question being asked. Is the issue whether an auto maker has monopolized the new car market for buyers or for sellers? In either case, however, the question is where is the locus of competition: for buyers it may well be limited to Peoria (except perhaps for commercial or fleet accounts); for sellers it is likely to be the entire nation or the world since interfirm rivalry is not confined to any geographic area.

The Supreme Court faced these issues in *Grinnell*. The district court had ruled that a national market existed in accredited central station protective services even though seller rivalry for sale of fire and burglar alarm systems was admittedly confined to individual metropolitan areas and customers in one city could not realistically transfer their patronage to sellers located in other cities. Accepting this determination, the Supreme Court relied on the defendant's national planning and price schedule, relations with other large businesses on a nationwide basis, and similar factors to find a national market. However this conclusion cannot withstand close analysis. Whether an individual firm operates on a national or local basis does not define a geographic market. Consider an example from a more familiar setting. Retail grocery competition exists between local stores and chains, as well as among large interstate chains. But competition between sellers and alternate sources of supply for buyers is invariably local. At the most, the geographic market embraces a metropolitan area.

As two of the dissenters convincingly explained, the same principle would seem to hold true in *Grinnell*. Grinnell faced no competition in at least 92 of the 115 cities in which it operated (i.e., if geographic markets were defined as the 115 metropolitan areas, Grinnell had 92 separate monopolies). Why, then, did the Court struggle so laboriously to find a national market? Perhaps the exclusionary practices (restrictive agreements and acquisitions) that supported the finding of illegal conduct could not be attached to each (or many) of the separate markets. The Court's approval of local divestiture to create localized competition in essence belied the existence of a national geographic market.

Cases since *Grinnell* generally reflect a consensus that where production outside a geographic area would be diverted to that area if a substantial price increase took place, then production from outside the area should be included (at least to some degree) in calculating the market share of local producers. See Consolidated Gold Fields PLC v. Minorco, S.A. (1989). Specific applications of this principle remain subject to considerable dispute, especially where the treatment of foreign imports into the U.S. is concerned. See George A. Hay, John C. Hilke & Phillip B. Nelson, *Geographic Market Definition in an International Context,* 64 Chicago–Kent L. Rev. 711 (1988). Although foreign producers can greatly constrain the ability of domestic firms to exercise market power, commentators disagree about whether geographic markets should be expanded to include foreign production or capacity in amounts greater than existing levels of imports into the U.S.

3. FEDERAL GUIDELINES

In 1992, the Justice Department and the FTC issued joint merger enforcement guidelines that outline how federal antitrust officials analyze the competitive effects of horizontal mergers.[4] The Guidelines present a useful approach to market definition and market power measurement that also is relevant for Sherman Act Section 2 cases. The Guide-

4. See *Symposium on New 1992 Merger Guidelines,* 38 Antitrust Bull. 473 (1993). The Justice Department first issued merger enforcement guidelines in 1968 and made revisions in 1982 and 1984. The FTC issued its own merger guidelines in 1982. The 1992 Guidelines are reprinted in 4 Trade Reg. Rep. (CCH) ¶13,104.

lines deeply influence enforcement policy and counseling and therefore warrant close consideration.

The 1992 Guidelines use demand substitution factors to define the relevant product market. Section 1.11 defines the relevant product market as "a product or group of products such that a hypothetical profit-maximizing firm that was the only present and future seller ('monopolist') likely would impose at least a 'small but significant and nontransitory' increase in price" (usually a 5 percent increase "lasting for the foreseeable future"). The process starts with the defendant's products. Next it adds products that the firm's customers view as good substitutes at "prevailing prices," although the government will use a price "more reflective of the competitive price" when circumstances are "strongly suggestive of coordinated interaction."[5] Finally, the Guidelines ask whether a small but significant and nontransitory price increase will cause a substantial shift of buyers to substitute products. To evaluate the likely response of buyers to a relative price increase, the government will account for a variety of factors, including:

(1) evidence that buyers have shifted or have considered shifting purchases between products in response to relative changes in price or other competitive variables;

(2) evidence that sellers base business decisions on the prospect of buyer substitution between products in response to relative changes in price or other competitive variables;

(3) the influence of downstream competition faced by buyers in their output markets; and

---

5. This formula attempts to avoid the *Cellophane* fallacy and address the possibility that the prevailing price already is supracompetitive.

(4) the timing and costs of switching products.

When switching by purchasers no longer occurs, a relevant product market has been identified.

Section 1.21 of the Guidelines defines the relevant geographic market as the region in which a hypothetical monopolist "was the only present or future producer of the relevant product at locations in that region" and "would profitably impose at least a 'small but significant and nontransitory' increase in price." Beginning with the location of the firm under consideration, one asks what would happen if the firm imposed a small but significant and nontransitory price increase. The government will add the location of additional production facilities if the firm's efforts to raise prices would induce buyer switching to other suppliers that renders the price increase unprofitable. In considering the buyers' likely response, the government will consider the four factors enumerated above. The government may define narrower markets where the firm can price discriminate against "targeted buyers" who cannot defeat the attempted price increase by substituting to more distant sellers.

The Guidelines account for supply side considerations in identifying participants in the relevant market. Section 1.32 provides that the federal agencies will identify firms "that are not currently producing or selling in the relevant product market in the relevant area as participating in the relevant market if their inclusion would more accurately reflect probable supply responses." These "uncommitted entrants" are included as market participants if their supply responses are "likely to occur within one year and without the expenditure of significant sunk costs of entry and exit, in response to a 'small but significant and nontransitory price' increase." Sunk costs are defined as "costs uniquely incurred to supply the relevant product and geographic market." An important set of uncommitted entrants consists of firms whose existing production and distribution assets could be used to produce and sell the relevant product. If the price of the relevant product rose, such firms might easily redeploy their assets to produce and sell the relevant product.

The uncommitted entry provisions address relatively short term supply responses in the absence of substantial sunk costs. Section 3.0 of the Guidelines separately accounts for the possible constraining effect of "committed entry" into the market—"new competition that requires expenditure of significant sunk costs of entry and exit." The Guidelines ask whether entry can achieve a significant market impact within a timely period, defined as two years from the initial planning period. The analysis then accounts for whether entry would be a profitable (and therefore likely) response to a merger resulting in a relative price increase. Finally, the government assesses whether entry would suffice to return market prices to their premerger levels.

The market definition approach of the 1992 Guidelines tends to yield broader markets (and smaller defendants' market shares) than were drawn by courts before the 1980s. See R. Pitofsky, *New Definitions of Relevant Market and the Assault on Antitrust,* at 1818–30. Although few judicial decisions fully have embraced the Guidelines' methodology, some courts have relied upon earlier versions of the 1992 Guidelines as an important point of departure for analysis. See United States v. Baker Hughes (1990); United States v. Waste Management, Inc. (1984).

4. MARKET SHARE MEASUREMENT AND THE TREATMENT OF PARTICULAR CLASSES OF INDUSTRY PARTICIPANTS

Market shares are antitrust's chief tool for assessing the competitive significance of firms in the relevant market. The validity of market shares as proxies for market power hinges on how closely the market definition reflects commercial realities. Once the product and geographic market boundaries are determined, market shares can be computed in one of several ways. See ABA Antitrust Section, Monograph No. 12, Horizontal Mergers: Law and Policy 153–61 (1986).

Market shares most often are calculated by setting the defendant's historical output (measured in production units or sales) as the numerator and then dividing that by the larger denominator constituting total production or sales in the defined area. Plant capacity (rather than actual output) may be a superior measure for homogeneous products, although capacity calculations can be problematic where the cost and quality of production facilities vary widely throughout the industry. For extractive industries, uncommitted physical reserves (rather than past or current output) may be a truer index of the firm's ability to compete for the next sale. See United States v. General Dynamics Corp. (1974). In commercial settings that feature competitive bidding for long-term increments of demand, it may be appropriate to use a bidding model that assigns equal shares to all qualified bidders on the theory that each firm is equally capable of competing for new contracts. Where the market consists mainly of R & D or a product undergoing rapid technological change, it may be necessary to use hybrid measures that account for the firm's technological acumen (e.g., R & D outlays) and its skill in translating new ideas into successful production programs (e.g., historical output). See William E. Kovacic, *Merger Policy in a Declining Defense Industry,* 36 Antitrust Bull. 543, 571–74 (1991). In all cases, the goal is the same: to select the measure of activity that best reflects the competitive significance of each market participant.

Choosing the right measurement yardstick is only one aspect of determining market shares. As *Alcoa* illustrates, a second, and often more demanding, task is to decide what market shares to assign various classes of industry participants. The parties in *Alcoa* generally agreed that ingot aluminum consumed in the U.S. was the appropriate market. Obviously this included all virgin ingot produced and sold on the open market. If this were all, Alcoa was conceded to be a monopolist, being the sole U.S. producer. But what of secondary aluminum—clippings, trimmings, and second-hand ingot available from aluminum fabrications previously sold and processed as scrap—which was an almost perfect substitute for virgin ingot? Or what of virgin ingot that Alcoa used in its own fabrication plants? Or imported ingot, both virgin and secondary? The extent to which this additional aluminum was included in the market (denominator) caused Alcoa's market share to swing between 33 and 90 percent. Thus, it is instructive to note why Judge Hand included some sources of the metal and excluded others, especially since his opinion is still a leading antitrust case.

The first issue was whether to include ingot that Alcoa produced and then consumed in its own fabrication plants. The trial court excluded this "captive" production because it was not available to buyers on the open market and hence, the court said, had no effect on price or output. Judge Hand rejected this premise because "[a]ll ingot—

with trifling exceptions—is used to fabricate intermediate, or end, products; and therefore all intermediate, or end, products which 'Alcoa' fabricates and sells, pro tanto reduce the demand for ingot itself." While this analysis seems unexceptional—Alcoa's control of ingot aluminum supply is unaffected by whether it is consumed internally or sold to other fabricators—it does not follow that captive production should always be included when totalling market shares. For example, in measuring a coal company's market power, it probably would be inappropriate to include all the production of coal mines owned by automobile or steel companies whose entire output is consumed by them. Output from these mines may reduce total demand for coal, but this production is often unavailable to the market unless the auto and steel makers also have a sales force and the other capabilities needed to sell coal. To include all their production would understate the defendant coal company's power.

By a parity of reasoning one might also assume that secondary (scrap) aluminum, salvaged from the virgin which Alcoa and others produced in the first place, also belongs in the market. Customers normally accepted secondary as a suitable substitute and paid the same price as they paid for virgin ingot. Again, Judge Hand reversed the trial court, but this time for including secondary in the market. Hand reasoned that Alcoa's awareness that "the future supply of ingot would be made up in part of what it produced at that time" must have "had its share in determining how much to produce." While Alcoa could only estimate the future impact of current production, experience would help it make this estimate and uncertainty would not forestall the impact. "The competition of 'secondary' must therefore be disregarded, as soon as we consider the position of 'Alcoa' over a period of years; it was as much within 'Alcoa's' control as was the production of the 'virgin' from which it had been derived." Rather than simply discount secondary, Hand completely excluded it. Had secondary been included, Alcoa's market share would have fallen from 90 to 64 percent (because, being out of Alcoa's control, the secondary would be included only in the denominator). It was unclear then that the latter figure amounted to monopoly power.

The total exclusion of secondary is questionable. Secondary and virgin aluminum were admittedly almost identical substitutes. Nor is Judge Hand's reference to Alcoa's original production of what later became secondary persuasive. Had another firm produced it instead, the competitive force of the secondary in the aluminum market would have been precisely the same. While this secondary supply was limited and therefore could not exert the same price check on Alcoa as could a competing producer, it nonetheless restrained Alcoa's power to set aluminum prices. Compare *United Shoe,* discussed pp. 131–32 infra (condemning a monopolist's lease-only policy and observing that, by refusing to sell shoe machinery equipment, the monopolizing manufacturer eliminates the competitive pressures otherwise presented by the second-hand market).

More compelling is the court's inclusion of imported virgin aluminum in the market; it cut Alcoa's market share by 10 percent. Under this approach it could also be argued that aluminum products fabricated abroad and imported into the U.S.—or, perhaps, even all foreign production regardless of where it was ultimately shipped—should also be included. However, substantial transportation and tariff barriers, as well as constant low import volume, support the court's ruling on this point.

When so able a judge as Learned Hand makes several disputed calls in solving the market share equation, one is alerted to the limitations of any market share determination. Even the most carefully defined market inevitably includes some firms or production whose impact on the defendant is insignificant, while excluding others having greater market force. Market shares are not synonymous with market power; they should mark the beginning for careful analysis, not the end of it. And courts generally have recognized this point. Compare *Grinnell* (monopoly power "ordinarily may be inferred from the predominant share of the market") with Shoppin' Bag of Pueblo, Inc. v. Dillon Cos. (1986) ("Market share alone . . . is not enough to determine a firm's capacity to achieve monopoly."); Hunt–Wesson Foods, Inc. v. Ragu Foods (1980) ("Blind reliance upon market share, divorced from commercial reality, could give a misleading picture of a firm's actual ability to control prices or exclude competition.").

Nor does the 90 percent figure in *Alcoa* set the floor of monopoly power. Later decisions frequently have concluded that a market share exceeding 70 percent supports an inference of monopoly power. Seventy-five to 95 percent of the shoe machinery market sufficed in United States v. United Shoe Machinery Corp. (1953), and *Grinnell* (1966) equated 87 percent of central station alarm systems with the requisite "predominant share of the market." In finding a conspiracy to monopolize violation in American Tobacco Co. v. United States (1946), the Court emphasized that the defendants accounted for "over two-thirds of the entire domestic field of cigarettes" and over "80 percent of the field of comparable cigarettes". See also Weiss v. York Hospital (1984) (market share exceeding 80 percent confers monopoly power).[6]

Courts rarely evaluate market shares in isolation when measuring the defendant's market power. Inferences from market shares typically are qualified by factors such as entry conditions, the size and stability of market shares over time, and profitability. See, e.g., Reazin v. Blue Cross & Blue Shield (1990) (considering entry barriers, supply and demand elasticities, the number of competitors, and market trends). Of these factors, entry is often paramount. Where entry is easy, courts have declined to infer monopoly power even from high market shares because actual or threatened entry will drive prices to competitive levels. See, e.g., Los Angeles Land Co. v. Brunswick Corp. (1993) (despite 100 percent market share, defendant lacked monopoly power due to ease of entry); United States v. Syufy Enters. (1990) (entry cut defendant's market share from 100 percent to 75 percent over four-year period and precluded finding of monopoly power); Ball Memorial Hosp. v. Mutual Hosp. Ins., Inc. (1986) (defendant with large market share lacked monopoly power due to ease of entry). By the same token, courts also have found monopoly power to exist at market shares under 70 percent when entry barriers are

6. At the other end of the spectrum courts routinely have held that market shares below 40 percent fail to support a finding of monopoly power. See, e.g., United Air Lines v. Austin Travel Corp. (1989) (31 percent held insufficient); Dimmitt Agri Indus., Inc. v. CPC Int'l Inc. (1982) (16 to 25 percent held insufficient); but see Energex Lighting Indus. v. North American Philips Lighting Corp. (1987) (defendant might possess monopoly power with a 25 percent market share). Between 40 percent and 70 percent, courts tend to find that monopoly power is lacking, although exceptions to this rule of thumb exist. Compare Twin City Sportservice, Inc. v. Charles O. Finley & Co. (1975) (50 percent held insufficient) with Broadway Delivery Corp. v. United Parcel Serv. (1981) (finding of monopoly power not precluded where defendant's share was less than 50 percent); see also Colorado Interstate Gas Co. v. Natural Gas Pipeline Co. (1989) ("lower courts generally require a minimum market share of between 70% and 80%").

high.   See Syufy Enters. v. American Multicinema, Inc. (1986).

The evaluation of entry as a qualifying factor depends on how the term *entry barrier* is defined.   Academic debate has focused on two principal approaches.   The first is attributed to Joe Bain, who defined entry barrier to encompass any market condition that enables an incumbent firm to charge monopoly prices without attracting new entry.   Joe S. Bain, Barriers to New Competition 3 (1956).   The second model is associated with George Stigler, who defined entry barrier as "a cost of producing (at some or every rate of output) which must be borne by firms which seek to enter an industry but is not borne by firms already in the industry."   George J. Stigler, The Organization of Industry 67 (1968).   Bain's approach includes a broader range of obstacles, particularly by evaluating the market as it exists today rather than by asking (as does Stigler's approach) whether the barrier is a cost that newcomers must incur and incumbents did not face when they entered.   For example, Bain's definition treats scale economies as an entry barrier (because incumbents with high ouput rates tend to have lower costs than newcomers with low output rates); Stigler's approach disregards this factor because the incumbent confronted similar challenges (the need to begin production and achieve lower costs through higher output) when it first entered.   Bain's concept of entry barriers generally has gained broader acceptance among courts and enforcement officials.   But see Echlin Manufacturing (1985) (merger decision endorsing Stigler's definition of entry barrier).

The weight given to market shares also should account for the the clarity of the market boundaries and the certainty with which individual products and producers have been included or excluded from the hypothetical circle that delineates the relevant market. Emphasis on market shares should vary directly with how accurately the market definition captures commercial realities and does not artificially exclude constraining forces or include products or suppliers of little competitive significance: the greater the doubts about the market definition, the more reason to consult other factors to measure market power.

B. MONOPOLIZATION: THE USES OF MONOPOLY POWER

The Sherman Act does not condemn the mere possession of monopoly power. Size alone is not an offense, mainly because it may result from natural or legal monopoly or from vigorous competition, which the Sherman Act encourages. Because Section 2 prohibits conduct which "monopolizes," courts focus instead on the monopolist's purpose and intent—on its positive drive to seize or exert monopoly power.

Distinguishing monopolizing intent from the permissible business activity of a firm with massive market power is not simple, especially since an unlawful purpose is generally inferred from the monopolist's conduct. Sound policy encourages all firms, regardless of size, to compete vigorously because competition gives consumers the desired quality of goods at the lowest price. On the other hand, allowing firms with market power to use any trade weapon available to firms without market power may result in the exclusion of competitors, the consolidation and persistence of monopoly power, and, ultimately, higher prices and reduced output. Debate over dominant firm conduct occurs at two levels: (1) whether the conduct is in fact exclusionary; and (2) if it is, whether that justifies an inference of illegal purpose and intent. To meet (or beat) the competition, how much freedom should a monopolist have to reduce prices, redesign products, restrict access to "essential" facilities, or otherwise refuse to deal with rivals?

1. CLASSIC TEST

The early foundation for Section 2 jurisprudence was set mainly in landmark cases that attacked the marauding practices of John D. Rockefeller's oil giant and of the tobacco trust. See Standard Oil Co. of N.J. v. United States (1911); United States v. American Tobacco Co. (1911). Both defendants unquestionably had monopoly power; Standard Oil controlled almost 90 percent of the nation's refining capacity, and the tobacco trust controlled 95 percent of cigarette sales. Nor did the Court doubt that each had engaged in unreasonable business practices which could not be justified as normal competition. Standard Oil forced railroads to give it preferential rates and engaged in local price discrimination and business spying, all to drive local competitors from the market. The tobacco trust's tactics, including its purchase of over 30 rival firms whose plants were immediately closed, were, in the Court's words, "ruthlessly carried out" to support the trust's monopoly.

These cases, then, presented the Supreme Court with classic examples of unsavory business practices by monopolists. There was no great dispute about whether the defendants had market power, or about how they attained and used that power. At issue, however, was the legal status of these findings. In stating the famous "rule of reason," the Court accepted the defendants' view that the Sherman Act did not condemn "reasonable" business practices. The Court went on to spell out the primary reach of Section 2's ban on monopolization. The Court held the latter to be an adjunct to Section 1, which prohibited unreasonable trade restraints resulting from collective action. (Section 1 did not reach single-firm conduct, which, said the Court, was the concern of Section 2.) *Standard Oil* and *American Tobacco* established that Section 2 condemned the abuse of monopoly power as evidenced by trade practices which would violate Section 1 if adopted by two parties acting jointly.

The Court's analysis was not so directly stated, however. Instead, it considered the defendants' business methods to attain power "solely as an aid for discovering [their] intent and purpose." The Court contrasted the defendants' abusive market practices with what it called "normal methods of industrial development." The difference between lawful and unlawful activity by a business with monopoly power was the presence of a positive drive to monopolize. Whether this positive drive existed was determined by examining the intent and purpose of the defendant's acts, not its market share or the market's structure. In upholding most of the district court's far-reaching divestiture decree, the Court in *Standard Oil* relied on the defendant's growth (which occurred mainly through acquisitions of rivals, illegal rebates from railroads, industrial espionage, and predatory pricing) as showing illegal intent.

The early approach to Section 2 is significant for many reasons. First, it establishes the minimum threshold for a Section 2 violation—a showing of monopoly power and of conduct involving a restraint of trade (such as would violate Section 1) which demonstrates illegal purpose and intent. The essence of the offense was not the defendants' particular acts—these merely evidence their intent—but rather their actual purpose or intent. Second, the Court did not condemn monopoly power alone. In considering defendants' positive drive for monopoly power, the Court seemed to rule that market power gained by "usual methods" was lawful. Third, the law's assessment of monopoly diverged from the economic concept, which focuses on the firm's ability to restrict output and raise price. From a legal standpoint, the firm's share of total output of a product is significant in judging monopoly only when accompanied by predatory practices affecting the ability of others to compete. The Court concluded that competition would prevent the rise of monopoly power in open markets. Unless protected by law, monopolies would arise only through deliberate acts. Thus, antitrust did not prohibit monopoly power (the economic concept); it punished only acts that created or sustained monopoly power. Power plus intent was condemned.

The limits (or, as critics charged, the limitations) of this "classic" test were exposed in a line of subsequent cases. First in United States v. United Shoe Machinery Co. (1918), and then in United States v. United States Steel Corp. (1920), the Court upheld acquisitions of complementary and competing companies even though done with an evident intent to obtain monopoly power. United Shoe's 50 acquisitions were considered separately (rather than as a group), and no single merger established the requisite intent. The lease-only policy also was upheld as within its patent grant, as assuring users of adequate service and of merely continuing the practice of the acquired firms before the merger.

U.S. Steel had accounted for 80–90 percent of domestic production at the time of its creation, but this amount had dropped to 41 percent at the time of trial. The company's market share and supporting testimony convinced the district court and the Supreme Court that U.S. Steel no longer had monopoly power. This was further supported, the Court noted, by government evidence of pricing agreements between the company and its rivals. In an analytical tour de force, the Court asserted that such collusion would have been unnecessary if U.S. Steel possessed effective power. The Court seemed to concede the likelihood of illegal intent in U.S. Steel's formation and growth. But in now famous dictum it concluded: "[T]he law does not make mere size an offense, or the existence of unexerted power an offense. It, we repeat, requires overt acts...."

This dictum proved troublesome later, but at the time it appeared to expand the rule of reason under Section 2. Power plus overt acts constituted a violation, and here the overt acts were benign. U.S. Steel had "resorted to none of the brutalities or tyrannies" relied upon by Standard Oil or the tobacco trust. To be sure, it had sought to fix prices with its competitors, but these efforts were ineffective. In a strange logical twist, the Court appeared to say that competition may have suffered, but competitors were not harmed. Collusion might violate Section 1, but, when ineffective, it would not establish illegal monopolization—at least where other practices were inoffensive. By implicitly approving U.S. Steel's price leadership and protection of smaller competitors, the Court also seemed to provide a protective cover (at least under Section 2) for the quiet life of the monopolist.

2. *ALCOA*

Between *U.S. Steel* in 1920 and Learned Hand's opinion in *Aloca*[7] in 1945, Section 2 was a dead letter. *Alcoa* dramatically shifted the foundation and reach of the anti-monopoly law. Rather than focus on the defendant's abusive market practices (since none were shown), *Alcoa* emphasized the defendant's market power. This moved the

7. The Second Circuit acted as the court of last resort because four Supreme Court justices recused themselves, denying the Court a quorum to hear the case. By statute Congress allowed the final appeal to be taken to the court of appeals in the circuit in which the trial took place.

law toward economist's concept of monopoly, which focuses on the existence of power to maintain prices above costs. *Alcoa's* treatment of the relationship between market power and conduct shaped Section 2 analysis for much of the post-World War II era and deserves close examination. See Frederick M. Rowe, *The Decline of Antitrust and the Delusions of Models: The Faustian Pact of Law and Economics,* 72 Geo. L.J. 1511, 1535 (1984).

When the government filed its monopolization suit in 1937, Alcoa had dominated aluminum production in the U.S. since the early 1900s and was still the sole domestic producer of virgin ingot. The court found that Alcoa's only competition was from imported virgin aluminum, and that its market share during the five years before trial always exceeded 90 percent. Alcoa argued that despite this market share it was not a monopolist because, as the district court found, its lifetime profits had been roughly 10 percent— hardly a monopolist's rewards. Judge Hand refused to accept this figure as evidence that Alcoa had not exerted monopoly control: a firm's overall profits do not necessarily reflect profits earned on one line (virgin ingot); nor is it an excuse that a monopoly has not used its power to extract monopoly profits.

Aside from showing Alcoa's market power, the government argued that Alcoa violated Section 2 by controlling aluminum production completely. The origin of this power and the reasonableness of its exercise were accordingly immaterial; Section 2 condemns "every person who shall monopolize." [8] Alcoa responded that it neither had inter-

8. The government also complained of Alcoa's purchase of patents and combination with foreign producers to restrain competition in the U.S., and of its cost squeeze of independent fabricators. The first charge failed of proof and the price squeeze, while unlawful, was not relied on in finding Alcoa guilty. Although the issue was not before the court, scholars have

fered with attempts by others to enter the virgin aluminum market nor had sought to eliminate smaller fabricators of aluminum products. Whatever monopoly power it had, Alcoa argued, resulted simply from reasonable, natural growth. Thus if Alcoa were restructured into several firms (as the government requested), the industry's efficiency and future progress would be jeopardized with no benefit to consumers.

In an elegant yet ambiguous opinion, Judge Hand rejected Alcoa's plea that it was a well behaved monopoly—that power had been "thrust upon it." Hand accepted the premise that a business which gains a monopoly "merely by virtue of his superior skill, foresight and industry" is not guilty of monopolization, but he reasoned that Alcoa nevertheless had transgressed Section 2. Three interrelated arguments formed the core of his analysis. First, since price-fixing among rivals is illegal per se (see Chapter 5), it would be illogical not to apply Section 2 to a dominant firm whose unilateral pricing choices could yield the same supracompetitive prices that a cartel imposes. Thus once a monopolist sets a price for its product and then sells it, the monopolist can be said to have acted unreasonably. Second, Alcoa had actively discouraged new entry into aluminum production by expanding its capacity more rapidly than the demand for its output warranted. Combined with substantial capital requirements, *Alcoa's* program of accelerated development effectively foreclosed entry. Third, the

debated whether Alcoa attained dominance by improperly foreclosing access by rival aluminum producers to supplies of electricity and bauxite. Compare Thomas G. Krattenmaker & Steven C. Salop, *Anticompetitive Exclusion: Raising Rivals' Costs to Achieve Power over Price*, 96 Yale L.J. 209 (1986) (advancing foreclosure hypothesis) with John E. Lopatka & Paul E. Godek, *Another Look at Alcoa: Raising Rivals' Costs Does Not Improve the View*, 35 J.L. & Econ. 311 (1992) (disputing foreclosure thesis).

possibility that condemning Alcoa might impair industry efficiency and progress was no defense, for the Sherman Act was designed to promote social and political as well as economic goals.

These arguments present at least two troublesome features. First, Judge Hand makes a weak case for condemning the behavior that is said to satisfy Section 2's conduct requirement. Price-setting by a monopolist is unavoidable, and the monopolist's position may merely reflect internal efficiencies unavailable to a cartel that fixes prices for its members. Disapproving capacity expansion to stimulate and meet customer demand risks discouraging desirable investment by firms that occupy most of the market. Is this not the behavior of the firm which, Judge Hand warned, having been urged to compete, should not be turned upon when it succeeds? Despite Hand's effort to identify avoidable acts, *Alcoa* reads like a no-fault monopolization theory—an attack on persistent monopolistic corporate size itself.

A second difficulty concerns Judge Hand's invocation of social and political values as supporting Section 2 liability. His opinion correctly observes that populist impulses helped motivate passage of the Sherman Act, but Hand provides no policy guidance as to when a preference for political and social decentralization should override efficiency concerns. Does attaining a dominant market position always pose an unacceptable threat to the social order, or should society sometimes tolerate massive corporate size because the possibility of achieving monopoly provides a crucial incentive to compete? If a jurist of Judge Hand's immense skills cannot supply a satisfying approach for resolving this tension, how are other judges to determine which values should control close cases?

Alcoa's true meaning remains a matter of dispute. From one perspective, the court said that Alcoa's stature—its sheer size—offended Section 2 because it allowed Alcoa to acquire monopoly profits and to discourage entry. From this perspective, the decision can be read as not applying the abuse theory (where an illegal intent to monopolize is inferred from predatory conduct) but instead what amounts to a no-fault structural test, where a showing of monopoly power creates a presumption of illegality. Read this way, *Alcoa's* radical departure from *U.S Steel* is obvious. Judge Hand appears to have rejected a no-fault standard, or at least did not rely upon it, because he also found that Alcoa abused its monopoly by anticipating demand and maintaining excess productive capacity.

Even so, *Alcoa* clearly established a new precedent. It moved the abuse theory to a different level, no longer requiring that the plaintiff prove predatory conduct violative of Section 1. After *Alcoa* the term "abuse" included acts which, taken alone, would generally be considered "honestly industrial," but when considered in their totality showed "no motive except to exclude others and perpetuate its hold upon the ingot market." The proof of intent was less demanding; the prerequisite was only a showing of deliberateness by the monopolist to maintain its monopoly position.[9] The requisite degree of deliberateness existed where the defendant's acts were legal in themselves but also tended to exclude competitors or potential entrants.

Even this less expansive reading of *Alcoa* is not immune from criticism. The broad suggestion that any practice

9. The court spoke generally of Alcoa's "intent," but indicated that such intent would readily be found. Alcoa was presumed to have "intended" the obvious consequences of its acts. However, this approach might absolve a temporary monopolist whose position is due solely to a head start from having first developed a new product. See Mobile CTS, Inc. v. NewVector Communications, Inc. (1989).

deterring competition may establish deliberateness confronts a monopolist with a Hobson's choice: if it responds to the threat of entry by pricing at competitive (marginal cost) levels, it violates Section 2; yet if it disregards potential entrants by charging a monopoly price, Judge Hand's opinion suggests that it has acted unreasonably and, therefore, illegally. In this regard the opinion invites a middle ground practice not dissimilar to oligopoly behavior (see Chapter 7). The court also seems to have misapplied the "thrust upon" defense by which a firm that prevails "merely by virtue of his superior skill, foresight and industry" is not guilty of monopolization. Is it not *skill* to have "the advantage of experience," trade connections, and "the elite of personnel"? What is *foresight* if not "anticipat[ing] increases in the demand for ingot and be[ing] prepared to supply them" or "embrac[ing] each new opportunity as it opened"? And what does *industry* mean, if it ignores Alcoa's investments "doubling and redoubling its capacity"? [10] Each factor was relied on to find that Alcoa deliberately maintained its monopoly power, yet each comes close to establishing the primary defense that Judge Hand recognized.

3. POST-*ALCOA* DEVELOPMENTS

In American Tobacco Co. v. United States (1946), the Supreme Court endorsed Judge Hand's opinion and established *Alcoa* as the framework for monopolization analysis in the post-World War II era. With occasional clarification,

10. At trial, the government argued that Alcoa's failure to expand capacity faster had created an aluminum shortage that was hampering military aircraft production in 1940. This view clashed with the basis on which Judge Hand ultimately found a Section 2 violation—that Alcoa purposefully had boosted capacity to accommodate all increases in demand. See II Simon N. Whitney, *Antitrust Policies* 112 (1958).

Hand's definition of monopolization as monopoly power plus exclusionary conduct has remained the point of departure for judicial analysis of single-firm behavior. What has changed over time, however, is the definition of conduct that is deemed to be unreasonably exclusionary. In general, the path of Section 2 jurisprudence since *Alcoa* has led toward allowing dominant firms greater discretion to choose and implement competitive strategies, even if specific tactics vanquish individual rivals.

This progression has not been straight or unwavering. Two years after *American Tobacco*, in United States v. Griffith (1948), the Court in dicta appeared to adopt some of *Alcoa's* broadest statements when it asserted that monopoly power, however acquired, "may itself constitute an evil and stand condemned under § 2 even though it remains unexercised." The Court, however, also relied on the defendants' use of their monopoly power; that is, their practice of buying film distribution rights for all their movie theaters as a block was condemned. Since some of their theaters had a monopoly and others did not, this block purchasing was an abuse of Griffith's monopoly power inasmuch as it was used to gain an advantage in competitive markets.[11]

Antitrust litigation against United Shoe Machinery illustrates the development of antitrust theory and its practical limitations. In 1918 the company successfully repelled a monopolization charge stemming from its acquisition of over 50 shoe machinery producers holding complementary

11. *Griffith* is questioned because monopoly profits can be extracted only at one level. Whether Griffith bargained with movie distributors as one or several units should not affect the terms on which they dealt—except, of course, that the savings of one negotiation for all Griffith theaters might be shared by lower prices to consumers, higher payments to distributors, or increased profits for itself. See also United States v. Loew's, Inc. (1962).

patents. United States v. United Shoe Machinery Co. (1918). Four years later, however, the Court prohibited (under Section 3 of the Clayton Act) United Shoe's use of tying clauses relating to supplies used in conjunction with its leases of shoe machinery equipment. United Shoe Machinery Corp. v. United States (1922). Then in United States v. United Shoe Machinery Corp. (1953), the government again challenged United Shoe's monopoly. While United Shoe's dominance derived mainly from its research and development, the court found that the company's policy of refusing to sell its machines and its imposition of specific lease provisions further enhanced its monopoly position. Entry by rivals was blockaded, the court concluded, by the lease-only policy and the lease terms. United Shoe's policy of repair without separate charges also was said to deter independent service organizations. Despite its exemplary record—"[p]robably few monopolies could produce a record so free from any taint" of predatory practices—United Shoe's lease policies were seen as restricting competition and supporting its monopoly. Accordingly, it had violated Section 2.

Whether United Shoe's restrictive leasing policies were improper or effective to continue its monopoly power is questionable. While raising entry barriers, each policy also may have served valid nonexclusionary ends—such as assuring the quality of the machines and fostering the provision of manufacturer services and information to customers. Compare Scott E. Masten & Edward A. Snyder, *United States v. United Shoe Machinery Corporation: On the Merits*, 36 J.L. & Econ. 33 (1993) (emphasizing efficiency rationales for disputed lease provisions) with Joseph F. Brodley & Ching-to Albert Ma., *Contract Penalties, Monopolizing Strategies, and Antitrust Policy*, 45 Stanford L.Rev. 1161 (1993) (rejecting efficiency interpretation of United

Shoe's contract terms). To the extent they limited customer choice, the lease restrictions are likely to have required United to give price concessions to its customers. R. Posner, *Antitrust Law*, at 203–04.

In any case, *United Shoe* resembles *Alcoa* on two counts. First, its analysis of the monopolist's business practices— effect and purpose—is questionable. Second, *Alcoa* and *United Shoe* found that practices that do not alone violate the antitrust laws may, in conjunction with overwhelming market power, violate Section 2. Restrictive leasing by a nonmonopolist is not contrary to the antitrust laws. See John Shepard Wiley, Jr., Eric Rasmussen & J. Mark Ramseyer, *The Leasing Monopolist*, 37 U.C.L.A. L.Rev. 693 (1990). For a monopolist, however, such practices which are not inevitable (and were thought to be unrelated to efficiency) are condemned because they might aid the monopoly position. *United Shoe,* therefore, reaffirmed *Alcoa's* retreat from the abuse theory by holding that it is enough to show that the continued monopoly power resulted from exclusionary practices that were deliberate even though not otherwise illegal. Occasional cases subsequently have extended *United Shoe* and ruled that dominant firms must conform to a more rigorous standard of conduct. Compare Grand Caillou Packing Co. (1964) (The Peelers case) (monopolist's unjustified discrimination between classes of users violates FTC Act) with Official Airline Guides, Inc. v. FTC (1980) (refusing to impose duty on monopolist not to be arbitrary in dealing with firms that compete in separate line of business).

Section 2 cases since the early 1970s generally have retreated from the stringent approach of *Alcoa* and *United Shoe* and have adopted a narrower view of behavior that satisfies the Section 2 conduct requirement. A major turning point occurred in Berkey Photo, Inc. v. Eastman Kodak

Co. (1979) (*Berkey*). In *Berkey*, the plaintiff alleged that Kodak had used a collection of exclusionary tactics to protect and extend its monopoly position in photographic film. Kodak had introduced a new type of amateur photographic film and had made it available in a configuration compatible only with a new design of Kodak instamatic camera. The plaintiff argued that Kodak violated Section 2 by failing to predisclose the new camera design to enable rival camera manufacturers to prepare similar designs to sell when Kodak began marketing its new film.

The Second Circuit rejected the plaintiff's contention and offered two bases for refusing to impose a predisclosure obligation on a monopolist. First, a predisclosure duty would enable competitors to free-ride on the dominant firm's R & D efforts, severely reducing its incentive to innovate. Second, the court noted the administrative difficulty of "discerning workable guidelines" for courts and businesses to follow in determining when predisclosure would be procompetitive and should be required.

Within the next year, two other influential decisions embraced *Berkey's* approach to exculpate monopolists accused of improper conduct. In California Computer Products Co. v. IBM Corp. (1979) (*CalComp*), the Ninth Circuit rejected claims that IBM violated Section 2 by redesigning its mainframe computers to render the products of rival manufacturers of peripheral products incompatible with the IBM mainframes. The Court stressed that the new IBM designs were qualitatively superior to earlier models and concluded that IBM had no duty to choose a new design that least restricted other producers of peripheral equipment. In E.I. du Pont de Nemours & Co. (1980), the FTC refused to condemn du Pont's aggressive expansion of production capacity in the titanium dioxide industry to capture all anticipated increases in demand. Like Learned Hand in

Alcoa, the Commission recognized the tension between preserving incentives to compete and controlling the growth and exercise of monopoly power. However, the FTC drew the balance between these concerns in a strikingly different way: "[T]he essence of the competitive process is to induce firms to become more efficient and to pass the benefits of the efficiency along to consumers. That process would be ill-served by using antitrust to block hard, aggressive competition that is solidly based on efficiencies and growth opportunities, even if monopoly is a possible result."

4. REMEDIES

Section 2 enforcement has featured many cases—e.g., *Standard Oil, Alcoa, United Shoe,* and *Grinnell*—in which the court has found illegal monopolization. Despite major victories in establishing liability, the government rarely has succeeded in restructuring dominant firms into two or more competing entities. Remedies in Section 2 cases often have taken the form of decrees barring specific exclusionary acts or dictating structural relief (e.g., divestiture or compulsory licensing of intellectual property) of questionable effect. Thus, the antitrust literature is replete with negative assessments of past efforts to use Section 2 to dissolve monopoly power. See W. Kovacic, *Failed Expectations,* at 1105–12.

Three major reasons explain why Section 2 has yielded relatively few remedial successes despite the historical breadth and flexibility of its liability standard. The first is that government enforcement agencies traditionally have devoted too little effort to devising plausible dissolution schemes and presenting them convincingly to the court. See Lawrence A. Sullivan, Antitrust 146 (1977). This lapse contributes to the second cause, which is judicial apprehension about imposing a dissolution plan that might sacrifice valuable efficiencies (especially inventive skill). See *United Shoe* (1953) ("Judges in prescribing remedies have known their own limitations."); United States v. American Can Co. (1916) ("I am frankly reluctant to destroy so finely adjusted an industrial machine as the record shows defendant to be.").

The third reason is that government monopolization lawsuits often take so long that ongoing industry changes severely undercut the suggested remedy. Dissolution ultimately was refused in *Alcoa*, partly because the sale of government-owned aluminum plants built during World War II had created two new rivals (Kaiser and Reynolds) to Alcoa. Government litigation against IBM provides a second example. After thirteen years of costly pre-trial and trial proceedings (the case consumed 700 trial days), the Justice Department in 1982 abandoned its effort to restructure IBM into four computer companies when, among other reasons, it became apparent that market forces had begun to unravel the firm's dominant position. See United States v. IBM Corp. (1982) (directing entry of stipulation of dismissal). The fruitless use of resources led one commentator to call the IBM case "the Antitrust Division's Vietnam." See Robert H. Bork, *The Antitrust Paradox* 432 (Revised Edition 1993).

The absence of many successful monopoly prosecutions does not mean that important accomplishments are lacking. On the day in 1982 that it dismissed its suit against IBM, the Justice Department also settled claims that AT&T had used various exclusionary tactics to impede competition in long-distance telephone service and in telecommunications equipment. See United States v. AT&T Co. (1982). The settlement triggered the most massive divestitures ever ordered in a Section 2 suit. The Bell System's regional operating companies and its equipment manufacturing arm (Western Electric) were divorced from AT&T's control, spawning a transformation of the telecommunications industry that appears to have improved performance. (Thorny issues remain, however, about the wisdom of decree provisions that bar the the regional operating companies from offering certain information services other than switched-voice communications and from competing with AT&T to provide long-distance service.) The Justice Department's experience in the AT&T case dictates caution in assuming that future government efforts to use Section 2 to dissolve monopolies will be nonexistent or unavailing.

5. RECENT APPLICATIONS

Modern monopolization litigation has focused on four types of conduct: predatory pricing, product innovation, refusals to deal (including denials of access to essential facilities), and the use of monopoly power in one market to achieve a competitive advantage in a separate market (leveraging). Cases since the mid–1970s generally have increased the ability of dominant firms to defeat Section 2 liability. Modern Section 2 jurisprudence gives dominant firms relatively broad discretion to implement preferred pricing, product development, and promotional strategies. See James D. Hurwitz & William E. Kovacic, *Judicial Analysis of Predation: The Emerging Trends*, 35 Vand. L. Rev. 63 (1982); Wesley J. Liebeler, *Whither Predatory Pricing? From Areeda and Turner to Matsushita*, 61 Notre Dame L.Rev. 1052 (1986). Courts have not adjusted the basic formula that monopolization consists of "the possession of monopoly power in the relevant market" and "the willful acquisition or maintenance of that power as distinguished from growth or development as a consequence of a

superior product, business acumen or historical accident."
Grinnell; but they have narrowed the range of behavior
that constitutes forbidden conduct by a monopolist.

Despite the trend toward greater permissiveness, some
recent decisions have reaffirmed potentially important limits on the monopolist's freedom of action.   These limits
derive strength from the earlier, more restrictive Section 2
case law tradition and from recent economic research whose
policy implications (see Chapter 3) dictate greater concern
with single-firm behavior than the non-interventionist
teaching of the Chicago School. Thus, the current equilibrium of Section 2 doctrine and policy, while more permissive than its 1960s resting point, is subject to change.

a. *Predatory Pricing*

For most of this century, antitrust case law failed to
provide a coherent basis for distinguishing legitimate pricing from unlawful predatory behavior. Judges recognized
that the monopolist must be allowed to set its own prices—
else the court would merely become a regulatory agency—
but offered only hazy guidance about the lower bound of
the firm's pricing discretion. Courts widely accepted the
idea that a monopolist with "deep pockets" could temporarily set prices below its own and its competitors' costs,
wait for chastened or bankrupt rivals to leave the market,
and then raise prices to supracompetitive levels.

The past two decades have featured enormous ferment in
judicial analysis of predatory pricing. Four schools of academic commentary on predatory pricing have influenced
this process. The first is the "cost-based school," which
emphasizes scrutiny of the relationship between the monopolist's costs and prices. Modern cost-based analysis originated in the work of Phillip Areeda and Donald Turner,
who argued that it is usually unreasonable for a competitive

firm to price below its short-run marginal costs unless it can expect to recover these costs through future monopoly pricing. See Phillip Areeda & Donald F. Turner, *Predatory Pricing and Practices Under Section 2 of the Sherman Act,* 88 Harv.L.Rev. 697 (1975), reformulated in 3 Phillip Areeda & Donald F. Turner, *Antitrust Law* ¶¶ 710–22 (1978). These scholars proposed that pricing by a monopolist below reasonably anticipated short-run marginal cost should be presumed unlawful, while a higher price should be presumed lawful. Because marginal costs are difficult to compute, they used average variable cost—i.e., dividing a firm's cost (less fixed charges) by the number of units produced—to determine whether the challenged prices were below cost.

The second school is the "structural filter school," which would apply cost-based rules only if the market's structural features indicate that the challenged pricing behavior is likely to injure competition. The structural filter approach emphasizes that successful predation is unlikely where ease of entry denies the predator the ability to recoup its investment in below-cost pricing. See Paul L. Joskow & Alvin K. Klevorick, *A Framework for Analyzing Predatory Pricing Policy,* 89 Yale L.J. 213 (1979); Kenneth G. Elzinga & Alan Mills, *Testing for Predation: Is Recoupment Feasible?,* 34 Antitrust Bull. 869 (1989).

The third school is the "no rule" school, which regards predatory pricing as so rare and irrational that antitrust law should ignore it. No-rule advocates argue that the possibility of successful resistance by the predator's target and the prospect of new entry or expansion by existing firms usually neutralizes predatory pricing strategies. Given the assumed infrequency of harmful exclusionary pricing, the no-rule school warns that antitrust intervention usually will chill price competition and deny consumers the benefit of low prices. See Frank H. Easterbrook, *Predatory Strategies and Counterstrategies,* 48 U.Chi. L. Rev. 263 (1981).

The fourth school is the "game-theoretic" school, which views predatory pricing as a rational strategy under some conditions and rejects the primacy of cost-based relationships for identifying illegal conduct. Game theorists emphasize the incumbent firm's exploitation of informational asymmetries to signal to the target firm that it should exit the market or reduce output. See Louis Phlips, *The Economics of Imperfect Information* 197–242 (1988). Related research argues that price-cost tests overlook "strategic entry deterrence" by which established firms warn prospective entrants that entry is unattractive and punish actual entrants. See Oliver E. Williamson, *Predatory Pricing: A Strategic and Welfare Analysis,* 87 Yale L.J. 284 (1977).

Modern academic commentary has led courts to reformulate standards for dominant firm pricing conduct in three basic ways. First, many courts have accepted the view of the cost-based school that the relationship between the monopolist's prices and its costs provides a useful starting point for evaluating predatory pricing claims. In general, courts have created a presumption that pricing below average variable cost is unlawful and have required the defendant to justify such pricing—for example, by showing that its pricing was promotional or that its costs were expected to fall. Most disputes focus on whether prices above this level—which is the usual case—also can be found to be unlawful. Most courts apply a rebuttable presumption of legality for prices at or above average variable cost and a conclusive presumption of legality for prices above average total cost. The evaluation of pricing at or above average variable cost but below average total cost depends mostly on an assessment of whether entry conditions would permit the defendant to charge monopoly prices after the plaintiff exits. See Phillip Areeda & Herbert Hovenkamp, *Antitrust Law* ¶ 711.1c (Supp.1993).

Two court of appeals decisions dealing with pricing above total cost reveal divergent applications of cost-based tests. The Ninth Circuit has ruled that prices above total cost can be unlawful if such prices tend "to eliminate rivals and create a market structure enabling the seller to recoup his losses." William Inglis & Sons Baking Co. v. ITT Continental Baking Co. (1981). The *Inglis* approach was subsequently rejected in an influential opinion by Judge Stephen Breyer because it would tend to push prices upward and did not effectively distinguish between pricing practices designed to discipline from those designed to compete. Barry Wright Corp. v. ITT Grinnell Corp. (1983). Reflecting the view of most courts, *Barry Wright* concluded that Section 2 did not prohibit prices that exceeded both incremental and average total costs.

The second judicial trend has been to focus on the structural prerequisites for successful predation. In Matsushita Electric Industrial Co. v. Zenith Radio Corp. (1986), the Supreme Court dismissed Section 1 conspiracy claims by two American electronics firms that a group of 21 Japanese-owned producers or sellers of television sets had conspired for over 20 years to charge predatorily low prices for goods sold in the U.S. The defendants allegedly colluded to charge monopoly prices in Japan and used monopoly profits earned in Japan to subsidize below-cost pricing in the U.S.

In concluding that summary judgment for the defendants was warranted, the Supreme Court echoed the no-rule school philosophy that "predatory pricing schemes are rarely tried, and even more rarely successful" and added that "[a] predatory pricing conspiracy is by nature speculative."

However, the Court stopped short of adopting a no-rule approach and indicated that pricing below some (unspecified) measure of the defendant's costs could be deemed unlawful. The Court also invoked the structural filter tenet that a rational investment in such a conspiracy required a reasonable expectation that competitors could be "neutralized," for "[t]he success of any predatory scheme depends on *maintaining* that power for long enough both to recoup the predator's losses and to harvest some additional gain" (emphasis in original). The Court stressed the absence of barriers to entry into the market, explaining that "without barriers to entry it would presumably be impossible to maintain supracompetitive prices for an extended time."[12]

The Supreme Court recently underscored the role of recoupment in rejecting predatory pricing allegations brought under the primary line price discrimination provision of the Robinson–Patman Act (see Chapter 11) in Brook Group Ltd. v. Brown & Williamson Corp. (1993). There Liggett & Myers alleged that Brown & Williamson (B & W) used below-cost pricing to subdue Liggett's efforts to sell generic cigarettes in competition with B & W's branded offerings. The Supreme Court sustained the dismissal of a $148.8 million jury award for Liggett, mainly because Liggett had failed to show how B & W (which had a 12 percent

12. In reviewing a merger under Section 7 of the Clayton Act, the Court soon reiterated the importance of structural conditions for successful predation. The plaintiff (a rival to the merging parties) had argued that the merger would enable the merged entity to engage in predatory pricing against it. In rejecting this argument, the Court said courts "should focus on whether significant entry barriers would exist *after* the merged firm had eliminated some of its rivals, because at that point the remaining firms would begin to charge supracompetitive prices, and the barriers that existed during competitive conditions might well prove insignificant." Cargill, Inc. v. Monfort of Colorado, Inc. (1986) (emphasis in original).

market share) could recoup its investment in below-cost sales. The Court reached this conclusion even though high level B & W corporate documents suggested that B & W recouped its investment in predation in the generics market instantaneously by halting the erosion of its sales of branded cigarettes. See William B. Burnett, *Predation by a Nondominant Firm: The Liggett Case (1993),* in The Antitrust Revolution 252 (John E. Kwoka, Jr. & Lawrence J. White eds.: 2d Edition, 1993).

The *Brook Group* Court said that plaintiffs who allege predatory pricing under Section 2 of the Sherman Act or under the Robinson–Patman Act must satisfy two requirements, which the Court called "not easy to establish." First, the plaintiff "must prove that the prices complained of are below an appropriate measure of its rival's costs." As in *Matsushita,* the Court declined to prescribe what measure of cost (average variable cost or average total cost) should be the threshold. In *Brook Group* the Court avoided the issue because the parties had agreed that the relevant measure of cost was average variable cost. The second requirement "is a demonstration that the [defendant] had a reasonable prospect, or under Section 2 of the Sherman Act, a dangerous probability, of recouping its investment in below-cost prices." The essence of recoupment is a showing that "the structure and conditions of the relevant market" would enable the alleged predator to engage in "sustained supracompetitive pricing" once its prey has been subdued.

Liggett's recoupment theory was that B & W priced below cost in the generic market to force Liggett to raise its prices for generics and to enable B & W and other sellers in the highly concentrated cigarette industry to stabilize generic prices at higher levels. Through tacit oligopolistic coordination (see Chapter 7), industry members then would sustain generic prices at supracompetitive levels. Recoupment would occur mainly by severely reducing the "cannibalization" (by low-cost generics) of sales of branded cigarettes. To the Court, the tacit coordination scenario was theoretically plausible, but it lacked a sufficient evidentiary basis to permit a jury to infer that B & W's conduct posed "an authentic threat to competition." The Court emphasized that relying on tacit coordination by oligopolists to achieve recoupment is highly speculative, given the difficulties that oligopolists face in orchestrating their behavior at arms length; here the Court saw no reasonable basis for inferring that B & W (and other industry members) had elevated prices above a competitive level for generics. As it had in *Matsushita* and *Cargill*, the Court in *Brook Group* did not preclude the pursuit of predatory pricing claims, but it endorsed a relatively permissive standard out of fear that stronger controls on pricing conduct might render antitrust suits "a tool for keeping prices high." In taking this approach, *Brooke Group* ensures that plaintiffs' victories in Section 2 predatory pricing cases will continue to be few and far between.

Brooke Group's emphasis on recoupment is consistent with a number of recent lower court predatory pricing decisions that have considered whether market conditions would permit a predator, regardless of its price-cost relationship, to exploit the demise of firms targeted by a below-cost pricing campaign. See A.A. Poultry Farms, Inc. v. Rose Acre Farms, Inc. (1989). However, the effect of applying a structural screen continues to depend on how courts define the relevant market and assesses the height of entry barriers within that market. Some cases have found predatory pricing liability after reaching debatable judgments about such issues. See, e.g., Kelco Disposal, Inc. v. Browning–Ferris Industries, Inc. (1988) (capital requirements of $300,000 deemed a substantial barrier to entry into local waste disposal market).

The third major effect of academic commentary in predatory pricing cases has been to lead courts to reevaluate the significance of subjective expressions of the defendant's intent. Despite careful counseling and expansive document retention programs, colorful statements of exclusionary purpose remain staples of predatory pricing cases and other Section 2 litigation. In an approach that borrows from the cost-based school and the no-rule school, a growing number of tribunals treat the "hot document" or testimony that captures exclusionary comments by defendants as inherently unreliable and ultimately meaningless. See Morgan v. Ponder (1989); *Barry Wright* (" 'intent to harm' without more offers too vague a standard"). This trend is not universal, however, as some courts have continued to allow juries to decide what importance to attach to expressions of the defendant's desire to overwhelm its rivals. See U.S. Philips Corp. v. Windmere Corp. (1988).

b. *Product Innovation*

Since the mid–1970s, courts generally have upheld aggressive dominant firm efforts to develop new products and to market such innovations. In *Berkey*, the Second Circuit ruled that "any firm, even a monopolist, may generally bring its products to market whenever and however it chooses" even though it may thereby make it more difficult for smaller firms to compete or survive. This position has gained widespread acceptance in subsequent litigation. See SCM Corp. v. Xerox Corp. (1981) (rejecting attack on Xerox' creation of a "patent thicket" around its dry paper copying process); Memorex Corp. v. IBM Corp. (1980) (rejecting claim that IBM had manipulated the design of its mainframe interfaces to defeat compatibility with peripheral equipment made by other firms); *CalComp* (1979) (rejecting claim that IBM had duty to predisclose design changes to rival producers of peripheral equipment).

As a rule of thumb, courts have immunized design or development activity so long as the monopolist can show that its inventive behavior improved its existing product offerings, even though one of the firm's aims was to exclude rivals. Courts and commentators have expressed concern that flawed judicial intervention might diminish dominant firm incentives to innovate and that no manageable test exists for distinguishing benign from pernicious behavior. Compare J. Gregory Sidak, *Debunking Predatory Innovation*, 83 Colum. L.Rev. 1121 (1983) (urging broad latitude for single-firm efforts to develop and market innovations) with Janusz A. Ordover and Robert D. Willig, *An Economic Definition of Predation: Pricing and Product Innovation*, 91 Yale L.J. 8 (1981) (favoring scrutiny of certain forms of dominant firm innovation).

Although *Berkey* adopted a relatively permissive view toward dominant firm inventive activity, the Second Circuit did not give monopolists unlimited discretion. *Berkey* stated that "[i]f a monopolist's products gain acceptance in the market ... it is of no importance that a judge or jury may later regard them as inferior, so long as that success was not based on any form of coercion." The court did not define what it meant by "coercion," and later cases provide little guidance about what behavior might be illegal. Some cases suggest that deliberate efforts to create incompatibility with a rival's products without offering performance enhancements or cost reductions for the monopolist's products might be actionable. See Northeastern Tel. Co. v. AT&T (1981).

c. *Refusals to Deal*

In United States v. Colgate & Co. (1919), the Supreme Court announced that "[i]n the absence of any purpose to create or maintain a monopoly, the [Sherman] act does not restrict the long-recognized right of trader or manufacturer engaged in an entirely private business, freely to exercise his own independent discretion as to parties with whom he will deal." Establishing when a monopolist may run afoul of Section 2 for refusing to deal with another firm is among the most difficult issues in antitrust today. One of the first cases to condemn a monopolist's refusal to deal under Section 2 is Eastman Kodak Co. v. Southern Photo Materials Co. (1927). Here Kodak had sought to integrate forward into the distribution of photographic supplies and had refused to provide supplies at wholesale to a retailer that had declined to be purchased by Kodak. The Supreme Court found illegal monopolization because Kodak had refused to deal "in pursuance of a purpose to monopolize." This result was seen as giving effect to *Colgate's* intent test, which asked whether the refusal stemmed from a "purpose to create or maintain a monopoly." Until recently, most "intent test" cases had arisen where a firm had monopoly power at one level of a chain of distribution and had refused to deal with firms at the next level in order to gain a monopoly position at both levels.

In Aspen Skiing Co. v. Aspen Highlands Skiing Corp. (1985), the Supreme Court accomplished a troublesome extension of the intent test. *Aspen* held that a monopolist's refusal to continue to participate in a joint marketing plan with its only rival could amount to monopolization. A unanimous Court ruled that the evidence supported a jury's determination that the refusal by the owner of three of four mountain slopes used for skiing in Aspen to cooperate with the owner of the fourth slope and continue their joint ski ticket reflected "a deliberate effort to discourage customers from doing business with its smaller rival." The Court emphasized that the defendant "was apparently motivated entirely by a decision to avoid providing any benefit to [the smaller rival] even though accepting [its] coupons would have entailed no cost" and would have benefited potential customers. The "decision by a monopolist to make an important change in the character of the market," coupled with the jury's conclusion that the defendant lacked a reasonable business justification, supported the conclusion that the behavior was unlawful.

Aspen's implication that a monopolist could violate Section 2 merely by changing its distribution pattern and, indeed, that the monopolist can be required to cooperate with its competitors in a joint marketing arrangement (itself questionable under Section 1 as an illegal market division, see Chapter 5) is disturbing. See Frank H. Easterbrook, *Monopolization: Past, Present, Future,* 61 Antitrust L.J. 99, 106–08 (1992). Perhaps most important, such a standard raises the risks associated with undertaking any form of legitimate collaboration with a direct rival (e.g., a research and development joint venture), as a lawsuit could accompany the decision to terminate or otherwise alter such an arrangement. By raising the potential costs of abandoning such relationships, *Aspen* makes it less likely that collaborative arrangements will be formed in the first place.

Some lower courts have sought to confine *Aspen's* reach by depicting its outcome as the product of unusual facts (i.e., a gerrymandered market definition and a frail defense by the monopolist). In Olympia Equipment Leasing Co. v. Western Union Tel. Co. (1986) the Seventh Circuit observed that "[i]f [*Aspen*] stands for any principle that goes beyond its unusual facts, it is that a monopolist may be guilty of monopolization if it refuses to cooperate with a competitor in circumstances where some cooperation is indispensable to effective competition." Successful defensive strategies by monopolists have consisted mainly of providing a business justification to excuse the challenged refusal to deal. See Trans Sport, Inc. v. Starter Sportswear, Inc. (1992) (emphasizing defendant manufacturer's effort to curb free-riding by plaintiff distributor); Oahu Gas Service v. Pacific Resources, Inc. (1988). However, in evaluating asserted efficiency rationales, courts will consider whether the record shows that theoretically plausible justifications in fact motivated the defendant's refusal to deal. See *Kodak* (1992).

The Supreme Court's *Kodak* (1992) decision reveals that *Aspen* remains important in defining a monopolist's duty to deal with rivals. See Stephen Calkins, *Supreme Court Antitrust 1991–92: Revenge of the Amici*, 61 Antitrust L.J. 269, 303–06 (1993). *Kodak* repeated *Aspen's* admonition that a monopolist may refuse to deal with rivals "only if there are legitimate competitive reasons for the refusal." *Kodak* sustained a reversal of summary judgment dismissing claims that Kodak had imposed an illegal tying arrangement (see Chapter 8) and had monopolized and attempted to monopolize. The case focused on Kodak's policy of selling replacement parts for Kodak photocopiers and micrographic equipment only to buyers of Kodak equipment who used Kodak service or who repaired their own machines. Image, an independent service organization (ISO), alleged that Kodak adopted the policy to preclude it from servicing Kodak equipment.

The record on appeal stipulated that Kodak lacked market power in the market for sales of original equipment. Kodak argued its need to compete for new equipment sales precluded it from charging existing, "locked-in" users of

Kodak machines supracompetitive prices for parts or service; if it acquired a reputation for gouging its customers in the aftermarket for parts and service, Kodak would lose new placements of its machines because prospective purchasers would account for the price of parts and service in estimating the life cycle cost of operating Kodak machines. Thus, unless it was planning to exit the market for new equipment sales (and did not care if it gained a reputation for post-sale opportunism), Kodak said it could not exercise power in a market defined as the supply of parts and service for Kodak equipment.

In rejecting this argument, the Supreme Court said "Kodak's theory does not explain the actual market behavior revealed in the market" and pointed to evidence showing that Kodak had raised service prices for its customers without losing equipment sales. The Court also emphasized that not all original equipment buyers were able to perform accurate life cycle cost studies. Some buyers (the Court singled out state and federal government agencies) could not acquire or comprehend information needed to calculate life cycle costs for copiers. This left a sizeable group of "locked-in" Kodak equipment owners who, without access to ISOs such as Image, would suffer from a serious informational disadvantage. The Court concluded that Kodak might be able to overcharge these vulnerable equipment purchasers for parts and service without significantly reducing the overall demand for new Kodak machines.

Kodak's importance for future Section 2 litigation is disputed. On the one hand, the case can be distinguished by its unusual facts and procedural history.[13] Moreover,

13. Kodak moved for summary judgment four months after Image filed its suit. The district court granted Kodak's motion without a hearing after letting Image file one set of interrogatories and take six depositions.

the substantive principle of *Kodak* appears to apply in the comparatively small set of instances where: (a) the matter involves a durable goods aftermarket; (b) the seller changes its policy and restricts the choices of existing equipment owners in obtaining aftermarket services; (c) ignorance by a significant group of buyers precludes effective pre-sale comparisons concerning the life cycle costs of various systems; and (d) switching from one system to another is relatively costly.

On the other hand, the Court's receptivity to arguments based on informational market power and supplier opportunism toward an installed base strengthens the hand of plaintiffs in pursuing refusal to deal claims and avoiding summary judgment. At a minimum, *Kodak* is likely to elicit additional suits that allege the monopolization or attempted monopolization of the aftermarket for parts or service for a single manufacturer's brand. As such, *Kodak* raises troublesome questions for future litigation and business planning. First, the Court said little about either the degree of Kodak's power over locked-in buyers or, more generally, about the circumstances in which it would be appropriate to treat producers of branded, durable goods as monopolists of their own brands. However, in its emphasis on the ability of sellers to exploit informational asymmetries, the decision could be read as a significant expansion of the concept of market power. See Herbert Hovenkamp, *Market Power in Aftermarkets: Antitrust Policy and the Kodak Case,* 40 U.C.L.A. L.Rev. 1447 (1993); Michael S. Jacobs, *Market Power Through Imperfect Information: The Staggering Implications of Eastman Kodak Co. v. Image Technical Services and a Modest Proposal for Limiting Them,* 52 Maryland L.Rev. 336 (1993).

Thus, appellate review occurred within an austere factual framework, with factual inferences drawn in favor of the opposing party (Image).

A second concern is the importance the Court attached to the fact that Kodak's refusal to sell parts to ISOs departed from its previous policy. Had Kodak never sold parts and service separate from its original equipment (for example, by bundling parts and service together with the copier in structuring the product's warranty), it would have faced no Sherman Act liability. Like *Aspen, Kodak* forces the firm to devote greater care in deciding whether to work with or supply competitors. The prospect of a treble damage award, or an injunction that forces continuation of an existing business relationship, may discourage firms from dealing with rivals, even when such undertakings otherwise would increase efficiency. This could create an unnatural bias in favor of vertical integration by inducing firms to internalize functions that they otherwise might perform through contracts with other entities. More generally, the Court's emphasis on a change of business patterns might deny firms valuable flexibility to experiment with different strategies (particularly for distribution) and to respond swiftly to changing conditions.

A second branch of the refusal to deal cases involves the "essential facility" or "bottleneck" doctrine. Under one widely-accepted modern articulation, the essential facility doctrine requires the plaintiff to prove (1) control of an essential facility by a monopolist, (2) the inability of a competitor reasonably to duplicate the essential facility, (3) the denial of use of the facility to a competitor, and (4) the feasibility of providing the facility. See MCI Communications Corp. v. American Tel. & Tel. Co. (1983). *Aspen* has been interpreted as adding a fifth ingredient to this test—namely, whether the defendant advanced a reasonable business justification for denying access or conditioning access on terms that the plaintiff deems to be excessively burdensome. See also P. Areeda & H. Hovenkamp, *Antitrust Law*, at ¶¶ 736.1 and 736.2.

If the essential facility doctrine is to be applied sensibly, three basic conditions must be satisfied. First, the court must ensure that access to the facility is truly "essential" and not merely "convenient" or "less expensive." See Twin Laboratories, Inc. v. Weider Health & Fitness (1990). Second, the court must take proper account of the monopolist's justifications for denying or restricting access. In Otter Tail Power Co. v. United States (1973), which found liability where an integrated electric utility refused to "wheel" bulk power to municipally-owned distribution systems, the Supreme Court arguably misapprehended legitimate business justifications arising from the defendant's efforts to fulfill its obligation (imposed by regulation) to provide universal service. Compare City of Anaheim v. Southern California Edison Co. (1992) (integrated utility had no duty to wheel power for municipally-owned distribution company where wheeling would simply shift costs from one set of customers to another); see also William E. Kovacic, *The Antitrust Law and Economics of Essential Facilities in Public Utility Regulation,* in Economic Innovations in Public Utility Regulation 1 (Michael A. Crew ed. 1992). Third, if access is mandated, the plaintiff should be required to pay the defendant an amount that covers the full cost of providing access. In setting appropriate access charges, courts may find themselves enmeshed in ratemaking exercises for which they are institutionally ill-suited.

d. Leveraging

In *Berkey* the court provided that "a firm violates Section 2 by using its monopoly power in one market to gain a competitive advantage in another, albeit without an attempt to monopolize the second market." A number of recent decisions involving leveraging claims have criticized the *Berkey* formula for dispensing with the need to show an attempt to monopolize or actual monopolization in the second market. A noteworthy example is Alaska Airlines, Inc. v. United Airlines, Inc. (1991), in which the Ninth Circuit rejected the *Berkey* approach and held that "[u]nless the monopolist uses its power in the first market to acquire and maintain a monopoly in the second market, or to attempt to do so, there is no Section 2 violation." Accord Fineman v. Armstrong World Industries (1992).

C. ATTEMPTS TO MONOPOLIZE

In addition to prohibiting monopolization and conspiracies to monopolize,[14] Section 2 proscribes attempts to monopolize. The attempt offense can be prosecuted as a felony, but few cases have explored this avenue of enforcement. Justice Holmes provided an early formative statement on attempts to monopolize in Swift & Co. v. United States (1905). Drawing closely on the criminal law analogue, he concluded that attempted monopolization consisted of conduct that closely approaches but does not quite attain completed monopolization, plus a wrongful intent to monopolize. Thus conduct amounts to an attempt to monopolize if there is a specific intent to monopolize and a dangerous probability that, if unchecked, such conduct will ripen into monopolization. Beyond these formulas lurk difficult questions: how much market power must a defendant have before it can be charged with an attempt to monopolize, and what conduct constitutes an attempt?

14. The Supreme Court recognized conspiracy to monopolize as a separate offense in American Tobacco Co. v. United States (1946). It differs from single firm monopolization by requiring collective action, by dispensing with proof of monopoly power, and by requiring a showing of specific intent (as in attempts). See ABA Antitrust Section, *Antitrust Law Developments* 270–73 (3d ed. 1992).

For most of this century, the Supreme Court shed little light on these issues, and lower court decisions reflected considerable disarray. As the offense of monopolization expanded—especially in *Alcoa*—the role of attempt to monopolize became cloudy. As with monopolization, efforts to develop a legal standard for illegal attempts have displayed a tension between prohibiting undesirable business conduct that is likely to result in monopoly and avoiding the suppression of desirable rivalrous conduct. Since many, if not most, business practices support both inferences, actions to punish attempts necessarily involve close scrutiny of the market context and justifications for the defendant's conduct. Moreover, by definition, an attempt case involves prosecution of the unsuccessful monopolist,[15] which increases judicial caution.

The Supreme Court's recent decision in Spectrum Sports, Inc. v. McQuillan (1993) provides needed direction to courts addressing the questions posed above. In *Spectrum Sports,* the Court stated that "it is generally required that to demonstrate attempted monopolization a plaintiff must prove (1) that the defendant has engaged in predatory or anticompetitive conduct with (2) a specific intent to monopolize and (3) a dangerous probability of achieving monopoly power." Repudiating the view that a dangerous probability of success could be inferred from proof of predatory conduct alone, the Court held that satisfying the dangerous probability element required an "inquiry into the relevant product and geographic market and the defendant's economic power within that market." An assessment of the defendant's market power was deemed essential if the purposes

15. A defendant can be convicted of both monopolization and an attempt to monopolize, United States v. General Elec. Co. (1948), but the more common view is that the attempt merges into the offense of monopolization. See American Tobacco Co. v. United States (1946).

of the Sherman Act, and Section 2 in particular, were to be served: "The purpose of the [Sherman] Act is not to protect businesses from the working of the market," the Court observed, "it is to protect the public from the failure of the market. The law directs itself not against conduct which is competitive, even severely so, but against conduct which unfairly tends to destroy competition itself."

A finding that the defendant possessed a dangerous probability of success can occur at market share thresholds well below those needed to establish actual monopolization. Although results in individual cases vary, courts appear to apply a rough presumption that market shares below 50 percent are insufficient to show the requisite dangerous probability of attaining a monopoly. See ABA Section of Antitrust, *Antitrust Law Developments,* at 263–65. As with monopolization cases, courts in attempt disputes adjust the inferences to be drawn from market shares depending on the height of entry barriers and the size and stability of competitors' market shares over time. See, e.g., Indiana Grocery v. Super Valu Stores (1989) (50 percent market share insufficient to show dangerous probability of attaining monopoly where plaintiff acknowledged that defendant "could never control" the market); United States v. Empire Gas Corp. (1976) (emphasizing ease of entry in rejecting attempted monopolization claim where defendant had 50 percent market share).

CHAPTER V

HORIZONTAL RESTRAINTS: THE EVOLUTION OF STANDARDS

The Sherman Act's primary role has not been to control single-firm monopolies, but rather to deal with concerted efforts by competitors to fix prices, to restrict output, to divide markets, or to exclude other rivals. These activities have been prosecuted under both Section 1 (as restraints of trade) and Section 2 (as conspiracies to monopolize). Unlike monopolization claims under Section 2, examinations of market-rigging practices under Section 1 usually have not focused on whether the defendants succeeded or failed to achieve monopoly power; instead, the judicial gaze has been directed, at least initially, toward the participants' conduct or actions, as distinct from their market power.

The policy behind Section 1 assumes that society may lose the benefits from competition if rivals are permitted to join together and to consolidate their market power. Agreements to restrict output and raise prices above competitive levels directly impair competition. Collective acts to exclude rivals from a market can achieve similarly deleterious effects. While courts readily assume the existence of these undesirable results, careful analysis of cartels also reveals that market-rigging arrangements are not self-policing. Moreover, joint research, production, or marketing agreements may reduce costs and increase competition. Thus, whether conduct should be condemned automatically or only when it in fact causes significant harm depends on the likelihood of economic harm as well as on other possible effects.

A. THE ECONOMICS OF CARTELS AND TRANSACTION COSTS

The rationale for industry cartels—agreements among rivals to restrict output and raise prices—flows from the model of perfect competition outlined in Chapter 3. Recall that we represented the market demand for widgets as a negatively sloped curve (i.e., as more is consumed, consumers will pay less—and vice versa), we observed then that a single-firm monopolist could increase its total revenues by cutting supply from 10 to 5 widgets while raising price from $.10 to $.60 per unit. (See Table 1, p. 61 supra.) Competitive firms or price-takers will quickly see that they also can increase profits by taking the same action collectively.

Assume that ten competing firms supplied a total of 10 widgets to the market weekly. According to the demand schedule (Table 1), the market price for widgets would be only $.10 and weekly revenues would be $1.00. However, acting in concert the ten firms could triple their weekly revenue by cutting production in half and selling their widgets at $.60 per unit. Each would agree to produce only one widget every other week, yet the industry's total revenue would now equal $3.00. This plan deprives consumers of two major benefits of a competitive market: lower prices and increased output. Not surprisingly, Congress sought to outlaw such conduct under the Sherman Act.

In light of these substantial rewards, the failure of industry members to cooperate so that their industry marginal revenue matches marginal cost may indicate merely that the firms understand such action is illegal. But we also know that not all business officials scrupulously follow the law.   Yet evidence of market-rigging, while not wholly absent, is not pervasive.   This is partly because such arrangements often are secret, but the more important reasons are problems that arise in forming and operating cartels, despite their promise of greatly increased revenues.

Modern scholarly analysis of cartel behavior originated in 1964 in an influential article by George Stigler.   See George J. Stigler, *A Theory of Oligopoly,* 72 J. Pol. Econ. 44 (1964). Stigler identified two formidable hurdles to successful cartel coordination.   First, cartel members must agree on the terms of their collaboration.   This seemingly simple task can pose a host of problems.   The parties must decide what they will produce, lest firms use product quality and service differences to divert sales away from other cartelists.   For much of the post-World War II era, the International Air Transport Association (IATA) lawfully fixed passenger fares on almost all international airline routes.   But the definition of a "sandwich" fed to passengers en route required a plenary session in 1958, and lengthy debate preceded IATA's decision to raise the surcharge for inflight movies.

Cartel members also must decide what their collective output should be and what price they should charge for their products.   Established firms may fear that if they raise their immediate profits, new producers will be encouraged to enter the industry.   Maintaining the cartel may require erecting barriers to new entry—or co-opting new entrants by admitting them into the cartel.   The latter policy will tend to unravel the cartel by eliminating the very reason for its existence; that is, the cartel's members will have to accept a smaller share of the market or output will increase and prices will fall.   Cartelists also may not know precisely what output level will maximize their profits over the short run.

After setting overall production levels and prices, the cartel must give each member a production quota. Cartel participants probably will have divergent costs and market shares. Consequently they will have different preferences concerning the appropriate price level and the correct distribution of market shares. See F.M. Scherer & D. Ross, *Industrial Market Structure and Economic Performance,* at 239–44. A growing firm will expect an increased share of the market in the future, and the declining firm will insist that the agreement maintain its existing share of sales. These and similar differences usually make it difficult to reach a consensus. Smoke-filled rooms and hard drinking may moderate disagreements, but they cannot eliminate differences in price and output preferences. IATA splintered into two camps almost from its inception. Low cost carriers demanded low transatlantic fares to encourage higher volume, and airlines with higher costs insisted on higher rates.

Suppose that the cartel achieves consensus on a plan to restrict output and raise prices. The cartelists then must solve a second basic problem that Stigler identified: they must adhere to the common plan in the face of incentives for each member to defect from the terms of their understanding. Once industry members agree to fix a price well above marginal cost, each firm will be tempted to cheat. As long as others honor their commitments, and as long as chiseling can be done covertly, honesty in observing the price-fixing agreement appears foolish.

The problems of reaching consensus and coping with cheating often interact. Cartelists who are least satisfied with the original agreement may be especially prone to chisel and may cause its disintegration. See Business Electronics., Inc. v. Sharp Electronics Co. (1988) ("Cartels are neither easy to form nor easy to maintain. Uncertainty over the terms of the cartel, particularly the prices to be charged in the future, obstructs both formation and adherence by making cheating easier."). Even during the celebrated price-fixing conspiracy of electrical equipment manufacturers in the 1950s, the conspirators often cheated and waged bitter price wars. See 1 Ralph G.M. Sultan, *Pricing in the Electrical Oligopoly—Competition or Collusion* 68 (1974). In explaining the cartel's temporary collapse in the early 1950s, one General Electric executive complained that "[n]o one was living up to the arrangements and we ... were being made suckers." R.A. Smith, *The Incredible Electrical Conspiracy,* Fortune 172 (Apr. 1961).

Cheating arises from each member's realization that she could boost her profits by undercutting the fixed price, gaining additional sales at a price equal to (or, perhaps, even above) her marginal cost. This is illustrated by Figure 9:

FIGURE 9: THE TEMPTATION OF CHISEL

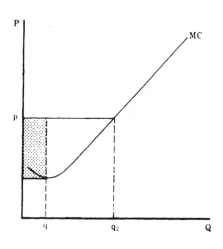

Here it is assumed that there are four firms in the industry with identical cost curves (MC), able to supply the entire market (q_2), but that the cartel limits each to one quarter of the output (q_1). Advantageous as the arrangement is to each participant, as reflected by the amount that the price (p) exceeds cost at the output (the shaded rectangle), this situation strongly tempts each firm to chisel since each could then raise its total revenues by increasing output to q_2. As long as the price at least equals marginal cost, increased revenues generally will bring increased profits. Pressure to prevent such chiseling encourages the cartel to lower the price nearer to the marginal cost.

Whenever the cartel price substantially exceeds a member's marginal cost, the cartel is likely to disintegrate unless it can effectively detect cheating and police its members. Detection can be aided by obtaining information about the pricing and sales decisions of competitors. Among other means, this can be done by directly contacting rivals, working through intermediaries such as trade associations, or giving buyers incentives to reveal the best offers of rivals. Detection alone, however, is not enough; firms also must devise credible strategies for punishing deviations. See Ian Ayres, *How Cartels Punish: A Structural Theory of Self-Enforcing Collusion*, 87 Colum. L. Rev. 295 (1987). For example, firms can commit themselves to punish cheaters by cutting prices below cost, or they can adopt contract terms such as "meet or release" clauses that assure buyers that if a rival seller offers a lower price, the firm with an existing contract will match the lower price or release the buyer from the contract.

Despite these difficulties, cartels can be profitable under some market conditions. Cartels are most likely to succeed in markets with high levels of seller concentration, substantial product homogeneity, high transaction frequency and visibility, and high entry barriers. See D. Carlton & J. Perloff, *Modern Industrial Organization,* at 216–23. However, where conditions are conducive to competition, the cartel is probably doomed, because policing numerous firms where entry is easy will prove impractical. Unless assured of protection from new entry, every cartel holds the seeds of its own destruction. Between these extremes (where many markets reside) the urge to create a cartel is enduring and universal as long as marginal revenue (price) exceeds marginal cost.

Cartels also are asserted to have beneficial effects in some cases. For example, a cartel may protect an industry from ruinous competition, thereby maintaining needed capacity, especially where fixed costs constitute a large percentage of the total costs (as with railroads). Insulated from certain competitive pressures, firms become free to finance desirable innovation and conduct other research as well as to protect the quality of their products from debasement. However, each of these alleged benefits is disputed. Ultimately the issue is whether the marketplace can fully assess the value or worth of a particular activity. Is it desirable, for example, to foster research that cannot support itself by useful products in the market? If consumers are unwilling, by their purchase decisions, to support quality, should industry groups impose minimum quality standards? Frequent government intervention to assure public health and safety reflects a judgment that the market does not adequately balance all interests. Nevertheless, it does not support private cartels as a substitute for market performance. These and similar issues, then, underlie the application of Section 1 to cartels.

Although some agreements among firms reduce competition, not all joint activity restricts output and raises prices. Firms frequently merge or integrate partially by contract to create partnerships and new firms or to achieve specific functions. Arrangements among noncompetitors, and even contracts among competitors, may foster a more efficient organization. Whatever the actual outcome, the driving purpose of the collaboration is that the new firm or organizational form will contribute to competition—the very opposite of a cartel. Ronald Coase first outlined these views over a half-century ago in pointing out that the distinction among contracts for a single transaction, the organization of a firm, or the structure of a market in which the first two operate, is not clear cut. Ronald H. Coase, *The Nature of the Firm,* 4 Economica (n.s.) 386 (1937). Rather, they are just points on a continuum of methods of organization.

Building on this understanding, scholars have developed the field of transaction cost economics to further explain alternative organizational forms. Economists have shown that firms do more than solve technical production problems; they also serve to reduce the costs of organizing and managing economic activity. Oliver E. Williamson, *Transaction Cost Economics,* in I Handbook of Industrial Organization Economics 136 (Richard Schmalensee & Robert D. Willig eds. 1989). Firms change their form, grow larger or smaller, or arrange with other firms to perform specific tasks to reduce costs, or otherwise improve the organization of economic activity. Curbing production costs (e.g., cutting the expense of running an assembly line) is important, but improved organization also translates into real cost savings.

Transaction cost economics has major antitrust implications. It illustrates that joint production or sales arrangements or other forms of cooperation may serve efficiency instead of cartel functions. For example, collaboration by rivals may facilitate the development of new products and services. See Thomas M. Jorde & David J. Teece, *Rule of*

Reason Analysis of Horizontal Arrangements: Agreements Designed to Advance Innovation and Commercialize Technology, 61 Antitrust L.J. 579 (1993). There is, in other words, no "right" degree of firm or interfirm organization in a market. The difficulty for antitrust is in discerning the objectives and likely effect of joint arrangements, and of deciding whether their probable benefits outweigh their likely competitive risks.

In the past fifteen years, the Supreme Court increasingly has accepted the view that markets and firms are part of the same continuum. See Copperweld Corp. v. Independence Tube Corp. (1984) (repudiating intraenterprise conspiracy doctrine). In several noteworthy cases, the Court has approved interfirm cooperation (by many, or even all, industry participants) where such action promises to increase efficiency. See Broadcast Music, Inc. v. Columbia Broadcasting System, Inc. (1979). However, broad generalizations about Section 1 doctrine can be treacherous. Some modern Supreme Court cases have condemned horizontal collaboration whose efficiency rationales seemed substantial. See Arizona v. Maricopa County Medical Soc'y (1982). Where the Court has treated horizontal collaboration tolerantly, its rulings have departed sharply from the spirit of less hospitable precedents without, in most cases, overruling them. The Court has neither reconciled inconsistencies in its recent decisions nor established a coherent framework that specifies which elements of its long, tortuous Section 1 jurisprudence retain vitality today. Consequently, major aspects of the doctrine governing relationships among direct rivals are among the most complex and unsettled areas of antitrust law today.

B. HORIZONTAL AGREEMENTS AND THE STRUCTURE OF LEGAL RULES: THE RELATIONSHIP BETWEEN PER SE RULES AND REASONABLENESS STANDARDS

Judicial efforts to interpret Section 1's condemnation of agreements in restraint of trade feature a basic tension between two approaches to structuring legal rules. The first adopts simple, bright-line tests ("per se" rules) that focus solely on whether certain conduct took place. The second uses multifactored reasonableness tests to evaluate the purpose and effect of challenged conduct. See Robert H. Bork, *The Rule of Reason and the Per Se Concept: Price Fixing and Market Division,* 74 Yale L.J. 775 (1965) and 75 Yale L.J. 373 (1966); Thomas J. Piraino, *Reconciling the Per Se and Rule of Reason Approaches to Antitrust Analysis,* 64 S. Cal. L. Rev. 685 (1991).

Several considerations account for the adoption in some Section 1 decisions of per se tests. The first is to give firms certainty about the legality of various acts and thereby enable them to plan and execute business practices without fear of subsequent legal attack, including private treble damage actions. Clear prohibitions also deter conduct known to pose severe competitive harms. The temptation to fix prices can be strong; if the legality of horizontal price-fixing were in doubt, or if such behavior might be justified, many would test the bounds of permissible conduct in the hope of either going unapprehended or of being able to explain the result as reasonable. Bright-line rules warn firms in advance that conduct is forbidden and discourage them from retesting the issue.

Clear prohibitions assume special importance where a statute (such as the Sherman Act) can be enforced criminally. Basic notions of fairness and justice would be offended, and the statute's perceived legitimacy would suffer, if firms and individuals were fined or imprisoned for transgressing murky legal commands. The steadfastness with which courts and enforcement agencies have struggled to preserve a distinct class of Section 1 offenses as per se illegal flows partly from the need to establish a politically and socially acceptable basis for punishing trade restraints as crimes.

A second rationale for simple tests is that they obviate the need for courts, businesses, and enforcement agencies to expend substantial resources in case-by-case evaluation of conduct whose effects are assumed to be, with negligible exceptions, pernicious. A bright-line rule that concentrates solely on whether or not the proscribed conduct occurred may be appropriate where the behavior far more often than not damages competition while offering no or few redeeming benefits to society. See Northern Pacific Railway Co. v. United States (1958). Where the possibility that conduct may have neutral or procompetitive consequences is extremely remote, the costs of condemning such behavior in the few instances in which it benefits society are substantially outweighed by the administrative savings (in judicial time and in the efforts of parties to assemble evidence of reasonableness) from the per se rule.

These rationales for per se prohibitions place a premium on determining that the forbidden behavior is indeed harmful in the vast majority of cases. Efficiency and justice are undermined when such determinations are not made carefully. Ill-conceived bright-line tests can discourage many instances of beneficial conduct. That judges may have trouble evaluating evidence is little excuse for summary prohibition where conduct often yields mixed competitive effects. It merely makes the case more pressing for competent tribunals with expertise in law and economics.

As this caution suggests, simplicity has its own drawbacks. Efforts to apply bright-line rules invariably yield an imperfect fit between the scope of their coverage and the conduct they seek to proscribe. Issac Ehrlich and Richard Posner observe that "[t]he inherent ambiguity of language and the limitations of human foresight and knowledge limit the practical ability of the rulemaker to catalog accurately and exhaustively the circumstances that should activate the general standard. Hence the reduction of a standard to a set of rules must in practice create both overinclusion and underinclusion." Issac Ehrlich & Richard A. Posner, *An Economic Analysis of Legal Rulemaking,* 3 J. Legal Stud. 257, 267 (1974). In the Section 1 context, overinclusion bars interfirm agreements that are procompetitive or benign, and underinclusion tolerates collaboration that harms competition. The challenge in devising simple rules is to reduce such errors to a tolerable minimum.

The inevitability of an imperfect fit between a bright-line rule and the behavior it seeks to attack elevates the importance of how courts classify conduct as falling within or beyond the rule's reach. See Paul T. Denis, *Focusing on the Characterization of Per Se Unlawful Horizontal Restraints,* 36 Antitrust Bull. 641 (1991). A per se rule that forbids "naked" price fixing requires the court to decide whether the price setting at issue is an unadorned output restriction (and warrants the label of naked price fixing) or helps achieve a legitimate business objective (thus dictating fuller analysis of competitive benefits and dangers). Classification enables the court to adjust a per se rule by stretching the rule's operative terms to encompass a broader range of conduct (thereby reducing underinclusiveness) or by concluding that such terms do not apply to conduct that facially seems covered by the rule (thereby reducing overinclusiveness). Thus, the classification process introduces some flexibility into the application of even the simplest and clearest per se tests.

The rationale for multi-factored reasonableness tests is rooted in the weaknesses of bright-line rules. Reasonableness tests minimize overinclusion and underinclusion by allowing courts to account for variations in commercial settings that defy satisfactory treatment through simple rules of thumb. However, this flexibility generates its own costs. Reasonableness tests consume more resources of courts and litigants because they expand the range of issues (and related information) that must be addressed. Reasonableness standards also reduce certainty about the legality of specific conduct, which can deter socially useful conduct and raise the frequency of litigated disputes. Finally, by increasing the discretion of judges and enforcement officials, such tests can yield greater inconsistency and unpredictability in the resolution of disputes and can increase the risk of error or misconduct by public decisionmakers.

The evolution of Section 1 doctrine has featured confusion and turmoil over when per se rules and flexible reasonableness tests, respectively, should determine the legality of collaboration by direct rivals. See Ernest Gellhorn & Teresa Tatham, *Making Sense Out of the Rule of Reason*, 35 Case W. Res. L. Rev. 155 (1984). The cases present essentially two models of analysis: a dichotomy model and a continuum model. Some decisions posit a sharp dichotomy between two polar forms of collective conduct. One pole consists of naked restraints on competition subject to outright, per se condemnation. The other pole contains agreements with mixed competitive consequences that warrant an expansive, openended reasonableness inquiry into the restraint's history, purpose, and market impact.

Other decisions disavow a sharp dichotomy between per se and rule of reason approaches and instead depict these tests as elements of a unified continuum. See Massachusetts Board of Registration in Optometry (1988). The unified model arrays business practices along a continuum that entails varying levels of inquiry depending on the nature of each type of behavior. The unified approach employs an abbreviated threshold inquiry to split horizontal restraints into two general categories. In one group are agreements that appear likely to reduce output with few (if any) offsetting efficiencies. Because such arrangements pose serious competitive dangers and have little procompetitive virtue, they can be condemned without further analysis. The inquiry for this category of conduct is similar to the approach applied to conduct deemed per se illegal in the dichotomy model.

The second category of behavior consists of collaboration that presents a mix of procompetitive and anticompetitive traits. Such behavior is subject to a multifactored inquiry that asks three basic questions. First, do the restrictions limit output and raise prices? Second, will the efficiency benefits of the restrictions outweigh their possible anticompetitive effects? Third, are the restrictions reasonably necessary to attain the efficiency goals? Courts also dispense with a more elaborate inquiry if certain industry characteristics are present. For example, a strong presumption of legality might be applied to the second category of restraints where the defendants have a trivial market share. See Capital Imaging Assocs. v. Mohawk Valley Medical Assocs., Inc. (1993) ("[I]n most cases where horizontal restraints on competition are alleged, market power remains a highly relevant factor in rule of reason analysis because market power bears a particularly strong relationship to a party's ability to injure competition").

C. PRICE–FIXING

Explicit agreements by competing firms to fix prices are a primary concern of Section 1. This was acknowledged in the earliest cases. Where evidence of agreement or conspiratorial conduct was not contested, courts concentrated on whether to consider evidence of economic injury or extenuating circumstances justifying the arrangement. Did the Sherman Act condemn every price-fixing agreement automatically? Must the plaintiff prove that the agreement harmed competition or competitors? Or, is the arrangement illegal unless the defendants can point to social benefits? The history of judicial treatment of price-fixing involves a typical ebb and flow process—of strict rules and encroaching exceptions. It is recounted below because the study of the judicial weaving is instructive for the application of the Sherman and Clayton Acts to other practices.

1. EARLY DEVELOPMENTS

The first Section 1 case to reach the Supreme Court, United States v. Trans–Missouri Freight Ass'n (1897), treated efforts by 18 railroads controlling traffic west of the Mississippi to eliminate fratricidal rate wars. The railroads created an association to set freight rates for all participants. When challenged by the government, they conceded that their contracts curbed each firm's commercial freedom. Nevertheless, the railroads argued that they were exempt from the Sherman Act as regulated carriers under the Interstate Commerce Act, and that in any case the rates they fixed were legal because these rates were reasonable and therefore valid under common law. The lower court sustained these arguments, but a closely divided Supreme Court reversed the decision. It held that the Sherman Act did not exempt railroads, and that it was unnecessary to consider whether the restraint was valid at common law. The Court said that Section 1 condemned "every" restraint of trade; it recognized no exceptions. By this literal reading, the Court appeared to condemn all agreements in restraint of trade, not just unreasonable ones. On the other hand, Justice Peckham's majority opinion also suggested that the agreement was illegal because it suppressed competition, and that this dictated prohibiting the arrangement regardless of whether the rates were reasonable.

Two cases decided in the following year further developed both sides of this analysis. The Court again ruled that price-fixing agreements were within the prohibition of "every" trade restraint (without regard to reasonableness). Nonetheless, the Court suggested that the statute would not be applied so sweepingly. In Hopkins v. United States (1898), the Court read *Trans–Missouri* as applying only to "direct" agreements in restraint of trade; only agreements whose main purpose was to fix prices were condemned. Covenants not to compete in connection with the sale of business goodwill and similar ancillary agreements, for example, were not barred. And in United States v. Joint–Traffic Ass'n (1898), the Court distinguished price agreements from ordinary sale, lease, partnership, and incorporation contracts because eliminating actual or potential rivalry was permissible where it supported an integration of the parties' productive economic activities or facilities. Thus, efficiency was recognized early on as justifying arrangements that might otherwise restrain trade. This placed the scope of *Trans–Missouri's* condemnation of "every" trade restraint in doubt.

The first phase in the Sherman Act's interpretation concluded with a suggestive opinion by William Howard Taft, then a circuit judge. He used an expansive (and, as suggested in Chapter 1, somewhat creative) reading of the common law to relate the rules of antitrust to Act's goals. In United States v. Addyston Pipe & Steel Co. (1898), six leading producers of cast iron pipe conceded that they had agreed among themselves to divide the southern and western markets into regional monopolies and had instituted a system of fixed prices for each territory. The fixed prices were just low enough to discourage entry by eastern producers; without the agreements, prices might have been lower if the local firms had competed among themselves. The defense emphasized two contentions. First, the arrangement's purpose was not to gain monopoly but to avoid ruinous price competition that had caused many cast iron pipe firms to disappear. Second, prices for pipe in each region were reasonable. Since consumers were not injured, there was no public harm for which the Sherman Act provided a remedy.

Neither defense convinced the circuit court. Instead, it held that the agreements deprived the public of the benefits of competition. Seeking to build an airtight per se ban against price-fixing agreements, Taft read the prevailing common law as voiding all price-fixing agreements unless they were ancillary to some legitimate cause. The law, as Taft saw it, made naked restraints in which the "sole object" is to eliminate competition per se illegal. Consequently, he ruled that even under *Joint–Traffic's* reading of Section 1, the defense of reasonableness was irrelevant. On the other hand, some restraints on competition are desirable, and here Taft drew from his reading of the common law the concept of "ancillary" restraints. Where the agreement served a legitimate end (such as the sale of a business or property or the creation of a partnership), the subordinate price restraint enhanced the basic arrangement and therefore should be preserved. In such cases, the benefits to society were likely to outweigh the losses, and such arrangements should not be automatically outlawed. When measured by this standard, the pipe producers' agreements were clearly not ancillary—and thus were illegal. Taft also acknowledged that some common law courts had applied a reasonableness test to nonancillary restraints, but he warned that such courts had "set sail on a sea of doubt."

Despite its force, Taft's analysis had a limited impact during the Sherman Act's formative years. Almost as an afterthought, Taft also noted in *Addyston Pipe* that "if it were important, we should unhesitatingly find that the prices charged in the instances which were in evidence were unreasonable." Latching on to this statement, the Supreme Court muted the significance of Taft's ruling by affirming (but modifying the decree of) the circuit court, and by emphasizing the finding that the prices fixed were in fact unreasonable. This implied that reasonableness might be sustained as a defense.

2. DEVELOPMENT OF THE RULE OF REASON

The Supreme Court seemed to reverse the trend toward a per se ban on price-fixing in Standard Oil of N.J. v. United States (1911). In a long, confusing opinion about Standard's efforts to monopolize the sale of petroleum products, Chief Justice White reread Section 1 as barring only *undue or unreasonable* restraints of trade. White had dissented in *Trans–Missouri* and *Joint–Traffic,* objecting to Justice Peckham's literalism in those cases. Here he asserted that to prohibit "every" trade restraint would be impractical and contrary to congressional intent. Applying a "standard of reason" to determine whether an agreement is prohibited as a restraint of trade depends, he concluded, on the arrangement's purpose, the character (i.e., power) of the parties, and the effect of their acts.

Standard Oil (N.J.) did not directly hold that price-fixing was permissible if reasonable, however. Standard's monopolizing activities were the Court's concern. Moreover, the Court noted that some conduct was conclusively presumed to be undesirable and harmful, but the scope and content of this unelaborated conclusion was unclear. Thus, in *Standard Oil (N.J.)* the Court created a new rule of uncertain content which emphasized behavior and recognized that agreements between firms have many possible effects; yet it also acknowledged that some conduct may be inherently unreasonable.

The next price-fixing case presented to the Supreme Court, Chicago Bd. of Trade v. United States (1918) (*CBOT*), is important for two reasons: it provides a much-cited, still influential recitation of the rule of reason's content, and it illustrates the general historical trend that the application of the rule of reason usually has exculpated the defendant. While the rule of reason standard no longer governs unadorned price-fixing agreements under the Sherman Act (if it ever truly did), this standard is used widely in antitrust. Its evolution, in theory and application, must be understood if one is to gain a sure foothold in antitrust.

In *CBOT* the government charged that a grain exchange rule requiring members to adhere to their closing bid on the "call" (which in effect confined price competition to the time the exchange was open) was illegal because it fixed prices during part of the business day. The call rule required exchange members to establish their off-hour trading price for "to arrive" grain at a special call session. The government claimed that the rule's purpose and effect was to fix the price for trading in "to arrive" grain after the exchange's daily and weekend closing times; members could not change their price during this time to reflect fluctuating conditions—as they would in an unregulated market. Yet the call rule did not seek to set the level of the "to arrive" price; participants in the call session were free to compete on the price for the "to arrive" grain.

Writing for the Court, Justice Brandeis rejected this claim of per se illegality in a famous statement of factors to be considered under the "rule of reason":

> [T]he legality of an agreement or regulation cannot be determined by so simple a test, as whether it restrains competition. Every agreement concerning trade, every regulation of trade, restrains. To bind, to restrain, is of their very essence. The true test of legality is whether the restraint imposed is such as merely regulates and perhaps thereby promotes competition or whether it is such as may suppress or even destroy competition. To determine that question the court must ordinarily consider the facts peculiar to the business to which the restraint is applied; its condition before and after the restraint was imposed; the nature of the restraint and its effect, actual or probable. The history of the restraint, the evil believed to exist, the reason for adopting the particular remedy, the purpose or end sought to be attained, are all relevant facts. This is not because a good intention will save an otherwise objectionable regulation or the reverse; but because knowledge of intent may help the court to interpret facts and to predict consequences.

Following these directions, the Court ruled in *CBOT* that the exchange requirement restricting its members' hours of operation and prices while the exchange was closed was reasonable. In doing so, the Court continued its practice of not examining actual prices or their reasonableness. Instead it found that the rules fostered the exchange market; and regulating competition, in contrast to preventing it, was not always to be discouraged. The critical factors for evaluating the call rule were its purpose and effect, which, according to the Court, were: to regulate the exchange's hours of business, to break up the monopoly previously held by a few warehouses willing to make evening purchases— which was thought to prey on unsuspecting country dealers and farmers—and to perfect the operation of the exchange by increasing the number of transactions made there. While analysis of each rationale suggests an equally persuasive contrary result,[1] the Court concluded that the call rule's primary aim was to create a public market where commodity prices could be determined competitively. To the Court, the rule sought to further rather than to suppress competition, and in this light it was reasonable.

CBOT has provided the starting point for many subsequent judicial efforts to conduct a rule of reason inquiry. The decision's much cited reasonableness formula has posed three interrelated difficulties in horizontal restraints analysis. First, the Court's comprehensive recitation of relevant criteria offered little guidance about how the factors mentioned in the passage quoted above should be considered in specific cases. Justice Brandeis did not rank

---

1. If monopolistic warehouse operators were exploiting country dealers or farmers, a response more consistent with the Sherman Act would be to increase competition by encouraging others to enter the off-hour market and offer competitive prices; to remedy the seller's lack of current price information, the exchange could circulate such data to these dealers and farmers. Note that these alternatives are less restrictive than the "call rule," which in effect prevented such sellers from selling their "to arrive" grain to member brokers at prices responsive to changing conditions. Cf. Peter C. Carstensen, *The Content of the Hollow Core of Antitrust: The Chicago Board of Trade Case and the Meaning of the "Rule of Reason" in Restraint of Trade Analysis,* 15 Res. in L. & Econ. 1 (1992) (challenged restraints seen as ancillary to proper functioning of the exchange and lacking cartelizing function).

these factors by their relative importance, nor did he suggest which party should bear the burden of coming forward with proof about the factors during the lawsuit. In later antitrust cases, the tendency to present unordered lists of criteria without discussing how such criteria should be administered by judges and litigants would characterize many of the Court's attempts to articulate reasonableness tests. See United States v. Penn–Olin Chemical Co. (1964) (joint venture); Brown Shoe Co. v. United States (1962) (merger). The failure to consider administrability can greatly increase the costs of applying reasonableness tests, both in litigation and counseling resources and in reduced predictability as individual tribunals devise idiosyncratic methodologies to apply *CBOT's* amalgam of criteria.

The second difficulty resulting from *CBOT* grew directly out of the first. To assess most or all of the factors in the decision's reasonableness calculus seemed an expensive, daunting task. *CBOT's* factors appeared to entail a wide-ranging industrial organization study that would examine the restraint's history and business context, and would measure its competitive impact. In this respect, *CBOT* helped engender the view that rule of reason analysis necessarily involved a costly, indeterminate evidentiary inquiry, which typically resulted in the defendants' exculpation. "Rule of reason" became a synonym for "legal per se."

The third difficulty with *CBOT* was that it indirectly fostered a harmful distortion in the evolution of Section 1 doctrine. Judges and plaintiffs came to perceive that Section 1 offered only two analytical tools: an administratively simple rule of per se illegality and an administratively hopeless rule of reason. Broad recognition of this dichotomy, coupled with the sense that there were no intermediate models between the per se and reasonableness poles, pressed courts to expand the category of conduct denominated illegal per se. From the late 1930s until the early 1970s, courts added substantially to the list of conduct subject to per se condemnation. Not until the late 1970s and early 1980s did courts moderate or, occasionally, reverse this process. The retreat from strained efforts to force conduct into the per se pigeon hole occurred only through a gradual judicial recognition that there were administrable, intermediate analytical alternatives between per se illegality and amorphous reasonableness tests.

The flexible view of the Sherman Act (even as applied to price-fixing) embodied in *Standard Oil (N.J.)* and *CBOT* dominated antitrust for a decade and continues to resurface regularly. Indeed, the rule of reason's subsequent application in monopolization (see Chapter 4) and trade association cases (see Chapter 6) shortly thereafter suggested to some that price-fixing might also survive Sherman Act scrutiny.

Before returning to the law of price-fixing, it is worth noting that the judicial treatment of the reasonableness defense to a price-fixing charge is typical of the evolution of antitrust law, and similar developments have occurred in most other areas where antitrust concepts have been applied. Defendants will first argue that their primary conduct was lawful—here, that price-fixing violates neither the common law nor the Sherman Act. After that contention is categorically dismissed, as in *Addyston Pipe,* the defense retreats to a second line of rebuttal. It asserts that the market-rigging in question does not violate the Sherman Act's prohibition of "undue" restraints because the arrangement (here, the fixed price) is reasonable. Not only is the agreement asserted to be harmless to consumers and competitors, but it is also said to help market participants avoid what are depicted as destructive effects of intense price rivalry.

In evaluating this claim in regard to price-fixing charges, several responses must be considered. No price is intrinsically reasonable, except by reference to its determination in a competitive market. Prices serve to allocate resources and production, and price-fixing distorts this market process. Courts are unable to measure marginal cost on which a theoretically reasonable price would be based. Price reasonableness is an ever changing concept responsive to market and cost conditions. What is reasonable one day may not be the next. To prevent abuse of the reasonableness defense, then, courts would have to supervise business pricing daily. Not only does this seem undesirable from the business manager's viewpoint, but it is also beyond judicial competence. Finally, price-fixing agreements concentrate market power and impair the competitive process. Unless the arrangement fulfills an overriding need, its effect is to destroy independent values worth preserving.

3.   THE RISE OF THE PER SE APPROACH

Perhaps recognizing some of these problems, at least for price-fixing, the Supreme Court seemed to dispel at its next opportunity any notion that price-fixing warranted a reasonableness standard. In United States v. Trenton Potteries Co. (1927), the makers of 82 percent of toilets and other bathroom fixtures belonged to an association that had fixed the prices of sanitary pottery and had limited sales to "legitimate" jobbers. Since the court of appeals had reversed a criminal conviction on the ground that the jury had not been allowed to consider the reasonableness of the prices fixed by the defendants, the issue of whether reasonableness constituted a defense was squarely before the Court. Justice Stone's response seemed unequivocal:

The aim and result of every price-fixing agreement, if effective, is in the elimination of one form of competition. The power to fix prices, whether reasonably exercised or not, involves power to control the market and to fix arbitrary and unreasonable prices. The reasonable price fixed today may through economic and business changes become the unreasonable price of tomorrow. Once established, it may be maintained unchanged because of the absence of competition secured by the agreement for a price reasonable when fixed. Agreements which create such potential power may well be held to be in themselves unreasonable or unlawful restraints, without the necessity of minute inquiry whether a particular price is reasonable or unreasonable as fixed and without placing on the government in enforcing the Sherman Law the burden of ascertaining from day to day whether it has become unreasonable through the mere variation of economic conditions.

Read literally, this analysis holds that proof of the mere existence of a price-fixing agreement establishes defendant's illegal purpose and that the prosecution need demonstrate nothing more. It need not show that the prices fixed are unreasonable, that the defendants had the power to impose their wishes on the market, or that the agreement injured anyone (by causing them to pay supracompetitive prices). That is, the action of agreeing to fix prices is in itself (per se) illegal. On the other hand, the defendants' control of 82 percent of the market itself evidenced market power (although the trial record suggested that pricing discipline was weak and that exhortations not to sell at off-list prices were often ineffective); nor did the Court apparently doubt that the arrangement had an undesirable impact.

These implicit limitations on the holding in *Trenton Potteries* were seized on by the Court only six years later in a price-fixing case presented in the midst of the Great Depression. To cope with plunging prices and falling output, 137 coal companies, which accounted for roughly 12 percent of all bituminous coal production east of the Mississippi River and almost 75 percent of all noncaptive bituminous output in Appalachia, formed a new company to act as the exclusive selling agent for member firms. The agency was instructed to get the "best prices obtainable" and if all output could not be sold, to allocate orders fairly among member firms. In effect it served as a sales cartel, but with far from complete control over the coal market.

Responding to the coal industry's "deplorable" economic condition, the Supreme Court in Appalachian Coals, Inc. v. United States (1933) reversed a lower court decision that had adhered closely to the analysis in *Trenton Potteries* and condemned the arrangement. Emphasizing the "essential standard of reasonableness," the Court called for "a close and objective scrutiny of particular conditions and purposes" in every case: "Realities must dominate the judgment. The mere fact that the parties to an agreement eliminate competition between themselves is not enough to condemn it." Starting from the premise that the proposed sales agency had no power either to fix or affect prices,[2] the Court accepted the defendants' argument that collaboration for legitimate ends—such as distributing "distress" (i.e.,

---

2. Commentary on *Appalachian Coals* usually assumes that the defendants had significant market power, but some observers doubt that the marketing agency and its members had the ability to cut output and raise prices. See Almarin Phillips, *Market Structure, Organization and Performance—An Essay on Price Fixing and Combinations in Restraint of Trade* 119–37 (1962).

odd-size) coal and preventing "pyramid" sales (i.e., multiple or fraudulent sales)—was lawful. It also accepted the defendant's professed intent to foster "a better and more orderly" marketing system rather than to restrict output. Finally, the Court held that legality ultimately rested on the likely effect of the agreement which had not yet been implemented; purpose or intent was not enough to condemn it.

Despite the Court's efforts to paper over the differences, *Appalachian Coals* clearly departed from *Trenton Potteries* and its per se rule. The question was which approach would prevail. Would *Appalachian Coals'* return to the rule of reason survive the Depression? The Court answered that question decisively—and negatively—in United States v. Socony–Vacuum Oil Co. (1940), which explicitly adopted a rigid per se rule condemning all price-fixing arrangements. With some exceptions, *Socony* remains a foundation for Sherman Act analysis of horizontal price-fixing cartels today.

Socony's facts strongly resembled those before the Court in *Appalachian Coals.* The oil refining industry was depressed, and independent producers faced panic market conditions. Decreased demand was aggravated by increased supplies of gasoline. Independent refiners lacked storage facilities and had been dumping gasoline at giveaway prices. In East Texas, crude oil prices fell to 10 to 15 cents per barrel, and gasoline was sold for 2½¢ per gallon. In response, a group of major refining companies agreed to buy surplus ("distress") gasoline from the independents, disposing of it in a more "orderly manner" so as not to depress prices. The arrangement assigned a major firm to each independent as a "dancing partner," and the major firm bought its partner's surplus gasoline. This gasoline eventually reached the market, but its effect on prices was thought to be weaker. The Court believed that the defendants, by manipulating the relatively thin spot market, kept gasoline prices above the level that competition would otherwise have yielded.

Although the defendants had not explicitly agreed on the price at which they would sell their gasoline, the Court easily found that the arrangement's purpose was to curtail competition and raise prices. Invoking *Appalachian Coals,* the defendants argued that their buying program served to stabilize the market by doing no more than curing "competitive evils." But the Court rejected this view as having "no legal justification"; the reasonableness of the fixed prices was no defense:

> Any combination which tampers with price structures is engaged in an unlawful activity. Even though the members of the price-fixing group were in no position to control the market, to the extent that they raised, lowered, or stabilized prices they would be directly interfering with the free play of market forces. The Act places all such schemes beyond the pale and protects that vital part of our economy against any degree of interference. Congress has not left with us the determination of whether or not particular price-fixing schemes are wise or unwise, healthy or destructive....

> Under the Sherman Act a combination formed for the purpose and with the effect of raising, depressing, fixing, pegging, or stabilizing the price of a commodity in interstate or foreign commerce is illegal per se.

Even the limited aim of price stabilization—i.e., of placing a floor under the market—was condemned as illegal:

> [M]arket manipulation in its various manifestations is implicitly an artificial stimulus applied to (or at times a brake on) market prices, a force which distorts those

prices, a factor which prevents the determination of those prices by free competition alone.

Finally, in rejecting the argument that the defendants lacked power to control prices, the Court, in its celebrated footnote 59, went so far as to indicate (in dicta) that effective power to implement the purpose was not necessary to prove illegal price-fixing; the offense is the illegal purpose as shown by the agreement. While the Court's language can be read as condemning any price-fixing agreement whether or not the parties could affect prices, a more sensible reading does not deny a de minimis limitation. The concern expressed by critics of this footnote is more theoretical than practical. If the parties' actions cannot affect prices, no reason would exist for them to agree to fix them. The Court's ruling sought to condemn market-rigging arrangements having less than total domination or control over a market; the latter may also cause at least temporary injury and are not tolerated under the Sherman Act.

Socony displaced *Appalachian Coals* and, for much of the post-World War II era, supplied the basic approach for judicial analysis of horizontal price-fixing claims. *Socony's* dicta that the Sherman Act condemns *any* price tampering moved courts to look suspiciously at all joint efforts by rivals to influence price levels. Thus, later cases applied a rule of per se illegality to maximum price-fixing, even though the potential public injury is less substantial and the economic rationale for condemnation is different.[3] In

3. The benefits from maximum price-fixing are: (a) consumers are protected from temporary exploitation; (b) public anti-inflation policy is served; (c) industry interests are served by increasing demand and re-assuring buyers against price disruptions; and (d) it allows low-price sellers to identify themselves and gives them a less costly way to make low price agreements with buyers. Among the possible harms from forced price ceilings are (a) the parties may select an entry-discouraging price; (b)

Kiefer–Stewart Co. v. Joseph E. Seagram & Sons, Inc. (1951), the Court relied on the principle of *Socony* to condemn as illegal per se an agreement by two distillers to set maximum prices that they would allow their distributors to charge.

The Supreme Court reaffirmed the per se rule against agreements to set maximum prices in Arizona v. Maricopa County Medical Soc'y (1982) when it struck down an agreement among physicians setting the maximum fees they would charge for their services. There 70 percent of the medical practitioners in Maricopa County (which includes Phoenix) established a plan whereby they agreed not to charge patients more than a specified fee for identified services; several insurance companies in turn agreed to pay the full cost of these services provided by the plan's participants. A list of the participating doctors was provided to consumers. The doctors argued that this agreement reduced prices to consumers by lowering information search costs, that the participating insurance companies were acting in the consumers' interests, and that the medical profession met higher standards and should not be subject to the usual antitrust (per se) rule. Although it acknowledged that the economic rationale for prohibiting maximum price agreements is distinct, the Court rejected the physicians' justifications. The Court believed that similar ends could be achieved without maximum price fixing and, fearing the competitive dangers of price fixing, concluded that these concerns justified per se condemnation. This approach is questionable. The insurers are unlikely to have participat-

the agreement may be an implicit arrangement to forego additional service or quality improvements; (c) the parties may be selecting some mechanism other than price for allocating short supplies; and (d) the price selected may become the minimum and in any case be an occasion for discussing prices generally. See Frank H. Easterbrook, *Maximum Price Fixing*, 48 U.Chi.L.Rev. 886 (1981).

ed in a physicians' cartel since it was not in their interest to increase their costs or protect the physicians. The program had genuine potential to lower consumer costs, and the use of a per se approach prevented consideration of the plan's effect on prices or output.

Nor is it permissible in most instances for rivals to form arrangements whose effect on price is indirect. Thus, agreements to set standard charges for check cashing or credit servicing, to change prices at the same time, or not to advertise prices are per se illegal. For example, in Catalano, Inc. v. Target Sales, Inc. (1980) (per curiam), the Court held that an agreement among beer distributors to eliminate free short-term credit on sales to retailers was "as plainly uncompetitive as a direct agreement to raise prices"—and hence was unlawful per se. Since extending interest-free credit is equivalent to giving the retailers a discount equal to the value of the use of the purchase price for that period, the credit terms were viewed as an inseparable part of the overall retail price. Similarly, in Plymouth Dealers' Ass'n of Northern California v. United States (1960), competing new car dealers were forbidden to agree on a "list price" even though customers invariably bargained over the price and the defendants almost never sold cars at that price—and the agreement responded to customer animosity over dealer pricing practices. By setting a standard starting price, the agreement affected prices even though it did not fix them—which violated *Socony's* airtight rule. Finally, an agreement among buyers of a product, rather than among sellers, to reduce the durum wheat content of high quality macaroni violates the per se rule. Durum wheat was in short supply, and the agreement's aim was to keep the price of wheat low. National Macaroni Mfrs. Ass'n v. FTC (1965). See also R. Blair & J. Harrison,

Monopsony, 68–78 (discussing adverse effects of monopsonistic buyers' cartels).

4. CURRENT DEVELOPMENTS

The formulation of the per se rule against price-fixing and the rigidity of its application have provoked extensive debate over Section 1 doctrine. By focusing almost exclusively on evidence of a conspiracy to fix prices, the law has made it relatively easy to prosecute unsuccessful cartels (where disgruntled participants testify against those who cheated or left the cartel) while providing no effective measure against cartels that have overcome the usual problems of reaching a consensus on terms, discouraging new entry, and detecting and punishing deviations from the cartel's terms. On the other hand, the per se rule also drives such cartels underground and makes it difficult for them to operate without the elaborate machinery needed to prevent evasion by low cost members with unused capacity. Thus, the elimination of formal cartels from American industry has been called antitrust's single most important achievement. R. Posner, *Antitrust Law,* at 39.

The dichotomy model of Section 1 analysis that distinguishes sharply between per se and reasonableness rules has proven unsatisfactory in a number of instances. It has perplexed courts where conduct that might be labelled "price-fixing" also may help expand output or provide a product that otherwise might not be available. Despite the nominally clear doctrinal division between per se and rule of reason requirements in cases such as *Socony,* Supreme Court antitrust opinions have not fit neatly into these two categories. See 7 Phillip Areeda, *Antitrust Law* ¶ 1511 (1986). Until the late 1970s, the Court softened the hard edges of the per se rule mainly by using the characterization process to except specific types of conduct that increased efficiency, even though such conduct in some sense fixed prices.

Since the late 1970s, some Supreme Court decisions have acknowledged the limitations of the dichotomy model and have suggested that per se and rule of reason analysis are not polar opposites but part of a single continuum. Such decisions have disavowed formalistic labels and have permitted an inquiry into competitive benefits and hazards without the full-blown reasonableness assessment suggested in *CBOT*. Cases consistent with this trend have used what has been termed a "structured" or "truncated" rule of reason test. In applying this approach, the Court has shown that a restraint can be found illegal without creating and evaluating a massive evidentiary record.

The modern blurring of Section 1 doctrinal boundaries between per se and rule of reason standards for horizontal restraints began indirectly in 1977 in a case dealing with vertical contractual restraints. In Continental T.V., Inc. v. GTE Sylvania Inc. (1977), the Supreme Court ruled that nonprice vertical restraints must be evaluated by a rule of reason. *Sylvania* not only transformed vertical restraints doctrine (see Chapter 8), but it also criticized the approach evident in many post-*Socony* decisions of using per se tests to condemn behavior whose economic effects are not immediately clear. The Court observed that early decisions such as *Standard Oil (N.J)* had "established the 'rule of reason' as the prevailing standard of analysis." The Court concluded that "[p]er se rules of illegality are appropriate only when they relate to conduct that is manifestly anticompetitive." The Court also described the per se rule as a "demanding standard" and emphasized that any "departure from the rule-of-reason standard must be based upon demonstrable economic effect rather than ... upon formalistic line drawing." See also *Business Electronics* (1988) (in Section 1 disputes, "there is a presumption in favor of a rule-of-reason standard").

Sylvania's caution against mechanistic application of the per se rule began influencing horizontal restraints analysis one year later in National Soc'y of Professional Engineers v. United States (1978). In *Professional Engineers,* the Court held that a professional society's canon of ethics prohibiting competitive bidding among its members violated Section 1. In doing so, it rejected defendant's claim that the restriction was justified "because bidding on engineering services is inherently imprecise, would lead to deceptively low bids, and would thereby tempt individual engineers to do inferior work with consequent risk to public safety and health." But the Court did not apply the per se rule even though the practice appeared to have a direct price effect, partly because a learned profession was involved. (In Goldfarb v. Virginia State Bar (1975), the Court had indicated that although covered by the antitrust laws the learned professions were subject to less rigorous rules.) Instead the Court engaged in a rule of reason analysis that, it said, required a balancing of the restraint's anticompetitive and procompetitive effects. Here the Court rejected the defendant's justification because the inquiry "is confined to a consideration of [the] impact [of the restraint] on competitive conditions," and the engineers had not claimed that their ban on competitive bidding enhanced competition. Compare United States v. Brown University (1993) (prescribing rule of reason analysis to evaluate efforts by private universities to jointly determine the amount of financial aid to be given to applicants admitted to more than one school; rule of reason inquiry should consider the defendants' "noneconomic justifications," including argument that the agreement made education at the participants' schools accessible to students from a wider range of socio-economic backgrounds).

Read literally, the Court seemed to take away with one hand what it was giving with the other. The Court's opinion could be read as narrowing the per se rule's application only to the most direct price-fixing agreements while more readily finding agreements not covered by the per se rule illegal under the rule of reason. Neither interpretation seems complete. As illustrated by the Court's per curiam decision in 1980 in *Catalano,* the per se rule still governs agreements (such as those restricting credit terms) which are inseparable from prices. Similarly, the Court in *Professional Engineers* specifically cited with approval the Third Circuit's decision in Tripoli Co. v. Wella Corp. (1970), that upheld marketing restraints related to product safety, even though the restraints did not necessarily enhance competition, because they were ancillary to the seller's purpose of protecting the public or shielding itself from product liability.

The idea in *Professional Engineers* that the Court might be prepared to retreat from the traditional per se/rule of reason dichotomy was confirmed the following year in Broadcast Music, Inc. v. Columbia Broadcasting System, Inc. (1979) (*BMI*). Since 1897, the copyright laws have protected musical compositions by giving owners the right to license the public performance of their works for profit. However, to collect royalties the owners must enforce their rights. This can be difficult—it is easy for performers to use a copyrighted work, and performances can be frequent, fleeting, and widespread. Individual composers seldom are able to negotiate with performers or to sue against unauthorized use. As a consequence, since 1914 owners of musical compositions have been organized, first into the American Society of Composers, Authors, and Publishers

(ASCAP), and since 1939 also in Broadcast Music, Inc. (BMI). A court order settling an earlier antitrust case had authorized ASCAP and BMI to grant blanket licenses for all works, provided that they held only a nonexclusive license that would allow users the option of contracting directly with individual composers. The effect was that the two organizations acted as a license clearing house for their members. Users dealing with ASCAP or BMI received a blanket license to perform the entire repertory as often as they wished. In return, each user paid a royalty measured either by a specified fee or by a percentage of the user's advertising revenues.

Deciding that the cost of its blanket contracts was rising unreasonably, CBS sought a license on a per use basis from both ASCAP and BMI. When they refused, CBS sued for violation of the Sherman Act, including price-fixing. The sole issue before the Court was whether the blanket license was per se illegal. On its face, the arrangement seemed to transgress *Socony's* sweeping ban against all arrangements having the purpose or effect of "raising, depressing, fixing, pegging, or stabilizing" prices.

In *BMI* the Court nonetheless opted for a modified rule of reason approach. The Court acknowledged that the blanket license arrangement melded the prices of differing compositions into a single fee, but it concluded that this pricing method is not plainly anticompetitive or without substantial justification. In explaining why it was using a rule of reason, the Court emphasized the Sherman Act's flexibility in responding to complex market situations:

> The Sherman Act has always been discriminatingly applied in light of economic realities. There are situations in which competitors have been permitted to form joint selling agencies or other pooled activities, subject to strict

limitations under the antitrust laws to guarantee against abuse of the collective power thus created.... This case appears to us to involve such a situation. The extraordinary number of users, spread across the land, the ease with which a performance may be broadcast, the sheer volume of copyrighted compositions, the enormous quantity of separate performances each year, the impracticability of negotiating individual licenses for each composition, and the ephemeral nature of each performance all combine to create unique market conditions for performance rights to recorded music.

Critical to the Court's choice between the per se and rule of reason standards was its conclusion that the marketing arrangements seemed reasonably necessary if the rights granted composers under the copyright laws were to be developed. The Court pointed to the arrangement's role in achieving market integration and creating related efficiencies in negotiating for and monitoring the use of the compositions. The alternative of individual negotiation and enforcement would be more costly and would delay the marketing of compositions and, in any case, was separately available to the plaintiff. Consistent with *BMI's* approach, subsequent lower court decisions have declined to condemn price-setting arrangements that are ancillary to achieving genuine efficiencies, including the creation of goods or services that would not be available (or available only at much higher cost) if the challenged practice were forbidden. See, e.g., National Bancard Corp. v. VISA USA (1986) (fixed fee assessed by credit card firm for processing charges throughout the firm's network treated as part of integrated arrangement that would not be available if the fee were not assessed).

BMI invited reassessment of the per se rule and its relationship to the rule of reason standard. Under *BMI's* framework, the court examines challenged agreements in varying levels of detail depending upon its initial assessment of the nature of the conduct. *BMI* suggests a threshold inquiry as to whether horizontal collaboration "facially appears to be one that would always or almost always tend to restrict competition and decrease output" or is designed to "increase economic efficiency and render markets more, rather than less, competitive." This permits the court to determine whether the conduct has procompetitive merit worthy of fuller analysis. In embracing this approach, *BMI* made explicit a process of evaluation that courts implicitly had performed in the past in deciding whether to characterize behavior as "price-fixing" and therefore subject to per se condemnation. The Court observed that not all forms of conduct that literally fix prices are "plainly anticompetitive" or likely to lack "redeeming virtue." For this reason, "it is necessary to characterize the challenged conduct as falling within that category of behavior to which we apply the label per se price fixing.' " With immense understatement, the Court said the characterization process "will often, but not always, be a simple matter."

BMI recognized that even price-fixing agreements may serve necessary and beneficial purposes. For example, would it truly be desirable for antitrust policy to prohibit firms from jointly setting the prices of products developed through joint research programs where such pricing facilitates the appropriation of gains from R & D and thereby provides a critical inducement for firms to engage in work they would not pursue unilaterally? *BMI* acknowledges that if a per se rule reaches such activities, the rule's cost may be too high.

The Court continued to blur the traditional per se/rule of reason dichotomy in NCAA v. University of Oklahoma (1984). In *NCAA*, the Court ruled that an agreement among member colleges of the National Collegiate Athletic Association to restrict how often each team's football games could be televised inhibited rather than enhanced competition, and thus violated Section 1. Despite the agreement's horizontal price-fixing and output limiting aspects, the per se rule was considered inappropriate. In deciding that the television agreement should be tested under a rule of reason, the Court emphasized that "horizontal restraints on competition are essential if the product is to be available at all"; the NCAA is a joint venture that required some collaboration to operate. The issues, therefore, were whether the television plan—an exclusive, joint marketing arrangement—was necessary for college football to exist (it was not, contrast *BMI*); whether college game attendance would suffer if the plan were unavailable (this defense failed, for it presumed the unreasonableness of competition, compare *Professional Engineers*); and whether the plan was needed to preserve competitive balance (again, this argument was rejected because it was unrelated to a neutral standard, any readily identifiable group of competitors, or the television plan). In finding a Section 1 violation, the Court indicated that applying a rule of reason did not invariably require an exhaustive, fact-intensive analysis of industry conditions and that plaintiffs could prevail in a rule of reason case.

NCAA reinforced *BMI's* teaching that various forms of competitor collaboration could offer substantial procompetitive benefits and warranted analysis beyond a superficial labeling exercise. Retreating from the dichotomy model implicit in *Socony* and its progeny, the Court acknowledged "there is often no bright line separating per se from Rule of Reason analysis. Per se rules may require considerable inquiry into market conditions before the evidence justifies a presumption of anticompetitive conduct." Regardless of the vocabulary used to describe the evaluation process, the Court observed that "the essential inquiry remains the same—whether or not the challenged restraint enhances competition." This view was a distinct and important advance in antitrust analysis.

NCAA constitutes the Court's most thoughtful modern effort to analyze the relationship between bright line tests of illegality and reasonableness inquiries. Its approach echoed dissatisfaction that the Court had displayed earlier in the same year with analytical models based on formalistic line-drawing. In Copperweld Corp. v. Independence Tube Corp. (1984), the Court expressly overruled the intra-enterprise conspiracy doctrine and held that a parent and its wholly owned subsidiary could not be "conspiring entities" for the purpose of satisfying Section 1's plurality requirement. Recognizing that prior doctrine had elevated form over substance, the Court emphasized that the parent and sub were one economic actor and that a firm cannot enhance its market power by separately incorporating a division. Stating that "it is sometimes difficult to distinguish robust competition from conduct with long-run anticompetitive effects," the Court embraced the view that antitrust should be wary of condemning horizontal agreements out of hand where there is uncertainty about the competitive effect of such behavior.

Since the late 1970s, with the notable exception of *Maricopa,* the Court's horizontal pricing jurisprudence has demonstrated a willingness to modify the traditional per se/rule of reason dichotomy. At a minimum, *BMI* and *NCAA* authorize courts to expand the characterization component of the traditional per se standard and explicitly entertain a fuller assessment of defendants' claims that the price-setting behavior has nontrivial procompetitive merit. See Edward J. Brunet, *Streamlining Antitrust Litigation by*

"Facial Examination" of Restraints: The Burger Court and the Per Se–Rule of Reason Distinction, 60 Wash. L. Rev. 1 (1984). As discussed below, however, other recent Court decisions indicate that the Court is as yet unwilling to abandon the language or framework of the dichotomy model in favor of a continuum approach that reconciles *Socony* with *BMI* and *NCAA.*

D. MARKET ALLOCATIONS AND PRODUCTION CONTROLS

Prices can be controlled not only by direct price-fixing agreements, but also indirectly by agreements among firms not to compete with one another. As Figure 10 illustrates, withdrawing supplies from a market moves the supply curve to the left, which raises the equilibrium price:

FIGURE 10: RESTRICTING OUTPUT

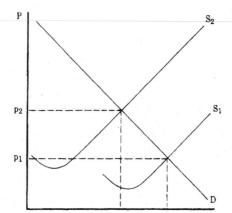

That is, if company Able withdraws from a market, available supply is reduced, and the supply curve will move from

S_1 to S_2. Without a change in demand, equilibrium will be achieved by an increase in price from p_1 to p_2.

Agreements to divide markets take many forms. Firms can agree to allocate markets geographically, for example, one serving the North and the other the South. Or they can agree to assign customers functionally by class (one serving wholesalers and the other retailers) or by product type (e.g., professional versus amateur video equipment). Such agreements are justified on the ground they permit more efficient production and marketing. Production facilities can be rationalized and scale economies achieved; distribution costs can be cut and transportation limited. The flaw in the argument for "more rational" organization of production is that if market efficiencies supported it, firms would seek such gains without market allocation agreements. Greater profits would justify specialization, making such agreements unnecessary.

In some respects, market division agreements can affect competition more severely than price-fixing. By eliminating competitors, the sole remaining market occupant—albeit in a limited territory—has a monopoly and is freed of competition not only with respect to prices but also with respect to service, quality, and innovation. Moreover, market allocations can avoid the internal divisions between different cost producers that often cause price agreements to crumble. On the other hand, many tensions that undermine price-fixing agreements also beset market allocations. If the remaining firm sets its price above marginal cost, new entrants appear; if entrants are "co-opted" by swift inclusion in the scheme, then the same spoils must be further split, making the arrangement less attractive.

In general, courts treat market division arrangements by the per se standard applied to price-fixing. The rule originated in *Addyston Pipe* (p. 172 supra), where the defendants agreed not to compete with each other in various areas and devised a system to allocate business among participants. While the *Addyston Pipe* Court seemingly would have condemned the market allocation agreement alone, the significance of its condemnation of the defendants' market division was diminished because the plan's price-fixing aspects dominated the Court's attention. Moreover, in National Ass'n of Window Glass Mfrs. v. United States (1923), the Court upheld an agreement by all manufacturers of hand-blown window glass to operate only one-half of the year because of a labor shortage. It ruled that the pact's legality depended on the particular facts, and here the agreement "to meet the short supply of men" was not a combination in unreasonable restraint of trade.

Not until Timken Roller Bearing Co. v. United States (1951) was a division of markets among competitors directly ruled unlawful. There the Court condemned a worldwide allocation of territories between the dominant American producer of tapered roller bearings and British and French firms (the latter controlled by Timken and its British rival). However, *Timken's* reach, and whether a per se or rule of reason approach was being applied, remained in doubt. The parties' market power and the agreement's effect on output and price were evident; thus the arrangement could not have survived under a rule of reason test, either. Moreover, the defendants were also convicted for fixing prices. In banning the arrangement, the Court emphasized the defendants' "aggregation of trade restraints," leaving unanswered whether a market allocation alone, without price-fixing, was per se illegal.

The next market division case to reach the Supreme Court, United States v. Sealy, Inc. (1967), moved closer to a per se rule for horizontal market division but still did not resolve how such conduct was to be assessed. Several mattress manufacturers formed a joint company which developed the Sealy trademark and advertised Sealy-brand mattresses regionally and nationally. The "parent" Sealy company licensed each shareholder-manufacturer to make and sell mattresses under the Sealy label. Each was also assigned an exclusive territory and was told the retail price at which it could sell Sealy-brand mattresses. The trial court held the price-fixing illegal but rejected the government's charge that the market division was unreasonable. Thus, the issue before the Supreme Court was the legality of the territorial allocation. The Court reversed the trial court, holding the arrangement did not warrant a rule of reason inquiry (i.e., it was apparently per se unlawful). Again, however, the Court did not rely solely on the market division's effect on competition; as in *Timken*, it looked at the "aggregation of trade restraints"—here the price-fixing in addition to the market division—even though the price-fixing was separately condemned.

Any remaining doubts about the standard for horizontal territorial restraints were eliminated in United States v. Topco Associates, Inc. (1972), which explicitly ruled that market allocations are per se illegal whether or not ancillary to price-fixing or other market-rigging arrangements. *Topco's* facts resembled *Sealy's* except for the absence of any price-fixing. In *Topco* a group of small- and medium-sized grocery chains with 6 percent of the market created a joint subsidiary to market private label (house brand) products through their stores in competition with larger supermarket chains such as A & P and Safeway. The latter each had their own branded goods, and the Topco participants were generally too small to market private label goods on their own. The formation of the joint venture to market goods under a private label was not challenged (see Chapter

6), but the arrangement was condemned for its dividing markets for the sale of Topco branded goods.

In reaching this result and applying a per se rule, the Court specifically rejected the lower court's analysis that the defendant supermarkets lacked market power, that the arrangement did not reduce competition among them or in the market, and that the restrictions were necessary for the joint venture to succeed. The Court said these arguments were for Congress to assess and observed that courts are ill-equipped to measure whether restraints on competition in one area are overcome by increased competition elsewhere. Since the market division necessarily eliminated competition among sellers of Topco private label products, the agreement restrained competition and was per se illegal. After remand to the trial court, the Supreme Court summarily affirmed a judgment that allowed Topco to designate areas of primary responsibility, specify warehouse sites, fix business locations for its licensees, cancel the membership of firms that promoted Topco products inadequately, and impose profit passovers, unless such practices achieved or sustained territorial exclusivity. See United States v. Topco Assocs. (1973).

Sealy and *Topco* warrant criticism on two related grounds: for (a) failing to evaluate the economic necessity and competitive benefits of the arrangements, and (b) ignoring that the participants lacked market power and therefore could not have affected competition adversely. Since both points have substantial economic support, and are consistent with the Court's decision in *Sylvania,* they deserve further explanation.

The first argument concerns the justification for the territorial allocation. Sealy and Topco feared that without the protection of exclusive territories, their retail participants would not promote the product aggressively, provide customer service, or otherwise seek to penetrate the market. Each licensee would be concerned that sellers of Sealy mattresses or Topco labels in adjoining areas would "free ride" on advertising or services that it provided. Not having incurred the advertising or other cost, neighboring sellers then would be able to undercut the price. Thus, the exclusive territories arguably were integral to the success of the Sealy and Topco ventures. Without them, competition would suffer from the loss or reduced vigor of the Sealy or Topco enterprises. This argument builds on the principle in *BMI* and *NCAA* that collaboration among competitors was an "essential element" of the product or service being marketed.

The second argument involves the defendants' stature in the market. Because the restraint had significant procompetitive merit, the Court should have considered the defendants' lack of market power in assessing the magnitude of possible anticompetitive effects from the arrangement. The Sealy and Topco licensees faced strong *interbrand* competition—rivalry from other firms selling similar products under different brands. An agreement dividing territories among those holding only 6 percent of sales (as in *Topco*) generally cannot force the sellers of the other 94 percent to follow its prices, quality, or service. Thus, not only did the joint arrangements offer genuine procompetitive benefits, but there was little reason to fear that their operation could curb interbrand competition.

By the mid–1980s, many scholars had concluded that cases such as *Sylvania, BMI,* and *NCAA* had discredited or overruled *Sealy* and *Topco*. See Martin B. Louis, *Restraints Ancillary to Joint Ventures and Licensing Agreements: Do Sealy and Topco Logically Survive Sylvania and Broadcast Music?,* 66 Va.L.Rev. 879 (1980). One noteworthy lower court decision, Rothery Storage & Van Co. v. Atlas Van Lines, Inc. (1986), has agreed. *Rothery* considered allegations that Atlas Van Lines, a national moving and storage company, had engaged in an illegal group boycott with some of its independent agent affiliates to deny the use of the facilities of Atlas or its affiliates to other independent movers. Deregulation of the moving industry had permitted the agents of Atlas to move goods interstate on their own accounts. In 1982 Atlas announced that it would cancel the agency contract of any affiliated mover who continued to handle interstate shipments on its own account as well as for Atlas. An agent could remain affiliated with Atlas and ship goods interstate on its own account only if the agent transferred its independent interstate authority to a separate corporation under a new name. Eight current and former Atlas agents attacked the policy as a per se illegal group boycott and horizontal pricing arrangement.

In an opinion authored by Judge Robert Bork and joined by Judge (now Justice) Ruth Ginsburg, the D.C. Circuit affirmed a grant of summary judgment for Atlas and ruled that the allegations should be evaluated under the rule of reason. After reviewing Taft's distinction in *Addyston Pipe* between "naked" and "ancillary" restraints, Judge Bork said that "[i]f *Topco* and *Sealy*, rather than *Addyston Pipe*, state the law of horizontal restraints, the restraints imposed by Atlas would appear to be a per se violation of the Sherman Act." From his reading of recent Supreme Court decisions such as *BMI* and *NCAA,* however, Bork concluded that "to the extent that *Topco* and *Sealy* stand for the proposition that all horizontal restraints are illegal per se, they must be regarded as effectively overruled."

No other lower court decision has stated the proposition as starkly as *Rothery,* but other decisions have refused to apply *Topco's* per se rule to horizontal market allocations that are shown to be ancillary to an efficiency-enhancing integration of the defendants' economic activities. See E. Thomas Sullivan & Jeffrey L. Harrison, *Understanding Antitrust and Its Economic Implications* 118–21 (1988). In Northrop Corp. v. McDonnell Douglas Corp. (1983), the Ninth Circuit held that the rule of reason should be used to evaluate a "teaming arrangement" (akin to a joint venture) that compelled the two co-venturers to abide by a horizontal allocation of customers for a new fighter aircraft that the firms were developing. In Polk Bros. v. Forest City Enters. (1985), the Seventh Circuit used a rule of reason analysis to uphold an agreement by two retailers to restrict the products that each could sell in stores that would be located within a new building which the firms had cooperated to construct. Both *Northrop* and *Polk Brothers* emphasized that the challenged market division facilitated the accomplishment of a productive endeavor (i.e., developing a new fighter and creating a new retailing facility) that would not have occurred without the restraint.

The Supreme Court has not upset these rulings, but neither has it abandoned *Topco.* In dealing with allegations of vertical price-fixing in *Business Electronics* (1988), the Court cited *Topco* without elaboration for the view that "a horizontal agreement to divide territories is per se illegal." More recently, in a short per curiam opinion in Palmer v. BRG of Georgia, Inc. (1990), the Court cited *Socony* and *Topco* as establishing that market division agreements involving actual or potential competitors are illegal per se. In *Palmer,* HBJ, a provider of bar review courses, agreed to give BRG an exclusive license to use HBJ's written materials and its trade name ("Bar/Bri") in Georgia. The agreement also provided that HBJ would not compete in Georgia and BRG would not compete outside

Georgia. The Court said the court of appeals "erred when [it] assumed that an allocation of markets or submarkets by competitors is not unlawful unless the market in which the two previously competed is divided between them." The Court held that an agreement by firms "not to compete in each other's territories" is anticompetitive and "unlawful on its face" without regard to "whether the parties split a market within which both do business or whether they merely reserve one market for one and another for the other."

E. BOYCOTTS

Since early in this century, courts have interpreted Section 1 to limit the ability of competing firms to agree not to deal with or to isolate another firm. Unlike many cartels, where all competitors voluntarily join to fix prices (and share monopoly rewards), concerted refusals to deal usually involve a subset of all market participants who band together to gain market power by destroying or coercing their rivals. Such organized refusals to deal with a particular firm are usually given the pejorative label of "group boycotts." [4]

1. PURPOSES AND ECONOMIC EFFECTS

Group refusals to deal with a competing firm serve various ends. One obvious and perhaps not infrequent aim is to eliminate or discipline troublesome rivals. See Timothy J. Brennan, *Refusing to Cooperate with Competitors: A*

---

4. Cf. Hartford Fire Ins. Co. v. California (1993) (in interpreting the McCarran–Ferguson Act's antitrust exemption for certain insurance activities, distinguishing between a "concerted agreement to terms," by which firms jointly refuse to deal except on specific terms, and a "conditional boycott," by which firms collectively use unrelated transactions as leverage to achieve desired terms for a specific transaction).

Theory of Boycotts, 35 J. L. & Econ. 247 (1992). Boycotts may, for example, serve to police a price-fixing agreement. More generally, they can punish maverick price cutters or others not adhering to industry custom. If concerted refusals to deal sought only to suppress rivalry, all boycotts probably would be deemed illegal per se under Section 1.

But not all refusals to deal can be classified so simply. Some serve economic efficiency or advance the group's general economic self-interest without seeking to diminish any other group's profits. Others even advance social and moral goals largely unrelated to the group's business or economic interests. For example, all used car dealers in a city might form a trade association to improve trading practices and their members' public image. Through the association, the dealers could agree to forego deceptive advertising, pressure sales tactics, or, for that matter, dealing with firms whose products pollute the atmosphere. Failure to abide by the agreement's terms could result in expulsion from the association and denial of its "fair dealer" seal of approval. Since the group is open to all used car dealers (and expulsion may inflict no actual economic penalty), its primary aim is not to punish nonparticipants. Reforming advertising and sales practices, instead, promotes the group's overall economic interest, not its immediate profits. In general, punishing polluters is unlikely to materially improve the group's profits. Because group refusals to deal have different purposes and because some serve public policy goals, it is doubtful that the Sherman Act should condemn them uniformly. It would seem necessary, at least initially, to assess their economic impact beyond the advantage they create for the group engaged in the boycott.

Three primary economic effects flow from a "successful" concerted refusal to deal that seeks to exclude or chasten competitors: (1) injury to the boycott's intended victim; (2)

injury to competition by forcing the victim to accept the boycott terms (reducing its competitive vigor) or by forcing the victim out of business; and (3) injury to innocent neutrals caught in the middle of a secondary boycott. These effects do not necessarily depend on the boycott's purpose. Whatever the group's goal, a successful boycott may force the intended victim out of business; not only is injury to the victim then complete, but competition also may suffer by the elimination of a significant firm—especially if entry into the field is limited. Alternatively, a successful boycott may make the victim acquiesce. For some boycotts, this will lessen the primary victim's competitive rivalry. And regardless of the group's goals, secondary boycotts impair the competitive vigor of the innocent neutral. If the neutral business accedes to the boycott demands (because of the group's superior economic power), it must forego the intended victim's business, the alternative being to lose the business of the boycotters. In either case, the neutral's business is likely to be reduced and its rivalry restricted.

2.   THE LEGAL STANDARD

The legal test for boycotts is far from clear, although it is still commonly said that such arrangements are judged by a per se rule. A more accurate appraisal is that where the boycotters possess market power or exclusive access to a critical competitive element and the boycott is directly aimed at limiting or excluding competitors, it is subject to per se treatment; otherwise concerted refusals to deal are tested under a rule of reason approach. Many concerted refusals to deal reflect mixed motives, and competitor agreements that serve legitimate purposes are treated under a rule of reason standard through which purposes and actual effects on competition are closely examined.

Early boycott cases revealed no clear line of decision. In Eastern States Retail Lumber Dealers' Ass'n v. United States (1914), the Court invalidated an implied agreement by retailers to boycott direct-selling suppliers. This arrangement seemed designed solely to exclude wholesalers from participating in the retail market. The retailers' argument that the direct selling wholesalers had infringed on their "exclusive right to trade" was properly dismissed, for the retailers had no rightful claim to control the retail trade. At this early stage, the Court did not focus on whether all boycotts were bad or only those without reasonable justification. Nor was attention given to whether the defendant retailers had market power or were simply defending themselves against free-riding interlopers. Instead, the violation's gravamen seemed to be the defendants' act of agreeing to coerce the wholesalers to leave the retail market, an analysis apparently borrowed from the labor boycott conspiracy cases then in the forefront of business regulation.

Other cases upheld the organized distribution of information about a firm or its orders as a means of curbing abusive business conduct. Cement Mfrs. Protective Ass'n v. United States (1925) suggested that a boycott designed to serve legitimate ends (such as preventing cement buyers from placing fraudulent orders) would be upheld. But the Court subsequently rejected agreements seeking to promote standard contracts with arbitration clauses or security provisions. In Paramount Famous Lasky Corp. v. United States (1930), for example, the Court rejected as irrelevant the industry's claim that the clause in the disputed agreement (no dealing with noncomplying film exhibitors) and its enforcement were necessary to protect the industry against undesirable practices: "It may be that arbitration is well adapted to the needs of the motion picture industry; but when under the guise of arbitration parties enter into unusual arrangements which unreasonably suppress normal competition their action becomes illegal." Any indication that a rule of reason was being applied was countered by a subsequent sentence (quoting from an earlier decision): "The law is its own measure of right and wrong, of what it permits, or forbids, and the judgment of the courts cannot be set up against it in a supposed accommodation of its policy with the good intention of parties, and, it may be, of some good results."

Cases such as *Cement Mfrs.* and *Paramount* are reconcilable if one follows the challenged arrangement's purposes and effects. In *Paramount,* agreements designed to stifle rivalry were condemned as illegal without consideration of justifications. By contrast, arrangements not aimed at suppressing lawful competition or merely ancillary to a valid purpose (as in *Cement Mfrs.*) were evaluated by balancing benefits against harms.

This framework does not answer all questions. For example, in Fashion Originators' Guild of America, Inc. v. FTC (1941) (*FOGA*), the Court faced a boycott whose aim was to eliminate troublesome competitors, enhance the group's general economic interests, and promote compliance with common law (and state) standards of business conduct. Women's garment manufacturers who claimed to be creators of original dress designs sought to curb "style piracy" by which other manufacturers copied their designs and sold these copies at much lower prices. To stop the practice the Guild's members agreed to refuse to sell to retailers who also sold garments copied from a Guild member's designs. The members were trying to prevent an allegedly illegal or tortious act (the copying of original designs); however, the Guild was taking the law into its own hands and, in the process, excluding rivals from the market. The Supreme Court declared that the Guild agreement was both an "unfair method of competition" proscribed by the FTC Act and a Sherman Act offense. Concerted action by a powerful combination could not be justified, according to the Court, and the FTC therefore correctly did not hear evidence of the evils of style piracy or of the illegality of the copying practice under state law.

FOGA has been read as applying a per se test to group boycotts. However, a close reading suggests that a narrow rule of reason (or only limited per se) approach was adopted. The Court considered the group's power (its market share) and its purpose (not public protection but self-interest as revealed by restraints on advertising, regulation of sale days, and limits on allowable discounts). It also noted the availability of a less restrictive alternative—relying on civil tort actions. What appeared to disturb the Court, and therefore may be the ultimate basis for its decision, was the elaborate private government that the defendants had formed to police the agreement. This machinery could readily be used to implement a boycott excluding lawful competitors. The social purpose of limiting style piracy appeared to be heavily outweighed by the dangers of an extralegal guild government.

In Klor's, Inc. v. Broadway–Hale Stores, Inc. (1959), the Court edged closer to a per se approach. The plaintiff, a San Francisco appliance store, alleged that the defendant department store chain had used its buying power to coerce ten national appliance manufacturers and their distributors from selling appliances to the plaintiff. The defendants did not deny the allegations, but moved for summary judgment arguing that there had been no public wrong—that the Sherman Act protects competition, not competitors. The defendants' affidavits showed that the boycott had no apparent effect on competition in appliance retailing. Finding enough public injury for Sherman Act liability, the Court explained: "Group boycotts, or concerted refusals by traders to deal with other traders, have long been held to be in the forbidden category. They have not been saved by allegations that they were reasonable in the specific circumstances, nor by a failure to show that they 'fixed or regulated prices, parcelled out or limited production, or brought about a deterioration in quality.' Even when they operated to lower prices or temporarily stimulate competition they were banned."

Despite this confirmation that group boycotts are in the "forbidden category" and cannot be redeemed by a showing that "they were reasonable in the specific circumstances," a close reading of *Klor's* again suggests a more limited principle. Since the *Klor's* defendants offered no justification for their conduct, one can read the case as involving only a summary rule of reason approach: the conduct poses substantial dangers, no benefit is asserted, and there is a less restrictive alternative—of individual refusals to deal, as *Colgate* allowed (see p. 319 infra). In this vein, a subsequent case involving exclusionary conduct acknowledged that boycott-type action would be illegal per se "absent any justification derived from the policy of another statute or *otherwise*." Silver v. New York Stock Exchange (1963) (dicta). A strict per se rule would not permit such "other" justification. These exceptions led some commentators to conclude that the Court had devised a "soft per se rule" for boycotts as distinguished from the more rigid rule applicable to price-fixing.

On the other hand, the Court in *Silver* held that the stock exchange had violated the Sherman Act because it excluded a broker from access to its facilities despite the absence of evidence that the plaintiff-broker's exclusion was designed to or would injure competition. The Court did not consider, for example, whether the exclusion was in retaliation for undercutting prescribed commission rates. It was enough that access had been denied without a hearing. The case thus can fairly be read as imposing a rigorous per se rule. It resembles *FOGA* in its hostility to private government action and the use of such uncontrolled power to discipline competitors (although here the 1934 Securities Exchange Act specifically authorized governance by the exchange). Another case supporting this alternative, more rigid reading of the Section 1 rule on boycotts is United States v. General Motors Corp. (1966). There the Court held that action by a group of automobile dealers urging GM to halt sales to a discount outlet was a "classic conspiracy" amounting to a group boycott and therefore per se unlawful.

A broad spectrum of commentators agrees that boycotts are a proper concern of Section 1 when used to enforce anticompetitive practices. Compare R. Posner, *Antitrust Law,* at 208–10 with L. Sullivan, *Antitrust,* at §§ 83–92. However, many observers have criticized the Supreme Court's apparent reliance on per se tests to condemn concerted refusals to deal in a number of its boycott cases. Most criticism focuses on *FOGA* and *Klor's* since neither boycotting group of defendants seems likely to have restricted output or adversely affected competition. In *FOGA,* the Guild included 176 participating original design manufacturers which continued to compete with each other and faced strong competition. Moreover there appear to have been legitimate reasons for their conduct. Guild members may have been trying to prevent copiers of their original designs from free riding on the product information made available by retailers to their consumers. By forcing retailers to deal exclusively with only the original products, they were preventing the copiers from getting the advantage of the promotional efforts of these retailers. The designers of original dresses also may have been seeking mainly to protect an investment in their dress designs by making it more costly for others to copy their ideas and sell pirated goods. See R. Bork, *Antitrust Paradox*, at 338–39. The Court should have used an ancillary purpose test that asked whether the benefit generated by protecting the designers' interest in their dress designs justified the means they used.

Similar analysis also provides a possible justification for the boycott in *Klor's*. Broadway (the defendant) might have been giving consumers demonstrations and product information on appliances; after examining the product at Broadway, customers might then have gone next door to Klor's, a discounter, and bought the products at lower prices. Broadway's response (to have Klor's cut off unless it also provided services) seems a less threatening response to free riders that deserves rule of reason rather than per se treatment.

Over the past decade, some Supreme Court decisions have retreated from an unqualified rule of per se illegality for concerted horizontal refusals to deal. In *NCAA,* the Court applied a rule of reason standard and closely evaluated proffered justifications before condemning the colleges' concerted refusal to televise games on other networks. More significantly, in Northwest Wholesale Stationers, Inc. v. Pacific Stationery & Printing Co. (1985), the Court distinguished *FOGA* as limited to boycotts "likely to restrict competition without any offsetting efficiency gains." Where the joint activity does not seek to disadvantage rivals, it is unlikely to have predominantly anticompetitive effects.

In *Northwest Wholesale* a seller of office supplies was expelled from a purchasing cooperative after it expanded its operations from retailing to include wholesale activities. The reason for the expulsion was disputed, and the district court granted the defendant summary judgment under the rule of reason because there was no evidence of anticompetitive effect. The Supreme Court unanimously upheld this ruling under what it called a per se test. In doing so, however, it substantially modified the per se rule for boycotts: "Unless the cooperative possesses market power or exclusive access to an element essential to effective competition, the conclusion that expulsion is virtually always likely to have anticompetitive effect is not warranted." The Court also emphasized that the cooperative raised efficiency by realizing scale economies in both buying and warehousing supplies and by ensuring that its members had ready access to these supplies on short notice. These features "enable smaller retailers to reduce prices and maintain their retail stock so as to compete more effectively with larger retailers."

Northwest Wholesale was a genuine improvement over the Court's earlier boycott decisions and their suggestion that Section 1 forbade all concerted horizontal refusals to deal. Like *BMI* and *NCAA*, *Northwest Wholesale* emphasized the arrangement's tendency to reduce transaction costs and otherwise increase efficiency. However, the *Northwest Wholesale* opinion was not flawless. In stating its "per se" group boycott test, the Court said the defendants must have "market power *or* exclusive access to an element essential to effective competition." These two conditions seem identical, as market power would appear to flow naturally from (or be necessary to attain) "exclusive access to an element essential to effective competition." The Court did not explain how (if at all) these concepts differed. A second problem arises from the Court's use of the term "per se" to describe its liability test. "Per se" illegality ordinarily entails no examination of structural market characteristics such as the defendant's market power; an evaluation of market conditions typically is an ingredient of a reasonableness test. In *Northwest Wholesale,* and in addressing other conduct that fits awkwardly into the per se/rule of reason dichotomy model,[5] the Court's use of the per se label to describe what is functionally a reasonableness inquiry has created substantial confusion among the lower courts. The *Northwest Wholesale* Court should have called its liability test a "structured" or "truncated" rule of reason rather than affixing the per se label to what actually was a reasonableness hybrid.

The Court reaffirmed the basic approach of *Northwest Wholesale* one year later in FTC v. Indiana Federation of Dentists (1986). There the Court upheld an FTC order that forbade a collective refusal by rival dentists to provide X-rays of patients to insurance companies that wanted the X-rays to evaluate the reasonableness of dentists' charges and to implement other cost containment measures. The Court's decision is important in two major respects. First, the Court used a rule of reason approach to evaluate the defendants' conduct. Acknowledging that decisions such as *Klor's* had "stated that group boycotts are per se unlawful," the Court "decline[d] to resolve this case by forcing the Federation's policy into the 'boycott' pigeonhole and invoking the per se rule." Referring to *Northwest Wholesale,* the Court explained that "the per se approach has generally been limited to cases in which firms with market power boycott suppliers or customers in order to discourage them from doing business with a competitor—a situation

5. See Jefferson Hosp. Dist. No. 2 v. Hyde (1984) (tying arrangements), discussed in Chapter 8.

obviously not present here. Moreover, we have been slow ... to extend per se analysis to restraints imposed in the context of business relationships where the economic impact of certain practices is not immediately obvious."

Second, the Court demonstrated that the rule of reason need not entail an exhaustive factual inquiry. Observing that "[a]pplication of the Rule of Reason to these facts is not a matter of any great difficulty," the Court began with a preliminary evaluation of the restraint's purpose and effect. Because the dentists' refusal to deal "impairs the ability of the market to advance social welfare by ensuring the provision of desired goods and services to consumers at a price approximating the marginal cost of providing them," the Court placed the burden on the defendants to come forward with proof that the conduct had "countervailing procompetitive virtue." The Court rejected as unsubstantiated the dentists' argument that quality of care concerns motivated the boycott, and, in light of direct record evidence of adverse competitive effects, dismissed the argument that the FTC was required to define a relevant market and evaluate the dentists' market power. Compare *Capital Imaging Assocs.* (1993) (to bear initial burden of showing anticompetitive impact of defendant's conduct, plaintiff must show actual detrimental effects or establish that defendant has market power).

Taken together, *Northwest Wholesale* and *Indiana Federation of Dentists* suggested that courts were to condemn group boycotts as illegal "per se" only where the defendants possessed market power or otherwise controlled access to some component essential to competition. Nonetheless, in a departure from earlier decisions in the 1980s, the Supreme Court appeared to reject this narrow conception of the per se rule in FTC v. Superior Court Trial Lawyers Association (1990) (*SCTLA*). In *SCTLA* the Court reviewed a court of appeals ruling that had reversed an FTC decision barring an agreement by attorneys not to represent indigent criminal defendants until the District of Columbia government increased the fees for such work. The Court appeared to use a per se test to uphold the FTC's condemnation of the lawyers' boycott. The *SCTLA* opinion placed Section 1 restraints in two categories (per se and rule of reason) and concluded that the lawyers' agreement easily fell within the first. The Court chastised the court of appeals for suggesting that per se rules are applied only for purposes of "administrative convenience and efficiency." Rather, per se rules "also reflect a long-standing judgment that the prohibited practices by their nature have 'a substantial potential for impact on competition.' " The Court added that the court of appeals' view that illegality required proof of the defendants' market power "is flatly inconsistent with the clear course of our antitrust jurisprudence."

SCTLA resembles the language and tone of boycott decisions that preceded *Northwest Wholesale.* The apparent return to the dichotomy model might be explained by the Court's view that the trial attorneys' boycott effectuated a price-fixing arrangement—i.e., to coerce the District of Columbia to pay higher fees. In a footnote, the Court "emphasize[d] that this case involves not only a boycott but also a horizontal price-fixing arrangement—a type of conspiracy that has been consistently analyzed as a per se violation for many decades." In the light of *SCTLA,* the Court's modern boycott decisions suggest the following standards: (1) an agreement by direct rivals to withhold their services until the price for such services is raised is a "naked" restraint on output and is condemned summarily, see *SCTLA;* (2) concerted refusals to deal that pose remotely plausible efficiency rationales are evaluated with a truncated rule of reason that begins (and sometimes ends) with a preliminary assessment of the conduct's purposes and effects, see *Indiana Federation of Dentists*; and (3) suits challenging membership policies of efficiency-enhancing collaborations require a fuller reasonableness inquiry, including a determination of the defendants' market power. See *Northwest Wholesale*.

The more flexible formulation of the boycott standard endorsed in *Northwest Wholesale* and *Indiana Federation of Dentists* seems a more accurate general restatement of the Court's own earlier jurisprudence and lower court decisions. See U.S. Healthcare, Inc. v. Healthsource, Inc. (1993). This view receives support from a number of cases—some upholding and others condemning group boycotts—that have applied what amounts to a more elaborate reasonableness test. Examples include cases involving actions arising from decisions on ethics by professional societies, especially when asserted quality control rationales appear to be spurious. See, e.g., American Medical Ass'n v. United States (1942) (condemning threatened secondary boycott by medical society against hospitals that opened their facilities to two physicians whom the society expelled for participating in a group medical practice). Where there is a close rational nexus between the professional rule and public protection, courts have upheld self-regulation even if enforced by a group boycott. See United States v. Oregon State Medical Soc'y (1952) (indicating, in dictum, that professional societies have substantial leeway in applying ethical constraints on their members).

Nor is this approach limited to the professions. One of its most frequent applications is in professional sports. For example, in Molinas v. National Basketball Ass'n (1961), a professional basketball player whom the NBA had suspended indefinitely for betting on his own team charged that the league and its members had engaged in an unlawful boycott. The court dismissed the complaint because "a disciplinary rule invoked against gambling seems about as reasonable a rule as could be imagined." Likewise the Professional Golfers' Association rules restricting eligibility in PGA events was justified by the need "to insure that professional golf tournaments are not bogged down with great numbers of players of inferior ability." Deesen v. Professional Golfers' Ass'n (1966).

In recognizing legitimate association objectives, courts have not given industry groups unlimited discretion to set and apply professional standards. The use, for example, of a trade association to test products and give a "seal of approval" may constitute an illegal boycott if nonobjective tests are used to drive out competitors. See Radiant Burners, Inc. v. Peoples Gas Light & Coke Co. (1961). Similarly, in Allied Tube & Conduit Corp. v. Indian Head (1988), the Supreme Court ruled that antitrust liability could attach to participants in a standard-setting organization where competitors of the proposed new standard controlled the process and abused it by rejecting the suggested standard for meritless reasons.

To survive antitrust scrutiny, the reason for the boycott must be closely related to a lawful purpose; and where the rule is essential for the enterprise (such as anti-gambling rules for professional sports), it will be viewed sympathetically. Rules whose primary aim is to increase the group's power vis-a-vis nonmembers are suspect. In cases where courts have considered noncommercial boycotts—concerted refusals to deal with social, moral, or other goals unrelated to the group's economic self-interest—they have been reluctant to interfere under the Sherman Act. See National Organization for Women, Inc. v. Scheidler (1992); Missouri v. National Organization for Women (1980).

F. SUMMARY

Supreme Court decisions since *Sylvania* and *Professional Engineers* generally have reflected the increasing importance of the rule of reason in analyzing agreements under the Sherman Act. The Court has acknowledged the limitations of an approach premised on a sharp dichotomy between the per se rules and the rule of reason. Indeed, after its decisions in *BMI, NCAA, Northwest Wholesale,* and *Indiana Federation of Dentists,* it seemed as though the Court might be prepared to break with the language and methodology of the dichotomy model that posits a sharp distinction between per se tests and rule of reason standards. In *SCTLA* and *Palmer,* the Court reaffirmed the usefulness of per se rules and suggested a reduced likelihood that the per se category will be abandoned in the immediate future.

The evolution of Section 1 horizontal restraints doctrine has featured several distinct historical phases: early interpretations that condemned "every" restraint of trade; the replacement of *Trans–Missouri's* literalism with the rule of reason in *Standard Oil* and *Chicago Bd. of Trade;* the gradual identification (see, e.g., *Trenton Potteries*) of highly suspect conduct within a broad rule of reason framework; after the Depression-era aberration of *Appalachian Coals, Socony's* enshrinement of bright-line rules and reliance on a sharp dichotomy between per se tests and full-blown reasonableness inquiries; a recognition since 1977 of the dichotomy model's limitations and the tentative emergence of a continuum model that calls for judges to apply a structured analysis of varying complexity after an initial assessment of the conduct's competitive qualities; and, unless it is an aberration, most recently a return in *SCTLA*

to opinion-writing that employs the language of the dichotomy model with little effort to acknowledge (as decisions
such as *BMI* and *NCAA* had done) the analytical rigidities
and distortions that can flow from giving decisive effect to
semantic characterizations.

The effect of this evolution is that Section 1 horizontal
restraints jurisprudence today continues to display a basic
tension between the post-*Socony* dichotomy model and a
post-*Sylvania* continuum approach.   Even if the Supreme
Court ultimately declines to reformulate Section 1 doctrine
along the lines of a continuum model, modern cases that
are hospitable to a continuum approach have reduced the
polarity of the per se and rule of reason approaches under
the dichotomy tradition.   They have done so in three ways.
The first is to produce a more candid recognition of the
importance of characterization in per se analysis and to give
courts more freedom to conduct a preliminary inquiry into
purpose and effect before assigning conduct to the per se or
rule of reason categories.   Characterization always has involved what amounts to a threshold reasonableness assessment.   In many instances, courts performed this task without acknowledging that not all "price-fixing" had identical
effects or without articulating why challenged behavior
should be termed "price-fixing" or called something else.
BMI and *NCAA* have improved the structure and quality of
analysis by forcing such choices into the open and increasing the likelihood that the selection among alternative
characterizations will be made wisely.

The second is to raise the awareness of courts and enforcement officials that per se tests can be unacceptably
crude tools for evaluating business conduct, particularly in
markets featuring rapid change in organizational forms,
technology, and product development.   With some exceptions, the Supreme Court's post-*Sylvania* jurisprudence has

revitalized the Court's longstanding admonition that per se condemnation is exceptional and is warranted only when the decisionmaker has the utmost confidence that the challenged behavior lacks redeeming merit. Cases consistent with the continuum approach wisely encourage the use of more cautious, reasonableness-oriented inquiries to assess behavior that is imperfectly understood. In doing so, the Court repeatedly has indicated that the focus of analysis— whether in the per se characterization process or a reasonableness evaluation—is the conduct's economic impact. In particular, the results in cases such as *BMI* and *Northwest Wholesale* have hinged upon transaction cost and other efficiency arguments.

Finally, decisions such as *NCAA, Northwest Wholesale,* and *Indiana Federation of Dentists* have inspired new methods for structuring reasonableness inquiries to permit decisionmakers to analyze conduct more fully without disappearing in the quicksand of *Chicago Bd. of Trade's* unordered rule of reason criteria. Many lower court decisions have recognized the availability of a truncated or "quick look" version of the rule of reason that requires the defendant to advance a legitimate justification for inherently suspect conduct as a condition for proceeding to a fuller assessment of competitive effects. See *Brown University; U.S. Healthcare.* Such methodologies promise to yield more accurate assessments of competitive effects while retaining many of the administrability benefits of bright-line standards. See James D. Langenfeld & John Morris, *Analyzing Agreements Among Competitors: What Does the Future Hold?,* 36 Antitrust Bull. 651 (1991). To the extent that it persuades courts that the rule of reason can be made manageable, the development of structured or truncated reasonableness methodologies may be the most influential force for gaining formal recognition of a continuum model of Section 1 horizontal restraints doctrine.

Thus, even if the dichotomy approach remains preeminent, there will continue to be pressure for greater doctrinal convergence between per se rules and the rule of reason. Such pressure will come from essentially the same sources that one scholar identified soon after the Supreme Court decided *NCAA*: "[T]hrough expansion of the characterization process, through contraction of the sorts of conduct to which [the per se rule applies], and through refinements of the alternative approach, the rule of reason." Diane Wood–Hutchinson, *Antitrust 1984: Five Decisions in Search of a Theory,* 1984 Sup. Ct. Rev. 69, 143.

CHAPTER VI

HORIZONTAL RESTRAINTS: PROBLEMS OF PROOF AND CHARACTERIZATION

Identifying the basic standards that courts use to distinguish prohibited from permitted conduct is simply the first step in determining the application of Section 1 of the Sherman Act to horizontal restraints. Given that business managers are under constant pressure to produce profits, the temptation to increase profits by whatever means is strong. Nevertheless, the likelihood that knowledgeable business managers openly will form agreements or conspiracies to fix prices, to allocate territories, or to boycott competitors is small; legal condemnation and the probabilities of detection and of subsequent harsh sentences undoubtedly deter many. Others perceive and prefer the possibility of securing the same ends by less direct methods. Consequently, enforcement questions arise essentially in two gray areas. First, how does one prove that the parties acted pursuant to an explicit or implicit agreement? Second, can their conduct reasonably be characterized as being seriously anticompetitive, or is it "legitimate" business activity that increases competition?

A. EVIDENCE OF AN AGREEMENT

Antitrust law draws a pivotal distinction between unilateral and collective conduct. Restrictions on unilateral conduct, imposed mainly by the Sherman Act's ban on monopolization and attempted monopolization, typically apply only when the defendant has attained a dominant position in the market. Firms acting alone face relatively few antitrust risks unless they have market power.

As indicated in Chapter 5, legal doctrine and government enforcement policy treat interfirm collaboration involving direct rivals with heightened suspicion. Some forms of joint horizontal action are condemned without regard to the defendants' market power. *Socony* and its progeny make it irrelevant in Section 1 litigation that the participants in a horizontal price-fixing scheme had little actual prospect of affecting prices through their joint efforts to curb output. When detected, such conduct often results in criminal prosecution.

The closer scrutiny of Section 1 applies only if the plaintiff first shows that the defendants acted jointly. Section 1 "reaches unreasonable restraints of trade effected by a 'contract, combination ... or conspiracy' between *separate* entities. It does not reach conduct that is 'wholly unilateral.'" *Copperweld* (emphasis in original). Because labeling behavior as "concerted" can have powerful consequences, litigants in Section 1 disputes devote great effort to determining whether conduct stemmed from an agreement. Evidence showing the existence of a conspiracy to restrain trade rarely is readily available, and defendants frequently contest charges that identical prices or similar business actions resulted from an agreement or combination. Thus, proving an agreement between competing firms is among the most important issues in a Section 1 trial.

1. THE REQUIREMENT OF AN AGREEMENT

Before examining cases involving agreement issues, we first consider why proof of an agreement is required. The language of Section 1 seems to address only concerted acts (i.e., contracts, combinations, or conspiracies), implicitly absolving individual conduct—a view that the legislative history supports. But the statutory term "combination" appears flexible enough to include interdependent yet still not concerted action. More persuasive, perhaps, is the argument that requiring evidence of agreement helps distinguish harmful conduct from harmless or unavoidable behavior. For example, identical pricing may only reflect similar product costs, intense rivalry, or other beneficial and nonconspiratorial factors. Nor could business managers be expected to compete vigorously if their reward for such activity could be a criminal sentence. This argument is not unassailable, however. As discussed in Chapter 7, requiring evidence of an agreement may place all oligopolistic coordination beyond the Sherman Act's reach, thus immunizing conduct whose market impact can mimic the results of express price-fixing arrangements.

Doctrines governing agreement issues in Section 1 cases strongly resemble standards used in conventional criminal conspiracy litigation. This simplified approach to the Sherman Act can be a mixed blessing. Proof of a conspiracy is often difficult even though the rules of evidence seem to favor the prosecution; juries can be wary of using broad, amorphous notions of "conspiracy" to impose criminal liability. Emphasizing the question of "agreement" also can deflect attention away from an evaluation of the impact of the defendants' actions, with the result that neither prosecutors nor courts consider the economic effects of challenged activities. Economically trivial conduct may be treated with great solemnity (and resource commitment) while instances of serious economic harm are overlooked. As Judge Posner points out, "[i]t is the large, unwieldly cartel that is most likely to collapse amidst mutual recriminations, thereby generating rich evidence of actual agreement. The cartel that requires minimum explicit coordination, perhaps because there are only a few sellers to coordinate, is apt to have a greater adverse effect on price and output and at the same time be in less danger of being detected and prosecuted." R. Posner, *Antitrust Law*, 95.

2. THE EVIDENTIARY REQUIREMENTS

A legal command triggered by collective action requires one to define what behavior constitutes an agreement.[1] Some cases involve a simple inquiry. The defendants collectively devise a plan and directly exchange assurances (e.g., in writing or in conversations) that they will travel a common path. The fact of collective efforts to fix prices or divide markets emerges clearly through documents circulated among the defendants or from testimony by a disgruntled participant who describes the concerted activity. If detected by public enforcement agencies or private plaintiffs, episodes of collective behavior involving per se offenses usually end in plea agreements, consent orders, or damage settlements.

Many cases, however, present harder analytical puzzles. In some instances, defendants expressly exchange assurances but do so covertly. The trial record contains no direct evidence of concerted action (e.g., a letter circulated among the defendants or testimony given by a renegade insider), and agreement must be proven through circumstantial evidence. In a second set of cases, the defendants

---

1. Related questions deal with whether rules of apparent authority from agency law apply in antitrust disputes to hold unincorporated associations liable for the misdeeds of their officers or whether corporations are bound by their officers' acts. Agency rules have been applied broadly, and liability readily has been found. See American Soc'y of Mechanical Engineers v. Hydrolevel Corp. (1982).

use subtle tactics to reach consensus. A firm may announce price increases well before their effective date in the hope that rivals will embrace similar strategies, or it may adopt policies that competitors interpret as commitments to forego rivalry on price or other terms of trade. Such policies might include placing "most favored nation" clauses in contracts with major customers. These clauses bind the firm to give favored buyers the benefit of any price reduction offered to another customer. By committing the firm to cut prices for much of its purchaser base, such clauses can discourage price reductions and thereby signal the firm's intent to avoid price cuts. In a third set of cases, firms coordinate their conduct simply by observing and anticipating their rivals' price moves. In oligopolies, such efforts may produce supracompetitive pricing similar to that generated by express cartel agreements. How antitrust should treat oligopolistic coordination is considered in Chapter 7.

a. Section 1 and the Endangerment of Overt Cartels

To understand the evolution of modern agreement doctrine, it is useful to consider how the application of Section 1 in the Sherman Act's early decades deterred the formation and operation of overt cartels. The first Section 1 cases rarely posed a question of whether the requisite agreement existed. In the late 19th Century, the central issue in Section 1 litigation was not the fact of concerted action but rather the legality of admittedly collective behavior.[2] For example, in *Trans–Missouri Freight* the defendant railroads conceded the existence of a collective rate-

2. As discussed in Chapter 1, the common law before 1890 did not flatly prohibit joint efforts by competitors to fix prices. The common law's ambiguous treatment of price-fixing and uncertainty about the Sherman Act's meaning led some firms to continue to coordinate their behavior openly after 1890.

setting agreement (its terms were reprinted with the Supreme Court's opinion) but urged that Section 1 did not condemn the challenged behavior. *Trans–Missouri* and other early Supreme Court decisions made clear that Section 1 applied to express agreements. The Court also established (and it remains true today) that Section 1 reaches exchanges of assurances—manifest through oral or written statements, physical conduct, or a course of dealing—that do not satisfy the formalities needed to obtain judicial enforcement under common law contract principles. See United States v. General Motors Corp. (1966) ("explicit agreement is not a necessary part of a Sherman Act conspiracy"); Esco Corp. v. United States (1965) ("A knowing wink can mean more than words.").

Until the late 1930s, most Section 1 litigation focused on the legality of admittedly concerted action. In *Socony* in 1940, the Supreme Court ruled that Section 1 barred all horizontal price-fixing arrangements and, by sustaining the defendants' convictions, indicated that cartelists faced unmistakable dangers, including successful criminal prosecution. The condemnation of horizontal price-fixing and increased recourse to criminal enforcement changed business behavior in several ways. As a matter of litigation strategy, firms mounted fuller efforts to show that the challenged conduct was unilateral and therefore outside Section 1's reach. As a matter of business planning, firms contemplating illicit cooperation with rivals took greater precautions to avoid detection—e.g., by avoiding written communications that might readily prove the existence of an agreement. Yet even paperless covert meetings and conversations were not riskless. The testimony of a participant-turned-informer could reveal how the conspirators formulated and executed a plan. Thus, firms devised more subtle ways to communicate their intentions and exchange assurances.

b. Modern Development of Formulas for Defining Concerted Action

Business efforts to disprove concerted action, to hide interfirm communications, and to devise indirect ways to exchange assurances have elevated the importance of the agreement issue in Section 1 cases. Courts have conceived various formulas to determine when conduct results from concerted, rather than unilateral, acts. Judicial attempts to define the Section 1 agreement requirement generally have failed to provide a satisfactory basis for distinguishing unilateral from concerted action where the trial record lacks direct evidence showing that the defendants acted jointly. See William E. Kovacic, *The Identification and Proof of Horizontal Agreements Under the Antitrust Laws*, 38 Antitrust Bull. 5 (1993).

Modern judicial efforts to define the elements of a Section 1 agreement originated in four Supreme Court decisions issued during a fifteen-year period beginning in 1939 with Interstate Circuit, Inc. v. United States (1939). In finding an illegal agreement by movie exhibitors to fix the prices to be charged for first-run films, the Court said that "[w]hile the District Court's finding of an agreement of the distributors among themselves is supported by the evidence, we think that in the circumstances of this case such agreement for the imposition of the restrictions upon subsequent-run exhibitors was not a prerequisite to an unlawful conspiracy. It was enough that, knowing that concerted action was contemplated or invited, the distributors gave their adherence to the scheme and participated in it." The Court added that "[a]cceptance by competitors, without previous agreement, of an invitation to participate in a plan, the necessary consequence of which, if carried out, is restraint of interstate commerce, is sufficient to establish an unlawful conspiracy under the Sherman Act."

Seven years later, in American Tobacco Co. v. United States (1946), the Court reviewed conspiracy to monopolize charges brought against the country's leading cigarette manufacturers under Section 2 of the Sherman Act. The Court said "[n]o formal agreement is necessary to constitute an unlawful conspiracy" and explained that a finding of conspiracy is justified "[w]here the circumstances are such as to warrant a jury in finding that the conspirators had a unity of purpose or a common design and understanding, or a meeting of minds in an unlawful arrangement."

This series of agreement decisions was capped by two cases involving the distribution practices of Paramount and its rival motion picture exhibitors. In United States v. Paramount Pictures, Inc. (1948), the Court largely reiterated the formula it had announced in *Interstate Circuit*: "It is not necessary to find an express agreement in order to find a conspiracy. It is enough that a concert of action is contemplated and that the defendants conformed to the arrangement." However, in a subsequent private challenge to Paramount and its competitors, the Court appeared to retreat from this expansive definition. In Theatre Enterprises, Inc. v. Paramount Film Distributing Corp. (1954), the Court cautioned that "[c]ircumstantial evidence of consciously parallel behavior may have made heavy inroads into the traditional judicial attitude toward conspiracy; but 'conscious parallelism' has not read conspiracy out of the Sherman Act entirely."

As a group, these decisions established three points of reference for Section 1 litigation. First, courts would apply the label of "concerted action" to interfirm coordination accomplished by means other than a direct exchange of assurances. Second, courts would allow agreements to be inferred from circumstantial proof suggesting that the challenged behavior more likely than not was the result of a jointly determined course of action. Third, courts would decline to find concerted action where the plaintiff showed only that the defendants recognized their interdependence and simply mimicked their competitors' conduct.

More recent cases have tried to capture these principles in a new formula. Through the early 1980s, many lower court decisions embraced the view that "[t]he substantive law of trade conspiracies requires some consciousness of commitment to a common scheme." Edward J. Sweeney & Sons, Inc. v. Texaco, Inc. (1980). In 1984 the Supreme Court seemed to endorse this formula while addressing vertical conspiracy claims in Monsanto Co. v. Spray–Rite Service Corp. (1984). There the Court said "[t]he correct standard is that there must be evidence that tends to exclude the possibility of independent action by the [parties]. That is, there must be direct or circumstantial evidence that reasonably tends to prove that [the parties] had a conscious commitment to a common scheme designed to achieve an unlawful objective." Yet neither *Monsanto* nor later case law has provided a satisfying analytical basis for distinguishing collective from unilateral behavior. While such tests make clear that the agreement concept encompasses more than a written document or spoken assurances, they offer no operational means for determining when the defendants have done more than merely observe and respond to their rivals' pricing moves.

The following example shows how mere "conscious parallelism" could be termed a "conscious commitment to a common scheme." Consider the behavior of oligopolists. Each firm knows that the effect of its actions depends on the actions and reactions of its rivals; price increases will stick only if all firms raise their prices. Recognizing this interdependence, but without consulting its competitors, each firm decides to match its rivals' price increases. Repeated efforts to match rivals' price moves arguably indicate the firm's "conscious commitment" to achieve higher prices. The firm "communicates" with its rivals only by observing and responding to their price moves. By calibrating its own pricing decisions to conform with its rivals' decisions, each firm might be said to have "consciously committed" itself to participate in a "common scheme." Yet such behavior also can be described as following that firm's self-interest in a wholly independent manner.

c. Evidentiary Standards

Outcomes in Section 1 litigation often depend on whether the plaintiff has supported its conspiracy claim with enough evidence to warrant a trial and to have its case submitted to the jury. The Section 1 plaintiff bears the burden of proving an agreement. In civil cases this burden is met only by introducing evidence that permits the factfinder to conclude that the existence of an agreement is more likely than not. Conclusory allegations of concerted action are prone to summary dismissal. See Gulf States Land & Development, Inc. v. Premier Bank N.A. (1992).

As *Monsanto* indicates, a "conscious commitment to a common scheme" can be shown by using direct or circumstantial evidence. Direct evidence consisting of documents or the testimony of a conspiracy participant sometimes establishes concerted action. Nonetheless, courts recognize that "[o]nly rarely will there be direct evidence of an express agreement" in Section 1 disputes. Local No. 189, Amalgamated Meat Cutters v. Jewel Tea Co. (1965). Plaintiffs therefore can use circumstantial evidence to show that the defendants acted concertedly.

In discussing the plaintiff's evidence, courts often distinguish between "express" and "tacit" agreements. These terms seem designed to acknowledge differences in the types of evidence used to prove concerted action. Cases that speak of "express" agreements ordinarily involve direct proof that the defendants have exchanged assurances. Documents and testimony typically stand atop the hierarchy of proof because they tend to give the court greater confidence that the defendants acted jointly. Cases that speak of "tacit" collusion use the term to describe two phenomena. One group of decisions uses "tacit" collusion to refer to alleged agreements which the plaintiff seeks to prove by introducing circumstantial evidence. Used in this manner, the "tacit" label acknowledges that such proof is inferior to direct evidence of concerted action. Many cases that use the terminology in this way find liability, with the crucial issue being to define what quantum of circumstantial proof will permit an inference of concerted action. The second group of cases that speak of "tacit" collusion uses the term to refer to parallel, interdependent conduct of the type addressed in *Theatre Enterprises.*[3] Cases that use "tacit collusion" as a synonym for "conscious parallelism" ordinarily do not find Section 1 liability.

Fear that mistaken inferences from ambiguous circumstantial evidence might deter procompetitive or benign conduct led the Supreme Court in *Matsushita* (1986) to extend *Monsanto's* agreement formula to the evaluation of horizontal conspiracy claims. The Court emphasized that "conduct as consistent with permissible competition as with illegal conspiracy does not, standing alone, support an inference of conspiracy." Quoting from *Monsanto,* the Court

3. See, e.g., *Brook Group* ("Tacit collusion, sometimes called oligopolistic price coordination or conscious parallelism, describes the process, not in itself unlawful, by which firms in a concentrated market might in effect share monopoly power, setting their prices at a profit-maximizing, supracompetitive level by recognizing their shared economic interests and their interdependence with respect to price and output decisions.").

explained that "[t]o survive a motion for summary judgment or for a directed verdict, a plaintiff seeking damages for a violation of Section 1 must present evidence that 'tends to exclude the possibility' that the alleged conspirators acted independently.... [Plaintiffs] in this case, in other words, must show that the inference of conspiracy is reasonable in light of the competing inferences of independent action or collusive action that could not have harmed [plaintiffs]." *Matsushita* ruled that the plaintiffs had failed to show that the defendants could reasonably expect to recoup the losses resulting from an alleged agreement to fix prices below the competitive level. Without such evidence, "[t]he alleged conspiracy's failure to achieve its ends in the two decades of its asserted operation is strong evidence that the conspiracy does not exist."

d. Interdependence and "Plus Factors"

The thorniest agreement issues have arisen in cases involving markets characterized by interdependence. This condition departs significantly from the model of perfect competition in which each firm is indifferent to its competitors' actions. In concentrated markets, the recognition of interdependence can lead firms to coordinate their conduct simply by observing and reacting to their competitors' moves. Such oligopolistic coordination sometimes generates parallel price movements that approach the market outcomes of traditional agreements to set prices.

Courts have struggled with whether parallel conduct that seems to flow from a recognition of interdependence suffices, without more, to support an inference of agreement. Three leading Supreme Court cases, pointing in somewhat divergent directions, establish the basic framework for analysis. In *Interstate Circuit* (1939), eight motion picture film distributors with 75 percent of the feature film market made identical changes in their contracts with two affiliated Texas exhibitors (theater owners) of first-run films. The complaint alleged that the distributors had violated Section 1 by jointly limiting the terms on which they would license subsequent runs of their films. However, there was no evidence of any express agreement among the eight *distributors*; the evidence instead showed that the *exhibitors* had made the initial request (and it was in each exhibitor's individual interest to limit competition from subsequent runs in the Texas market, and the contract modifications served this interest).

In upholding the district court's finding that there had been an agreement among the distributors, the Supreme Court relied on four factors: (1) One exhibitor had made its request in a letter addressed to all distributors, ensuring that each distributor knew that all were being asked to make the same changes in the contract; each defendant knew that the same "offer" had been communicated to the others. In dictum, the Court said "[i]t was enough that, knowing that concerted action was contemplated and invited, the distributors gave their adherence to the scheme and participated in it." (2) Largely identical alterations were made in each contract, and the modifications were complex; these changes were no coincidence. (3) The contract changes were major (especially compared to the price increase) and could be implemented only if all agreed to them; and the initial communication assured that each distributor understood this. (4) The defendants failed to call their top officers as witnesses to deny the existence of an agreement, suggesting that their testimony would have proved unfavorable. This omission left the Court "unable to find in the record any persuasive explanation, other than agreed concert of action, of the singular unanimity of action on the part of the distributors."

The approach in *Interstate Circuit* was reinforced by *American Tobacco* (1946), where the Court found that three firms accounting for 90 percent of cigarettes made in the U.S. had violated Section 2 of the Sherman Act by conspiring to monopolize. For twenty years the defendants had maintained virtually identical price lists and discounts; on many occasions, defendants had raised prices in lockstep fashion, even during the Depression when their costs had fallen. From this evidence the Court upheld a finding that the conduct resulted from a conspiracy, emphasizing that the defendants had not offered an "economic justification" for their behavior.

The Court soon retreated from the broad implications of *Interstate Circuit* and *American Tobacco*. In *Theatre Enterprises* (1954), the Court upheld a verdict that distributors of first-run films had not conspired to deny first-run rights to a suburban exhibitor. The Court emphasized several considerations: (1) The defendants advanced sound economic reasons why each distributor independently took the same action; licensing the plaintiff would have reduced revenues from competing downtown theaters; and the plaintiff's offer did not appear genuine. (2) There was no evidence that all defendants knew that the others had received or spurned the first-run offer; the firms' prior antitrust convictions did not constitute evidence of misconduct in this instance. (3) The distributors' officers specifically denied any collusion. Responding to the overdrawn reaction to its dictum in *Interstate Circuit,* the Court now declared (in equally famous language): "Circumstantial evidence of consciously parallel behavior may have made heavy inroads into the traditional judicial attitude toward conspiracy; but 'conscious parallelism' has not yet read conspiracy out of the Sherman Act entirely."

The divergent results in *Interstate Circuit* and *Theatre Enterprises* also can be explained by the procedural posture of the two cases. In both instances the Court upheld a lower court decision. *Interstate Circuit's* seemingly radical departure from previous thinking may have reflected judicial reluctance to overturn a decision where purpose is significant and where the trial court's proximity to the witnesses was undoubtedly of influence. Cf. Poller v. Columbia Broadcasting System, Inc. (1962) ("summary procedures should be used sparingly in complex antitrust litigation where motive and intent play leading roles, the proof is largely in the hands of the alleged conspirators, and hostile witnesses thicken the plot"). The different outcomes also might be attributed to the type of remedy sought in each case. The Justice Department's suit in *Interstate Circuit* was for injunctive relief only, whereas the private plaintiffs in *Theatre Enterprises* sought treble damages.

The meaning of the *Interstate Circuit, American Tobacco,* and *Theatre Enterprises* trilogy remains a matter of active debate. It is possible, however, to discern some rough guidelines from subsequent judicial decisions. Courts generally have held that "conscious parallelism" or oligopolistic interdependence, without more, does not permit an inference of conspiracy. Courts typically require plaintiffs who rely on parallel conduct to introduce additional facts, often termed "plus factors," to justify an inference of agreement. See Petruzzi's IGA Supermarkets, Inc. v. Darling–Delaware Co. (1993); Reserve Supply Corp. v. Owens–Corning Fiberglas Corp. (1992); Clamp–All Corp. v. Cast Iron Soil Pipe Inst. (1988).

Courts have used various plus factors to illuminate the source of parallel conduct. Section 1 cases often ask whether defendants had a rational motive to engage in a conspiracy. In a closely related inquiry, other decisions consider whether the disputed conduct would have contradicted the defendants' self-interest if pursued unilaterally. In applying the "motive to conspire" and "contrary to self-interest" factors, many cases have dismissed claims that rest chiefly on the fact of parallelism without a showing that defendants could expect to gain from concerted action. See, e.g., First National Bank of Arizona v. Cities Service Co. (1968).

Plus factors that have supported an inference of conspiracy include proof that defendants priced uniformly where price uniformity was improbable without an agreement; committed past antitrust violations involving collective action; directly communicated with competitors, and then made simultaneous, identical changes in their behavior; or agreed to adopt common practices, such as product standardization, whose implementation helped achieve pricing uniformity. Defendants have rebutted an inference of concerted action where they have demonstrated that their conduct either was consistent with independent choice or accomplished procompetitive or competitively neutral objectives.

Decisions analyzing plus factors generally have failed to establish a clear boundary between tacit agreements—to which Section 1 applies—and parallel pricing stemming from oligopolistic interdependence, which *Theatre Enterprises* regards as insufficient to support an inference of agreement. Courts seldom rank plus factors by their probative value or specify the minimum critical mass of plus factors that will sustain an inference of concerted conduct. The failure to rigorously analyze the competitive significance of each plus factor can be attributed in part to the Supreme Court's decision in Continental Ore Co. v. Union Carbide & Carbon Corp. (1962), which admonished courts to give plaintiffs "the full benefit of their proof without tightly compartmentalizing the various factual components and wiping the slate clean after scrutiny of each." This condition often makes judgments about future litigation outcomes problematic and imparts an impressionistic quality to judicial treatments of agreement issues.

Variation in judicial analyses of plus factors suggests that decisions often depend on the court's unarticulated intuition about the likely cause of observed parallel behavior. Judges seem to vary in their acceptance of the proposition in *Theatre Enterprises* that conscious parallelism does not necessarily indicate concerted action. Courts that appear to regard pricing uniformity as a sign of collaboration and market failure tend to expand the range and reduce the quantum of conduct that, when added to parallel behavior, can support a finding of agreement. Thus, some decisions go to great lengths to characterize proof as suggesting collective activity. See, e.g., In re Petroleum Products Antitrust Litigation (1990); City of Long Beach v. Standard Oil Co. of California (1989). On the other hand, judges who see parallelism as benign—e.g., a natural result of the tendency of supplier prices to converge in competitive markets—implicitly hold the plaintiff to more rigorous standards of proof and display a greater reluctance to infer an agreement on the basis of asserted plus factors. See, e.g., Reserve Supply Corp. v. Owens–Corning Fiberglas Corp. (1992); Market Force Inc. v. Wauwatosa Realty Co. (1990).

B. PROBLEMS OF CHARACTERIZATION

Establishing the existence of collective action is the threshold inquiry in Section 1 horizontal restraints cases. An equally important task is to characterize the nature of challenged behavior. Vexing classification issues can arise as courts attempt to determine whether specific business conduct is designed to perfect the operation of a freely competitive market or serves mainly to fix prices or allocate sales territories.

1. INFORMATION EXCHANGES

Exchanges of information between competing or related businesses often raise antitrust problems. Information exchanges have Section 1 implications in essentially two settings—where data is disseminated through the assistance of a trade association, and where firms obtain or provide information by contacting competitors directly.

a. *Trade Associations*

Business officials selling the same product may cooperate for a number of reasons, many of which the antitrust system views as promoting competitive markets. Primary among the possibly valid bases for meetings between competitors is the dissemination of trade information among producers. Knowledge concerning current inventory levels or the availability of raw materials, for example, may help a firm to plan its production and to develop its market strategies, thereby reducing costs, increasing profits, and possibly intensifying competition. The extensive scope and impact of government economic regulation has made it increasingly important for business, with its experience and expertise, to participate in planning and implementing such regulation. Trade associations also may promote the industry to potential customers where free rider problems may make it more efficient for industry groups to advertise rather than for individual firms to do so. Firms also join trade bodies to improve technology by sharing information, to encourage standardization, and to enjoy advantages of large-scale organization, such as establishing an industry credit bureau.

On the other hand, trade associations or similar information exchanges can also serve as vehicles for firms to fix
prices, allocate sales opportunities, or boycott others. As
Adam Smith noted long ago: "People of the same trade
seldom meet together, even for merriment and diversion,
but the conversation ends in a conspiracy against the public, or in some contrivance to raise prices." [4] For example,
trade association activities such as reporting prices can help
firms detect off-list prices and enforce collusive pricing.
Still, it is the agreement to fix prices (not the opportunity)
that arguably should be banned, especially since trade
groups serve desirable ends.

Firms need not always state their desire to fix prices in
order for trade meetings to have this effect. Industry
managers often come from similar social strata; their bonds
of friendship, group similarity, and identical interests are
likely to discourage maverick (competitive) action, especially where common meetings are frequent and the ensuing
discussions address sensitive pricing and production issues.
Thus, trade meetings and information exchanges may facilitate oligopolistic price coordination by making a rival's
decisions more predictable and providing common guidelines as to "appropriate" price levels. If all prices are
publicized, rivals can retaliate more readily against secret
price-cutting, thus denying the benefits (additional orders)
to the price-shading firm. Thus, in an oligopoly, information exchanges may encourage price stability and fix prices

4. Adam Smith, *The Wealth of Nations* 128 (Canaan ed. 1937) (1st ed.
1776). Smith added that "though the law cannot hinder people of the
same trade from sometimes assembling together, it ought to do nothing to
facilitate such assemblies; much less to render them necessary." This
admonition is often ignored. Many public policies encourage or compel
private entities to collaborate in setting terms of trade, causing frequent
collisions with antitrust doctrines that ban certain agreements among
rivals. Doctrines for resolving such conflicts are discussed in Chapter 13.

by aiding the detection and punishment of deviations from a desired norm. Indeed, this possibility helped spawn the trade association movement and inspired its promotion of "open price plans." See Arthur Jerome Eddy, *The New Competition* (1912).

Membership in a trade association and the exchange of information concerning prices, output, inventories, or any other aspect of the business is covered by Section 1 because an agreement or combination is present. Trade associations in themselves are statutory combinations. They may also involve agreements by members to exchange information and accordingly meet the traditional definition of a contract. Or, as suggested in the preceding paragraph on oligopoly coordination, a tacit agreement among trade association members may be inferred from their conduct. Whatever the jurisdictional basis, a central question under Section 1 is whether this information exchange tends to restrain trade unreasonably.

Where there is no apparent (and effective) purpose to fix prices or otherwise limit competition among its members, the exchange of information facilitated by a trade association is usually tested under a rule of reason approach. Even though, as the Court acknowledged in Maple Flooring Mfrs. Ass'n v. United States (1925), it is not "open to question that the dissemination of pertinent information concerning any trade or business tends to stabilize that trade or business and to produce uniformity of price and trade practice," the mere exchange of information is not "an unreasonable restraint, or in any respect unlawful." This position has survived the rule of *Socony* which found it illegal per se to agree on prices or otherwise tamper with the price system. At first glance, this conclusion may seem anomalous, since the exchange of trade information itself alters how firms set price and production levels; nonetheless, the mere exchange of information does not in itself require the recipients to follow a particular policy. And antitrust law generally relies on that basic distinction to differentiate between price agreements and information exchanges.

Of course, even under a rule of reason approach, programs for data dissemination still can be condemned as unreasonable trade restraints. Early cases dealing with "open competition" plans (which admittedly sought to "keep prices at reasonably stable and normal levels") found that such plans violated the Sherman Act. Thus, in American Column & Lumber Co. v. United States (1921) (the *Hardwood* case), a trade association whose members produced one-third of the nation's hardwood lumber had adopted a plan requiring member firms to submit price lists, detailed daily sales and shipment reports (including invoice copies), monthly production and stock reports, etc. The plan as implemented was held to violate Section 1. The association's central office summarized the reported data and sent the membership weekly reports that listed each transaction, the parties, and the price, and noted whether the price departed from the member's listed price. Moreover, in frequent meetings the members not only discussed market conditions but strongly urged each other to restrict output and maintain prices. By any standard, the Court concluded, this was "not the conduct of competitors but is ... clearly that of men united in an agreement, express or implied, to act together and pursue a common purpose under a common guide."

Nonetheless, the *Hardwood* case was not easily decided. There was no agreement to limit production or charge a fixed price, as the Court openly acknowledged, and the contention that it is shown by "the disposition of men to follow their most intelligent competitors" hardly supplies the missing link—especially since market conditions were not conducive to price leadership or other efforts to curb output. (The plan involved only one-third of the industry and 365 sellers.) In pointed dissents, Justices Brandeis and Holmes argued that the Sherman Act should not be used to stifle discussion or require business rivals to compete blindly without relevant trade information.

After striking down a similar open price plan in the linseed oil industry in United States v. American Linseed Oil Co. (1923), the Supreme Court approved the plans of two trade associations. In Maple Flooring Mfrs. Ass'n v. United States (1925) the trade association disseminated information detailing members' average costs and summarizing all sales, prices, and stocks—but not identifying current individual transactions; a single base point freight rate booklet (which would facilitate uniform pricing) was also distributed to them. But the Court said this information exchange did not unreasonably restrain trade, noting that after the *Linseed Oil* case the association's members stopped discussing prices and after the complaint was filed here the weekly summary no longer linked specific sellers with particular transactions. Other evidence established that the members' prices were not uniform and actually were lower than those of nonmember producers. The Court was, it appears, influenced by the association's effort to stay within the letter of the antitrust laws.[5] The Court also stressed the conduct's positive traits, stating that

5. The evidence also seemed to support the inference that the association sought to facilitate an express price agreement or oligopoly pricing by exchanging average cost data and distributing a single base point freight rate book. But see Thomas W. Gilligan, *Imperfect Competition and Basing–Point Pricing*, 31 Econ. Inquiry 394 (1993); David D. Haddock, *Basing Point Pricing: Competitive vs. Collusive Theories*, 72 Am. Econ. Rev. 289 (1982). Moreover, the market presented a ready opportunity for collusion. The association had only 22 members, and their aggregate market share was 70 percent.

"[c]ompetition does not become less free merely because the conduct of commercial operations becomes more intelligent through the free distribution of knowledge of all the essential factors entering into the commercial transaction."

On the same day as its decision in *Maple Flooring,* the Court approved a second trade association's plan in *Cement Mfrs.* (1925). There the Court upheld an elaborate statistical program that involved the incidental disclosure of price information among cement manufacturers. Despite "substantial uniformity" of prices and other industry trade practices, the Court sustained the plan on the grounds that product homogeneity forced competing sellers to meet price changes and that the data was needed to counter fraud by some buyers.

Maple Flooring and *Cement Mfrs.* were authored by Justice Harlan Fiske Stone, who had served as Attorney General in the Coolidge Administration. In these cases Stone displayed his enthusiasm for the "associationalism" policies of Herbert Hoover, who used his position as Secretary of Commerce in the early 1920s to encourage industry leaders to form trade associations to collect and disseminate data on prices, production, and inventories. As reflected in *Maple Flooring* and *Cement Mfrs.,* associationalists believed that the wide availability of statistical data on business transactions would reduce operational inefficiency, faulty investment, and the misuse of resources. The trade association antitrust cases of the 1920s stemmed largely from Hoover's efforts to encourage businesses to cooperate at a time when the emerging body of Sherman Act precedents were subjecting collaboration among rivals to antitrust scrutiny. See Ellis W. Hawley, *Herbert Hoover and the Sherman Act, 1921–1933: An Early Phase of a Continuing Issue,* 74 Iowa L. Rev. 1067 (1989).

The Court returned to the question of open price plans in *Sugar Institute, Inc. v. United States* (1936). The principal association of sugar refiners devised an open price plan which (a) assured that price reductions would be promptly met by all members, (b) provided that price increases would be announced in advance but could later be withdrawn unless all sugar refiners followed suit, and (c) resulted in an agreement that no refiner would make secret concessions from announced prices. The Court condemned only the last item—the agreement to abide by list prices until a new price was publicly announced. Otherwise the Court accepted the parties' justification for advance announcement of price moves (an industry custom which gave customers a grace period in which to buy sugar at the former price).

One might be tempted to dismiss *Sugar Institute* as another Depression-inspired opinion by Chief Justice Hughes, whose antitrust views (see *Appalachian Coals*) generally have not survived *Socony's* per se ban on all agreements that tamper with prices. However, such a characterization would not be fully accurate in this case, as the basic rule of reason standard for information exchanges antedated *Sugar Institute* and was long accepted by the Supreme Court. Thus, the *Maple Flooring* rule largely survives, despite *Socony's* per se prohibition of price-fixing and price stabilization agreements. See United States v. Citizens & Southern Nat'l Bank (1975) ("the dissemination of price information is not itself a per se violation of the Sherman Act."). Furthermore, this conclusion is buttressed by the economic and social values provided by trade exchanges, especially for smaller firms. As the Supreme Court later observed: "The exchange of price data and other information among competitors does not invariably have anti-competitive effects; indeed such practices can in certain circumstances increase economic efficiency and render markets more, rather than less, competitive." United States v. United States Gypsum Co. (1978).

To be sustained, information exchanges carried out by trade associations should adhere to several guidelines. See Brian Henry, *Benchmarking and Antitrust,* 62 Antitrust L. J. 483 (1994). Such exchanges should be limited to past prices, should be aggregated to avoid identifying particular transactions or parties, and should not bind the members to abide by announced prices. In addition, the data should be publicly available. See Wilcox v. First Interstate Bank of Oregon (1987); Tag Mfrs. Institute v. FTC (1949).

b. Verification and Exchange of Prices By Direct Rivals

The Supreme Court has established more stringent controls on the verification of prices directly between suppliers. In United States v. Container Corp. (1969), 18 firms shipped 90 percent of the cardboard cartons supplied in the Southeast. They established an informal price exchange whereby suppliers gave each other, on request, price information on their most recent sales to a particular customer. Not surprisingly, once a firm had received this information, it would often (but not always) quote the same price to that customer, and buyers commonly divided orders among suppliers. The market loosely resembled an oligopoly (18 of the 51 firms in the market controlled 90 percent of the sales, and the six largest controlled almost 60 percent); and the industry had excess capacity despite rapid increases in demand. On the other hand, entry was easy and frequent, and capacity had expanded rapidly. Conceding that these facts fit none of the precedents, the Court condemned this information exchange because "[t]he exchange of price data tends toward price uniformity." The Court explained that Section 1 bans "[s]tabilizing prices as well as raising them" and, quoting *Socony,* added that "stabilization is but one form of manipulation."

Despite the harshness of this language, the Court's subsequent opinions made clear that *Container* was not announcing a new per se rule for price exchanges. See *Citizens & Southern Nat'l Bank* (1975). Nevertheless, it seems clear that a stricter test for price verification between sellers was to be applied in some circumstances. Viewing the market as an oligopoly, the Court observed that price exchanges identifying particular parties, transactions, and prices could foster interdependent pricing (by preventing secret price concessions). Thus, the opinion could be read as applying a rule of presumptive illegality to specific price exchanges among oligopolists. The difficulty with this view of *Container* is that the market did not really fit the Court's analysis. There were too many firms, entry was too easy, and excess capacity pressed too hard on the market, for oligopoly pricing as it is normally understood to occur—and the dissent made this clear. The Court's reasoning also would apply to generalized price exchanges, yet it left undisturbed its precedents in *Cement Mfrs.* (exchange of price to specific customers) and *Maple Flooring* (exchange of generalized price data).

This set the stage for United States v. United States Gypsum Co. (1978). Here the government charged that gypsum board producers had engaged in per se illegal price-fixing by checking current and future prices with rivals before giving price concessions to buyers. (The government read the per se-type language of *Container* as overruling *Maple Flooring* and as creating a new test for information exchanges.) The defendants said they had consulted competitors on prices and sales terms only to comply with the meeting competition requirements of the Robinson–Patman Act (see Chapter 11). They contended that the Sherman

Act could not condemn out of hand what the Robinson–Patman Act authorized, and that this was a "controlling circumstance" that *Container* recognized as a defense to a Sherman Act charge.[6]

Although unrelated aspects of the *Gypsum* opinion were not supported by all Justices, those participating agreed that the mere exchange of price information without intent to fix prices is not criminal price-fixing per se and must be tested under the rule of reason. They also ruled that a seller could usually satisfy the requirements of the Robinson–Patman Act's meeting competition defense without direct price checking; and the dangers presented by interseller verification in an oligopoly (here the eight largest companies had 94 percent of national sales) outweighed the benefits that could occur from allowing this exchange. Thus the Court held that the meeting competition defense was not an exception to the *Container* rule prohibiting direct price exchanges.

c. *Implications for Future Information-Sharing*

Modern information technology such as computer-based networks has increased the ability of firms to monitor their rivals' conduct and to share information about specific transactions and business practices generally. Improvements in information technology have coincided with recent developments that have spurred firms to pursue new initiatives that involve intra-industry data sharing. See David J. Teece, *Information Sharing, Innovation, and Antitrust,* 62 Antitrust L.J. 465 (1994). These trends promise to make information-sharing issues prominent elements of future antitrust analysis.

6. *Container* had noted that the exchange of prices in *Cement Mfrs.* (1925) had been justified partly by a "controlling circumstance"—i.e., to prevent buyer fraud.

The legal doctrines discussed above have at least four major implications for the emerging business environment. First, one still cannot confidently state the legal test applicable to the dissemination of pricing data. The Supreme Court used the language of a per se test in *Container* but dealt with the case under a narrower-than-usual rule of reason standard. By contrast, *Gypsum* spoke in the measured terms of the rule of reason, yet its treatment of the facts left little doubt that price exchanges were disfavored among oligopolists. This suggests that the Court may have adopted a modified rule of reason approach that entails a fuller, fact-based inquiry in competitively structured industries and employs a less hospitable presumption of illegality for information exchanges in highly concentrated markets.

Second, *Container* and *Gypsum* severely limited the circumstances in which competitors can share price data directly. *Container's* suspicion of price exchanges in concentrated markets has led some lower courts to treat price exchanges among rivals as a plus factor from which a jury could infer an agreement to fix prices. See In re Coordinated Petroleum Products Litigation (1990). This does not mean, however, that all price exchanges are forbidden. Courts have upheld exchanges of pricing data where defendants have shown that the exchange served a legitimate business objective and the exchange was not designed to stabilize prices. See *Wilcox* (1987).

Third, it is unclear from the standpoint of economic analysis that price verification is likely to lead to higher prices, even in oligopolies. If a seller has excess capacity and lacks other reasonable means to check on alleged price concessions—probably a common situation, even in concentrated markets—price rivalry may occur only if a seller can check on whether the lower price was offered; otherwise the seller may lose more in profits than it gains in sales from a price cut. We still do not know, despite the assumption in *Gypsum,* whether price exchanges in oligopolies cost consumers more because of interdependent pricing than they gain from the price rivalry that results.

Fourth, even though the market impact of price verification may be ambiguous, it is clear that antitrust concerns are less acute when firms exchange data other than current or future prices. There is growing recognition that information exchanges involving historical costs and production techniques can increase the ability of firms to compete more effectively. For example, collaboration by health insurers to pool information on the outcomes of specific forms of medical treatment can play an important role in enabling insurers to implement cost containment programs. See Kathryn M. Fenton, *Antitrust Implications of Joint Efforts by Third Party Payors to Reduce Costs and Improve the Quality of Health Care,* 61 Antitrust L.J. 17, 19–22 (1992). A second illustration is the practice of "benchmarking," by which firms compare their production, quality control, and sales techniques with those of successful firms within the same industry or in other sectors. Benchmarking data is sometimes accumulated and disseminated by third parties such as trade associations and management consulting firms, but it also involves direct contacts and information exchanges by competitors. Identifying "best practices" within other companies can reveal a firm's shortcomings and suggest possible paths for improvement. See T. Jorde & D. Teece, *Rule of Reason Analysis of Horizontal Arrangements: Agreements Designed to Advance Innovation and Commercialize Technology,* at 596–98. A reasonableness standard that gives heavy weight to the potential benefits of these types of information-sharing seems best suited to yield a proper assessment of competitive effects.

2. JOINT VENTURES AND THE APPLICATION OF THE RULE OF REASON

Cases dealing with joint ventures provide instructive examples of how courts have applied the rule of reason to horizontal restraints. The term "joint venture" describes a variety of cooperative arrangements that fall short of an outright consolidation of the participants' operations. Joint ventures ordinarily consist of contractual relationships, although the parties sometimes create a new corporate entity whose stock is held by the participating firms. These arrangements present legal and economic analytical challenges that are largely similar to those discussed in Chapter 5 where firms collaborate rather than compete. Most joint ventures are measured under a rule of reason unless the "joint venture" consists of little more than a transparent arrangement to fix prices or allocate markets; in the latter case, per se condemnation is common.

Joint ventures can serve a variety of socially desirable ends. Joint ventures can enable the participants to unify complementary technical and managerial capabilities to perform projects whose requirements exceed the expertise of any single firm. By facilitating the transfer of know-how and technology, joint ventures also can improve the skills of individual venture participants and thereby overcome barriers to entry and expansion in specific markets. Collaboration can permit firms to realize R & D scale economies by avoiding duplication of effort and assembling a critical mass of R & D resources that might exceed the reach of individual companies; allowing cooperation on R & D projects also may elicit higher levels of investment in inventive activity by increasing the ability of the venture's participants to appropriate the returns to innovations that the venture generates. Finally, joint ventures can enable firms to spread the risk associated with undertaking financially ambitious projects.

Against these benefits one must weigh some potentially serious competitive risks. Collaboration among direct rivals may discourage the pursuit of promising independent approaches to solving product design, development, or marketing problems, although this danger is diminished if a sufficient number of independent centers of design, production, and sales activity is preserved. Cf. United States v. Automobile Mfrs. Ass'n (1969) (consent decree barring cooperative efforts to delay and obstruct development of automobile pollution control devices). Cooperation on one project also might cause spillovers of cost, pricing, and design information that reduce the participants' inclination to compete aggressively against each other on other fronts. See United States v. Minnesota Mining & Mfg. Co. (1950).

To evaluate these alternative possibilities, antitrust law applies two related inquiries to joint ventures or similar forms of collaboration. The first is whether the act of joining together itself violates the antitrust laws. Detailed consideration of this subject is postponed until Chapter 9, which examines Section 7 of the Clayton Act—the principal anti-merger provision of the federal antitrust laws. Under Section 7, the focus is whether the new "partnership" will create market power or reinforce existing market power by eliminating actual or potential competition among the venturers. Note that joint ventures and mergers both are approaches for integrating the activities of distinct firms. Joint ventures differ from mergers mainly in the scope and duration of the parties' integration: joint ventures generally involve a less sweeping convergence of the parties' activities and a shorter unification of efforts. Each method has strengths and weaknesses as a solution to transaction cost problems that arise in organizing economic activity. Where superior efficiency is the parties' goal, antitrust policy should avoid creating incentives for firms to favor one organizational method over the other. This requires care to ensure that rules governing joint ventures and mergers, respectively, do not distort the choice between contracts or consolidations.

The second basic inquiry (and the object of the discussion below) concerns the venture's purposes and effects. Analysis usually centers on whether group's objectives are legitimate, whether the venture unduly restricts the freedom of action of its participants, and whether the venture may properly refuse to grant access to new participants.

a. Characterizing the Venture and Evaluating Collateral Restraints

The threshold issue in evaluating a collective arrangement asserted to be a joint venture is to characterize the concerted activity. Arrangements characterized as unadorned efforts to fix prices or allocate markets typically are subject to summary condemnation. On the other hand, behavior with plausible efficiency rationales is treated by a fuller reasonableness test whose complexity varies according to the degree of potential anticompetitive danger and the strength of claimed efficiencies.

Since World War II, joint venture cases have varied enormously in the skill with which courts have performed the characterization process. An important starting point is *Timken* (1951). In *Timken* the Supreme Court refused to accept the defendant's "joint venture" characterization of its agreement with a British entrepreneur to buy the stock of a British producer of roller bearings. After studying the arrangement's terms, which included worldwide price agreements and market allocation covenants, the

Court concluded that "prior decisions plainly establish that agreements providing for an aggregation of trade restraints such as those existing in this case are illegal under the [Sherman] Act." *Timken* remains sound authority for the proposition that firms cannot avoid summary condemnation for horizontal price-fixing or market allocation schemes simply by labelling their activities a "joint venture." See United States v. Dynalectric Co. (1988).

Several later cases applying *Timken* performed the characterization analysis with little comprehension of the business phenomena under consideration. In *Sealy* (1967), the Supreme Court examined the collective activities of a group of small manufacturers of mattresses which created the "Sealy" trademark and exploited it through joint advertising. The Court seemed to regard the combination as a legitimate collaboration, yet it classified as horizontal territorial divisions the contract provisions by which each participant agreed to confine its sales to an assigned area (in conjunction with a retail price-fixing clause). The Court treated these restrictions as forbidden under the rule in *Timken*. To the Court, the territorial division offered no benefits to be weighed against its harm to competition.

The Court took an even more rigid and questionable approach in *Topco* (1972). There a group of regional grocery chains formed a joint buying association to promote and market private label goods in competition with similar goods offered by the national food chains. As in *Sealy,* the Court assumed the combination itself to be lawful. Here also the Court used a per se rule to strike down territorial restrictions that assured each participant that its co-venturers would not use the private brand to compete with it. The Court scorned suggestions that it assess the justifications for the challenged restrictions, stating that a more elaborate reasonableness standard would "leave courts free to ramble through the wilds of economic theory in order to maintain a flexible approach."

Sealy and *Topco* have been analyzed and criticized sharply (see Chapter 5), and that examination will not be repeated here. Note, however, that in each case a group of smaller firms had combined to obtain efficiencies enjoyed by larger competitors, but without permanently merging into a larger firm. The economic question which the Court declined to consider [7] was whether the restrictive provisions (protecting the territorial allocation to each joint venturer) were necessary for the venture to operate effectively and whether the harms of those provisions outweighed their gains.

The main analytical flaw of these decisions is their failure to appreciate how contractual restrictions can increase the efficiency of cooperative activity. Both *Sealy* and *Topco* recognized that the transaction in question involved more than a "naked" restraint on output. In neither case, however, did the Court apprehend that the territorial restrictions were *collateral* to and supportive of the venture's legitimate aims. Any cooperative activity entails difficult transactional problems because the co-venturers bring differing capabilities, firm cultures, and management styles to bear on the governance and operation of a collective enterprise. See Armen A. Alchian & Harold Demsetz, *Production, Information Costs, and Economic Organization,* 62 Am. Econ. Rev. 777 (1972); Joseph F. Brodley, *Joint Ventures and Antitrust Policy,* 95 Harv. L. Rev. 1521, 1529 (1982). Contractual restrictions in joint ventures often increase the efficiency of the collaboration by reducing

---

7. Later Supreme Court decisions have taken a more sanguine view of the courts' ability to evaluate efficiency claims. See *Sylvania* (1977); cf. *Aspen* (1985) (emphasizing absence of efficiency justification for dominant firm's exclusionary conduct).

transaction costs—particularly by discouraging opportunism (e.g., free-riding) by the venture's participants. See Oliver E. Willamson, *The Economic Institutions of Capitalism* 85–130 (1985); Benjamin Klein, Robert A. Crawford & Armen A. Alchian, *Vertical Integration, Appropriable Rents, and the Competitive Contracting Process,* 21 J.L. & Econ. 297 (1978).

Much of the academic scholarship that demonstrates how collateral restrictions can serve legitimate ends in a joint venture began to emerge in the 1960s. However, even some earlier joint venture cases grasped the basic intuition of what became known as transaction cost economics and applied it in a way that contrasts starkly with the reasoning of *Sealy* and *Topco.* One example is United States v. Morgan (1953), where the court examined the practice of investment bankers of forming underwriting syndicates when they sell new issues of securities. During the initial offering, the syndicate agrees with the issuer on the price at which the security will be offered to the public; this supports their effort to attract capital by marketing the stock in "an orderly way." The court held that this joint support of the new issue market did not unreasonably restraint trade. The court relied on the combine's short-term nature and its necessity. After the issue was "floated," the combine ended, and new syndicates comprised of differing firms constantly were formed. Even more significant, the syndicate helped raise entrepreneurial capital at a low cost. The government was unable to point to any equally efficient alternative for raising capital; without the price-fixing provisions, it was highly unlikely that an investment banker would take the risk of underwriting a major issue.

Morgan anticipated analytical developments that increasingly have come to shape the evaluation of joint ventures. The Supreme Court has not overruled its cases that tend to equate collateral restraints with naked price-fixing or market allocation schemes. Nonetheless, the Court's decisions since the mid–1970's have adopted an economically oriented approach that takes a more tolerant view of restrictions that are ancillary to an integration of economic activities. See Joseph Kattan, *Antitrust Analysis of Technology Joint Ventures,* 61 Antitrust L.J. 937, 956–63 (1993). The Court has not invariably sustained such restrictions, but it has relied more heavily on the rule of reason to determine their legality. See *BMI* (rejecting per se illegality for horizontal agreement setting prices for copyrighted materials); *NCAA* (applying rule of reason to assess horizontal output restrictions imposed by a joint venture). These decisions have caused lower courts to assess collateral restraints in similar ways. See, e.g., *Northrop* (1983) (rejecting rule of per se illegality to assess joint venture that compelled a horizontal allocation of customers).

The emerging rule of reason inquiry for collateral restraints has essentially three elements. First, do the joint venture participants have market power? If not, competitive hazards arising even from seemingly onerous collateral restrictions are likely to be small. See *Rothery* (1986) (defendant's 6 percent market share permitted conclusive presumption of validity for collateral restrictions ancillary to bona fide joint venture). Where the market power of the venture participants is substantial, courts treat collateral restrictions more skeptically. See *Berkey* (1979).

Second, do the collateral restrictions serve to increase or reduce the joint venture's total output? In *BMI* the Supreme Court refused to apply a per se rule to price setting in blanket licenses for musical compositions because "the agreement on price is necessary to market the product at all." The challenged restrictions in *BMI* boosted the use of compositions by reducing transaction costs that parties otherwise would incur in obtaining individual licenses. In many instances, restrictions on the participants' ability to engage in competing projects may improve the venture's performance by discouraging each firm from shirking in its contributions to the venture and from trying to free-ride on its partners' efforts. For example, without such limits, a participant in an R & D joint venture might seek to reduce promised contributions (e.g., data, know-how, and first-rate personnel) to the venture and instead devote its best resources to projects whose returns it can appropriate exclusively. See William B. Burnett & William E. Kovacic, *Reform of United States Weapons Acquisition Policy: Competition, Teaming Arrangements, and Dual–Sourcing,* 6 Yale J. Reg. 249, 276–77 (1989). However, collateral restraints that limit the participants' independent behavior and lack a substantial connection to the attainment of the venture's legitimate goals remain vulnerable to successful attack.

Third, could the participants have used less restrictive means to achieve the venture's valid aims? The need to ensure the venture's efficient operation ordinarily will not justify unlimited restrictions on the participants' discretion. See, e.g., Los Angeles Mem. Coliseum Comm'n v. National Football League (1984) (collateral limitation equivalent to horizontal allocation of territories unjustified where less restrictive alternative existed). The co-venturers generally will not be required to choose the *least* restrictive means for accomplishing legitimate purposes, but the venture may be required to show that its choice of restrictions was reasonable, given an array of possible approaches for reducing intrateam transaction costs. See Robert Pitofsky, *A Framework for Antitrust Analysis of Joint Ventures,* 54 Antitrust L.J. 893, 911 (1986).

b. *Treatment of Outside Entities*

Cooperative ventures that develop commercially useful products or production processes may attract demands by nonparticipants for inclusion in the joint venture or access to the fruits of its work. As a venture becomes increasingly successful and attains a degree of market power, the group may be required to accept competing firms as members or adequately explain why it refused to do so. In Associated Press v. United States (1945), the publishers of 1,200 newspapers who had formed a newsgathering organization were ordered to eliminate restrictive membership rules that gave each member exclusive rights to AP stories in its locale and authorized each member to exclude competitors from membership. The Supreme Court viewed the arrangement as an agreement to exclude competitors, noting that the parties had not demonstrated that the restrictions were needed to achieve newsgathering scale economies. On the other hand, neither the parties nor the Court considered the influence of this restriction in providing members with incentives to gather local news for the AP. Nor was there evidence that AP's market power was so great that the denial of access to nonmembers of AP-developed news could suppress competition; without market power the exclusive dealing provision would generally be upheld. In *Silver* (1963), the Court used the Sherman Act to impose a due process-type "duty to explain and afford an opportunity to answer [charges]" before the Exchange could sever private telephone wire connections with a nonmember broker.

More recent decisions have suggested that a refusal to allow participation or access might provoke an antitrust challenge based on two related theories. The first is the essential facility theory (see Chapter 4) which prohibits a monopolist's refusal to allow access to a facility whose availability is vital to the ability of rival firms to compete in upstream or downstream markets. The second is the ban on group boycotts (see Chapter 5), which prohibits certain collective refusals to deal. See SCFC ILC, Inc. v. Visa U.S.A., Inc. (1993) (refusing to reverse jury verdict against credit card joint venture for excluding the owner of a competing credit card from participating in the joint venture).

The specific requirements of these theories of liability differ, but they share two important operative ingredients. Both rely on a showing of market power to trigger close scrutiny unless the specific aim of the challenged activity is to restrict output and raise prices. Thus, if the venture lacks market power with respect to some important competitive characteristic (e.g., a technology or manufacturing process), it is unlikely that a denial of a demand for access will create liability. Both theories also foreclose liability when the defendant can establish a reasonable business justification for an outright refusal to allow access or for imposing terms of access that the nonparticipant deems oppressive. Joint ventures are allowed to set and enforce membership rules as long as the rules are fair, reasonable, and "substantially related to efficiency enhancing or procompetitive purposes that otherwise justify the [venture's] practices." *Northwest Wholesale* (1985). For example, charging a substantial entry fee for access may be appropriate to prevent free-riding by risk-averse outsiders who wait until the venture's success is assured before seeking to join. In general terms, the emphasis on market power and business justifications coincides with the approach the Supreme Court has taken in *Aspen* (1985) and *Kodak* (1992) in determining the duty of individual firms to continue to deal with their rivals under Section 2 of the Sherman Act.

c. *Recent Representative Illustrations*

The modern direction of joint venture analysis can be discerned from two noteworthy matters. The first is the FTC's decision approving a consent settlement that allowed the *GM–Toyota* joint venture. General Motors Corp. (1984). The Commission permitted GM, the largest seller of passenger cars in the U.S. and the world, to form a joint venture with Toyota, which was the third largest seller of passenger cars world-wide, the largest foreign seller in the U.S., and the fourth largest seller in the U.S. Under the agreement, the venture would manufacture between 200,-000 to 250,000 subcompacts at an idle GM plant in California; the price was to be set by the parent companies. As a condition of its approval, the FTC limited the agreement to 12 years and otherwise sought to keep the parent companies competitive. The FTC emphasized the arrangement's procompetitive features, especially the opportunity for GM to learn about more efficient Japanese manufacturing and management methods. See John E. Kwoka, Jr., *International Joint Venture: General Motors and Toyota,* in The Antitrust Revolution 46 (John E. Kwoka, Jr. & Lawrence J. White eds. 1989). The *GM–Toyota* decision marked a major departure from earlier, more hostile FTC treatments of joint ventures. See Yamaha Motor Co. v. FTC (1981) (enforcing FTC order barring joint venture on ground that the venture illegally divided markets). In 1993 the FTC granted General Motors' request to set aside the 1984 consent order, emphasizing the reduction in automobile industry concentration since 1984 and the efficiency gains that continuation of the joint venture would produce. See General Motors Corp., 5 Trade Reg. Rep. (CCH) ¶ 23,491 (FTC: Oct. 29, 1993).

The second illustration is Chicago Professional Sports Ltd. Partnership v. NBA (1992). Here the Chicago Bulls and WGN–TV used Section 1 to challenge the National Basketball Association for limiting "superstations" such as WGN to 20 broadcasts of NBA games per season. The plaintiffs argued that the NBA should be viewed as a cartel that had committed a per se violation of Section 1 by imposing a direct limit on the output of broadcast games. The NBA responded that it should be treated as a joint venture and that its broadcasting restrictions were lawful ancillary restraints. To begin its analysis, the Seventh Circuit said "[c]haracterization is a creative rather than exact endeavor" and noted three possible labels to apply to a sports league for Section 1 purposes: a single entity immune under Section 1 by reason of *Copperweld*; a joint venture whose activities largely enhance efficiency; or a joint venture whose conduct principally serves to reduce output. The Seventh Circuit concluded that the district court reasonably applied the third characterization to the NBA—"a joint venture in the production of games but more like a cartel in the sale of its output."

Because the NBA properly had been characterized as a joint venture, the Seventh Circuit said "the Rule of Reason supplies the framework for antitrust analysis" to evaluate the broadcast restrictions. Judge Easterbrook's opinion for the court relied on *NCAA* in concluding that "any agreement to reduce output measured by the number of televised games requires some justification—some explanation connecting the practice to consumers' benefits—before the court attempts an analysis of market power. Unless there are sound justifications, the court condemns the practice without ado, using the 'quick look' version of the Rule of Reason...." The court then assessed the NBA's asserted justifications, focusing on the league's claim that its television policy curbed free-riding by individual franchises on investments made by the league as a whole. Agreeing in principle that "[c]ontrol of free-riding is ... an accepted justification for cooperation," Judge Easterbrook nonetheless concluded that the avoidance of free-riding did not justify the broadcast limits, because the league could use (and sometimes did use) other mechanisms for charging individual teams for benefits conferred by the league. Thus, the court used a rule of reason approach to evaluate the challenged restrictions, but it applied a structured inquiry that focused initially on the adequacy of the defendant's justification for the restraints.

d. Legislative Reforms

Responding to concerns that antitrust horizontal restraints doctrine unduly discourages desirable collaborative R & D activity, Congress in 1984 enacted the National Cooperative Research Act. 15 U.S.C.A. §§ 4501–4505. To qualify for protection, co-venturers must notify the Justice Department and the FTC about the venture's content and goals. The statute provides that courts are to evaluate qualifying R & D joint ventures under a rule of reason, "taking into account all relevant facts affecting competition, including, but not limited to, effects on competition in properly defined relevant research and development markets." The statute limits the liability of co-venturers to actual (rather than treble) damages in successful private lawsuits where the challenged conduct falls within the scope of the statutory notification, and permits the taxing of attorneys fees against plaintiffs if the defendant substantially prevails in a litigated challenge against a notified venture.

In 1993, Congress extended the protection of the 1984 legislation to cover joint production ventures in what is now designated as the National Cooperative Research and Production Act. Protection for joint production ventures is available only if the venture's principal production facilities are located in the U.S. and the venture's participants are U.S. persons or foreign persons from countries that treat U.S. companies fairly under their antitrust laws governing joint production ventures.

CHAPTER VII

THE OLIGOPOLY PROBLEM

In Chapter 5, we briefly considered how oligopoly markets could generate supracompetitive pricing even though the sellers in such markets do not expressly agree on prices. The possibility that oligopolists might realize supranormal returns by recognizing their interdependence and accounting for their competitors' reactions when making output or pricing decisions poses a fundamental problem for antitrust rules designed to control, respectively, dominant firm exclusionary conduct and concerted action. No single firm has, or threatens to obtain, monopoly power; thus, the prohibitions of Section 2 of the Sherman Act are unavailing. At the same time, the mere fact of conscious parallelism does not constitute evidence of an agreement that would implicate Section 1.

Recognition of oligopoly's awkward place in antitrust analysis is roughly a half-century old. Intellectual and legal developments in the 1930s and 1940s converged to place the oligopoly question on antitrust's active agenda. One stimulus was the research of Edward Chamberlin and Henry Simons on firm behavior in concentrated industries. In describing pricing by oligopolists, Chamberlin concluded that "[s]ince the result of a cut by any one is inevitably to decrease his own profits, no one will cut, and although the sellers are entirely independent, the equilibrium result is the same as though there were a monopolistic agreement between them." Edward H. Chamberlin, *The Theory of*

Monopolistic Competition 48 (1933). One year later Simons proposed a program to restructure concentrated industries into smaller independent units. Henry C. Simons, *A Positive Program for Laissez Faire* (1934).

These works soon were followed by cases that meant courts would face more disputes involving oligopoly behavior. In *Interstate Circuit* (1939) and *American Tobacco* (1946), the Supreme Court suggested that Section 1 might supply a flexible tool for attacking interdependent parallel conduct. These decisions straddled *Socony* (1940), which banned all express agreements to "tamper" with prices and upheld a criminal conviction of the defendants. *Socony* raised the hazards of direct horizontal coordination and impelled firms to pursue more subtle ways to enlist the participation of rivals in foregoing aggressive price competition.

Since the 1940s, the Sherman Act's oligopoly gap has commanded considerable attention. This pattern promises to persist. Modern antitrust enforcement trends have made it likely that businesses often will operate in the gray fringe of doctrine that forbids rivals to act jointly to set prices or other terms of trade. Since the late 1970s, the Justice Department has devoted extensive resources to criminal prosecution of price-fixing and other per se illegal horizontal offenses. In the same period Congress raised the minimum Sherman Act fine for individuals from $100,-000 to $350,000 and for corporations from $3 million to $10 million. Congress also increased the maximum prison term for individuals from one year to three years, and guidelines promulgated by the United States Sentencing Commission have ensured that convicted antitrust defendants usually will serve time in prison. As a group, these measures have raised the likelihood that efforts by competitors to coordinate their conduct through a direct exchange of assurances will be detected, prosecuted, and penalized severely.

The growing dangers of explicit coordination have given firms strong incentives to rely more heavily on tactics that are less likely to elicit a government inquiry—especially a grand jury investigation—and may help achieve the same results as direct discussions of prices and output. Moreover, as explained below, there is an emerging scholarship that explains how indirect means of coordination may be effective substitutes for a direct exchange of assurances about future behavior.

A. ECONOMISTS AND THE OLIGOPOLY PROBLEM

Since the work of Chamberlin and Simons, economists have been instrumental in shaping antitrust's treatment of oligopolies. The past fifty years embrace three distinct phases in economic thinking about oligopoly. See Jonathan B. Baker, *Two Sherman Act Section 1 Dilemmas: Parallel Pricing, the Oligopoly Problem, and Contemporary Economic Theory*, 38 Antitrust Bull. 143 (1993). From the late 1940s through the 1960s, structuralist perspectives dominated industrial organization economics (see Chapter 4) and guided antitrust policy toward concentrated industries. The structural model viewed supracompetitive pricing in oligopolies as nearly inevitable because the small number of industry members either would expressly agree to raise prices or would achieve the same result solely through interdependent, follow-the-leader reactions to the conduct of rivals. To address the latter phenomenon—often termed "tacit collusion" or "administered pricing"—structuralists proposed a three-pronged antitrust strategy: (1) redefine the concept of "agreement" under the Sherman Act to reach purely interdependent parallel behavior; (2) strictly prohibit horizontal mergers that would create new, or reinforce existing, oligopolies; and (3) deconcentrate existing oligopolies by enforcing Section 2 or enacting a new law. The first and third methods received serious attention in the 1960s and 1970s, and the second approach animated horizontal merger policy until the 1980s.

In the 1970s and 1980s the structuralist consensus among economists crumbled, and Chicago School perspectives ascended. The Chicago School raised two basic objections to structuralist diagnoses of oligopoly. As described in Chapter 5, George Stigler's research in the mid–1960s on collusion underscored the difficulties that competitors face in forming and executing express agreements to curb output. Stigler pointed out that cartelists not only must choose a common price but also must detect and punish cheating. By implication, his work undercut the structuralist assumption that mere recognition of interdependence would move firms inexorably to raise price in parallel. If inherent centrifugal forces disintegrated *express* cartels, then *tacit* efforts to coordinate pricing were even more likely to unravel as industry members cheated on the "agreements" formed at arms-length. Cf. *Brook Group* ("Uncertainty is an oligopoly's greatest enemy."). The second objection came from Harold Demsetz, Yale Brozen, and others who cast doubt on earlier studies that posited a strong positive link between industry concentration and profitability. Their research demonstrated that not all firms in oligopoly markets enjoyed supranormal profits, suggesting that companies which achieved higher returns and larger market shares did so through superior performance—and not industrywide coordination.

Chicago School views had important policy implications and helped recast antitrust doctrine and enforcement policy toward concentrated industries in the late 1970s and throughout the 1980s. Because indirect coordination was deemed problematic and prone to fail, the federal antitrust agencies focused horizontal restraints enforcement on prosecuting direct agreements to restrict output. Courts and enforcement officials increasingly accepted the idea that large corporate size and concentration reflected superior efficiency. This induced caution in pursuing initiatives to disassemble firms in concentrated industries and prompted a relaxation of horizontal merger controls.

Since the early 1980s, many economists have reexamined Chicago-oriented assumptions about tacit coordination among oligopolists. See Dennis A. Yao & Susan S. DeSanti, *Game Theory and the Legal Analysis of Tacit Collusion,* 38 Antitrust Bull. 113 (1993). Stigler's model studied cartel coordination in the context of a single interaction among firms. More recent research treats the coordination problem not as a "one-shot" encounter, but as a "repeated game" in which industry participants expect to face each other again and again over time. In some economic models, moving from a one-shot game to a repeated game makes it more likely that firms will coordinate their behavior without an express agreement. See C. Shapiro, *Theories of Oligopoly Behavior,* at 356–81.

Successful coordination in such models depends on how well firms perform two basic tasks. The first is to identify observable principles ("focal points") around which firms can organize their pricing decisions. See D. Kreps, *Course in Microeconomic Theory,* at 414–16. For example, a firm might publish a price book listing the formulas it uses to compute prices for its various products and might then introduce price increases by announcing that it will impose a common percentage increase for a given group of products. The price book tells rivals how the firm will compute its prices, and the common percentage increase shows how much it will raise prices. This reveals the specific pricing "solution" that the firm seeks to achieve among all possible price hikes. The second task is to convince competitors that the firm will punish rivals who do not organize their behavior according to suggested focal points. As noted in Chapter 5, firms can use various tactics to make credible threats to punish deviations. Thus, by putting "meeting competition" or "meet or release" clauses in its contracts, a supplier can detect price cuts by rivals and commit itself to respond in kind. See Steven C. Salop, *Practices that (Credibly) Facilitate Oligopoly Co-ordination,* in New Developments in the Analysis of Market Structure 279–82 (Joseph E. Stiglitz & G. Frank Mathewson eds. 1986).

Recent refinements of Stigler's model of collusion are influencing antitrust policy toward oligopolies in two basic ways. One is to increase attention to tactics that firms can use to signal their intent to adhere to a course of conduct and facilitate coordination with other industry members. Tacit collusion mechanisms and facilitating practices have figured prominently in recent federal enforcement initiatives and will receive close attention from the FTC and the Justice Department in the future. See American Home Products (1992) (alleging conspiracy to raise prices of infant formula); United States v. Airline Tariff Publishing Co. (1992) (alleging conspiracy to raise commercial airline ticket prices). A second effect has been to alter the analysis of mergers between direct rivals. As discussed in Chapter 9, the federal Merger Guidelines account for the amenability of post-merger markets to interfirm coordination that does not involve a conventional exchange of assurances.

B. LEGAL APPROACHES TO THE CONTROL OF OLIGOPOLIES

Antitrust doctrine and enforcement policy have taken several paths to frustrate efforts by oligopolists to coordinate their behavior by means other than a direct exchange of assurances.

1. EXPANDING THE DEFINITION OF "AGREEMENT" UNDER SECTION 1 OF THE SHERMAN ACT

The oligopoly problem has focused attention on whether parallel pricing that flows from the oligopolists' recognition of interdependence constitutes concerted behavior within the meaning of Section 1. For a brief period, the Supreme Court suggested that it could. In *Interstate Circuit* (1939), after ruling that the trial court properly found an agreement among the film distributors, the Court said that "in the circumstances of this case such agreement ... was not a prerequisite to an unlawful conspiracy. It was enough that, knowing that concerted action was contemplated and invited, the distributors gave their adherence to the scheme and participated in it." This comment suggested that Section 1 might reach oligopoly pricing because each seller knows that its rivals account for its reactions and that oligopoly pricing succeeds only if all firms "participate" by selling above their marginal costs. Such an interpretation seemed the only way to explain why the Court stated an alternative basis for the decision since, as the Court acknowledged, circumstantial evidence in the record sustained the trial court's finding of a conspiracy.

The Court again highlighted the elastic potential of the agreement concept in *American Tobacco* (1946) where, in considering conspiracy to monopolize charges under Section 2, it held that a finding of concerted action is justified if the "conspirators had a unity of purpose or a common design and understanding, or a meeting of minds in an unlawful arrangement." Perhaps a pattern of follow-the-leader pricing in a concentrated industry could supply acceptable proof of the requisite "unity of purpose."

The possibility that the Supreme Court would pull purely interdependent parallel pricing within Section 1's reach was short-lived. In *Theatre Enterprises* (1954), the Court disavowed the expansive implications of its earlier decisions: "[T]his Court has never held that proof of parallel business behavior conclusively establishes agreement or, phrased differently, that such behavior itself constitutes a Sherman Act offense. . . . 'conscious parallelism' has not yet read conspiracy out of the Sherman Act entirely." *Theatre Enterprises* was widely seen as an important shift in judicial analysis of oligopolistic behavior. Later Supreme Court decisions displayed the continuing influence of the structuralists' view of oligopoly, but none posed difficult problems in finding an agreement.

The progression from *Interstate Circuit* to *Theatre Enterprises* inspired a famous debate in the 1960s about the application of Section 1 to oligopoly behavior. The contestants were Donald Turner, a Harvard Law School professor who served as Assistant Attorney General for Antitrust in the mid–1960s, and Richard Posner, a professor at the University of Chicago Law School and subsequently a court of appeals judge. Endorsing the approach of *Theatre Enterprises,* Turner argued that interdependent behavior should not be interpreted as an illegal conspiracy under Section 1. Donald F. Turner, *The Definition of Agreement Under the Sherman Act: Conscious Parallelism and Refusals to Deal,* 75 Harv. L. Rev. 655 (1962). Turner argued that an oligopolist behaves exactly as a seller in a competitive industry, except that it also accounts for its rivals' reactions. From this he concluded that it would be unreasonable to interpret the Sherman Act to condemn rational and unavoidable behavior.

Even if oligopoly behavior were held illegal, Turner doubted that any remedy available under Section 1 would prove effective. Injunctive relief that directed defendants to ignore their rivals would be anomalous, for it would order them to make irrational price and output decisions. Commanding firms to price their goods at their marginal costs (i.e., as if the market were competitive) would involve the courts in continuous regulation for which they are ill-equipped. Cf. *Alcoa* (1945). Nor would dissolution or other structural solutions seem appropriate since the essence of the Section 1 offense would be the interdependence theory, and this relies on the seller's conduct (interdependent pricing) rather than market structure as ultimately being responsible for the result. In a separate paper, Turner contended that the proper solution to the oligopoly problem would be to restructure oligopolists into smaller units, either by charging them with joint monopolization under Section 2 or by adopting special legislation. See Donald F. Turner, *The Scope of Antitrust and Other Economic Regulatory Policies,* 82 Harv. L. Rev. 1207, 1217–31 (1969).

That these analytical difficulties might be overcome by an alternative theory was suggested by Judge Posner. See Richard A. Posner, *Oligopoly and the Antitrust Laws: A Suggested Approach,* 21 Stan. L. Rev. 1562 (1969). Posner pointed out that oligopoly markets involve concerted action in that they manifest a tacit output agreement among sellers. In a concentrated market, sellers must act voluntarily to translate their mutual dependence into oligopoly prices. This constitutes a meeting of the minds even though there is no overt communication among sellers. Each seller communicates its offer to the others by restricting output (and thereby maintains its prices above marginal cost). If oligopoly pricing is to succeed, the seller's rivals must cooperate by curbing their output, as well. Therefore Posner argued that since "tacit collusion or non-competitive pricing is not inherent in an oligopolist market structure but, like conventional cartelizing, requires additional, voluntary behavior by the sellers," it violates Section 1. Id. at 1578.

Nor did Posner find the problem of formulating an effective remedy under Section 1 insoluble. Such tacit collusion is not significantly different from formal cartel arrangements supported by an express agreement—other than it is easier to conceal. He contended that simple remedies might increase the costs of tacit collusion. Oligopoly behavior is avoidable; fearing that rivals will cheat or otherwise not react "rationally," firms in such markets constantly face a choice of whether to participate whenever they make output and pricing decisions. Consequently, injunctive relief would not be unwieldy or impractical. Oligopoly compliance could be tested by the seller's rate of return as compared with the risk and return in other markets. As Posner conceded, this raised the difficult question of what proof establishes tacit collusion that violates Section 1 since, by definition, evidence of explicit communication will be unavailable.

On the whole, Turner's position in the debate has prevailed in subsequent judicial treatments of the agreement issue in Section 1 litigation involving oligopolies. Courts consistently have held that conscious parallelism alone does not support an inference of agreement. It bears repeating, however, that judges enjoy substantial discretion to define the "extra ingredient of centralized orchestration of policy which will carry parallel action over the line into the forbidden zone of implied contract and combination." Louis B. Schwartz, John J. Flynn & Harry First, *Free Enterprise and Economic Organization: Antitrust* 439 (6th ed. 1981). After reciting the *Theatre Enterprises* admonition that conscious parallelism is not enough, some decisions have gone to great lengths to identify additional behavior from which an inference of agreement might be inferred.

Despite reluctance to accept his prescription, Posner's proposal has not wanted for influence. His views have helped lead antitrust officials to reexamine business behavior at the periphery of Section 1's agreement requirement. In the mid–1970s, for example, the Justice Department charged that General Electric and Westinghouse had curtailed price competition in the sale of turbine generators through the "conscious adoption and publication of identical pricing." The two firms were alleged (a) to have used price books that covered all features of the complex electrical machinery and provided formulas for computing prices, (b) to have routinely made public announcements concerning all outstanding orders and prices, and (c) to have adopted "price protection plans" that ensured all customers that they would receive the benefit of discounts given to any one purchaser. The government argued that such behavior supported an inference that the two firms had agreed to pursue a common strategy to eliminate price rivalry. The defendants accepted a consent decree that barred them from disseminating pricing information from which each company could monitor its rival's pricing practices. United States v. General Electric Co. & Westinghouse Elec. Corp. (1977). The firms admitted that they charged identical prices, but contended that this resulted simply from conscious parallelism.

If *GE–Westinghouse* had been litigated to a conclusion on the merits, each side would have had high cards to play at trial. The government was prepared to introduce internal company documents showing that GE regarded its public announcements as invitations for Westinghouse to cooperate and that Westinghouse understood them to be so. On the other hand, GE and Westinghouse could have pointed to a recent decision in which government failed in an effort to depict a pattern of public price announcements by rival automobile producers as an agreement to fix prices. In United States v. General Motors Corp. (1974), the court exonerated the defendants, observing that "[t]he public announcement of a pricing decision cannot be twisted into an invitation or signal to conspire; it is instead an economic reality to which all other competitors must react."

2. SECTION 2 OF THE SHERMAN ACT

Section 2 has proven a largely unsuitable means for attacking oligopoly pricing. The ban against monopolization seems unavailing since no single oligopolist ordinarily has monopoly power. Section 2's ban against conspiracies to monopolize briefly emerged as a possibility in *American Tobacco* (1946), but the Supreme Court's restrictive interpretation of the agreement requirement in the Section 1 context in *Theatre Enterprises* logically extended to Section 2 conspiracy claims, as well. One modern decision suggests that the Section 2 offense of attempted monopolization reaches direct interaction between firms in concentrated markets even though such interaction does not result in an agreement. In United States v. American Airlines, Inc. (1984), the Fifth Circuit sustained an attempted monopolization claim against American Airlines arising from a failed effort by American's chief executive officer to persuade his counterpart at Braniff Airlines by telephone to collaborate in setting prices for routes on which the two firms competed. The Braniff executive rejected the proposal, but taped the telephone conversation and gave the tape to the Justice Department. American argued that an illegal attempt could be found only if the two executives had agreed to raise prices. In rejecting this view, the Fifth Circuit stated that if the Braniff official had accepted the American executive's offer to set prices, "the two airlines, at the moment of acceptance, would have acquired monopoly power. At the same moment, the offense of joint monopolization would have been complete."

3.   SECTION 5 OF THE FEDERAL TRADE COMMISSION ACT

The FTC has authority under Section 5 of the FTC Act to prosecute conduct that violates the Sherman Act. Section 5's ban upon "unfair methods of competition" also enables the Commission to challenge conduct that infringes the "spirit or policy" of the Sherman Act or constitutes an "incipient" violation of the Sherman Act. See FTC v. Sperry & Hutchinson Co. (1972).

Section 5's elastic properties have made it a recurring source of interest as a means to challenge interfirm coordination that eludes the Sherman Act. The FTC has tried several approaches to apply Section 5 against oligopolistic behavior. One group of cases has used Section 5 to challenge express and tacit agreements to implement facilitating practices such as the industry-wide use of base-point pricing. In these cases, the conduct arguably also was amenable to challenge as an illegal agreement under Section 1 of the Sherman Act, and reliance on Section 5 was not essential to successful prosecution of the FTC's complaint. In a second group of disputes, the FTC has mixed conspiracy counts with claims that the behavior violated Section 5 even if undertaken unilaterally. When liability has been established, such cases have relied heavily on the finding of an agreement and usually have failed to indicate clearly which liability standard is being applied (Section 1 or Section 5), or to specify what evidence would establish a violation of Section 5 alone. In a third set of cases, the FTC has attacked conduct without seeking to prove an agreement. Courts in these cases have acknowledged that the FTC has authority to condemn purely unilateral conduct, but no decision has found liability on the evidence advanced by the Commission.

Several cases illustrate the application of Section 5 and the FTC's limited success in using this measure to address oligopoly behavior. In FTC v. Cement Institute (1948), the Supreme Court upheld an FTC order barring cement producers from using delivered prices that included transportation calculated from a standard point (often a location other than where the goods were made and shipped). While the Court ruled that there was substantial evidence in the record to support the FTC's conclusion that cement sellers had agreed with each other to establish this pricing system, it also observed (in footnote 19) that this "does not mean that existence of a 'combination' is an indispensable ingredient of an 'unfair method of competition' under the Trade Commission Act." The Court went on to acknowledge "marked differences between what a court must decide in a Sherman Act proceeding and the duty of the Commission in determining whether conduct is to be classified as an unfair method of competition." However, the Court gave no further guidance about what criteria should be applied when the FTC proceeds under Section 5 without relying on Sherman Act jurisprudence.

In the 1970s the Commission initiated a number of matters to challenge oligopoly behavior. The FTC charged leading makers of ready-to-eat cereals and the nation's eight leading petroleum refiners with the collective possession of monopoly power and exclusionary activity in violation of Section 5. The complaints in the cereal and petroleum cases sought divestitures that would have restructured the affected industries into a larger number of business units. Both initiatives were conceived as innovative efforts to undo oligopoly market structures and eliminate supracompetitive pricing. Instead, each consumed massive resources and ended in sobering failure. In Exxon Corp. (1981), after eight years of pretrial proceedings, the Commission dismissed its complaint, conceding that the completion of pretrial discovery alone was "at least several years away." In Kellogg Co. (1982), the administrative law judge dismissed the FTC's complaint after a full trial on the merits; the Commission later vacated the ALJ's decision and dismissed the complaint without an opinion.

In Boise Cascade Corp. v. FTC (1980), the Commission renewed its assault on delivered pricing by challenging softwood plywood producers for using rail freight charges from the Pacific Northwest in determining the price of plywood produced in the southern United States. The Ninth Circuit ruled that the industry-wide basing-point scheme did not violate Section 5 because the Commission had failed to provide evidence of either an "overt agreement" to engage in basing-point pricing or proof that the challenged scheme "actually had the effect of fixing or stabilizing prices." Soon afterwards, in a private treble damage case involving the same conduct, the Fifth Circuit ruled that evidence of identical delivered pricing practices *plus* contacts among the participants showing they had an opportunity to conspire was enough to allow a jury to find an agreement under Section 1 of the Sherman Act. See In re Plywood Antitrust Litigation (1981). However, the significance of this ruling may be limited by the the subsequent procedural history of the case. The Justice Department filed an amicus brief in the Supreme Court arguing that additional evidence was necessary before mere tacit collusion could support the finding of a conspiracy (for example, that the action served the participants' self-interest only if all went along). The parties reached a settlement, and the writ was dismissed.

The FTC's efforts to use Section 5 to attack facilitating practices without collusion culminated in Ethyl Corp. (1983). In *Ethyl* the Commission alleged that the nation's four producers of gasoline antiknock compounds had engaged in various facilitating practices, including 30-day advance announcements of price changes, "most favored nation" clauses in sales contracts assuring buyers the benefit of subsequent price cuts, and uniform delivered prices. The FTC conceded that each firm adopted the practices "independently and unilaterally." Nonetheless, the agency concluded that, by removing some uncertainty from the market, the practices had facilitated parallel pricing at supracompetitive levels. The Second Circuit denied enforcement of the FTC's order, ruling that "noncollusive, nonpredatory and independent conduct of a nonartificial nature" did not violate Section 5. Before a practice could be deemed "unfair" under Section 5, the Commission was required to establish that the behavior was "oppressive"—a condition that could be inferred only from "(1) evidence of an anticompetitive intent or purpose on the part of the producer charged, or (2) the absence of an independent legitimate business reason for the conduct." Thus, the court held that "[t]he mere existence of an oligopolistic market structure in which a small group of manufacturers engage in consciously parallel pricing of an identical product does not violate the antitrust laws."

4. INVITATIONS TO COLLUDE

As noted above, *American Airlines* established the availability of the attempted monopolization cause of action under Section 2 of the Sherman Act as a basis for challenging invitations by firms in concentrated markets to engage in collusive pricing. Recent FTC and Justice Department enforcement initiatives have used novel approaches to address invitations to collude where conduct does not constitute an agreement subject to Section 1 scrutiny. Although these matters do not deal specifically with oligopolies, they use liability theories that could readily be applied to firms in such markets.

In Quality Trailer Products Corp. (1992), the FTC charged a producer of axles with violating Section 5 by inviting a competitor to fix prices. The Commission alleged that the defendant had criticized its rival for charging low prices and had suggested that the two firms agree to maintain their prices above specific levels. In announcing a consent agreement, the FTC called the invitation to collude an unfair method of competition even though the competitor had spurned the request. The FTC emphasized that such requests, in the absence of a plausible efficiency rationale, posed serious anticompetitive risks.

In United States v. Ames Sintering Co. (1990) (per curiam), the Justice Department used the federal wire fraud statute to challenge a firm's effort to use interstate telephone calls to enlist a competitor's participation in a bid-rigging plan. Noting that "Section [1] of the Sherman Act does not proscribe attempts," the Sixth Circuit upheld the defendant's conviction on the wire fraud counts.   Taken together, the *Quality Trailer* and *Ames Sintering* cases are suggestive of what is likely to be a continuing effort on the part of the federal enforcement agencies to challenge invitations to collude without resorting to Section 1.

5.   MERGER POLICY

Merger policy is a major element of antitrust's campaign against supracompetitive oligopolistic pricing.   Although detailed analysis of merger standards is reserved for Chapter 9, several preliminary observations are appropriate. Given difficulties in addressing interdependent parallel behavior in existing oligopolies, an important purpose of merger policy since the Celler–Kefauver Act of 1950 has been to discourage consolidations that would spawn new oligopolies or solidify already substantial levels of concentration.   While this general aim has remained largely constant, refinements of oligopoly theory have changed merger policy in two important ways.   Recognition of the difficulty that firms face in trying to coordinate behavior without directly exchanging assurances has helped move courts and enforcement agencies to tolerate greater concentration (and larger horizontal mergers) than were deemed acceptable twenty years ago.

A second effect has been to focus merger analysis more precisely on the evaluation of firm and industry characteristics that facilitate or frustrate explicit or tacit coordination. Current merger policy still rests heavily on the longstanding tenet of oligopoly theory that greater aggregate concentration yields a greater probability of successful interfirm coordination.   Although this assumption is the subject of extensive, contentious debate, merger analysis has become more sophisticated in seeking to explain why specific transactions would or would not be likely to facilitate a unilateral or collective exercise of market power.

6. PROPOSED LEGISLATIVE REFORMS

A final strategy that periodically has commanded close attention is to enact new legislation to deconcentrate oligopolies or directly attack instances of persistent monopoly power (see Chapter 4). Modern consideration of proposals to deconcentrate oligopolies originated in Carl Kaysen's and Donald Turner's *Antitrust Policy,* which appeared in 1959. Viewed as the leading synthesis of antitrust law and economics of its time, the Kaysen–Turner volume declared that "[t]he principal defect of present antitrust law is its inability to cope with market power created by jointly acting oligopolists." Id. at 110. The two scholars called for new legislation to restructure concentrated industries and provided the foundation for similar recommendations by a host of legislative committees, blue ribbon task forces, and individual commentators in the 1960s and 1970s. See W. Kovacic, *Failed Expectations: The Troubled Past and Uncertain Future of the Sherman Act as a Tool for Deconcentration,* at 1136–39. In general terms, the deconcentration proposals would have broken up oligopolistic industries unless existing concentration resulted solely from lawful patents or unless dissolution would cause the loss of substantial scale economies.

These deconcentration proposals yielded no legislation, but they had a powerful (and unintended) impact on the future direction of antitrust. These measures galvanized research and discussion concerning the structuralist assumptions that had guided antitrust policy since *Alcoa.* As the evidence (much of it assembled by Chicago School figures such as Yale Brozen, Harold Demsetz, and Richard Posner) began to mount that broad-based assaults on concentration were neither analytically justified nor costless, serious opposition arose within academia, government agencies, and the business community.

An important catalyzing event took place in 1974 in what came to be known as the Airlie House Conference. See *Industrial Concentration: The New Learning* (Harvey J. Goldschmid, H. Michael Mann & J. Fred Weston eds. 1974) (collecting papers and proceedings from the Airlie House Conference). At the Airlie House meeting, critics of structuralism synthesized a developing literature that challenged the economic basis for deconcentration. The results of the conference and related research were widely seen as refuting major elements of structuralist oligopoly theory and discrediting deconcentration. By drawing critical scrutiny to structuralism, the deconcentration proposals indirectly helped inject Chicago School views into the mainstream of antitrust analysis and thus helped foster a broader conservative redirection of antitrust.

CHAPTER VIII

VERTICAL RESTRAINTS

To this point, our examination of agreements between firms has focused on horizontal agreements—concerted acts that restrain competition between firms at the same level of production or distribution. We now shift to restraints imposed by the seller on the buyer (or vice versa) or on what is called a vertical relationship. For example, a car manufacturer usually operates at one level—production. The firm sells the cars it builds to dealers who, in turn, sell the vehicles to consumers at retail. Other industries feature extensive vertical integration through which firms operate at more than one level of commercial activity. Thus, many oil companies not only produce and refine crude oil, but also distribute gasoline through a mix of company-owned and franchised service stations.

Antitrust principles governing vertical arrangements have undergone extraordinary adjustment in the past thirty years. See E.T. Sullivan & J. Harrison, *Understanding Antitrust and its Economic Implications,* at 147. In 1966, as Assistant Attorney General for Antitrust, Donald Turner remarked that he approached vertical "territorial and customer restrictions not hospitably in the common law tradition, but inhospitably in the tradition of antitrust law." Donald F. Turner, *Some Reflections on Antitrust,* in 1966 N.Y. State Bar Association Antitrust Law Symposium 1, 1–2 (1966). Turner's comment captured the the prevailing attitude toward vertical restraints in an era in which the

Supreme Court expanded prohibitions against resale price maintenance (RPM) and tying arrangements and imposed draconian limits on vertical territorial restrictions, exclusive dealing agreements, and other distribution tactics. The Court's favored tool for condemnation often was a rule of per se illegality.

In Continental T.V., Inc. v. GTE Sylvania, Inc. (1977), the Supreme Court drew the era of acutely "inhospitable" antitrust treatment of vertical restraints to a close. In terms of doctrine, *Sylvania* held that the rule of reason governed vertical restraints other than RPM; more generally, the decision admonished judges to apply a rule of per se illegality only where the challenged conduct posed grave competitive dangers. As a model of analysis, *Sylvania* injected price theory into the mainstream of antitrust policy. Justice Lewis Powell's opinion for the Court drew heavily on recent, economically-oriented literature, observing that "an antitrust policy divorced from market considerations would lack any objective benchmarks."

Sylvania unquestionably improved antitrust analysis of vertical restraints. Nonetheless, *Sylvania* also has created—or at least contributed to—four basic problems treated in this Chapter. First, *Sylvania* drew a doctrinally important but logically frail distinction between resale price maintenance and so-called "nonprice" restraints. Subsequent decisions acknowledge that RPM and nonprice restrictions have similar economic effects, yet the Court repeatedly has upheld the per se rule for RPM first adopted in Dr. Miles Medical Co. v. John D. Park & Sons Co. (1911). Though it still pays homage to *Dr. Miles,* the Court has weakened the effect of the per se ban against RPM by putting formidable evidentiary and antitrust injury hurdles before plaintiffs who seek to avail themselves of *Dr. Miles* and its progeny.

Second, *Sylvania* extensively discussed the respective antitrust roles of per se rules and reasonableness tests. In doing so, the Court spoke of the two approaches as antonyms rather than as related elements of a unified analytical structure. Here the Court missed an opportunity to develop a new vocabulary that would help eliminate analytical distortions caused by the use of a binary classification scheme that channels conduct toward either summary condemnation or, as commonly perceived, an indeterminate reasonableness inquiry. This is more than a semantic quibble. Particularly in tying cases, the failure to recognize intermediate standards between these polar options has led courts to use the label of "per se illegality" to describe what should instead be called a structured rule of reason standard. The lack of a suitable nomenclature and related analytical framework poses a true risk of yielding perverse outcomes in specific cases.

Third, in prescribing a reasonableness standard for nonprice vertical restraints, *Sylvania* offered little guidance about the appropriate content of the rule of reason in vertical cases. Since *Chicago Bd. of Trade,* the Achilles heel of the rule of reason has been the lack of administrable approaches for ordering the analysis of relevant criteria. *Sylvania* failed to grapple with this issue, but subsequent lower court decisions have explored interesting approaches for structuring the rule of reason inquiry to minimize litigation costs while retaining a high probability of achieving economically sound results.

Finally, *Sylvania's* endorsement of an efficiency-based methodology for evaluating vertical restraints focused attention on the question of what goals antitrust should pursue. Justice Byron White's concurring opinion in *Sylvania* placed this adjustment in perspective:

[W]hile according some weight to the businessman's interest in controlling the terms on which he trades in his own goods may be anathema to those who view the Sherman Act as directed solely to economic efficiency, this principle is without question more deeply embedded in our cases than the notions of "free rider" effects and distributional efficiencies borrowed by the majority from the "new economics of vertical relationships." Perhaps the Court is right in partially abandoning this principle and in judging the instant nonprice vertical restraints solely by their "relevant economic impact"; but the precedents which reflect this principle should not be so lightly rejected by the Court.

As this comment suggests, vertical restraints disputes often highlight the tension between efficiency and the populist vision of ensuring the well-being of individual entrepreneurs, especially small firms. *Sylvania* and later Court decisions have strengthened the hand of large consumer goods manufacturers in their dealings with small retailers. In doing so, such cases have unleashed strong political forces to reverse the post-*Sylvania* judicial retrenchment of vertical restraints doctrine and to reinvigorate public enforcement against restrictive distribution practices. See Jean Wegman Burns, *Vertical Restraints, Efficiency, and the Real World*, 52 Fordham L.Rev. 597 (1993).

Thus, perhaps more than any other area of antitrust law, the evolution of vertical restraints doctrine displays the influence of economics on legal standards and reveals the collision of rival views about antitrust's proper goals. The development of standards for vertical practices also illuminates issues that we first encountered in examining horizontal restraints in Chapters 5 and 6 above—particularly the tension between per se and rule of reason tests, the content of a reasonableness inquiry, and the Supreme

Court's recent tendency to adjust evidentiary and antitrust injury requirements to moderate the effect of nominally potent liability standards.

A. TRANSACTION COST ECONOMICS AND VERTICAL RELATIONSHIPS

Whether or not a firm integrates vertically by owning and operating assets in two or more stages of production or levels of distribution usually depends on relative operating costs or efficiencies.[1] If internal integration is cheaper, the firm will tend to integrate and operate at both the manufacturing and retailing levels; on the other hand, the firm will operate at only one level and will not expand vertically if recourse to intermediate market transactions is less costly. See O. Williamson, *Transaction Cost Economics,* at 150–59. Vertical integration usually results from the firm's effort to achieve efficiencies—i.e., lower costs—not available to it with other market arrangements such as contracts. Other reasons may exist, but they are less likely to be controlling.

Similar transactional savings frequently are sought by firms that integrate vertically on a less formal basis—that is, through contracts. A firm may seek a stable supply or output by arranging a long-term exclusive dealing agreement or by requiring that dealers buying its product for resale concentrate sales and advertising efforts within assigned territories. On the other hand, such restraints—especially where they seek to restrict the price at which the dealer may resell the product—may merely mask efforts by manufacturers or dealers to fix prices horizontally. Or the

1. This discussion assumes a simple two-level distribution model consisting of manufacturers and retailers. More complex industry configurations that include wholesalers, jobbers, and other service providers are common.

producer may attempt to extract a monopoly price at retail because it cannot do so at the manufacturing point.

Vertical contractual arrangements often serve to increase efficiency. Occasionally they may be part of an effort to enhance a firm's market power, while others lie somewhere between these poles. Until 1977, antitrust cases often ignored such distinctions and presumed that vertical contractual restraints had sinister aims. See United States v. Arnold, Schwinn & Co. (1967). Courts often evaluated vertical restraints by applying rules that governed similar conduct in a horizontal context; thus, vertical price-fixing and territorial restraints were generally prohibited under a per se-type rule. Since *Sylvania* in 1977, vertical restraints other than RPM have been judged under a rule of reason standard.

The vertical restraints considered here fall into two categories: those restricting the distribution of a product and those excluding or foreclosing competing firms from a market. Typical of the former is RPM by which a manufacturer specifies a minimum price at which her product can be resold to retail consumers. Examples of the latter are tying clauses in which the manufacturer conditions the sale of one product on the buyer's purchase of a second product from her. Conceptually these practices are distinct, even though antitrust law often lumps them together. Distribution restraints in essence are agreements by firms to eliminate some competition among themselves; thus they are analogous to price or territorial cartels. On the other hand, exclusionary practices are attempts to exclude rivals through agreements between buyers and sellers rather than by a seller offering products at lower prices. Many boycott cases examined in Chapter 5, therefore, fall in this category.

As a final preliminary point, one should keep in mind that vertical contractual restraints and vertical integration often are substitutes for one another. In organizing production and distribution, the firm must decide which activities it can best conduct internally and which functions are best contracted out to separate business entities. Antitrust policy should treat these approaches consistently to permit the firm to choose the mix of strategies that minimizes transaction costs. See M. Katz, *Vertical Contractual Relations,* at 715.

B. RESTRICTIONS ON DISTRIBUTION

1. RESALE PRICE MAINTENANCE (RPM)

The earliest vertical restraints antitrust cases involved efforts by manufacturers to set prices below which retailers could not subsequently resell their products. In the still leading case of Dr. Miles Medical Co. v. John D. Park & Sons Co. (1911), a manufacturer of a proprietary medicine (produced by a secret, but unpatented, formula) sued a wholesaler on the ground that the latter obtained the plaintiff's medicine at cut prices by inducing others to breach their price agreements with Dr. Miles. The Court ruled that a manufacturer who sells goods to a wholesaler may not restrict their resale by constraining the buyer's pricing decisions. Relying on the common law's hostility towards equitable servitudes on chattels, the Court noted that "a general restraint upon alienation is ordinarily invalid" and where its purpose is to destroy competition by fixing prices the restraint is "injurious to the public interest and void."

The Court's views of common law doctrines governing the alienability of property rights and the legal status of RPM were questionable. RPM is not a "general restraint upon alienation," for it does not bar the transfer of the retailer's property interest; it only limits pricing opportunities, not resale. Moreover, equivalent common law protections are still available to limit the purchaser's "freedom"—namely, the purchaser cannot disparage the goods, and she is also liable to her customers for any defects even though the latter resulted from defective design or manufacture. Finally, as Justice Holmes' dissent in *Dr. Miles* pointed out, the common law regarded RPM tolerantly, and courts reviewing such agreements at the turn of the century often upheld them.

The antitrust significance of *Dr. Miles* lies in its formalistic reliance on property law doctrines to decide whether a vertical restraint violates the Sherman Act. The Court seems to have ignored the arrangement's economic purpose and its effect on consumer welfare, except indirectly in its assertion that once a product has been sold (and title passed) "the public is entitled to whatever advantage may be derived from competition in the subsequent traffic." Although the majority opinion does not make this explicit, the outcome in *Dr. Miles* may have been guided by a concern that RPM facilitated horizontal collusion at either the manufacturing or retailing levels. See H. Hovenkamp, *The Sherman Act and the Classical Theory of Competition*, at 1057–65; cf. Andrew N. Kleit, *Efficiencies without Economists: The Early Years of Resale Price Maintenance*, 59 Southern Econ. J. 597 (1993) (documenting early 20th Century awareness of efficiency rationales for RPM).

The *Dr. Miles* rule of per se illegality for RPM agreements has inspired vigorous criticism and debate, yet it remains a fixture of antitrust doctrine. Some observers perceived that *Sylvania* foreshadowed the demise of *Dr. Miles*, yet several times since 1977 the Supreme Court has reiterated that RPM is per se violation of Section 1. See

Business Electronics Corp. v. Sharp Electronics Corp. (1988); 324 Liquor Corp. v. Duffy (1987); Monsanto Co. v. Spray–Rite Service Corp. (1984); California Retail Liquor Dealers Ass'n v. Midcal Aluminum, Inc. (1980). Despite its well-established character, the per se ban on RPM agreements is worth discussing since it raises many issues that arise regularly in antitrust analyses of other vertical transactions.

RPM agreements between a manufacturer and her dealers may serve several functions. Most antitrust decisions have focused on RPM's likely harms. For example, retailers may form a cartel to fix the prices at which they would sell certain products; because of the legal difficulty of enforcing that agreement, they pressure the manufacturer to enforce it for them. Or the manufacturer may impose RPM on her dealers to assure adherence to a price-fixing conspiracy (or tacit oligopolistic collusion) with other producers; with industry-wide RPM, a manufacturer seeking to cheat on the cartel would gain no advantage through shading prices to her dealer since increased sales would not result. Commentators who endorse a per se ban against RPM often emphasize the usefulness of such a rule in deterring and attacking horizontal cartel behavior. See John J. Flynn & James F. Ponsoldt, *Legal Reasoning and the Jurisprudence of Vertical Restraints: The Limitations of Neoclassical Economic Analysis in the Resolution of Antitrust Disputes,* 62 N.Y.U. L. Rev. 1125 (1987).

If these were the only reasons for a manufacturer to participate in an RPM agreement, the result (although not the reasoning) in *Dr. Miles* would be unassailable. On the face of it, it seems questionable whether RPM agreements could benefit the producer since setting a *minimum* resale price above the competitive level places a floor on retail prices, while setting the resale price below the competitive price would render the RPM agreement superfluous. Recalling our earlier analysis that when price goes up demand is necessarily reduced (see pp. 47–48 and Figure 1, p. 46, supra), RPM seems to reduce a manufacturer's sales and correspondingly her profits; without the RPM price retailers would sell more at a lower retail price—but pay the same wholesale price.

There are, however, other reasons for a manufacturer to seek an RPM arrangement with her dealers. Three possible procompetitive justifications stand out. It may be to a manufacturer's advantage that the retailers provide effective service to their customers (e.g., personal computers) or that the product be better promoted throughout a sales area in order to attract buyers (e.g., cosmetics and other drug store items). Creating an effective minimum retail price induces dealers to compete more aggressively on nonprice criteria such as service (repairs, returns, credit) and promotion (advertising). See Benjamin Klein & Kevin M. Murphy, *Vertical Restraints as Contract Enforcement Mechanisms,* 31 J.L. & Econ. 265 (1988); Victor Goldberg, *The Free Rider Problem, Imperfect Pricing and Economics of Retailing Services,* 79 Nw. L. Rev. 736 (1984); Lester G. Telser, *Why Should Manufacturers Want Fair Trade?,* 3 J.L. & Econ. 86 (1960). Nonprice competition would increase each seller's costs until, in a competitive retail market, the dealers' marginal cost equalled the RPM price. Figure 11 illustrates this effect.

FIGURE 11: RIVALRY AMONG DEALERS UNDER RPM

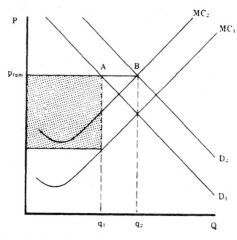

Initially, the RPM price (P_{rpm}) will intersect the demand curve (D_1) and clear the market at a level (Point A) well above the retailer's marginal cost (MC_1); resulting in consumers demanding the limited quantity (q_1) with the retailer's supracompetitive return equalling the shaded area. But such supranormal returns would dissipate quickly under the pressure of nonprice competition. A new, expanded demand (D_2) would occur because increased service and promotion makes the product more valuable to a larger group. As dealers competed with each other by service and promotion, marginal cost would rise (MC_2); the new equilibrium (Point B) would eliminate the "excess" profits as output rose (to q_2).

The second beneficial purpose of RPM is to protect the signal of high quality created by a retailer's approach to doing business. Retailers with a reputation for providing attractive sales displays and excellent service indicate to customers that the products they carry have high quality. Sending this high quality signal helps manufacturers by "certifying" that the manufacturers' goods also have high quality. One retailer could free-ride on the quality certification efforts of another retailer; it could gain increased sales of a manufacturer's product whose reputation has improved because a rival retailer invested in sales and service attributes that imbued the manufacturer's goods with an aura of high quality or stylishness. Manufacturers might use RPM to encourage retailers to devote resources to activities that help certify quality. See Howard P. Marvel & Stephen McCafferty, *Resale Price Maintenance and Quality Certification,* 15 Rand J. Econ. 346 (1984).

A third procompetitive goal of RPM is to facilitate entry by new firms and the introduction of new products. New, unknown firms may face difficulty in persuading store owners to allocate scarce shelf space and inventory capacity to stock their goods. New or existing companies seeking to introduce new products may believe that detailed explanations and demonstrations at the point of sale will be essential to attract customers. Ensuring generous resale margins with RPM can induce retailers to carry a new entrant's goods or to stock a product early in its life cycle. See Ronald N. Lafferty, Robert H. Lande & John B. Kirkwood, *Introduction and Overview,* in Impact Evaluations of Federal Trade Commission Vertical Restraints Cases 1, 30–34, 44–45 (FTC: 1984).

Whether RPM agreements generally enhance efficiency is much debated. Lack of competition at retail may protect supranormal returns for retailers until "corrected" by new entrants. See Robert L. Steiner, *Sylvania Economics—A Critique,* 60 Antitrust L.J. 41 (1991). RPM also may deny customers a broader desired array of price-quality options, including the option of buying the product at a lower price through foregoing service or advertising. For example, an avid reader of computer magazines may not need elaborate presentations by a knowledgeable sales staff and would prefer not to pay higher prices associated with a computer retailer's efforts to recruit or train such personnel. Unlike the "marginal" customer who wants a detailed description of a desktop computer's features, the "inframarginal" user may regard such point-of-sale services as superfluous. See William Comanor, *Vertical Price Fixing, Vertical Market Restrictions, and the New Antitrust Policy*, 98 Harv. L. Rev. 983 (1985); William Comanor & John B. Kirkwood, *Resale Price Maintenance and Antitrust Policy*, 3 Contemp. Pol'y Issues 9 (1985). Other commentators argue that RPM elicits retailer promotional activities that serve mainly to steer consumers toward high-margin items and away from other merchandise that may offer a price-quality mix more to the purchaser's tastes. See Warren S. Grimes, *Spiff, Polish, and Consumer Demand Quality: Vertical Price Restraints Revisited*, 80 Cal. L. Rev. 815, 828–32 (1992).

Yet, suppose there is a significant group of consumers who do not value extensive point-of-sale services and would rather buy lower-priced, non-serviced goods. One ordinarily would expect one or more existing manufacturers to offer this option (e.g., as with separate service contracts for large household appliances) or that new entrants would emerge to satisfy this demand. See Don Boudreaux & Robert B. Ekelund, Jr., *Inframarginal Users and the Per Se Legality of Vertical Restraints*, 17 Hofstra L. Rev. 137, 150–51 (1988). And since a manufacturer is free to integrate forward and to impose similar conditions on sales in her own outlets, it seems futile to prevent the same result through the less restrictive means of contract. The adoption of RPM may avoid problems from free riders (e.g., from appliance sales by discount stores with the product returned for warranty service to established department stores). See Kenneth Kelly, *The Role of the Free Rider in Resale Price Maintenance: The Loch Ness Monster of Anti-*

trust Captured, 10 Geo. Mason L. Rev. 327 (1988). Finally, note that vertical restraints such as RPM at most limit *intra*brand competition. In general, *inter*brand competition—the focus of horizontal price-fixing—is unaffected.

All this does not mean that the result in *Dr. Miles,* and later cases condemning RPM, is always erroneous. Nonetheless, modern empirical studies and theoretical research have raised grave doubts about the wisdom of a rule that categorically forbids RPM. See Pauline M. Ippolito, *Resale Price Maintenance: Economic Evidence From Litigation,* 34 J. L. & Econ. 263 (1991). Indeed, most (though hardly all) commentators agree that an unconditional rule of per se illegality is inappropriate. See Barbara Ann White, *Black and White Thinking in the Gray Areas of Antitrust: The Dismantling of Vertical Restraints Regulation,* 60 Geo. Wash. L. Rev. 1, 53 (1991). Even observers who view RPM suspiciously and endorse a strict standard to prohibit it would recognize exceptions from per se condemnation for new entrants, new products, or failing companies. See Robert Pitofsky, *In Defense of Discounters: The No–Frills Case for a Per Se Rule Against Vertical Price Fixing,* 71 Geo. L.J. 1487, 1495 (1983); but cf. W. Grimes, *Spiff, Polish, and Consumer Demand Quality,* at 853–54 (concluding that RPM can cause serious consumer injury even when imposed by firms with small market shares).

Modern government enforcement policy at least implicitly recognizes the efficiency rationales for RPM. As mentioned in Chapter 5, the Justice Department often prosecutes horizontal price-fixing criminally. RPM has been per se illegal for over eight decades, yet criminal prosecutions for vertical price-fixing are exceedingly rare. From 1974 (when Congress amended the Sherman Act and raised the violation of the statute from a misdemeanor to a felony) through 1993, the Justice Department initiated a single criminal case against an episode of purely vertical price-fixing. See United States v. Cuisinarts, Inc. (1981). In the same period, the Department commenced over 1000 criminal cases against horizontal price-fixing. If RPM were widely seen as being as pernicious as horizontal price-fixing, the Department presumably would have mounted a far more aggressive effort to fine or imprison vertical price-fixers.

The *Dr. Miles* rule ignores relevant efficiency considerations and, in effect, treats vertical price-fixing more harshly than modern antitrust doctrine evaluates horizontal price collaboration, which is seen as posing greater competitive dangers than RPM agreements. The Supreme Court's decision in *BMI* (see Chapter 5) suggests how the Court might end this anomaly and extricate RPM from the rigid approach of *Dr. Miles*. See Wesley J. Liebeler, *Resale Price Maintenance and Consumer Welfare: Business Electronics Corp. v. Sharp Electronics Corp.*, 36 U.C.L.A. L. Rev. 889 (1989). In evaluating the blanket horizontal licensing arrangement in *BMI*, the Court said that "easy labels do not always supply ready answers" and warned that a literal approach in applying per se rules is "overly simplistic and often overbroad." In characterizing conduct for the purpose of applying a per se rule, the inquiry must focus on "whether the practice facially appears to be one that would always or almost always tend to restrict competition and decrease output ... or instead one designed to 'increase economic efficiency and render markets more, rather than less, competitive.'" Current antitrust learning generally discourages a conclusion that RPM "facially appears to ... always or almost always tend to restrict competition and decrease output." Under the *BMI* approach, procompetitive explanations for RPM often would justify the application of a structured rule of reason that examines competitive effects more fully. A useful threshold criterion in such an evaluation would be the effect of RPM on output. As Roger Blair and David Kaserman explain, "[i]f minimum resale prices are imposed to assure the provision of commodity-specific services, the result should be an expansion of output. In contrast, if either a dealer cartel or a producer cartel is behind the resale price maintenance scheme, the industry output will fall." R. Blair & D. Kaserman, *Antitrust Economics*, at 360.

Criticism of the per se ban against minimum RPM pales when compared to the opprobrium heaped on the Supreme Court's extension of the *Dr. Miles* rule to the fixing of maximum resale prices. In Albrecht v. Herald Co. (1968), the Court ruled that the defendant newspaper violated Section 1 by refusing to sell to the plaintiff-distributor when the latter resold the papers to customers at more than the suggested retail price. The Court stated that "agreements to fix maximum prices 'no less than those to fix minimum prices, cripple the freedom of traders and thereby restrain their ability to sell in accordance with their own judgment.' " Maximum RPM endangered competition, the Court added, "by substituting the perhaps erroneous judgment of a seller for the forces of the competitive market" and thereby impeding "the ability of buyers to compete and survive in that market." See also Arizona v. Maricopa County Medical Soc'y (1982).

In reaching this result, the Court majority overlooked important ways in which maximum RPM can enhance distributional efficiency and increase interbrand competition. The complaining distributor in *Albrecht* had an exclusive territory in which it alone delivered the defendant's paper. Unless otherwise constrained, the distributor could exploit its exclusive franchise by charging a monopoly price for newspaper subscriptions within its territory. The supracompetitive price would depress circulation, causing the publisher to lose subscription revenues and, more important, to reduce advertising rates which were pegged to total circulation. See Herbert Hovenkamp, *Vertical Integration by the Newspaper Monopolist,* 69 Iowa L. Rev. 45 (1984). Maximum RPM helped the publisher prevent the distributor from setting prices that reduced the output of the newspaper.

The Supreme Court's analysis in *Sylvania* (1977), which reaffirmed the *Dr. Miles* rule against RPM primarily because of its stabilizing effect on retail prices, underscores the need to reevaluate *Albrecht.* The automatic prohibition of maximum RPM seems inconsistent with *Sylvania's* holding that dealers can be granted exclusive territories; because *Sylvania* lets the manufacturer protect dealers against intrabrand competition, courts eventually may find it appropriate to let manufacturers control the maximum price their dealers charge. By denying manufacturers the use of maximum RPM to constrain opportunism by dealers with exclusive territories, *Albrecht* creates an artificial bias favoring the substitution of vertical integration for contractual distribution arrangements. Thus, firms may resort increasingly to vertical integration, even though the cost of doing so exceeds the cost they would incur if such firms could enforce maximum RPM contracts. See R. Blair & D. Kaserman, *Antitrust Economics,* at 347; cf. Paschall v. Kansas City Star Co. (1984) (en banc) (rejecting Section 2 monopolization challenge by independent carriers to a newspaper publisher's plan to replace all independent carriers with delivery agents who would be employees of the publisher).

Decisions since *Albrecht* have adhered to the nominal principle that maximum RPM is illegal per se. Nonetheless, the practical impact of this rule in private treble damage litigation was attenuated severely in Atlantic Richfield Co. v. USA Petroleum Co. (1990) (*Arco*). In *Arco* the Supreme Court ruled that the plaintiff gasoline retailer failed to establish compensable antitrust injury by alleging that a competitor and its refiner/supplier agreed to set a nonpredatory maximum resale price for gasoline. In the Court's view, only a predatorily low maximum price could cause the requisite antitrust injury—harm that results from reduced competition and not simply from the diminished profits of individual market participants (see Chapter 12). If the maximum price were set relatively high, the plaintiff would be better off because it could undercut its rival's high price and capture more sales. If the maximum price were set at low but nonpredatory levels, the plaintiff might lose sales or be forced to reduce its margins, but only because the defendant was behaving in ways that benefit consumers by providing low prices.

Arco is important for two reasons. First, the antitrust injury requirement greatly reduces the ability of private plaintiffs to recover damages for maximum RPM. To obtain treble damages, future private plaintiffs must prove that the maximum price was set at a predatorily low level—probably by reference to price-cost standards that courts have used in evaluating predatory pricing claims under Section 2 of the Sherman Act (see Chapter 4). This evidentiary requirement weakens the practical effect of the nominally strict per se liability standard.

Second, the *Arco* majority opinion is laden with footnotes suggesting that the Court doubts the wisdom of the per se rule against maximum RPM. The Court prefaced its analysis of antitrust injury by saying "We assume, *arguendo,* that *Albrecht* correctly held that vertical, maximum price-fixing is subject to the per se rule." Justice William Brennan's opinion for the Court explained that "*Albrecht* is the only case in which the Court has confronted an unadul-

terated vertical, maximum price-fixing arrangement" and
observed that "[v]ertical, maximum price-fixing ... may
have procompetitive interbrand effects even if it is *per se*
illegal because of its potential effects on dealers and consumers." Citing extensively to critics of *Albrecht,* the
Court noted that "[m]any commentators have identified
procompetitive effects of vertical, maximum price-fixing"
and stated that the "procompetitive potential of a vertical
maximum price restraint is more evident now than it was
when *Albrecht* was decided, because exclusive territorial
arrangements and other nonprice restrictions were unlawful *per se* in 1968." These comments may induce lower
courts to chop away at *Albrecht* through restrictive con-
structions or to question its holding directly. If *Albrecht's*
validity is placed squarely before the Supreme Court in the
future, *Arco* suggests that the Court might withdraw the
per se ban against maximum RPM.

2. CONSIGNMENTS AND DISTRIBUTION
THROUGH AGENTS

Dr. Miles condemned the challenged price restraint because it denied the retailer-purchaser her common law
"right" to resell (i.e., alienate) her property. This analysis
emphasized that the purchaser was a separate legal and
economic entity and that she had bought and taken title to
the product. The question then arose as to whether the per
se rule against RPM applied where the retailer was the
manufacturer's agent and, instead of taking title to the
products, received them on consignment. Could the manufacturer then set the resale price? In United States v.
General Elec. Co. (1926), the Court answered that where it
is clear that the arrangement is legitimate and the manufacturer both retains title and bears substantial risks of

ownership (e.g., losses from acts of God), the antitrust laws allow her to dictate the terms of sale—including retail prices. Under *GE,* a manufacturer can avoid the rule of *Dr. Miles* by appointing retailers as her agents and by selling to them under a consignment agreement.[2]

GE, in other words, continued the formalism of *Dr. Miles,* focusing on the *method* of the producer's control and not its *effect* on competition or consumer welfare. *GE* reached a contrary result, but its analysis is equally unsatisfactory. GE had an agency rather than a sales relationship with its retailers, yet GE and its retailers were separate legal entities, and the agreements between them seemed designed to restrain trade—with the same effect as resulted under the RPM agreements condemned in *Dr. Miles.* To be sure, once the rule against RPM is adopted, courts must draw a line somewhere to recognize the authority of a vertically integrated manufacturer to set prices in her retail outlets. But neither distributional efficiency nor logic support drawing the line at the agency relationship—except that it is somewhat consistent with the property law rule and rationale that the Court applied in *Dr. Miles.*

Case law since *GE* has featured a continuing judicial retreat from the rule and an unrequited search for a reasonable justification for the result. Some cases attacked the legitimacy of the consignment, questioning whether the retailers were truly the manufacturer's agents. See United States v. Masonite Corp. (1942). In Simpson v. Union Oil Co. (1964), the Court ruled that Union Oil violated the Sherman Act by fixing retail prices for its service station-consignees. *Simpson* distinguished *GE* on the ground that

---

2. GE probably used this arrangement to price discriminate between its industrial and retail customers; it wanted to prevent arbitrage—to keep industrial customers from buying electric lamps at lower prices and reselling them to retail users in competition with GE but at a lower price.

a patentee was entitled to restrict its licensee's prices— although Justice Potter Stewart's dissent correctly noted that this argument related to a wholly separate ruling in *GE* (see p. 416–19 infra). Nor could the Court effectively distinguish the legitimacy of the agency relationship. About the only reason the Court offered for invalidating the vertical price restraint was that Union Oil used it to "coerce" nominal agents "who are in reality small struggling competitors seeking retail gas customers." At the same time, the Court sought to provide assurance that at least some consignment arrangements still would be upheld. Justice William O. Douglas stated that "an owner of an article may send it to a dealer who may in turn undertake to sell it only at a price determined by the owner. There is nothing illegal about that arrangement."

Simpson posed many analytical difficulties. The decision suggested that dealer-imposed price restraints would be upheld, but this clashed with horizontal price-fixing case law. Nor was the Court presented with any evidence that Union Oil held substantial market power vis-a-vis its retailers. The Court used antitrust to redress a perceived inequity in the bargaining power of an integrated oil company with its retail service stations, but without considering how its decision might reduce distributional efficiency. If the Court's ruling imposes significant costs, the oil company is likely to integrate forward and establish company-owned retail outlets—which hardly supports the retailers whom the Court sought to protect. Indeed, only fifteen years earlier, in Standard Oil Co. v. United States (1949), Justice Douglas had dissented from the Court's decision to ban an exclusive dealing arrangement between a major refiner and its independent gasoline retailers (see infra pp. 341–43). Justice Douglas warned that imposing stringent limits on exclusive dealing would lead refiners to integrate forward into retailing and would stifle opportunities for independent retailers.

Despite its skepticism toward consignments, *Simpson* has not led courts to condemn all vertical price-fixing by contract except where the manufacturer clearly controls the retail outlet. The legal distinction between ownership (or agency control) of goods and their resale, recognized in *Dr. Miles* and repeated since then, was not disturbed by *Sylvania's* change of course insofar as the Court had held that the owner of goods or her agent can set the price and other terms under which they are sold. Lower courts today usually uphold RPM when adopted as part of a good faith agency or consignment arrangement. See Illinois Corporate Travel, Inc. v. American Airlines, Inc. (1989); Mesirow v. Pepperidge Farm, Inc. (1983).

3. TERRITORIAL AND CUSTOMER RESTRICTIONS

With the opportunity for RPM first narrowed in *Dr. Miles* and then seemingly foreclosed in *Simpson,* attention shifted to other contractual means for attaining similar or additional distributional advantages. Judicial concern with the "costs" of such devices on competitive price and output levels sharply limited vertical restraints until, in 1967, the Court ruled in *Schwinn* that territorial or customer restrictions on the resale of goods were per se illegal. The ruling raised a storm of criticism for its archaic legal analysis. New economic insights into vertical distribution arrangements further undermined this rigid rule. Thus, only a decade later, the Supreme Court reversed direction in *Sylvania* and adopted a rule of reason test for nonprice vertical restraints. A closer look at these devices is necessary to understanding their legal control.

In distributing her products, a manufacturer may wish to insulate appointed dealers from competition from others who sell her product. Where the manufacturer relies on the dealer to promote her products by local advertising, dealer protection from intrabrand competition is likely to be essential to the latter's efforts. (See pp. 200–201 supra discussing *Sealy* and *Topco* and the "free rider" problem in a horizontal context.) Likewise the manufacturer already may have developed sales contacts in the dealer's territory and thus be unwilling to appoint a dealer who might capture such sales. Consequently customer limitations are also commonly included in dealer franchise agreements. Note that some reasons for these limits resemble justifications already rejected by the Supreme Court in banning RPM agreements. There is, perhaps, a basic difference between RPM and territorial restraints in the type of products affected. RPM agreements typically involve convenience goods such as proprietary drugs where the manufacturer seeks to assure that branded goods are available even through low volume outlets. On the other hand, nonprice distribution restraints are normally applied to larger specialty items, such as cars or bicycles where dealer promotion of the producer's brand is important. Customers generally shop for the latter products, and the manufacturer desires that they be attracted to her product by intensive sales and service efforts by her dealers. A dealer's greater investment in promoting specialty goods may suggest why courts have generally been more receptive to non-price vertical restraints.

Manufacturers argue that dealers need protection from intrabrand competition to support desired activities and, sometimes, to gain a greater return on investment. In this way superior dealers are attracted, they respond to manufacturer suggestions, they will carry larger inventories (and thus better satisfy customer needs), they will increase market penetration through greater advertising and sales efforts, and they will provide higher quality maintenance and repair, which are important for continued sales of complex durable goods. Dealer rationales are often the other side of the same coin. Dealers contend that, freed from intrabrand competition, they can exploit the product more fully through specialized sales and service; they can assure greater promotional and service efforts since they are protected against invasions by free riders; and they can reduce their investment risk and increase the scope of those investments.

Whether these arguments are persuasive depends on several unanswered questions. If *inter*brand competition is vigorous, it would seem unimportant what restraints a manufacturer or retailer imposes on the other—as long as such restraints do not mask a horizontal price or territorial cartel. Unless vertical integration—at least by internal growth—is restricted, and that is generally *not* the case, a manufacturer's choice of distribution techniques seemingly should go unobstructed; such techniques probably are designed to increase productive efficiency, ultimately lowering prices and increasing output. Rules inhibiting integration by contract may force the manufacturer to select less efficient (i.e., more costly) methods such as internal expansion or merger. Allowing a manufacturer to design her own distribution system should invigorate interbrand competition and facilitate new entry—especially since smaller scale enterprises can be designed; that is, the alternative of forward vertical integration is likely to require greater capital investment.

An example sharpens this point. Assume that you manufacture bicycles and want to compete with Fuji and other major bicycle producers. By shielding your dealers from competition from other sellers of your bicycles, each dealer will work harder to advertise your brand in its territory and to service your products to gain repeat business. In this way you can limit your capital investment to that needed to produce bicycles; you will not have to establish and maintain numerous retail outlets.

This analysis suggests that whether vertical restraints on distribution by customer and territorial devices should be allowed is unrelated to whether the manufacturer retains title or whether the dealer is her agent. Rather, it invites a rule of reason test that weighs the potential harms against the benefits (and possibly the less restrictive alternatives), unless it is clear that in the vast majority of cases the costs of such restraints greatly outweigh the benefits. This seemed to be the Supreme Court's approach when it first considered the issue in White Motor Co. v. United States (1963). In appearing to overturn the Justice Department's long-standing contention (since 1948) that vertical territorial allocations were illegal per se, the Court reversed the lower court's grant of summary judgment for the government. White Motor sold its trucks to dealers who agreed to resell them only to customers not otherwise reserved to the manufacturer and who had a place of business or purchasing headquarters within the assigned territory. Because of the meager record and the Court's own inexperience with franchise limitations, the Court concluded that it did not "know enough of the economic and business stuff out of which these arrangements emerge" to be certain whether they stifle or promote competition.

White Motor was widely seen as adopting a rule of reason approach to vertical territorial restraints, although the Court noted that "[w]e only hold that the legality of the territorial and customer limitations should be determined only after a trial." Shortly thereafter lower courts assessed such restraints on a rule of reason basis, evaluating their purpose, power, and effect, and usually upholding the particular schemes. See Sandura Co. v. FTC (1964). Unlike *Dr. Miles* and *Simpson*, these decisions paid no notice to whether there were restraints on the alienation of property, or whether title had passed to the dealer.

The suggestion that antitrust analysis of vertical restraints was moving to a more rational ground proved a vain hope. In United States v. Arnold, Schwinn & Co. (1967), the Court examined Schwinn's scheme for distributing its bicycles. Once the leading U.S. producer of bicycles, Schwinn had seen its market share almost halved in the preceding decade as competitors selling to Sears and other mass merchandisers captured an increasing share of sales. Schwinn distributed most of its bicycles in two ways: through sales to wholesale distributors who resold them to franchised distributors (for resale to the public); and under the "Schwinn Plan," by direct sale to franchised retailers after paying commissions to wholesalers who placed the orders. The "Schwinn Plan" was a consignment arrangement through which Schwinn shipped bicycles directly to franchised retailers. Distributors and retailers were restricted as to the class of persons to whom they could sell: distributors could sell only to retailers within their exclusive territories, and retailers could sell only to ultimate customers and not to other unfranchised retailers.

The fundamental question, therefore, was whether the vertical territorial restrictions on the distributors and retailers were lawful—and whether they would be tested on a rule of reason or a per se basis. The Court seemed to announce a partial per se standard: where the manufacturer sells the product subject to territorial or other restraints upon resale, she violates the Sherman Act. Much as it had in *Dr. Miles*, the Court relied on the concept of restraints on alienation to support its holding that nonprice contractual restraints were suspect "[o]nce the manufacturer has parted with title and risk." However, if the manufacturer retained title, dominion, and risk and the distributor took the goods on consignment, the territorial restriction would violate Section 1 only when the restraint on competition was unreasonable.

Schwinn was criticized from almost every corner. From academia, the new transaction cost economics—especially in its analysis of free-riding—played a key role in showing how *Schwinn* had erred. Transaction cost reasoning revealed that "nonstandard vertical contracts are not inherently mysterious, suspect, and indicative of market power" and created a "framework for understanding why particular types of contractual arrangements have evolved for reasons other than market power." P. Joskow, *The Role of Transaction Cost Economics in Antitrust and Public Utility Regulatory Policies,* at 60. In the business community, manufacturers, distributors, and retailers quickly found the rule in *Schwinn* difficult to accept since it often imposed higher costs on them depending on the form of organization or the character of the distribution transaction. They sought to avoid its reach by alternative but similar devices: assigning areas of "primary responsibility" to dealers, including "location clauses" in franchise agreements, providing for "profit passovers," and so forth. Lower courts frequently aided this process through often-tortured efforts to limit *Schwinn* to its facts or to distinguish its treatment of territorial allocations from these supposedly less inclusive alternatives. Faced with this two-pronged attack of direct and indirect criticism, the Supreme Court, in the next vertical distribution case to reach its docket, overruled *Schwinn,* and announced a rule of reason standard.

Continental TV, Inc. v. GTE Sylvania Inc. (1977) is the most important antitrust case since *Socony* and *Alcoa* in the

1940s. It deserves close analysis. As a manufacturer of television sets, Sylvania had a miniscule share (1–2 percent) of the U.S. market when compared to RCA (60–70 percent), Zenith, and Magnavox. In 1962 Sylvania abandoned its saturation distribution through independent or company-owned wholesalers and moved to sell directly to a smaller group of franchised retailers. These dealers were free to sell and ship their goods anywhere and to all classes of customers. But Sylvania determined how many retailers it would appoint in any geographic area and required its dealers to agree to operate only from approved locations.

The new marketing approach appeared to succeed. Within three years Sylvania's share of national television set sales increased to 5 percent. However, a dispute arose with one of its franchisees when Sylvania, dissatisfied with over-all San Francisco sales of its television sets, appointed an additional dealer to serve that area. The plaintiff, a nearby Sylvania dealer, objected and, after failing to reach an understanding with Sylvania, moved its store to Sacramento. This violated the franchise agreement's location clause, and Sylvania terminated the franchise, prompting a lawsuit. Before the Supreme Court, the issue was whether the location clause was permissible or was per se illegal as the trial court had ruled.[3] After a careful review of *Schwinn* and the economic criticisms of its analytical approach, the

3. The trial judge in *Sylvania* was retired Supreme Court Justice Tom Clark, sitting by designation. He had served on the Court in 1967 when *Schwinn* was decided but had not participated in that case. Justice Clark's dissent in *White Motor* had urged adoption of the per se standard that *Schwinn* later approved. Partly as a result of Clark's role in the trial, *Sylvania* involved several antitrust firsts: it was the first time the Court expressly overruled a major antitrust doctrine; it was the first time the Supreme Court reversed a former colleague sitting as a trial judge for an error of law; and, as noted in Chapter 3, it was the first explicit adoption by the Court of the Chicago School approach for testing business conduct under the antitrust laws.

Court endorsed a case-by-case balancing of competitive effects to test nonprice vertical restraints. Although *Sylvania* involved location clauses often said to be less inclusive and therefore not as restrictive as the territorial restraints in *Schwinn,* the Court found no basis for distinguishing the two restrictions since both involved franchise systems that effectively foreclosed significant *intra*brand competition.

In holding that vertical nonprice territorial restraints must be tested under a reasonableness standard, the Court's new analysis emphasized the arrangement's redeeming purposes and possible benefits. Sylvania was allowed to seek more efficient distribution methods because *inter*brand rivalry—competition among different television manufacturers—would thereby be enhanced. And, as long as there was competition at the *inter*brand level, these benefits would probably outweigh the necessarily less significant limitation of *intra*brand rivalry—rivalry among dealers of Sylvania television sets.

The Court relied on economic theory to demonstrate that the location clause would increase Sylvania's ability to compete against other television manufacturers. Assuring dealers of Sylvania sets some insulation from other Sylvania dealers would elicit aggressive dealer efforts to advertise the product and provide customer services; the location clauses protected dealers from "free-riding" retailers who might seek to reap the benefits of these activities—and thereby discourage the initial dealer's effort to advance Sylvania's product. Furthermore, the Court argued that consumers will be protected from excessive prices or services by competition from non-Sylvania television set sellers and because each manufacturer has an independent interest in maintaining as much intrabrand rivalry as is consistent with efficient distribution. Thus the Court concluded that, on balance, nonprice distribution restraints yield sufficient economic benefits to warrant a rule of reason analysis. The Court did "not foreclose the possibility that particular applications of vertical restrictions might justify per se prohibition," but it emphasized that any "departure from the rule of reason standard must be based upon demonstrable economic effect rather than—as in *Schwinn*—upon formalistic line drawing."

Sylvania is important because it reversed a major legal doctrine and explicitly adopted price theory as the basis for the Court's decision. However, the decision left many questions unresolved and raised new problems of its own. See Ernest Gellhorn & Kathryn M. Fenton, *Vertical Restraints During the Reagan Administration: A Program in Search of a Policy,* 33 Antitrust Bull. 543 (1988). Perhaps most important, *Sylvania* gave little persuasive basis for distinguishing between "price" and "nonprice" restraints. Many commentators have pointed out that price and nonprice restraints have similar effects on competition and ought to be evaluated under the same standard. See, e.g., William F. Baxter, *The Viability of Vertical Restraints Doctrine,* 75 Calif. L. Rev. 933 (1987). For example, exclusive territories can have a greater impact on price than most RPM arrangements because, if effective, the former prevent goods from being available from multiple sources at any price. Since *Sylvania,* the Court itself has acknowledged that creating exclusive territories in many circumstances is no less restrictive in its competitive effect than RPM. See *Business Electronics* (1988); Monsanto Co. v. Spray–Rite Service Corp. (1984). Applying different legal standards to conduct with largely similar competitive effects unnaturally distorts the manufacturer's choice of distribution strategies and generates pressure to manipulate related legal doctrines to harmonize the law's treatment of price and nonprice restraints. See George A. Hay, *Observations: Sylva-*

nia in Retrospect, 60 Antitrust L.J. 61, 63–64 (1991). As discussed below, courts indirectly have reduced the practical significance of the price/nonprice distinction by imposing heavy evidentiary burdens on plaintiffs who seek to prove the existence of an illegal RPM agreement.

Nor did *Sylvania* make clear how the rule of reason was to be applied, who was to bear the burden of persuasion on measuring intra- and interbrand effects, or which justifications deserved special consideration. In discussing the rule of reason, Justice Powell quoted extensively from Justice Brandeis' openended rule of reason formula in *Chicago Bd. of Trade* and gave scant additional guidance concerning the rule's meaning or the appropriate approach for its implementation in evaluating nonprice vertical restraints. The *Sylvania* Court recited various efficiency rationales that might justify nonprice restraints (e.g., prevent free-riding, facilitate market penetration, assure product quality and consumer safety), but it emphasized no one factor over another. Rather, the Court said the factfinder must weigh "all the circumstances" in analyzing the restraint.

Many observers have criticized *Sylvania's* failure to define rigorously the content and framework of a rule of reason inquiry for nonprice restraints. See Assam Drug Co. v. Miller Brewing Co. (1986); H. Hovenkamp, *Economics and Federal Antitrust Law,* at 271. Subsequent lower court decisions have focused on two major criteria identified by Justice Powell in *Sylvania* to determine whether the challenged conduct is reasonable. See Richard M. Steuer, *The Turning Points in Distribution Law,* 35 Antitrust Bull. 467, 513–18 (1990); E. Gellhorn & T. Tatham, *Making Sense Out of the Rule of Reason,* at 170–77. The first is whether the arrangement is likely to have a "permanent effect" on interbrand competition. Many cases have endorsed the use of a market power "filter" to assess the defendant's ability to undermine interbrand competition. Courts generally have upheld nonprice restrictions employed by firms that lack substantial interbrand market power. See Murrow Furniture Galleries v. Thomasville Furniture Indus. (1989); Valley Liquors, Inc. v. Renfield Importers, Ltd. (1982); but see Eiberger v. Sony Corp. of America (1980) (invalidating territorial restriction in a warranty imposed by manufacturer with a 12 percent market share).[4]

If the supplier has market power, courts will consider a second criterion derived from *Sylvania*—whether the restraint has "redeeming virtues." Many cases have interpreted this factor as precluding a finding of liability when the defendant establishes a plausible business rationale for the challenged restraint. Courts have relied on evidence of legitimate business justifications to validate restraints even when such restrictions are imposed by a firm assumed to have substantial market power. See Trans Sport, Inc. v. Starter Sportswear (1992). By introducing proof of justifications, defendants shift the burden of proof back to the plaintiff to show that the asserted rationales are either ad hoc rationalizations or are outweighed by other evidence of harmful competitive effects. In one of the few post-*Sylvania* decisions to find liability on a nonprice vertical restraint claim, the plaintiff established that the defendant had 70–75 percent of the relevant market and showed that the defendant's justifications for imposing exclusive territories lacked factual support. See Graphic Prods. Distribs., Inc. v. Itek Corp. (1983).

4. The pro-plaintiff outcome and reasoning of *Eiberger* may be an anomaly even in the Second Circuit. See, e.g., New York v. Anheuser-Busch (1993) (criticizing *Eiberger* and rejecting challenge to vertical territorial restraints imposed by defendant brewer which accounted for 40 percent of sales in an assumed market).

Several years after *Sylvania,* Richard Posner proposed a rule of per se legality for all vertical restraints. See Richard A. Posner, *The Next Step in the Antitrust Treatment of Restricted Distribution: Per Se Legality,* 48 U. Chi. L. Rev. 6 (1981). Courts have not formally endorsed this view, but outcomes in reported decisions since 1977 indicate that the application of the rule of reason to nonprice vertical restraints has nearly amounted to a rule of per se legality for such conduct. Since *Sylvania,* nonprice vertical restraints rarely have failed to survive scrutiny under the rule of reason test. See Douglas H. Ginsburg, *Vertical Restraints: De Facto Legality Under the Rule of Reason,* 60 Antitrust L.J. 67 (1991). This suggests that courts generally presume that nonprice vertical restraints are designed to increase efficiency and should be permitted except in extraordinary circumstances.

4.   UNILATERAL AND CONCERTED ACTION DISTINGUISHED: SUBSTANTIVE PRINCIPLES AND EVIDENTIARY STANDARDS

The continuation of the price/nonprice distinction in vertical restraints doctrine has elevated the importance of the process by which courts decide whether the challenged conduct constitutes an agreement to set resale price levels. If conduct is labelled an RPM agreement, the *Dr. Miles* rule of per se illegality applies. If the behavior is characterized as virtually anything else—for example, a unilateral refusal to deal or a vertical agreement to impose nonprice restraints—a more lenient rule of reason standard is used, usually with the result that the defendant is exculpated. Thus, how courts define terms such as "agreement" and "price restraint" and specify the plaintiff's evidentiary burden are central issues in vertical restraints cases. A legal scheme that creates an apparent dichotomy between per se illegality (the plaintiff always wins) and the rule of reason (the defendant generally wins) magnifies characterization and evidentiary issues.

We previously explored these issues in Chapter 5 in studying concerted refusals to deal ("group boycotts"), which sometimes involve vertical relationships and are scrutinized with varying degrees of strictness according to the comparative dangers presented by their means and ends. Compare ES Development, Inc. v. RWM Enterprises, Inc. (1991) (finding illegal horizontal conspiracy where rival automobile dealers combined to pressure manufacturers not to extend franchise commitments to competing dealers seeking to operate in a proposed auto mall). Courts use a different analytical approach where firms decide unilaterally whether to deal with another party. Traditional concepts of "freedom of contract" are followed when a manufacturer unilaterally decides that she will no longer deal with a particular retailer. At least that is the basic theory. But reality is seldom so simple, and many cases have questioned whether a particular manufacturer's actions were unilateral or constituted an exclusionary agreement with some of her dealers.

A much debated starting point for characterization in vertical restraints cases is United States v. Colgate & Co. (1919). Bound by the trial court's interpretation of a criminal indictment which charged Colgate only with refusing to sell to a dealer (but not pursuant to a resale price agreement), the Court ruled that a manufacturer's mere advance announcement that it would not sell to price-cutters did not violate the Sherman Act. In the Court's view, the missing element was that no agreement existed between Colgate and its other dealers (who adhered to the announced RPM plan): "In the absence of any purpose to create or maintain a monopoly, the act does not restrict the long recognized right of trader or manufacturer engaged in an entirely private business, freely to exercise his own independent discretion as to parties with whom he will deal."

The rule seems at once both necessary and illogical. On one hand, a competitive market relies on the individual manufacturer's choice of how best to distribute her products to ensure productive efficiency. As a practical matter the case also may have great significance in limiting specious private treble damage claims. *Colgate* is not important in upholding the manufacturer's freedom to suggest prices, because its facts are limited to Colgate's action to cease supplying the dealer. But without the *Colgate* rule, a manufacturer's termination of a dealer (e.g., for inadequate sales) could be perilous. Citing *Dr. Miles* (and *Interstate Circuit*) the terminated dealer otherwise could file a private treble damage suit claiming that the termination violated Section 1 by seeking to enforce an illegal RPM system. As discussed below, recent cases interpret *Colgate* to require the terminated dealer to show that the manufacturer and her dealers have agreed to enforce RPM or some other restrictive plan. See Monsanto Co. v. Spray–Rite Serv. Corp. (1984).

The *Colgate* rule is limited to situations where the person refusing to sell lacks a "purpose to create or maintain a monopoly." Although seldom noted or analyzed, this limitation is consistent with other rules in antitrust imposing an obligation on a monopolist not to act discriminatorily (see Chapter 4). Where the buyer has no other readily available source, the seller may lose her freedom to refuse to deal, at least insofar as she cannot show a valid basis for any refusal. In this limited circumstance, the balance may favor the purchaser. However, where the monopolist can establish a legitimate basis for the refusal or where no monopoly exists and the buyer has alternatives for the seller's product or service, an individual refusal to deal may still be upheld. See *Aspen* (1985) (discussed in Chapter 4). Thus, in Official Airline Guides, Inc. v. FTC (1980), the Court ruled that a monopoly publisher's refusal to publish commuter flight schedules was not illegal. The FTC failed to show that the publisher tried to exclude the commuter airlines or otherwise sought to enlarge or entrench its monopoly (or that of its customers).

The illogic of *Colgate,* though, is its apparent inconsistency with *Dr. Miles,* its formalism and unreality, and the narrowness with which it interprets the meaning of agreement under the Sherman Act. *Dr. Miles* struck at RPM accomplished by direct agreement; but *Colgate* seems to permit a manufacturer to achieve the same result (for that was Colgate's admitted purpose), though indirectly, by allowing Colgate to announce an RPM policy and then to act unilaterally to enforce it. It is unsurprising, therefore, that after *Colgate* retailers frequently followed the resale price policies urged by manufacturers. *Colgate's* rationale seems equally unsatisfactory. Emphasizing that Colgate's dealers were under no formal constraint and could sell the product at any price without fear of suit for a breach of contract, the Court found that no agreement existed and hence there was no Sherman Act violation. Again this formalism ignores apparent reality.

Colgate has been questioned since its inception, and its subsequent history is one of limitation and exception. Almost immediately the Court itself said the ruling was "misapprehended" and distinguished it to invalidate an RPM system enforced by a "course of conduct" or "tacit understandings." See FTC v. Beech–Nut Packing Co. (1922). In United States v. Parke, Davis & Co. (1960), a drug manufacturer sought to obtain compliance with its RPM plan by bargaining and mediating with retailers in order to gain their adherence and trade. In effect, the manufacturer sought and received promises of future compliance. In general terms, the goal and primary effort of Parke, Davis was indistinguishable from that of Colgate: the only evident difference was that the dealer in *Colgate* did not comply and was cut off, whereas in *Parke, Davis* the manufacturer succeeded and did not need to terminate the dealer. Later cases such as *Albrecht* (1968) appeared to remove even this distinction, finding an agreement whenever a dealer succumbs to manufacturer pressure or other dealers adhere to the manufacturer's announced policy— even though no express understanding is shown.

From the early 1960s through the early 1980s, cases sometimes cited *Colgate* with approval, but the safe harbor *Colgate* created for unilateral conduct had grown small and perilous to navigate. Unilateral refusals to deal with retailers in support of a manufacturer's announced policy were lawful only if the facts were "of such Doric simplicity as to be somewhat rare in this day of complex business enterprise." George W. Warner & Co. v. Black & Decker Mfg. Co. (1960). A manufacturer could invoke *Colgate* with success "only so long as no step in addition to announcement of policy and withdrawal of trade from violators is taken by the manufacturer." L. Sullivan, *Antitrust,* at 393. So convinced was the FTC that *Colgate* had been fatally weakened that the Commission filed a test case (ultimately unsuccessful) to extend the rule of *Dr. Miles* to the "unilateral" conduct that *Colgate* had protected. See Russell Stover Candies, Inc. v. FTC (1983).

By the early 1980s, a number of lower courts had held that an RPM agreement could be inferred where a manufacturer terminated a price-cutting dealer after receiving complaints from nondiscounting dealers. In Monsanto Co. v. Spray–Rite Service Corp. (1984), the Supreme Court repudiated this approach and revitalized *Colgate*. In *Monsanto*, a herbicide manufacturer terminated a cut-rate distributor for not complying with service obligations after also receiving price complaints from other distributors. The Seventh Circuit upheld a jury finding of a price conspiracy from "proof of termination following competitor complaints." This did not satisfy the Supreme Court. Reaffirming the principle of *Colgate*, the Court stated that a manufacturer has "legitimate reasons" to exchange information with its dealers about their resale prices. Because "distributors are an important source of information for manufacturers" in their efforts to achieve an "efficient distribution system," it was natural for a manufacturer and its dealers to communicate constantly about prices and sales tactics. Thus, "[p]ermitting an agreement to be inferred merely from the existence of complaints, or even from the fact that termination came about 'in response to' complaints, could deter or penalize perfectly legitimate conduct." Before a conspiracy to fix prices can be inferred, there must be evidence that tends to exclude the possibility of independent action by the manufacturer and distributor: "[T]here must be direct or circumstantial evidence that reasonably tends to prove that the manufacturer and others had a conscious commitment to a common scheme designed to achieve an unlawful objective." While the Court found such evidence in *Monsanto* on an ambiguous record, later cases have reflected judicial skepticism that price-fixing was the manufacturer's aim.

The Supreme Court reiterated and extended the principle of *Monsanto* four years later in Business Electronics Corp.v. Sharp Electronics Corp. (1988). *Sharp* involved the termination of a discounting distributor following complaints of price-cutting by a rival, nondiscounting distributor. The Fifth Circuit had reversed a jury verdict for the terminated distributor, finding that the plaintiff had failed to prove an agreement to set a particular resale price or to set a specific resale price level. The Supreme Court affirmed, stating that its "approach ... is guided by the premises of *GTE Sylvania* and *Monsanto:* that there is a presumption in favor of a rule-of-reason standard; that departure from that standard must be justified by demonstrable economic effect, such as the facilitation of cartelizing, rather than formalistic distinctions; that interbrand competition is the primary concern of the antitrust laws; and that rules in this area should be formulated with a view towards protecting the doctrine of *GTE Sylvania*." The Court went on to explain that, without a common understanding about specific prices or price levels to be charged, an agreement to terminate a dealer creates no greater competitive risk than an agreement to impose nonprice vertical restraints. However, the Court provided no guidance for determining what evidence would establish the requisite agreement on prices.

Taken together with the Court's subsequent decision in *Arco* (1990), which imposed strict antitrust injury requirements on plaintiffs challenging maximum RPM, *Monsanto* and *Sharp* have increased the difficulty of mounting a successful attack on RPM under Section 1 of the Sherman Act. None of these decisions rejects the substantive liability rule of per se illegality or abandons *Sylvania's* formal distinction between price and nonprice restraints. Yet, the Court has minimized discontinuities in antitrust's treatment of price and nonprice restraints by reducing the likelihood that challenged behavior will be deemed a concerted vertical "price" restraint and summarily condemned. Compare Lovett v. General Motors Corp. (1993) (refusing to find that automobile manufacturer conspired with dealers to curtail deliveries to price-cutting retailer) with Big Apple BMW, Inc. v. BMW of North America, Inc. (1993) (reversing summary judgment for defendant on plaintiff's claim that defendant engaged in vertical conspiracy to terminate plaintiff's dealership). The Court has achieved this harmonization by requiring plaintiffs who seek to invoke the per se rule of *Dr. Miles* to prove the existence of (1) an agreement (2) that establishes specific resale prices or price levels (3) and, where the plaintiff is a private party, causes antitrust injury.

The Supreme Court's efforts to delimit the reach of *Dr. Miles* have created the anomaly of having two distinct legal tests for determining whether there is an price-related "agreement" under Section 1 of the Sherman Act, depending on whether the conduct is horizontal or vertical. As discussed in Chapter 6, a horizontal price-fixing agreement subject to per se prohibition under *Socony* can be inferred from consciously parallel pricing conduct accompanied by one or more plus factors. By contrast, per se condemnation for RPM applies only if the plaintiff proves an agreement to set specific prices or price levels. The bifurcation of agreement tests for horizontal and vertical price-fixing arrangements, respectively, is partly a result of historical accident. At the same time, this pattern also can be explained as the result of efforts by courts to accommodate historical interpretations and legal constructs to a developing understanding of economics. The establishment of more rigorous criteria for vertical price agreements may reflect a growing judicial awareness that price-related vertical arrangements have greater procompetitive merit than horizontal price agreements.

C. LIMITS ON SUPPLIER POWER: EXCLUSIONARY PRACTICES

1. TYING ARRANGEMENTS

Under a tying arrangement, the seller of a product conditions the sale of one product upon the buyer's agreement to purchase a second product. Assume that a producer of photocopiers requires purchasers to buy their copy paper from the seller. Under a tying agreement, the copier manufacturer sells the *tying* product (the copier) to the buyer only if the buyer agrees to purchase a *tied* product (e.g., copy paper or toner). Section 1 of the Sherman Act applies to tying arrangements that involve either goods or services, and Section 3 of the Clayton Act covers tying arrangements that involve goods only.

Tying arrangements are evaluated under two standards. Courts have applied what commonly is called a "per se" rule of illegality to tying arrangements where the plaintiff proves that (1) there are two distinct products, (2) the seller has required the buyer to purchase the tied product in order to obtain the tying product, (3) the seller has market power in the market for the tying product, and (4) the tying arrangement affects a substantial amount of commerce in the market for the tied product. See Grappone, Inc. v. Subaru of New England, Inc. (1988). Such a test plainly does not use the characterization of "per se" in the same manner as *Socony*, where the defendants' power in the affected market was irrelevant to the determination of liability. A more suitable description would be to call this approach a "truncated" or "structured" rule of reason standard; such a characterization would indicate that the legal review does not involve broad inquiry into a multitude of potentially relevant factors but instead employs structural screens (e.g., the requirement that the defendant have market power in the tying product) to identify the subset of conduct to be banned. Nonetheless, the per se label continues to be used despite wide recognition that the "per se" test for tying differs greatly from the per se test for horizontal price-fixing.

Early judicial scrutiny of tie-ins involved the patent laws and efforts by the owner of a patented product to assert a right (under the patent grant) to tie a second, usually unpatented article to the tying product. In Motion Picture Patents Co. v. Universal Film Mfg. Co. (1917), the patentee of a motion picture projector sold it on the condition that it would be used only to project the patentee's films. When a licensee used the projector to show other films, the patentee sued for contributory infringement—an invasion of the patentee's rights under the patent grant. In denying the infringement claim, the Court ruled that the patent grant did not entitle the patentee to restrict the machine's use to particular materials; the Court expressed concern with attempts to extend the patent's monopoly grant.[5] The tying arrangement, in other words, was banned because the holder of a legal monopoly in one market (projectors) used that leverage to monopolize another market (films). In ruling that the mere existence of a patent does not entitle the patentee to impose a tie on the purchaser of a patented product, the Court's reliance on the "leverage" rationale suggested that tying arrangements would be vulnerable to attack under the antitrust laws.

This reasoning was first applied to tying arrangements under Section 3 of the Clayton Act, which makes it unlawful to lease or sell

5. Under patent law, tying provisions in a patent license constitute patent misuse and can operate to deny the patentee relief for infringement of the tying clause and of the patent itself. The doctrine of patent misuse may have a broader scope than an antitrust violation since the former does not depend on a showing of anticompetitive effect.

goods, wares, merchandise, machinery, supplies, or other commodities, whether patented or unpatented, ... on the condition ... that the lessee or purchaser thereof shall not use or deal in the goods [etc.] ... of a competitor or competitors of the lessor or seller, where the effect of ... such condition ..., may be to substantially lessen competition or tend to create a monopoly in any line of commerce.

In International Business Machines Corp. v. United States (1936), the Supreme Court enjoined the two leading producers of business machines from leasing their machines subject to the condition that their lessees purchase unpatented tabulating cards exclusively from the lessors. Since IBM and Remington Rand alone made machines that could perform mechanical tabulations and computations without intervening manual operation, the Court apparently concluded that the companies had monopoly power in the tying (business machine) market and had used this power to monopolize the manufacture and sale of tabulating cards. Looking at IBM's business alone, the commerce in the tied product (cards) was substantial—sales of over three billion cards involving more than $3 million annually; therefore the Court found that the effect of the condition "may be to substantially lessen competition." The Court also rejected the defense that each firm made its cards specially for its machines and that other cards might cause the machines to malfunction and therefore damage the machine producers' business reputations. The evidence had shown that others were able to produce suitable cards for use in the machines, just as the government had done for the machines it leased (at a 15 percent higher lease price). There was a less restrictive alternative: neither company was "prevented from proclaiming the virtues of its own cards or warning against the danger of using, in its machines, cards which do not conform to the necessary specifications, or even from making its leases conditional upon the use of cards which conform to them."

In *IBM* the Court seemed to follow a rule of reason approach in deciding whether a tie-in condition covered by Section 3 adversely affected competition. First it examined whether the seller (or lessor) had power in the tying product—since without such market power the tie-in could have no effect on the tied product. Then it considered, if only briefly, the quantitative impact of the tie-in on sales in the tied market. Finally, in reviewing IBM's assertion that the condition was necessary for the efficient distribution of the tying product, the Court held that a defense would apply only if no other reasonable and less harmful alternatives were available.

However, the Court applied a stricter legal standard a decade later in International Salt Co. v. United States (1947). There International Salt, the largest producer of salt for commercial use, tied the lease of two patented machines (one for dissolving rock salt into brine for use in industrial processes, and the other for injecting salt into canned products) to the lessee's purchase from it of all the salt used in operating the machines. In finding that these leases violated Section 3 of the Clayton Act, the Court relied on International Salt's patents as creating market power in the tying product's (the machines') market and on the substantial dollar volume of business in the tied product which was foreclosed to competitors (here about $500,000 per year) as providing the requisite competitive effect. Once these minimum threshold elements were shown, the Court held that a violation was proven: "[I]t is unreasonable, per se, to foreclose competitors from any substantial market. The volume of business affected by these contracts cannot be said to be insignificant or insubstantial and the tendency of the arrangement to accomplishment of monopoly seems obvious." Again the defense that the condition was needed for quality control was rejected: "But it is not pleaded, nor is it argued, that the machine is allergic to salt of equal quality produced by anyone except International."

Because *IBM* and *International Salt* form the foundation of later applications of the antitrust laws to tie-ins and because the legal standard in *International Salt* amounts to a per se-type ruling (i.e., anticompetitive effects are presumed from foreclosure of a certain dollar volume), the cases and the standard deserve close analysis. Both cases rely on the leverage theory—that the tie-in enabled the firms to extend monopoly power from one product market to another. See Ward S. Bowman, Jr., *Tying Arrangements and the Leverage Problem*, 67 Yale L.J. 19 (1957); Louis Kaplow, *Extension of Monopoly Power Through Leverage*, 85 Colum. L. Rev. 515 (1985).

In neither case is the factual analysis or the theory fully persuasive. For example, it does not follow that International Salt's patents on salt dispensing machines necessarily gave it a monopoly in that (the tying product) field. The Court did not consider how many other machines were available, what International Salt's market share was, or the alternatives available to users of brine and to canners. More important, the leverage theory itself seems faulty. Due to the extent that IBM (and Remington Rand) occupied the tabulating machine market, they probably also gained a monopoly in the sale of tabulating cards—at least for use in tabulating machines. But it does not follow, as the Court also assumed, that the firms earned monopoly *profits* in the second market. Since the two products (machines and cards) were complementary, and therefore both were necessary for any tabulating service, the firm that monopolized either product could extract the full monopoly profit obtainable from the monopolization of the entire service. Here IBM's lawful patent on tabulating machines justified its extraction of monopoly profits from the tabulating service, and whether it extracted that profit through the rental price of the machines or through the sale of punch cards seems unrelated to the Court's expressed leverage theory.

This raises the question of why sophisticated firms such as IBM and International Salt would impose tying conditions when they could lawfully obtain monopoly profits on the sale or lease of the tying product. One reason is that these conditions enable a manufacturer to discriminate among users in relation to the intensity of their use of the product—to charge users different prices according to their use of the machines. By tying card purchases to the rental of the machine, IBM was thus able to meter the degree of use and then price the service so that low as well as high intensity users would find it attractive. Scholars have actively debated whether firms should be allowed to use tying to facilitate price discrimination. Some emphasize that price discrimination encourages the monopolist to increase output and thereby results in a smaller misallocation of resources than unitary monopoly pricing would. See Henry M. Butler, W.J. Lane & Owen R. Phillips, *The Futility of Antitrust Attacks on Tie-in Sales: An Economic and Legal Analysis,* 36 Hastings L.J. 173 (1984). Others point out that price discrimination can result in a substantial transfer of wealth from consumers to producers and thus contradicts the congressional aim of reserving such surplus for consumers. See R. Lande, *Chicago's False Foundation: Wealth Transfers (Not Just Efficiency) Should Guide Antitrust,* at 643–44.

Nor is it conclusive that the tying provision foreclosed competing sellers of cards from entering the market. Since

IBM's interest lies in obtaining the monopoly profit on the tabulating service, it will either make the cards itself or buy them from others depending on which alternative offers the lower price; that is, IBM has no incentive to disturb the market structure of the tied product except to keep it competitive. This further suggests that concerns that tying creates entry barriers because it forces competing producers of tabulating machines to enter a second market, and thereby increases their capital costs, are overstated; it seems more likely that these others would use the same suppliers of tabulating cards. Not all such explanations are benign, however. The tie in *International Salt* required users to buy International's salt unless another firm's salt was cheaper. This may have helped International to monitor its rivals' current prices and use this information to enforce a cartel among salt producers. See John L. Peterman, *The International Salt Case,* 22 J.L. & Econ. 351 (1979). However, if this were the case, the objection should be with the cartel, not the tie-in, unless one concludes that tie-ins serve no valid end.

Because the Clayton Act applies only to the sale or lease of commodities, tie-ins have also been judged under Section 1 of the Sherman Act. For a time these standards appeared to diverge. For example, in Times–Picayune Publ. Co. v. United States (1953) a publisher of both a morning and evening newspaper faced competition from only one other evening paper. The government challenged, as a Sherman Act violation, the defendant's "unit plan" which required advertisers to take space in both morning and evening papers, and not in either separately. It contended, inter alia, that this tie-in foreclosed the competing afternoon newspaper from advertising lineage. While concluding that the defendant did not occupy a "dominant" position in the tying product—and therefore could not have foreclosed advertising markets to competitors—the Court also stated that under the Sherman Act the plaintiff must show both a monopolistic position in the tying product and that a substantial volume of commerce in the tied product was restrained. The Court observed that the rule of *International Salt* found a Clayton Act § 3 violation if *either* ingredient was present.

The case seemed significant for several reasons. The Sherman Act standard was less likely to hold tie-ins illegal. Here, not only must power in the tying product be present, but competitive effects must be shown. And neither was presumed from minimal evidence as in *International Salt*. Mere market power such as that indicated by a patent for the tying product was insufficient; dominance or overwhelming power was also required. Likewise competitive effect in the tied product could not be presumed from dollar volume; rather, actual market effects had to be proven. In addition, the Court focused extensively on the valid business aims that motivated the unit price offering, including the overhead savings and other efficiencies from eliminating repetition of 30 separate steps in the publishing process. Finally, the Court refused to consider this a real tie-in case since only one product (readership of newspaper advertising in the New Orleans market), and not two separate products, was involved, and there was as a consequence no tying of one product to another.

This rule of reason approach to tie-ins under the Sherman Act proved short-lived as the Court moved toward a per se-type rule. First, in Northern Pac. Ry. Co. v. United States (1958), the Court applied Section 1 to condemn the defendant's sales (and leases) of land adjoining its rail lines because the contracts contained preferential routing clauses requiring the purchasers to ship commodities produced on such land over Northern Pacific's rails. (Section 3 of the

Clayton Act did not apply since the tying product was land, which is not a commodity.) Several aspects of the Court's analysis stand out. The Court expressly labeled the rule of *International Salt* as a per se test and restated the rule as requiring a showing that "a party has sufficient economic power ... to appreciably restrain free competition in the market for the tied product" and a showing that "a 'not insubstantial' amount of interstate commerce was and is affected" in the tied product. That standard was then held fully applicable to Sherman Act cases. Despite its faint efforts at reconciliation, the Court seemed to abandon the view in *Times–Picayune* that the Clayton and Sherman Acts applied different standards of legality. And without requiring specific proof of substantial market power in the tying product (such power was inferred from vastness of NP's land holdings and from the fact that without power the tie-in would not benefit NP), the Court deemed the arrangement unreasonable and sustained the district court's grant of summary judgment for the government.

It is unclear whether the *Northern Pacific* Court would have permitted NP to raise any defenses. Unlike the *Times–Picayune* defendant, NP offered no business justification for the tie-ins. One possible explanation for the challenged tie-in was that NP was using the device to avoid price controls imposed by the ICC on freight transportation. See also F.M. Scherer & D. Ross, *Industrial Market Structure and Economic Performance,* at 567 (describing incentives for regulated firms to impose tying arrangements). Later decisions have treated the use of tying to evade price controls or other forms of regulation as an important rationale for finding liability. See Litton Systems, Inc. v. American Tel. & Tel. Co. (1983); Sandoz Pharmaceutical Corp. (1991). Other scholars have suggested that NP's tying contracts served to police price-fixing agreements among railroads by requiring a buyer or lessee not using the NP line to disclose the lower rate or service available elsewhere. F. Jay Cummings & Wayne E. Ruhter, *The Northern Pacific Case,* 22 J.L. & Econ. 329, 342 (1979).

In United States v. Loew's, Inc. (1962), the Supreme Court applied a similarly rigid per se approach, presuming economic power from the copyright of popular films, to bar block booking. The Court objected to the selling of packages of motion pictures to television where buyers were "coerced" into taking bad as well as good pictures in the sale. Several explanations have been offered for this practice, including a reduction in the costs of information and simulated price discrimination. See Roy W. Kenney & Benjamin Klein, *The Economics of Block Booking,* 26 J.L. & Econ. 497 (1983). In any event, there seems little economic basis for condemning the transaction where many competing films and other programs were available for sale to television.

An even stricter per se approach to tying agreements was revealed in Fortner Enterprises, Inc. v. United States Steel Corp. (1969) (*Fortner I*). U.S. Steel offered attractive credit services to home builders who agreed to buy prefabricated houses (which the plaintiff claimed were over-priced and defective) from U.S. Steel. The defendant's special credit terms, such as 100 percent financing at rates below market levels, were said to be unique, thus demonstrating U.S. Steel's special economic power in the credit market; and sales of more than $9 million of prefabricated houses by U.S. Steel in three years across the country, allegedly foreclosed by the tying arrangements, were not an insubstantial effect. The Court curtly rejected U.S. Steel's argument that the tie-in was, in effect, a competitive price cut made possible through scale economies resulting from both the tie-in and avoided costs, such as credit controls otherwise imposed on lenders. The Court asserted that the tied product should instead have been offered at a lower price. Because the Court was reviewing a grant of summary judgment, the decision established only that a violation of the Sherman Act could be found if the plaintiff proved that U.S. Steel had economic power in the credit (tying product) market. Thus, the case was remanded to the trial court for further evidence.

Eight years later the matter returned to the Supreme Court in United States Steel Corp. v. Fortner Enterprises, Inc. (1977) (*Fortner II*). Technically it now involved only a review of the lower court's decision that U.S. Steel indeed had economic power in credit. On this question the Supreme Court read its earlier standard narrowly and ruled that there was no evidence that U.S. Steel had "significant" economic power in the credit market. Here the Court appeared to move away from a rigid rule against tying. To be sure, bound by the law of the case, it restated the per se rule. But its approach to plaintiff's evidence suggested a new direction. It seemed to reflect a "partial per se" test similar to that applied to group boycotts. The Court now viewed the evidence as showing only that the purchase requirement was part of the price of the loan—and nothing else. Fortner was not forced to accept the advantageous terms; rather, these terms were the best arrangement Fortner could make.

In the mid–1980s, the Court had a major opportunity to clarify tying doctrine in a case where the tie-in seemed to be a cheaper way to bundle and sell a package of services. In Jefferson Parish Hosp. Dist. No. 2 v. Hyde (1984), a large acute-care hospital required patients wanting operations to use the hospital's anesthesiologists. The hospital claimed that this bundling of services reduced costs and improved the quality of care; an excluded anesthesiologist complained that the tie prevented him from obtaining privileges of practice. A unanimous Court upheld the arrangement but could not agree why. Five justices said that the per se rule still applied generally to tie-ins. Justice Stevens' opinion for the Court said "[i]t is far too late in the history of our antitrust jurisprudence to question the proposition that certain tying arrangements pose an unacceptable risk of stifling competition and therefore are unreasonable per se." However, after reasserting the importance of a per se test in tying jurisprudence, the Court conducted an elaborate inquiry in which it concluded that there were two separate products, that the hospital lacked enough market power to invoke the per se rule (since it attracted only 30 percent of the patients in its district), and that there had been no showing of an adverse effect on competition.

In an opinion by Justice O'Connor, four justices concurred in the result, concluding that surgery and anesthesia were not separate products for tying purposes. However, the concurring justices unsuccessfully urged the Court to abandon the per se label for tying arrangements and acknowledge that it had adopted a rule of reason approach. In effect, the concurring justices would have collapsed the existing "per se" and "rule of reason" tests into a single structured rule of reason that would employ the market power screens now used in the "per se" standard to organize the analysis. The Court majority had displayed a somewhat greater appreciation of the economic rationale for tying, but the Court's refusal to abandon the per se label constitutes one of the more deliberate missed opportunities in modern antitrust decisionmaking.

Among its failings, *Jefferson Parish* leaves in place an ill-defined rule of reason theory that the plaintiff apparently can pursue even if the defendant falls short of the market power threshold employed in the per se test. Plaintiffs generally have failed to establish liability under the rule of reason test, but the persistence of a rule of reason standard distinct from the existing hybrid per se approach has confused the lower courts and led them to spend much effort to identify what the residual rule of reason requires and how it should be applied. See, e.g., Town Sound & Custom Tops, Inc. v. Chrysler Motors Corp. (1992). Moreover, although *Jefferson Parish* appeared to create a safe harbor under the per se test for firms with 30 percent or less of the relevant market for the tying product, the Court failed to offer a rigorous definition of what market power means for tying analysis. Not surprisingly, lower courts have found the market power standard difficult to apply. See, e.g., Digidyne Corp. v. Data General Corp. (1984) (market power presumed from copyright).

The Court's most recent tying decision has not clarified these issues. In Eastman Kodak Co. v. Image Technical Services (1992), the Court affirmed a reversal of summary judgment for Kodak against charges that Kodak illegally tied the sale of replacement parts for its photocopiers and micrographic equipment to the purchase of its repair services. After holding that a genuine issue of fact existed as to whether parts and repair services constitute two distinct products, the Court considered whether a seller without market power in the market for the sale of original equipment can possess market power in the aftermarket of parts and services for that product. In examining this question, the Court appeared to assume (although it did not expressly state) that it was applying the per se standard of illegality for tying.

The Supreme Court accepted the lower court's conclusion that Kodak lacked market power in the original equipment market. Kodak had argued that this fact alone was dispositive; due to its lack of market power in copiers and micrographic machines, if Kodak tried to charge supracompetitive prices for parts or service, it would lose new placements of original equipment as purchasers switched to suppliers who offered equipment with lower total life-cycle costs. Even though Kodak held over 80 percent of the market for parts and service for its own machines, competition for new sales of original equipment would preclude it from extracting excessive prices from the owners of its installed base. The Court rejected this argument for essentially two reasons. First, the Court found that the cost and difficulty of obtaining meaningful life-cycle cost data would create a substantial pool of vulnerable equipment purchasers whom Kodak could exploit. Sophisticated buyers who could gather and assimilate such data could protect themselves as Kodak suggested, but others might not. Second, the costs of switching would preclude existing owners of Kodak equipment from buying machines from other manufacturers. Kodak might exploit these "locked-in" customers by charging supracompetitive prices for parts and services, especially if the percentage of locked-in users was high relative to potential new purchasers. Compare Richard Craswell, *Tying Requirements in Competitive Markets: The Consumer Protection Issues,* 62 B.U.L.Rev. 661 (1982) (proposing that consumer protection laws, rather than antitrust enforcement, be used to redress harm from tie-ins resulting from information asymmetries). The Court also rejected, as unsubstantiated by record evidence, Kodak's argument that its sales policies were justified by valid quality control concerns.

The Court stressed that it was reviewing the case in a summary judgment context and that, with a fuller evidentiary record at trial, Kodak might prevail on the issues of whether there were two products, whether it could exercise market power in aftermarkets for its copier and micrographic equipment, and whether its justifications outweighed any anticompetitive effects of the tie-in. The implications of *Kodak* generally expand the possible reach of tying law—especially in its suggestion that a firm might readily be deemed to have market power over the aftermarket for parts and services for original equipment over which it has no market power. See Virtual Maintenance, Inc. v. Prime Computer, Inc. (1993); see also Warren S. Grimes, *Antitrust Tie–In Analysis After Kodak: Understanding The Role of Market Imperfections*, 62 Antitrust L.J. 263 (1994). At the same time, however, the Court appeared to recognize a quality control defense to liability under the "per se" rule. This seems to confirm the view of earlier cases that have ruled that tying could be justified as providing a necessary avenue for entry or as a valid means for ensuring quality control for the tying product. See, e.g., *Grappone* (1988); United States v. Jerrold Electronics Corp. (1960).

2. EXCLUSIVE DEALING

Another way to secure vertical integration through contract is exclusive dealing. Instead of relying on her economic power in the tying product to obtain sales of a second or tied product, the manufacturer offers a sales contract conditioned on the buyer's agreement not to deal in the goods of a competitor. That is, the dealer purchasing women's shoes from a footwear producer must promise to promote and market only the seller's brand of shoes; the dealer is "tied" to a particular supplier. Alternatively, the arrangement may reflect the buyer's desire to obtain an assured source of supply—she seeks the producer's agreement to provide her with the producer's entire output or at least her (the buyer's) requirements.

Exclusive dealing is another variant of partial vertical integration designed to facilitate the distribution of products to the ultimate consumer. See Howard P. Marvel, *Exclusive Dealing*, 25 J.L. & Econ. 1 (1982); Oliver E. Williamson, *Markets and Hierarchies: Analysis and Antitrust Implications*, 82–131 (1975). It differs from tie-ins in that a second (tied) product is not involved, and from refusals to deal in that the primary focus is not on maintaining a selected resale price. But exclusive dealing arrangements all involve the use of economic power in the sale or purchase of one product as leverage to affect intrabrand sales and, if effective, they foreclose that opportunity to interbrand competitors. When an oil company obtains exclusive dealing contracts from its service station operators, it "denies" these outlets to sellers of competing brands of gasoline, just as the tie-in in *International Salt* limited the sales opportunities of competing sellers of industrial salt. These business arrangements have similar economic effects, but exclusive dealing has long been subject to a modified rule of reason approach that examines the effect of foreclosure on other sellers.

The origin for modern exclusive dealing analysis is Standard Oil Co. of California v. United States (1949) (*Standard Stations*). There the largest seller of gasoline in seven western states made exclusive dealing contracts with independent stations constituting 16 percent of all retail outlets, whose sales involved almost 7 percent (or $58 million) of all retail gas sales in the area. Attacked under Section 3 of the Clayton Act, the arrangement clearly met the "quantitative substantiality" test applied in *International Salt* (where foreclosure of $500,000 violated Section 3). Nonetheless, the Court applied a different standard that considered but did not closely examine the foreclosure's economic effects. It ruled that in measuring the impact of an exclusive dealing arrangement, the market in the foreclosed line of commerce (here retail gasoline sales in seven western states) should be reviewed. The Court noted that the market was concentrated since the seven largest firms, all of which used exclusive dealing contracts, controlled 65 percent of the market and that entry was apparently restricted since market shares had stabilized after the contracts were introduced. The Court found liability because agreements relating to 7 percent of retail sales created a potential clog on competition which was "foreclosed in a substantial share" of the market.

Standard Stations is important because the decision enunciates a distinctive "quantitative substantiality" test for exclusive dealing contracts under Section 3. Under *Standard Stations,* exclusive dealing is not presumed to suppress competition, and the adverse effects of exclusive dealing arrangements are not assumed merely from the dollar volume impact on competitor opportunities to make sales to the foreclosed retailers. The Supreme Court held that foreclosure of a substantial share of the retail market (here almost 7 percent) where the market is otherwise concentrated and entry is restricted, establishes a sufficient basis for a court to infer that the arrangement may substantially lessen competition.

This "partial" per se ruling seems questionable from two perspectives. Although it treats exclusive dealing contracts more favorably, as having potentially beneficial effects, it operates from the doubtful assumption that they are somehow substantially different and less harmful than tie-ins. This suggests, perhaps, that legal doctrine governing partial vertical integration by contract should be more receptive to tying arrangements. As Justice Douglas noted in a separate opinion in *Standard Stations,* if the vertical arrangement reflects substantial gains in efficiency, denying firms this opportunity by contract will only force them to achieve these ends by acquiring the formerly independent outlets or, if that is prohibited by the antimerger laws (see Chapter 9), by forward vertical (i.e., internal) expansion.

Second, the Court's sole reliance on market shares as demonstrating market foreclosure and competitive effect also seems misplaced. Whether an exclusive dealing contract can foreclose competitors depends not only on the number of outlets or the share of sales foreclosed but also on the agreement's length. If the agreement can be terminated on short notice, as in *Standard Stations,* and there are available outlets, the exclusionary effect is likely to be minimal because a competitor could enter simply by offering the retailers better terms.

Subsequent cases have retreated from this position. In Tampa Elec. Co. v. Nashville Coal Co. (1961), a coal supplier argued that its agreement to fill an electric utility's "total requirements" for coal for 20 years should not be enforced because it violated Section 3. (Coal prices had jumped, making the contract less profitable for the coal company.) The Court upheld the contract after analyzing its economic impact more intensively, both as to the affected markets and as to the probable foreclosure, than the arrangement in *Standard Stations.* Foreclosure in the coal market was only 0.77 percent, but the Court went on to consider qualitative factors (including entry conditions and "particularized considerations of the parties' operations") to assess the market impact of the arrangement.

Tampa Electric appeared to move toward a less rigid rule of reason approach. Yet in FTC v. Brown Shoe Co. (1966), the Court upheld the FTC's condemnation of a franchise plan where a shoe supplier's dealers promised not to carry shoes competing with the franchisor's lines even though the record contained no evidence of the market share affected or of the extent to which competing shoe suppliers were foreclosed—and the dealers could terminate the agreements at any time. Relying on the broader reach of Section 5 of the FTC Act, the Court ruled that competitive effects did not have to be shown. *Brown Shoe* has been heavily criticized for ignoring the franchise plan's benefits in stimulating retail competition and for finding liability where the actual foreclosure effect was less than 1 percent and both the manufacturing and retailing tiers of the shoe industry were unconcentrated. See John L. Peterman, *The Federal Trade Commission v. Brown Shoe Company*, 18 J.L. & Econ. 361 (1975); cf. Brown Shoe Co. (1984) (vacating *Brown Shoe* exclusive dealing order; emphasizing respondent's lack of market power and ease of entry).

Due to its weak logic and reliance on Section 5, *Brown Shoe* has not guided subsequent case developments. Instead, lower courts have followed *Tampa Electric's* more relaxed treatment of exclusive dealing. See U.S. Healthcare, Inc. v. Healthsource, Inc. (1993). Modern cases focus on three principle criteria in evaluating the reasonableness of exclusive dealing arrangements. The first is the extent of market foreclosure. Lower court decisions generally refuse to find liability where the foreclosure is less than 20 percent of the market. See Satellite Television & Assoc. Resources, Inc. v. Continental Cablevision (1983) (foreclosure of 8 percent held insufficient). The Supreme Court's use of a 30 percent market share threshold in *Jefferson Parish* suggests that foreclosure up to this level is likely to be deemed acceptable in future cases. The second major criterion is the duration of the exclusive arrangement. Agreements that provide short terms and specify short notice for termination frequently are presumed to be reasonable. See, e.g., Roland Mach. Co. v. Dresser Indus.

(1984) (calling agreements terminable in less than one year "presumptively lawful"). The third major factor is the height of entry barriers, with courts tending to uphold the challenged practice where the defendant shows that entry into the affected market is easy. See Beltone Elecs. Corp. (1982).

D. CONCLUSION

Antitrust policy today regards vertical contractual restraints far more favorably than it did twenty years ago. As reflected in *Sylvania* and its progeny, transaction cost economics has attuned courts to the procompetitive aims of many vertical arrangements (such as territorial divisions) once subject to per se condemnation. The rule of reason now provides the basic standard for nonprice vertical restraints, and recent cases have shown more willingness—mainly through the use of market power screens—to cull out claims that pose few dangers to interbrand competition. Even for RPM agreements, the Supreme Court has reduced the impact of the *Dr. Miles* per se rule by forcing plaintiffs to satisfy demanding evidentiary and injury requirements.

Beyond a general trend toward more permissive doctrinal treatment of vertical restraints, several other identifiable concerns promise to occupy the attention of courts, enforcement officials, and practitioners in the coming years. One is antitrust's continued distinction between price and nonprice restraints. Many observers believe that there is little reason to evaluate price and nonprice restraints, respectively, by different legal standards, as both forms of restrictions tend to have the same competitive effects. Cf. Rudolph J. Peritz, *A Geneology of Vertical Restraints Doctrine*, 40 Hastings L.J. 511 (1989) (favoring retention of price/nonprice distinction). Supreme Court decisions such as *Monsanto* and *Sharp* have indirectly recognized and addressed this anomaly by making it more difficult for plaintiffs to invoke the harsher standards applicable to vertical price maintenance agreements.

A second, related problem results from the heavy emphasis that antitrust doctrine now places on characterizing collective action subject to Section 1 of the Sherman Act as being horizontal or vertical. The fundamental question in reviewing any form of conduct under the antitrust laws should be whether the restraint has a positive or negative impact on output and prices within the relevant market. Denominating conduct as "horizontal" or "vertical" is only a rough, initial step toward predicting the likely competitive effects of challenged behavior. The failure to go beyond the preliminary labeling exercise and focus on the ultimate question of market impact has created analytically unsupportable discontinuities in Section 1 doctrine. One disturbing consequence is that cases such as *BMI* and *NCAA* encourage a more discriminating analysis of horizontal agreements with price and output restrictions, but modern Supreme Court vertical restraints decisions continue to adhere to the view that all RPM agreements are forbidden.

A final problem deals with the future vitality of several formative Supreme Court vertical restraints decisions. The pillars of the Court's exclusive dealing jurisprudence are *Standard Stations* (1949) and *Tampa Electric* (1961). Justice O'Connor's concurring opinion in *Jefferson Parish* (1984) analyzed the anesthesiologists' contract as an exclusive dealing arrangement, but the Court majority only considered the tying implications of the agreement. Thus, aside from the Court's cursory affirmance of the FTC's order under Section 5 of the FTC Act in *Brown Shoe* (1966), the Court has not addressed substantive exclusive dealing standards in over 30 years. This leads one to ask whether *Standard Stations* and *Tampa Electric* are true indicators of how the Supreme Court would decide an exclusive dealing case today, given the upheaval in the Court's treatment of nonprice restrictions since *Sylvania* in 1977. In the absence of recent guidance from the Court, both the lower courts and the FTC have moved steadily toward embracing more permissive tests that require market foreclosure of 20 percent or more to establish liability.

CHAPTER IX

MERGERS

Beyond considering how antitrust limits the attainment and use of monopoly power, this text has concentrated on contractual or similar arrangements between independent firms. In this Chapter we examine measures by which firms integrate their operations more completely and permanently—usually through the purchase by one company of the stock or assets of another company. We use the terms *merger* and *acquisition* interchangeably to denote all methods by which firms legally unify ownership of assets formerly subject to separate control. It is difficult to overstate the importance of antimerger policies to the U.S. antitrust system. No area of antitrust activity commands closer scrutiny and or arouses more impassioned debate.

A. TENSIONS IN MODERN MERGER ANALYSIS

In reviewing agreements between independent firms, we saw that cases applying Section 1 of the Sherman Act generally view such arrangements as posing greater competitive dangers than unilateral conduct. This concern is most acute where the participants are direct rivals, for courts often presume that such arrangements are more prone to restrict output and increase prices. At first glance, consistency in approach might seem to forbid almost every merger—the formal and complete integration of one firm into another. Such arrangements lack the limited duration and substantive scope of most contracts. Unlike cartels or boycotts (which are temporary and subject to internal pressures that ultimately can force their disintegration), mergers inevitably eliminate competition between the merging firms. Thus, if antitrust principles prohibiting cartels and other partial integration through contract are to be consistently applied to functionally similar transactions, one might conclude that merger doctrine should be simple and straightforward—and most mergers (especially transactions involving direct rivals) should be condemned by a simple per se rule.

However, closer study of the motives that lead firms to merge suggests a more cautious approach. It is true that mergers can and do pose competitive hazards. Mergers of direct rivals may yield substantial single-firm market power or, by reducing the number of participants in a concentrated industry, may increase the likelihood that the remaining firms will expressly or tacitly coordinate pricing and output decisions. Transactions between vertically-related firms may foreclose opportunities for equally or more efficient non-integrated firms to gain sales. Though serious in some instances, these adverse possibilities do not warrant a policy of categorical prohibition. Just as Section 1 doctrine tolerates many concerted business efforts to stimulate demand and seek customers (despite their facial similarities to the actions of price-fixing cartels or their potential to create monopoly power), merger policy also recognizes that consolidations often serve useful social ends without impairing competition.

Several considerations suggest why society has a strong stake in leaving firms relatively free to buy or sell entire companies or specific assets. First, mergers can bring superior managerial or technical skill to bear on underused assets. Second, mergers can yield economies of scale and scope that reduce costs, improve quality, and boost output. Third, the possibility of a takeover can discourage incumbent managers from behaving in ways that fail to maximize profits. Fourth, a merger can enable a business owner to sell her firm to someone who is already familiar with the industry and who would be in a better position to pay the highest price. The prospect of a lucrative sale induces entrepreneurs to form new firms and thereby spurs competition by facilitating entry and exit. Finally, many mergers pose few risks to competition. For example, a merger is unlikely to undermine competition where the merging firms are relatively small or entry into their markets is easy.

Antitrust merger law seeks to weed out transactions whose probable anticompetitive consequences outweigh their likely benefits. Because courts seldom undo mergers which go unchallenged at their inception, the critical time for review usually is when the merger is first proposed. This requires enforcement agencies and courts to forecast market trends and future effects. Merger cases examine past events or periods, not so much to gather proof of misconduct, but to understand the merging parties' position in their markets and to predict the merger's competitive impact. In reviewing mergers, courts and enforcement agencies often have relied on structural criteria (is the market concentrated?) and on devising relatively clear rules (based mainly on the merging firms' market shares) which inform business managers in advance about which mergers are likely to be challenged. Formative Supreme Court merger decisions during the 1960s strongly encouraged such techniques.

Since the 1960s, however, there has been a growing recognition that merger standards which give decisive effect to structural criteria not only demand unattainable precision in delineating relevant markets and measuring market power, but also slight vital qualitative considerations. The tension between bright-line structural rules and multi-factor reasonableness tests has injected instability into merger analysis. See ABA Antitrust Section, *Monograph No. 12, Horizontal Mergers: Law and Policy* 1–4 (1986). Merger jurisprudence of the past decade has featured a divergence between cases that adhere to Supreme Court precedents from the Warren Court Era and give dispositive weight to market concentration data, and cases that expand the range of qualitative evidence that can rebut presumptions based solely on post-acquisition market shares. Since the early 1980s, the Justice Department and the FTC have disavowed reliance on bright-line structural rules and have embraced a fuller assessment of other criteria bearing upon the merger's competitive effects.

Several other developments have contributed to instability in modern merger analysis. First, the Supreme Court has not issued an opinion concerning substantive merger standards since 1975. See United States v. Citizens & Southern National Bank (1975). In the intervening years, the Court's decisions dealing with Section 1 claims have abandoned or modified per se rules governing nonprice vertical restraints, tying arrangements, group boycotts, and certain horizontal price and output restraints. Whether the Court might endorse a similar retreat from structural rules that it endorsed in the 1960s for merger analysis is unknown. What is clear, however, is that many lower court decisions since 1975 have embraced analytical techniques that are favored by some of the Court's more recent Section 1 cases but deviate greatly from the rules embodied in the Court's merger decisions.

Second, economic learning relevant to mergers has undergone major changes in the past 30 years. Economists generally have rejected the structure-conduct-performance model that animated merger policy in the 1960s and have developed more complicated approaches for determining when specific transactions are likely to reduce competition. Despite substantial progress, the existing tools for estimating price and output effects of mergers, assessing efficiency claims, and predicting entry responses in the post-merger market remain relatively crude and often are unreliable. See Richard Schmalensee, *Horizontal Merger Policy: Problems and Changes,* 1 J. Econ. Perspectives 41, 42–43 (1987); Dennis A. Yao & Thomas N. Dahdouh, *Information Problems in Merger Decision Making and Their Impact on the Development of an Efficiencies Defense,* 62 Antitrust L.J. 23 (1993). Moreover, there remain important theoretical disagreements about the ability of firms in the post-merger market to exercise market power unilaterally, to coordinate behavior through signaling or other tacit methods of interaction, or to raise prices through noncooperative forms of oligopolistic coordination.

A third destabilizing force is a continuing debate over the appropriate goals of merger policy. Since the early 1980s, federal enforcement policy and some judicial decisions have given primacy to economic efficiency as the organizing principle for merger analysis. This orientation has been criticized for slighting legislative history and earlier Supreme Court merger precedents that emphasize the decentralization of economic, social, and political power. Although efficiency considerations form the mainstream of merger analysis today, populist currents can and do influence the evaluation of specific transactions.

The fourth development relates closely to the third. The retrenchment of federal merger enforcement during Ronald Reagan's presidency inspired state governments to scrutinize mergers more actively. Compared to the federal agencies, state antitrust officials have tended to define relevant markets more narrowly, to rely more heavily on structural presumptions, to treat efficiency arguments more skeptically, and to give greater effect to non-efficiency factors (e.g., a transaction's potential impact upon employment within the state) in deciding whether to prosecute. See David W. Barnes, *Federal and State Philosophies in the Antitrust Law of Mergers,* 56 Geo. Wash. L. Rev. 263 (1988). Recent efforts by federal and state antitrust officials to revise their respective merger guidelines have produced some convergence of publicly stated enforcement plans, but important differences are likely to persist.

The instability generated by these developments is keenly felt by antitrust specialists because merger policy is the most politically sensitive area of antitrust enforcement. Antitrust-relevant behavior usually unfolds in obscurity, but mergers often are front-page news. For competitors, suppliers, customers, and local communities, the announcement of a major transaction is an easily-grasped portent of change in the balance of industry power and in the geographic distribution of employment and company expenditures. Large "deals" quickly focus the attention of rival companies, employees, private citizens, and elected officials on the decisions of public enforcement officials and antitrust courts. When added to the task of analyzing inherently difficult legal and economic issues, coping with this political dimension makes forecasting the outcome of an antitrust merger proceeding as difficult as any assignment an antitrust counselor performs.

B. COMPETITIVE EFFECTS OVERVIEW

Merger analysis classifies transactions into three categories according to the competitive relationships between the merging parties. In a *horizontal* merger, one firm acquires another firm that produces and sells an identical or similar product in the same geographic area, and thereby eliminates competition between the two firms. In a *vertical* merger, one firm acquires either a customer or supplier. *Conglomerate* mergers encompass all other acquisitions, including *pure* conglomerate transactions where the merging parties have no evident economic relationship (e.g., a steel producer buys a petroleum refiner); geographic extension mergers, where the buyer makes the same product as the target firm but does so in a different geographic market (e.g., a baker in Atlanta purchases a bakery in Honolulu); and product extension mergers, where a firm producing one product buys a firm which makes a different product that requires the application of similar manufacturing or marketing techniques (e.g., a producer of household detergents buys a producer of liquid bleach). Each form of merger raises distinctive competitive concerns.

1. HORIZONTAL MERGERS

Horizontal mergers pose three basic competitive problems. The first is the elimination of competition between the merging firms which, depending on their size, may be significant. The second is that the unification of the merging firms' operations may create substantial market power and could enable the merged entity to raise prices by reducing output unilaterally. The third problem is that, by increasing concentration in the relevant market, the transaction may strengthen the ability of the market's remaining participants to coordinate their pricing and output decisions. Here the concern is not so much that firms will collude expressly; rather, the fear is that the reduction in the number of industry members will facilitate the arms-length, tacit coordination of behavior. By barring transactions that would make tacit coordination more effective, horizontal merger policy is central to antitrust's effort to address the problem of oligopolistic interdependence (see Chapter 7).

Horizontal transactions that pose competitive dangers also may create significant efficiencies—e.g., by generating economies of scale and scope. Scholars have proposed three approaches to treat efficiency claims in merger analysis. One is to forego case-by-case evaluation in favor of setting concentration enforcement thresholds high enough to permit firms to realize most (if not all) efficiencies likely to flow from mergers. See Alan A. Fisher & Robert H. Lande, *Efficiency Considerations in Merger Enforcement*, 71 Calif. L. Rev. 1582 (1983). A second technique supplements structural criteria by incorporating an efficiency defense directly into judicial and enforcement agency analysis of proposed transactions. See Timothy J. Muris, *The Efficiency Defense Under Section 7 of the Clayton Act*, 30 Case W. Res. L. Rev. 381 (1980); Oliver E. Williamson, *Economies as an Antitrust Defense Revisited*, 125 U. Pa. L. Rev. 699 (1977). The third method is for enforcement agencies to weigh the merging parties' efficiency claims heavily ex ante (and approve a larger number of transactions) and to conduct an ex post review to determine whether such efficiencies were realized in practice. By this approach, the government might impose ex post structural relief where anticipated efficiencies fail to materialize. See Joseph F. Brodley, *The Economic Goals of Antitrust: Efficiency, Consumer Welfare, and Technological Progress*, 62 N.Y.U. L. Rev. 1020 (1987).

The second of these approaches—recognizing an efficiencies defense to rebut a presumption of liability based on market shares data and other structural factors—is the most widely accepted technique for treating efficiency concerns in horizontal merger analysis today. This technique promises to gain more acceptance as courts and enforcement agencies respond to concerns that merger controls ignore efficiency claims which, if accepted, would enable American firms to compete more effectively in global markets. See Robert Pitofsky, *Proposals for Revised United States Merger Enforcement in a Global Economy,* 81 Geo. L.J. 195 (1992).

2. VERTICAL MERGERS

Vertical mergers take two basic forms: forward integration, by which a firm buys a customer, and backward integration, by which the firm acquires a supplier. Various efficiency rationales can motivate vertical mergers. The most important is to reduce transaction costs. See O. Williamson, *Markets and Hierarchies: Analysis and Antitrust Implications,* at 82–105. Replacing market exchanges with internal transfers can offer at least two major benefits. First, the vertical merger internalizes all transactions between the manufacturer and its supplier or dealer, thus converting a potentially adversarial relationship into something more akin to a partnership. This can help eliminate problems created by the tendency for vertically-aligned independent entities to behave opportunistically during a contractual relationship. Second, internalization can give management more effective ways to monitor and improve performance—for example, ensuring that customer service departments fulfill the firm's warranty commitments.

Vertical integration by merger does not reduce the total number of economic entities operating at one level of the market, but it may change patterns of industry behavior. Whichever direction (upstream or downstream) a vertical merger takes, the newly acquired firm may decide to deal only with the acquiring firm, thereby altering competition in three markets: among the acquiring firm's suppliers, customers, or competitors. The adjustment toward greater reliance on internal transfers is unremarkable; if efficiencies can be gained from internalization, one would expect the newly integrated firm to resort more to internal transfers and to rely less on open market transactions. (Similarly, of course, if such purchases are more costly, they are likely to decline.) However, not all market participants may regard a switch to fewer outside purchases favorably. Suppliers may lose a market for their goods, retail outlets may be deprived of supplies, and competitors may find that both supplies and outlets are blocked.

This phenomenon raises the same concern that attends antitrust analysis of vertical contractual restraints (see Chapter 8)—the possibility that vertical integration will foreclose competitors by limiting their access to sources of supply or to customers. But the foreclosure theory of competitive harm also has attracted extensive criticism. See P. Joskow, *The Role of Transaction Cost Economics in Antitrust and Public Utility Regulatory Policies,* at 58–59. Economists emphasize that the foreclosure hypothesis mistakenly assumes that internalization from a vertical merger completely shields internal transfers from the discipline of market forces. Vertically integrated firms ordinarily will buy products from related companies only if they offer a quality and price superior to that attainable through external transfers.

Some courts have expressed concern that vertical mergers may raise barriers to entry and expansion by other firms. Vertical integration may force other firms to integrate vertically in order to compete; this may delay entry and increase the risk premium for the capital which such entrants need. Firms with market power sometimes may invest in vertical integration to retard entry that might erode supracompetitive profits. Thus, antitrust intervention may be appropriate to discourage vertical mergers where integration entrenches existing market power by impeding new entry. See R. Blair & D. Kaserman, *Antitrust Economics,* at 314–16.

In examining vertical merger policy, recall that a merger is not the only way to integrate vertically. See Martin K. Perry, *Vertical Integration: Determinants and Effects,* in 1 Handbook of Industrial Organization 183, 185–87 (Richard Schmalensee & Robert D. Willig eds. 1989). A firm can accomplish vertical integration, and produce the same market effect, by expanding internally—i.e., developing its own source of supply, opening new retail outlets, and channeling its purchases or sales through them. Cases applying Section 2 of the Sherman Act have imposed modest limits on the pricing behavior of a vertically integrated monopolist (see Chapter 4), but antitrust law generally tolerates vertical integration by internal expansion. See United States v. Philadelphia Nat'l Bank (1963) ("one premise of an anti-merger statute ... is that corporate growth by internal expansion is socially preferable to growth by acquisition"). There is no sound policy basis for treating integration accomplished through merger or internal growth differently. Thus, with the qualifications noted above, lenient antitrust treatment for both forms of vertical integration generally is appropriate.

3. CONGLOMERATE MERGERS

Conglomerate transactions take many forms ranging from short-term joint ventures to complete mergers. As noted above, conglomerate acquisitions generally are classified as either product line extensions, geographic market extensions, or "pure" conglomerates. Whatever form it takes, a conglomerate merger involves firms which operated in separate markets; thus, a conglomerate transaction ordinarily has no direct effect on competition. There is no reduction or other change in the number of firms in either the acquiring or acquired firm's market. Foreclosure is generally absent, except insofar as the merging parties may engage in reciprocal dealing or supply each other's needs. Nor is there any change in the market structure, the firms' market shares, or concentration levels.

Conglomerate mergers can serve desirable social ends as well as impair competition. See ABA Antitrust Section, *Monograph No. 14, Non–Horizontal Merger Law and Policy* 27–35 (1988). On the positive side, as with all other types of mergers, they supply a market or "demand" for firms, thus giving entrepreneurs liquidity at an open market price and with a key inducement to form new enterprises. Again, the threat of a takeover may press existing managers to increase efficiency in imperfectly competitive markets. Conglomerate mergers also provide opportunities for firms to reduce capital costs and overhead and achieve promotional (advertising) efficiencies.

On the negative side, conglomerate acquisitions sometimes are feared because they may lessen future competition by eliminating the possibility that the acquiring firm would have entered the acquired firm's market independently. A conglomerate merger also may convert a large firm into a dominant company with a decisive competitive advantage or otherwise raise entry barriers. A conglomerate merger may also reduce the number of smaller firms and increase the merged firm's political power, thereby impairing the social and political goals of retaining independent decision making centers, guaranteeing small business opportunities, and preserving democratic processes.

C. THE SHERMAN ACT AND MERGERS TENDING TO MONOPOLY

Antitrust merger law began with the early application to horizontal consolidations of the Sherman Act's ban on combinations in restraint of trade and combinations to monopolize. The first effort to apply the new antitrust statute to a horizontal merger failed miserably. In 1895 in *E.C. Knight* (see Chapter 2), the Supreme Court ruled that manufacturing was not "commerce" under the Sherman Act and rejected the government's challenge to a series of acquisitions that gave the Sugar Trust control of 98 percent of the country's sugar refining capacity. *E.C. Knight* suggested that the Sherman Act would tolerate mergers yielding absolute control of an industry's productive capacity. This helped trigger the era of "merger for monopoly"—a wave of consolidations that saw many small and medium size companies combined into dominant or near-dominant enterprises. George J. Stigler, *Monopoly and Oligopoly by Merger,* 40 Am. Econ. Rev. 23, 27 (1950).

The turn of the century merger movement ended in 1904 with the Supreme Court's decision to invalidate the consolidation of the Northern Pacific and Great Northern Railroads. In the celebrated *Northern Securities* case (see Chapter 2),[1] the Supreme Court took the position that all mergers between directly competing firms constituted a combination in restraint of trade and therefore violated Section 1. Coupled with the stock market crash of 1903, *Northern Securities* stymied the creation of new monopolies through horizontal mergers. On the other hand, many mergers—indeed, thousands—were never challenged, and

---

1. *Northern Securities* provided the occasion for Justice Holmes' famous dissent and observation that "Great cases, like hard cases, make bad law."

others were upheld under the Sherman Act. In 1911, in *Standard Oil (N.J.)* (see Chapter 4), the Supreme Court appeared to substitute a not-too-stringent rule of reason test by which mergers yielding monopoly (as well as combinations creating cartels) were to be evaluated. In applying this rule of reason standard in United States v. United States Steel Corp. (1920) (see Chapter 4), the Court held that a consolidation of most of the steel industry into one firm that initially held 80 to 90 percent of industry capacity and held 41 percent at trial did not violate Section 2 of the Sherman Act. The Court found that the mergers were undertaken to gain monopoly control, but concluded that U.S. Steel had not actually achieved monopoly power and had then abandoned its original goal.

U.S. Steel signaled that the Sherman Act was a frail tool for preventing mergers which might yield market power. Along with a booming stock market, tolerant judicial and executive branch attitudes toward corporate size created a favorable climate for mergers in the 1920s. From 1924 to 1928, the country witnessed a wave of acquisitions equal in intensity to the merger movement at the turn of the century. The second wave's main characteristic was the creation of oligopolistic market structures through mergers that formed strong "number two" firms in industries formerly controlled by a single company and tightened some existing, comparatively weak oligopolies. See F.M. Scherer & D. Ross, *Industrial Market Structure and Economic Performance*, at 156.

Renewed efforts to use the Sherman Act to control mergers occurred after the price-fixing (e.g., *Socony*), boycott (e.g., *FOGA*), and monopolization (e.g., *Alcoa*) cases of the 1940's indicated that the Supreme Court might scrutinize large acquisitions more rigorously. In United States v. Columbia Steel Co. (1948), the government challenged U.S.

Steel's purchase of Consolidated Steel, a competitor in steel fabrication. In a relevant geographic market consisting of 11 western states in which Consolidated sold all of its output, the market shares of the merging firms were 13 and 11 percent. In holding that the merger did not violate the Sherman Act, however, the Court did little more than conclude that a merger bringing 24 percent of the market under one firm's control was not unreasonable. The Court revealed little awareness of how a merger that did not create a single-firm monopoly could affect market prices. If the largest company in an industry not known for robust price competition could buy its largest steel fabrication competitor, it became evident that the Sherman Act would not forbid a merger unless the parties were on the verge of obtaining substantial monopoly power.

Columbia Steel confirmed the Sherman Act's weakness as a merger control device, yet the decision indirectly bolstered antitrust prohibitions against mergers by spurring Congress in 1950 to strengthen the Clayton Act's antimerger provision (Section 7). The amended Clayton Act became antitrust's principal tool for merger control, but it did not completely eliminate recourse to the Sherman Act. The jurisdictional reach of the amended Section 7 originally was narrower than the coverage of Section 1 of the Sherman Act. However, more recent legislative extensions of the Clayton Act's jurisdiction have severely reduced the number of transactions to which Section 1 alone applies. Recent cases generally have concluded that mergers challenged under Section 1 should be evaluated by the same substantive standards as those applied under Section 7. See United States v. Rockford Memorial Corp. (1990).

D. THE ENACTMENT AND AMENDMENT OF SECTION 7 OF THE CLAYTON ACT

The announcement of the rule of reason standard in *Standard Oil (N.J.)* aroused congressional concerns that a largely conservative judiciary might exploit the Sherman Act's generality to undermine the ban against trade restraints and monopolization. To counteract this tendency, Congress in 1914 enacted the Clayton Act, which forbade specific forms of illegal conduct. Among these was Section 7, which barred anticompetitive stock acquisitions. Known as the "holding company" section, its aim was to arrest "trusts" in their incipiency. See ABA Antitrust Section, *Monograph No. 7, Merger Standards Under U.S. Antitrust Laws* 6–16 (1981).

In practice, the original Section 7 was a feeble antimerger safeguard. Because Section 7 banned only purchases of *stock,* businesses soon realized that they could evade this measure simply by buying the target firm's assets. The Supreme Court further undermined Section 7 by allowing a firm to escape liability if it bought a controlling interest in a rival firm's stock and used this control to transfer to itself the target's assets before the government filed a complaint. See Thatcher Manufacturing Co. v. FTC (1926). Thus, a firm could circumvent Section 7 by quickly converting a stock acquisition into a purchase of assets. The Court also required that the competitive impact of a merger under Section 7 be shown to be almost as substantial as that required in Sherman Act cases. See International Shoe Co. v. FTC (1930).

By the early 1930s, it was apparent that the original Section 7 was a nullity. Between the passage of the Clayton Act in 1914 and the amendment of Section 7 in 1950, only 15 mergers were overturned under the antitrust laws, and 10 of these dissolution orders were based on the Sherman Act. See F.M. Scherer & D. Ross, *Industrial Market Structure and Economic Performance,* at 175. Two events in 1948 galvanized Congress to demand curative legislation. First, *Columbia Steel* showed that the Sherman Act could not serve as a strong merger control device. Second, an FTC study concluded that the country was undergoing an alarming wave of corporate acquisitions and warned that "no great stretch of the imagination is required to foresee that if nothing is done to check the growth in concentration, either the giant corporations will ultimately take over the country, or the Government will be impelled to step in and impose some form of direct regulation in the public interest." [2]

In 1950 Congress enacted the Celler–Kefauver Act, which amended Section 7 of the Clayton Act to close the assets loophole. After a minor jurisdictional change in 1980, Section 7 of the statute now reads as follows:

No person engaged in commerce or in any activity affecting commerce shall acquire, directly or indirectly, the whole or any part of the stock or ... assets of another person engaged also in commerce or in any activity affecting commerce, where in any line of commerce in any section of the country, the effect of such acquisition may be substantially to lessen competition, or to tend to create a monopoly.

2. FTC, *The Merger Movement: A Summary Report V* 68 (1948). Many observers discredited the FTC's analysis and conclusions, yet harsh contemporaneous criticism of the FTC report had no apparent impact on how Congress viewed the study. See Derek Bok, *Section 7 of the Clayton Act and the Merging of Law and Economics,* 74 Harv. L. Rev. 226, 231–33 (1961).

Congress intended the amended section to reach vertical and conglomerate transactions, as well as horizontal mergers. The revised provision also sought to prohibit a greater range of mergers than prevailing interpretations of the Sherman Act condemned; under the new Section 7, mergers could be forbidden when the trend toward lessening competition was still incipient and had not ripened into monopoly power. The phrase "may be substantially to lessen competition" lowered the standard of proof so that only probable anticompetitive effects need be shown.

In seeking to stem a trend toward economic concentration, Congress sought to achieve a variety of objectives. Chief Justice Warren's majority opinion in Brown Shoe Co. v. United States (1962), the first Supreme Court decision to interpret the amended Section 7, noted that Congress in 1950 sought to retain " 'local control' over industry" and to protect small business. Congress "feared accelerated concentration of economic power on economic grounds, but also for the threat to other values a trend toward concentration was thought to pose." In an influential analysis of Section 7, Derek Bok found that, during congressional consideration of the Celler–Kefauver amendment, "[e]fficiency, expansion, and the like were ignored or simply brushed aside in the deliberations. . . . [T]here is every reason to believe that Congress preferred the noneconomic advantages of deconcentrated markets to limited reductions in the cost of operations." Derek Bok, *Section 7 of the Clayton Act and the Merging of Law and Economics*, 74 Harv. L. Rev. 226, 307, 318 (1960). However, the Celler–Kefauver legislative history provides scant guidance about how courts should convert Congress' social and political concerns into operational rules of law, or balance such objectives against economic goals with which they may conflict. Many observers have concluded that courts and enforcement agencies are unlikely to devise administrable standards for applying non-economic factors and therefore should develop merger standards solely by reference to economic concerns such as efficiency.   See 4 Phillip Areeda & Donald F. Turner, *Antitrust Law* ¶ 904 (1980).

E. THE SUPREME COURT AND MERGER ANALYSIS SINCE 1950

The Supreme Court has not spoken on issues of substantive merger policy since 1975, leaving a crucial basis for judicial analysis of mergers unaltered for nearly two decades.   The Court's silence since 1975 has posed a major challenge to the antitrust community.   The past 20 years have featured great ferment in commentary relevant to merger policy and a broad reformulation of the federal merger guidelines which were first issued in 1968.   Modern commentary has discredited or qualified some of the central analytical assumptions that guided Supreme Court merger jurisprudence after 1950, and the federal enforcement guidelines today reflect this scholarship.   The new commentary and federal guidelines, in turn, have influenced the lower courts, whose decisions have modified the analytical methodologies and liability thresholds that prevailed in 1975.   In important respects, lower court rulings and federal enforcement policy today diverge significantly from the spirit (if not the letter) of many of the Supreme Court's merger decisions since the Celler–Kefauver Act.   To illuminate the context and importance of recent developments in enforcement policy and judicial analysis, we begin with the Supreme Court cases.

1. VERTICAL MERGERS

The Supreme Court has decided only three vertical merger cases under Section 7 since 1950, and one of these was decided under the original Section 7. All three are relevant to understanding the statute's application to vertical mergers. They illustrate problems the Court has encountered in defining and applying the "relevant market," and they demonstrate its reliance on market shares to infer adverse competitive effects. They also establish a strict but not necessarily rigid standard for measuring the legality of vertical mergers under the Clayton Act.

Until United States v. E.I. du Pont De Nemours & Co. (1957) (*du Pont–GM*), it was generally assumed that the original Section 7 did not apply to vertical transactions. Nevertheless, the Supreme Court ruled that du Pont's purchase of 23 percent of GM stock before 1920 foreclosed sales to GM by other suppliers of automotive paints and fabrics between 1920 and 1949 (the time of the lawsuit) and thus had an illegal anticompetitive effect. *Du Pont–GM* remains significant because the legal focus on foreclosure to measure anticompetitive effect has continued.

As the *du Pont–GM* Court observed, delineating the relevant market is necessary to determine whether the merger will "substantially lessen competition" under Section 7. Du Pont sold finishes and fabrics to GM, which used them to paint and upholster its cars. GM's purchases accounted for a negligible part of total sales of these materials, yet the Court ruled that "automotive finishes and fabrics have sufficient peculiar characteristics and uses" to make them a distinct "line of commerce." The record of the case casts doubt on this finding. Du Pont's competitors made similar (and interchangeable) finishes and fabrics and sold them to

GM and its competitors, as well as to nonautomotive firms. Thus, du Pont's sales to GM did not significantly foreclose sales to du Pont's rivals, and there was no compelling reason to limit the relevant market to automotive sales. See Jesse W. Markham, *The du Pont–General Motors Decision,* 43 Va. L. Rev. 881, 887 (1957). By confining the market to automotive finishes and fabrics, the Court unduly emphasized the merger's impact on these sales—and hence upon du Pont's rivals. The foreclosure of paint sales was only 3.5 percent of total industrial finishes but 24 percent of automotive uses. Similarly, GM's purchases of 19 percent of all automotive fabrics from du Pont might appear significant until it is noted that this represents but 1.6 percent of all uses of this type of fabric.

In deciding whether du Pont had violated Section 7, the Court established two requirements. First, the affected market must be substantial. The antimerger law did not reach consolidations involving trivial firms or markets. Whatever the correct product market, GM's size and du Pont's annual sales of over $26 million to GM easily met this test. Second, the government must show that competition would likely be "foreclosed in a substantial share" of the relevant market.[3] The Court relied on GM's substantial purchases of paints and fabrics from du Pont to infer that du Pont's stock ownership in GM was a decisive factor in GM's decision to buy du Pont products. It then concluded that the stock acquisition had foreclosed a substantial share of the market to du Pont's competitors and therefore had the necessary anticompetitive effect. This analysis is questionable. As the District Court had noted in reaching a contrary opinion, GM's varying purchases from du Pont over the years suggested that the commercial merit of du Pont's products and prices governed such decisions. Other

3. Quoting from *Standard Stations* (1949) (see Chapter 8).

facts, such as GM's purchases before the stock acquisition and purchases from du Pont by other auto companies, reinforced the trial court's reasoning. (It would generally be in GM's and du Pont's interests—the latter as a stockholder—for GM to buy inputs at the best price, regardless of who supplied them.)

Still the *du Pont–GM* case was sui generis. All other things being equal, GM would of course buy its supplies from stockholders. Each firm's size and the oligopolistic structure of their industries seemed to make any further interconnection between the two companies undesirable. The decision can therefore be rationalized as requiring strict scrutiny of vertical mergers involving companies already powerful in their relevant markets, at least when they buy stock in a leading customer.

The Supreme Court's first opportunity to interpret the amended Section 7 came in Brown Shoe Co. v. United States (1962). Both of the merging firms (Brown and Kinney) manufactured shoes and distributed them through their respective retail outlets. The merger's primary vertical impact was likely to be in the foreclosure of Kinney's retail outlets to other shoe producers. Kinney's manufacturing operation was small; its outlets had bought 80 percent of their shoes from manufacturers other than Brown. Of U.S. manufacturers, Brown was the fourth largest, producing about 4 percent of the country's footwear; Kinney was the eighth largest retailer and operated over 350 shoe stores.

An analysis of the vertical merger's effect on competition among shoe manufacturers, which would be adversely affected by a shift of purchases by Kinney outlets to Brown (Brown's president admitted in testimony that "we hoped" to use the ownership of Kinney to introduce Brown's shoes into Kinney stores), again required consideration of the product market. Looking at various factors (see infra pp. 376–77), the Court adopted the District Court's finding that men's, women's, and children's shoes were separate product markets. After completing this exercise, however, the Court ignored these findings and lumped all shoes together in examining the merger's vertical effects.

In this unconcentrated market, the Court extended the *du Pont–GM* standard by relying primarily on the potential foreclosure of Kinney outlets to other shoe producers. The Court explained that the "primary vice of a vertical merger or other arrangement tying a customer to a supplier is that, by foreclosing the competitors of either party from a segment of the market otherwise open to them, the arrangement may act as a 'clog on competition,' which 'deprive[s] ... rivals of a fair opportunity to compete.' " (quoting *Standard Stations*). The Court buttressed this conclusion by emphasizing (1) Section 7's role in halting market concentration in its "incipiency," (2) the trend toward mergers and market concentration in the shoe manufacturing and retailing industries, (3) the merger's effect on shoe styles and customer preferences, on nonintegrated manufacturers and retailers, and on middlemen, and (4) the absence of any apparent justification for the merger. On close examination, however, much of this analysis seems misguided.

The actual and likely vertical foreclosure from the merger was minimal—however one measured it. See John L. Peterman, *The Brown Shoe Case,* 18 J.L. & Econ. 81 (1975). Kinney's 350 retail outlets constituted less than one-half of one percent of all retail outlets selling shoes (of which there were 70,000) and less than 2 percent of stores selling shoes only (there were 22,000 of these). Looking at actual sales, Kinney sold 1.6 percent of all shoes (or 1.2 percent of dollar volume)—and 20 percent of these sales had not been open to other manufacturers since they were supplied from Kinney's plants before the merger. Thus, *the maximum possible foreclosure from the vertical merger was 1.3 percent of shoe sales* (80 percent of 1.6 percent) without regard to actual relevant product market data. In a deconcentrated market this hardly portended a substantial lessening of competition. Indeed, two years after the merger, footwear made by Brown constituted under 8 percent of Kinney sales—that is, the merger actually affected less than .1 percent of nationwide shoe sales.

The Court's other arguments did not fortify the foreclosure evidence. Kinney's status as the largest remaining family-style shoe store chain (whatever that means) neither added nor detracted from these figures since there was no evidence that retail competition extended beyond a shoe store's immediate locality. Nor was the Court's recitation of recent declines in the number of shoe manufacturers or of separate owners of retail shoe outlets important since a vertical merger merely *substitutes* a new owner (here at the retail level). Such substitution does not affect market concentration unless, of course, the transaction also features a horizontal overlap.

At first glance the Court seemed on more solid ground in questioning the merger because the defendant offered no economic justification for it. Harlan M. Blake and William K. Jones offer an interesting explanation for this omission. The two scholars point out that "[t]he Government had urged that the Brown–Kinney consolidation was a menace to competition because the integrated company would have been more efficient, and would have been able to sell shoes of equal appearance and quality at a lower price than its unintegrated competitors." In response, Blake and Jones explain, "Brown's counsel, apparently applying the well-known legal principle that every Government action demands an equal and opposite reaction, found himself in the incomprehensible position of arguing that the merger produced no such economies or likelihood of benefit to the consumer." The Court proceeded to endorse the government's view that the merger would improve efficiency and that this effect counted against the merger. Harlan M. Blake & William K. Jones, *Toward a Three–Dimensional Antitrust Policy,* 65 Colum. L. Rev. 422, 456–57 (1965). This reasoning, Blake and Jones find, was the "real vice" of the decision, as "the claims of increased efficiency should have been considered on their merits; if found to be valid and sufficiently substantial, they should have resulted in approval of the transaction."

In Ford Motor Co. v. United States (1972), the Court emphasized heightened barriers to entry in condemning Ford's attempted acquisition of Autolite, a spark plug manufacturer. Autolite sold spark plugs for use by automobile manufacturers in producing new cars—the original equipment (OE) market—and for sale in the replacement aftermarket. Spark plug producers ordinarily sold spark plugs at low prices to car manufacturers because they expected to charge higher prices for aftermarket replacement sales. (Automobile mechanics usually replaced spark plugs with the same brand as the car maker had installed as OE.) The Court warned that, if Ford entered the spark plug aftermarket by acquiring Autolite, "it would have every incentive to perpetuate the OE tie and thus maintain the virtually unsurmountable barriers to entry to the aftermarket." This argument is unpersuasive, however, and like the foreclosure argument is increasingly challenged. See R. Blair & D. Kaserman, *Antitrust Economics,* at 331–32. The Court offered no economic evidence that the spark plug aftermarket was functioning badly. Rather, the Court noted that large-scale retailers such as Sears and Montgomery

Ward had experienced noteworthy growth in aftermarket spark plug sales. If the merger made Ford a more efficient and stronger competitor, the opinion provided no basis for concluding that other firms could not duplicate Ford's integration and compete effectively.

As a group, the Court's vertical merger cases encouraged lower courts to focus mechanically on: (1) what percentage of the market the merger foreclosed (recall how low *Brown Shoe* had set the threshold of competitive concern) and (2) whether the market featured a trend toward vertical integration (suggesting that entry barriers had increased dangerously). Following the Supreme Court's lead, lower court decisions tended to recite the presence or absence of these factors, rather than explain their competitive significance. As Lawrence Sullivan observes, a deterministic application of foreclosure data, rather than a coherent analysis of competitive harm, characterized many decisions: "If the share foreclosed is high enough, the prosecutor need not articulate any particular theory about why the merger is injurious; it need only insist that it is." L. Sullivan, *Antitrust,* at 663.

2. HORIZONTAL MERGERS

The Celler–Kefauver Act sought to arrest what Congress saw as a rising tide of economic concentration—a trend that the FTC had attributed mainly to horizontal mergers. Some observers feared the apparent trend toward concentration because it would facilitate direct and indirect collusion among rival sellers. Such collusion is often difficult— sometimes impossible—to detect. And if identified, prosecution under the Sherman Act was sometimes uncertain (see Chapter 7). In addition, concentration was likely to result either in fewer firms or in the smaller firms having a reduced share of the market; mergers could therefore impair felt needs to preserve small businesses and local control over industry.

The Supreme Court's horizontal merger decisions have sought to address these concerns, but not always with satisfactory results. Again, the first decision, and in some respects still the benchmark for horizontal mergers in unconcentrated markets, is *Brown Shoe*. The Supreme Court's analysis of the merger's horizontal aspects focused on retailing. Brown was the third largest shoe retailer (by dollar volume) with 1,230 stores while Kinney ranked eighth; between them they would control some 1,600 shoe stores throughout the nation and would become the second largest shoe retailer having 7.2 percent of all shoe stores and 2.3 percent of total retail shoe outlets.

In deciding whether the Brown–Kinney retail merger violated Section 7, the Supreme Court announced a functional standard for determining whether a horizontal merger adversely affected competition. Rather than establishing specific tests such as the market shares of the merging firms[4] or the degree of industry concentration, the Court said it would look at the merger's actual and likely effect:

[P]roviding no definite quantitative or qualitative tests by which enforcement agencies could gauge the effects of a given merger to determine whether it may "substantially" lessen competition or tend toward monopoly, Congress indicated plainly that a merger had to be function-

4. The Court noted that the House Report on the bill to amend § 7 reflected "a conscious avoidance of exclusively mathematical tests." The Court added: "Statistics reflecting the shares of the market controlled by the industry leaders and the parties to a merger are, of course, the primary index of market power; but only a further examination of the particular market—its structure, history and probable future—can provide the appropriate setting for judging the probable anticompetitive effect of the merger."

ally viewed, in the context of its particular industry. That is, whether the consolidation was to take place in an industry that was fragmented rather than concentrated, that had seen a recent trend toward domination by a few leaders or had remained fairly consistent in its distribution of market shares among the participating companies, that had experienced easy access to markets by suppliers and easy access to suppliers by buyers or had witnessed foreclosure of business, that had witnessed the ready entry of new competition or the erection of barriers to prospective entrants, all were aspects, varying in importance with the merger under consideration, which would properly be taken into account.

Despite its apparent adoption of an economic impact test for horizontal mergers, the Court spelled out no guidelines for implementing this approach. And its application of this standard to the facts of the Brown–Kinney merger seemed to betray the announced "rule of reason" approach.

In considering the merger's horizontal effect, the Court first defined the geographic market. As a general principle, the Court observed that in amending Section 7 "Congress prescribed a pragmatic, factual approach to the definition of the relevant market, not a formal, legalistic one. The geographic market selected must, therefore, both 'correspond to the commercial realities' of the industry and be economically significant." The Court noted that shoe store customers shopped only within their cities of residence. But it rejected Brown's further argument for a detailed analysis of buying patterns in particular cities as impractical and unwarranted. It therefore concluded that the relevant geographic market consisted of cities of over 10,000 in which both Brown and Kinney operated stores.

As noted above, the Court found that men's, women's, and children's shoes constituted separate product markets. In reaching this result, the Court articulated the following standard for identifying the relevant product market:

> The outer boundaries of the product market are determined by the reasonable interchangeability of use or the cross-elasticity of demand between the product itself and substitutes for it. However, within this broad market, well-defined submarkets may exist which, in themselves, constitute product markets for antitrust purposes.... The boundaries of such a submarket may be determined by examining such practical indicia as industry or public recognition of the submarket as a separate economic entity, the product's peculiar characteristics and uses, unique production facilities, distinct customers, distinct prices, sensitivity to price changes, and specialized vendors.

Segmenting the shoe industry into separate men's, women's, and children's product markets was justified because "[t]hese product lines are recognized by the public; each line is manufactured in separate plants; each has characteristics peculiar to itself rendering it generally noncompetitive with others; and each is, of course, directed toward a distinct class of customers."

The Court's relevant product market analysis is questionable in two major respects. First, the Court overlooked supply substitution—the possibility that production lines configured to produce one type of shoes (e.g, men's shoes) could easily be rearranged to produce another type of shoes (e.g., women's footwear). As Justice Harlan's concurring opinion pointed out, "taking into account the interchangeability of production, the complete wearing apparel shoe market ... would seem a more realistic gauge of the possible anticompetitive effects" of the merger.

Second, and more problematic, was the Court's introduction of the concept of "submarkets" into market definition analysis. Soon after *Brown Shoe* was decided, economists George Hall and Charles Phillips called the submarket idea "an intellectual monstrosity" with "little economic justification."[5] Other observers warned that the submarket concept would invite analytical confusion and mischief by encouraging "the broadening and narrowing of product definitions in order to achieve desired results in calculating market shares." G.E. Hall & Rosemary Hall, *A Line of Commerce: Market Definition in Anti–Merger Cases,* 52 Iowa L. Rev. 406, 426 (1964).

In the abstract, one could argue that these critiques of the Court's submarket approach were unduly harsh. The Court may have been trying to acknowledge that the products included in the relevant product market may differ in their attractiveness to users. Differentiated products often are imperfect substitutes for each other, and the size of gaps between differentiated products in the "product space" can vary (see Chapter 4). Even after careful analysis, the relevant product market may include some comparatively weak substitutes for the merging parties' products, while other products that exercise a nontrivial constraint upon the merging parties' pricing discretion are left outside the artificial bounds that demarcate the product market. In theory, the submarket approach might be seen as a way to address these discontinuities among substitute products by determining demand elasticities more precisely and by

---

5. George R. Hall & Charles F. Phillips, *Antimerger Criteria: Power, Concentration, Foreclosure, and Size,* 9 Vill. L. Rev. 211, 219–20 (1964). For similar later assessments, see 2 Phillip Areeda & Donald F. Turner, *Antitrust Law* ¶ 535b (1978); R. Posner, *Antitrust Law,* at 129.

pinpointing significant groups of consumers who might be vulnerable to post-acquisition price discrimination by the merged entity. Cf. Donald I. Baker & William Blumenthal, *The 1982 Guidelines and Preexisting Law*, 71 Calif. L. Rev. 311, 326 (1982); Thomas J. Campbell, *Predation and Competition in Antitrust: The Case of Non-fungible Goods,* 87 Colum. L. Rev. 1625 (1987).

In practice, however, the critics' diagnoses hit the mark. For many courts, *Brown Shoe's* submarket concept reduced the urgency to define product markets rigorously; the option of denominating weakly reasoned "submarkets" became a seductive alternative to the laborious, difficult effort required to assess demand and supply substitution possibilities. Cf. White and White, Inc. v. American Hosp. Supply Corp. (1983) ("the analysis employed below suggests that the task of defining the relevant market may be abandoned in favor of a less demanding determination of submarkets"). *Brown Shoe* also invited lax analysis through its recitation of the "practical indicia" by which submarkets might be identified. The Court failed to explain the economic significance of each criterion to the market definition process, and it offered no framework for evaluating these factors. From this formless collection of considerations, judges soon discovered that they often could find something to justify even the most analytically suspect submarkets.

As a more important consequence, the submarket concept too often served as an irresistible tool for courts and enforcement agencies to gerrymander markets to achieve preferred outcomes. See Lawrence C. Maisel, *Submarkets in Merger and Monopolization Cases,* 72 Geo. L.J. 39 (1983). Justice Harlan's concurring opinion in *Brown Shoe* warned that "[i]f the Government were permitted to choose its 'line of commerce' it could presumably draw the market narrowly in a case that turns on the existence *vel non* of monopoly power and draw it broadly when the question is whether both parties to a merger are within the same competitive market." The *Brown Shoe* submarket criteria supplied an elastic device for enforcement agencies to narrow or stretch the product market's boundaries and thereby generate an increase in concentration sufficient to warrant the merger's condemnation.

No less controversial than its definition of the relevant market was the Court's assessment of the Brown–Kinney merger's horizontal competitive effects. In analyzing its chosen product markets, the Court emphasized that "[i]n 118 separate cities the combined shares of the market of Brown and Kinney in the sale of one of the relevant lines of commerce exceeded 5 percent." Aware that a 5 percent national market share constituted weak evidence of market power, the Court argued: "In an industry as fragmented as shoe retailing, the control of substantial shares of the trade in a city may have important effects on competition. If a merger achieving 5 percent control were now approved, we might be required to approve future merger efforts by Brown's competitors seeking similar market shares."

A comparison of what the *Brown Shoe* Court *said* with what it *did* reveals its competitive effects analysis to be schizophrenic. On the one hand, the Court called for an analysis of the merger's actual and likely competitive impact in the market. This would have required scrutiny of the merged firm's ability to restrict output and raise price, the opportunity for collusion, and the effect on entry or expansion by others. On the other hand, the Court in fact studied none of the merger's economic consequences save one—the structural effect. It found that a merger creating a firm with 5 percent of an atomistic market is, by itself, likely to diminish competition. Not even an expectation of improved efficiency would have prevented its invalidation under Section 7.

Aside from this contradiction between the Court's theory and its application of Section 7, two other aspects of *Brown Shoe* warrant attention. First, even though the Brown–Kinney merger formed the industry's second largest firm, a merger creating a company with only 5 percent of sales is unlikely to increase the dangers of collusion in a fragmented industry. The record does not indicate the degree of concentration at the retail level, but there were at least 20 competing firms in the market and probably many more. Oligopolistic or collusive pricing is unlikely in an industry of 20 firms where none is dominant. The second point is the Court's view that a merger controlling 5 percent of the market is more significant *because* the industry is fragmented. The less concentrated the market, the less weight should be attributed to the market shares of the merging firms. If a merger yielding a firm controlling 5 percent is not worrisome, such a merger cannot possibly be more dangerous to competition because the market is unconcentrated.

One year later, in United States v. Philadelphia Nat'l Bank (1963) (*PNB*), the Court applied Section 7 to bank mergers and held that a merger creating the largest bank in the Philadelphia area with almost one-third of the market in a highly concentrated industry (the two largest firms would have nearly 60 percent and the top four almost 80 percent) would probably substantially lessen competition. In so doing, the Court outlined a market share threshold above which mergers were presumed to be illegal without a showing of their economic impact:

[The] intense congressional concern with the trend toward concentration warrants dispensing, in certain cases, with elaborate proof of market structure, market behavior, or probable anticompetitive effects. Specifically, we think that a merger which produces a firm controlling an undue percentage share of the relevant market, and results in a significant increase in the concentration of firms in that market is so inherently likely to lessen competition substantially that it must be enjoined in the absence of evidence clearly showing that the merger is not likely to have such anticompetitive effects.

Under this test, the plaintiff established a prima facie case of illegality under Section 7 by showing that the merging firms' combined market shares and overall concentration in the relevant market exceeded specified levels. Here the merger created a firm having 30 percent of the relevant market, and the concentration among the leading firms increased as the combined postmerger market shares of the top two firms jumped from 44 to 59 percent. The Court proceeded to reject PNB's efforts to rebut the presumption of illegality based on market shares. To no avail, PNB argued that creating a larger bank in Philadelphia would draw more business to the metropolitan area and increase economic activity. The Court responded that "a merger the effect of which 'may be substantially to lessen competition' is not saved because, on some ultimate reckoning of social or economic debits and credits, it may be deemed beneficial." Cf. *National Society of Professional Engineers* (1978) (a showing of anticompetitive effects from a trade restraint under Section 1 is not overcome by evidence suggesting other possible benefits); but cf. *Brown University* (1993) (allowing noneconomic factors to be weighed against anticompetitive effects of horizontal restraint challenged under Section 1.)

Although its legal test is very different from that announced in *Brown Shoe*, *PNB* is not necessarily inconsistent. *Brown Shoe* involved a deconcentrated industry where the Court at least said that an examination of economic factors was required, whereas *PNB* relied heavily on market share thresholds to set an outside limit of presumptive illegality for horizontal mergers in concentrated markets. And if a horizontal merger in a concentrated market does not violate Section 7 under the *PNB* test, it must still survive the economic impact scrutiny of *Brown Shoe*. On the other hand, *PNB* did not state a rigid per se rule. Its second requirement—that a merger involving 30 percent of the market was unlawful if the merger also raised concentration significantly—was designed to allow large firms in concentrated markets to buy minor firms without violating Section 7. The *PNB* Court also allowed that its presumption of illegality might be rebutted by "evidence clearly showing" the likely absence of anticompetitive effects.

PNB's test of presumptive illegality suggested that the plaintiff's prima facie case was rebuttable in theory, but subsequent Supreme Court horizontal merger decisions in the 1960s indicated that market share and concentration data would be virtually conclusive in practice. In giving decisive effect to quantitative measures of illegality, the Court often relied on highly questionable market definitions to proscribe challenged transactions under Section 7. When market shares are relied on to evidence market power and used to infer competitive effects, the drawing of the market's boundaries is crucial. As discussed in Chapter 4, the market should include all products having a high demand cross-elasticity (i.e., those which could be readily substituted at a small price increase) with the merging firms' product.

Under the stress of deciding particular cases, however, the Supreme Court often lost sight of this standard when delineating the relevant product and geographic markets. In United States v. Aluminum Co. of America (1964) (*Alcoa–Rome*), the nation's leading producer of aluminum and aluminum conductor was prohibited from acquiring Rome, one of the largest producers of copper conductor and also a "substantial" manufacturer of aluminum conductor. In the aluminum conductor "market" Alcoa's share was 27.8 percent; Rome accounted for 1.3 percent; and the nine largest firms, which included Alcoa and Rome, produced 95.7 percent. The Court held that the dominant firm in a concentrated industry could not purchase a significant competitive factor (Rome having been a dynamic force) without unlawfully impairing competition.

In *Alcoa–Rome,* the Court used tortured logic to determine that all types of aluminum conductor were a separate submarket in which the merger should be tested. After concluding that bare and insulated aluminum conductors were separate markets, the Court held that together they also constituted a separate *all* aluminum market. This market definition has little to commend it. The Court's primary argument that both bare and insulated aluminum are used to conduct electricity is unpersuasive since that would also require the inclusion of copper conductor. Why then did the Court ignore the high cross-elasticity of copper and exclude it from the market? The only plausible reason appears to have been a need to find a market in which the *PNB* test could be applied to find illegality. Neither the bare nor the insulated market alone would have justified finding a Section 7 violation under the *PNB* framework. With only .3 percent of the market, Rome was a trivial entrant in the bare aluminum conductor market. The merged firm's share in the insulated aluminum conductor market totaled 16 percent—only halfway to *PNB's* 30 percent threshold.

In United States v. Continental Can Co. (1964), the Court enjoined the merger of the second largest manufacturer of metal containers with the third largest producer of glass containers. Compared to its market definition analysis in *Alcoa–Rome,* the Court in *Continental Can* took a wholly different—and inconsistent—approach. This time metal cans and glass jars were lumped into one container market even though the cross-elasticity of demand among different types of jars or of cans was substantially greater than between jars and cans. By distorting the product market and treating the case as a horizontal transaction, the Court in effect overstated the merger's impact; in fact the merger directly affected only substitute competition. Consequently, the Court failed to focus on the real issue before it—namely, how to test mergers between firms producing distant substitute products. In the combined "container" market, Continental ranked second with 21.9 percent; Hazel–Atlas, the acquired firm, had 3.1 percent; and the six largest firms held 70.1 percent of the market. While the Court also emphasized the merger's impact on future and potential competition, it relied mainly on the total market share (of 25 percent) and the increasing concentration in the industry. Viewed together, *Continental Can* and *Alcoa–Rome* lowered the percentages at which mergers were presumptively illegal.

In United States v. Von's Grocery Co. (1966), the Court appeared to abandon *PNB's* standard of presumptive illegality in favor of an even more stringent rule which would forbid almost all mergers of consequence. Von's, the third largest retail grocery chain in the Los Angeles market, with 4.7 percent of all sales, acquired the sixth largest retailer. Together they accounted for 7.5 percent of all grocery store sales in the area, which was only slightly less than the leader, Safeway. In finding a Section 7 violation, the Court emphasized the trend toward mergers and chains and the decline of independent firms in the market. From 1950 to 1963 the number of owners operating a single grocery store in the Los Angeles retail market fell from 5,365 to 3,590; the number of food chains with two or more stores increased between 1953 and 1962 from 96 to 150; and between 1949 and 1958 nine of the top 20 chains acquired 126 stores from their smaller competitors. The Court relied primarily on the Clayton Act's purpose of preventing powerful combinations from driving out smaller rivals; since this merger would further reduce the number of independent firms in the market, it violated Section 7.

In *Von's,* the Court interpreted the antimerger law as a mandate to encourage markets composed of small competitors. The Court said "[i]t is enough for us that Congress feared that a market marked at the same time by both a continuous decline in the number of small businesses and a large number of mergers would slowly but inevitably gravitate from a market of many small competitors to one dominated by one or a few giants, and competition would thereby be destroyed." *Von's* appeared to make all but the most trivial horizontal mergers illegal per se. The result and reasoning in *Von's* provoked a celebrated dissent from Justice Stewart, who observed that "the Court pronounces its work consistent with the line of our decisions under Section 7 since the passage of the 1950 amendment. The sole consistency that I can find is that in litigation under Section 7, the Government always wins."

Justice Stewart's impression was confirmed in United States v. Pabst Brewing Co. (1966), which used a contorted definition of the relevant geographic market to condemn the acquisition by Pabst (the nation's tenth largest brewer) of Blatz (the eighteenth largest). The district court had dismissed the complaint because the government had failed to show either that Wisconsin or the three-state area of Wisconsin, Illinois, and Michigan, were relevant geographic markets. The merging parties accounted for 4.49 percent of nationwide beer sales, 23.95 percent of sales in Wisconsin, and 11.32 percent of sales in the Wisconsin–Illinois–Michigan area. The Supreme Court reversed the decision and scolded the district court for asking too much from the government, observing that Section 7 "does not require the delineation of a 'section of the country' by metes and bounds as a surveyor would lay off a plot of ground." The Court declined to specify any relevant geographic markets and appeared to hold (contrary to *Brown Shoe*) that the government need prove only that the merger had a substantial effect somewhere in the country. Yet without first defining a market in which to measure competitive effects, any prediction of a merger's impact on competition is meaningless. By ruling that the transaction was illegal for its effect on competition in the national market—where the merging firms accounted for 4.49 percent of all beer sales—the Court suggested that only the most trivial horizontal mergers would escape risk. See 4 Phillip Areeda & Donald F. Turner, *Antitrust Law* ¶ 909b (1980) (table of cases listing market shares of merged companies, market structure, and court decision).

The Court's post-*PNB* decisions from *Alcoa–Rome* through *Pabst* were heatedly criticized as being inconsistent and economically unsound. Such criticism appears to have affected the Supreme Court's analysis of horizontal mergers. By the early 1970s, commentators had raised serious doubts about the structure-conduct-performance model on which the Court's merger jurisprudence had relied. Moreover, by the early 1970s, the Court's composition changed significantly with the departure of Chief Justice Warren and Justices Black and Fortas, all of whom had fostered the application of populist values in interpreting Section 7. During the tenure of Chief Justice Warren Burger and other of President Richard Nixon's appointees, the Court embraced a more economically-oriented approach in antitrust cases and retreated from the use of bright-line tests in favor of more elaborate reasonableness standards.

The impact of these adjustments on merger analysis began to emerge in United States v. General Dynamics Corp. (1974). In *General Dynamics* the Court upheld a district court decision approving a merger of two leading coal producers even though a rapid decline in the number of coal producers had occurred. The merger increased the concentration of the top two firms in the market by over 10 percent and resulted in the two largest firms now controlling about half of all sales. In an opinion by Justice Stewart (an acerbic dissenter in *Von's* and many other of the Court's earlier merger decisions), the Court repeated its admonition in *Brown Shoe* that "statistics concerning market share and concentration, while of great significance, were not conclusive indicators of anticompetitive effect." Market share was only the beginning place for analyzing a merger's competitive impact, for "[e]vidence of past production does not, as a matter of logic, necessarily give a proper picture of a company's future ability to compete." The Court concluded that the acquired firm's exhausted coal reserves, combined with long-term contract commitments, indicated it was no longer a significant force in the market—and its disappearance as an independent firm would not adversely affect competition. Thus, the Court did more than apply a rigid test predicated on market share data; instead, it accounted for important qualitative factors in concluding that market shares based upon historical sales data would not give a "proper picture of [the merging parties'] future ability to compete."

Given the decision's narrow facts, it was not immediately clear whether *General Dynamics* suggested a new trend. The case involved the unusual situation of an exhaustible resource rather than a replenishable product, and for this reason the Court viewed the market as uncommitted coal reserves rather than, as the government urged, coal production. In retrospect, however, it is evident that the *General Dynamics* Court did more than address the proper method for calculating market shares and measuring the parties' competitive significance. Instead, the decision emphasized language in *Brown Shoe,* ignored during the turbulent preceding decade in the Court's Section 7 decisions, regarding the limitations of market share data as a conclusive index of competitive effect. In doing so, *General Dynamics* rehabilitated the rebuttal opportunities suggested in *PNB* in holding that defendants in fact could defeat the plaintiff's prima facie case by showing that the merger was unlikely to have anticompetitive effects. More generally, the retreat from populist-influenced structuralism foreshadowed the revolution in analysis that the Court would unleash in 1977 with *Sylvania* and *Brunswick*. Thus, *General Dynamics* signaled a major adjustment not only in merger analysis, but in antitrust policy as a whole.

Following *General Dynamics,* the Court's merger decisions required an economically more rigorous definition of the relevant market and assessment of the future competitive capability of the merging parties. In United States v. Marine Bancorporation (1974), a Seattle bank's acquisition of a Spokane bank in the State of Washington was upheld because state law prohibited the former from establishing a branch in Spokane. The Government's argument that the relevant market was the entire state where the two banks might otherwise have been potential competitors was unpersuasive because the Seattle bank was not a competitor, actual or potential, in the Spokane metropolitan area. Similarly, in United States v. Connecticut Nat'l Bank (1974), the Court held that commercial and savings banks could not be simply aggregated into a single product market. Careful analysis, the Court ruled, requires specific evaluation of competition with other credit suppliers as well as more rigorous examination of the overlap between commercial and savings banks.

3. CONGLOMERATE MERGERS, POTENTIAL COMPETITION, AND JOINT VENTURES

The legal mainstay of attack upon conglomerate mergers under Section 7 has been the potential competition doctrine. This theory has had a checkered and not wholly satisfactory history. Its first application in connection with conglomerate acquisitions was to a joint venture between two chemical companies in United States v. Penn–Olin Chem. Co. (1964). Pennsalt, an Oregon producer of sodium chlorate (a bleaching agent used mainly in the pulp and paper industry) which it sold in the West, joined Olin Mathieson, an industrial chemical firm which was an intermediate user of sodium chlorate, to build a sodium chlorate plant in Kentucky and to sell that product in the Southeast. Before Penn–Olin entered this market, only two firms had plants in the Southeast and controlled over 90 percent of all sales. Before forming the joint venture, both Pennsalt and Olin Mathieson had considered but not completely rejected the possibility of entering the Southeast independently. Relying on the competitive value of an additional entrant, the district court upheld the joint venture. The government had not shown "as a matter of reasonable probability" that both firms would have entered the market if Penn–Olin had not been created. The court reasoned that one actual entrant was worth more than two on the sidelines.

On review the Supreme Court remanded the case for further findings and ruled that if one of the firms probably would have entered with the other remaining "at the edge of the market, continually threatening to enter," the venture should be disapproved. The Court concluded that the possible elimination of a potential entrant, even if the evidence failed to show a reasonable probability of entry by the second firm, would violate Section 7. On remand, the district court determined that independent entry by either of the two firms was improbable and that therefore the "merger" did not violate Section 7. An equally divided Supreme Court upheld this decision (1967).

The potential competition theory applied in *Penn–Olin* can be questioned on three grounds. First, the Supreme Court ignored the effect of the joint venture's actual entry into the market. This entry increased the number of firms in the Southeast (by 50 percent) and reduced the other firms' share of productive capacity, thus diminishing the likelihood of price collusion. Second, the assumption that once one venturer enters the market the other will remain a potential entrant overlooks how the new entrant is likely to change the market and affect the attractiveness of further entry. The joint venture (or one of the partners) would enter in the first place because the product's price is supranormal, permitting increased profits to be earned. Once an additional firm enters, prices should fall with increased output, and the market would no longer be as attractive to new entrants. Third, even if the market still appeals to new entrants because prices do not fall (e.g., demand rises or the new entrant joins in collusive pricing), the significance of the remaining venturer(s) as potential entrant(s) depends on a factor slighted by the Court—the number of other chemical firms with interest and ability to enter the Southeast market. Penn–Olin's entry and its possible elimination of one venturer as a potential entrant matters only if there were no other possible entrants.

The Court next considered the legality of a conglomerate merger in FTC v. Procter & Gamble Co. (1967) (*P & G*). Procter, a large, diversified producer of detergents and other household products sold in supermarkets, bought Clorox, the largest seller of household liquid bleach. Procter accounted for 54 percent of detergent sales, but it neither made nor sold bleach. Clorox controlled almost 49 percent of the bleach market; its nearest rival (Purex) had less than 16 percent of bleach sales. In ruling that Procter's acquisition of a producer of complementary products violated Section 7, the Court relied on two somewhat contradictory grounds: first, that the merger would give Clorox (supported by Procter) a decisive competitive advantage in the bleach market, allowing it to discipline competitors and raise new barriers to entry; and second, that Procter was the leading, and perhaps only, potential candidate for entry into the bleach market. For these reasons, the Court held that the merger adversely affected actual and potential competition.

Neither basis for its decision is compelling. The first ground presumes that Procter had both the ability and desire to drive out competing bleach producers. Yet, if the entry was as desirable to Procter as the Court assumed, Procter could have achieved that end through internal expansion and then driven Clorox and others from the market.[6] The second ground—that the merger eliminated

6. In finding that a Procter-owned Clorox would have an unfair advantage, the Court focused chiefly on Procter's promotional efficiencies— which, to the Court, were not socially desirable economic efficiencies and therefore counted against the merger. The Court cast doubt on the availability of any efficiencies defense under Section 7, stating that "[p]ossible economies cannot be used as a defense to illegality. Congress was

Procter, the leading and perhaps only potential market entrant—is contradicted by the available evidence. Entry into bleach production was not impeded by technical barriers; the market contained many small firms; retail distribution was possible by any of the large retail chains; large scale economies did not bar smaller firms. Nor did the Court consider whether other large detergent producers could have entered the market. Procter was probably only one of several (perhaps many) possible entrants, and its elimination as a potential competitor through the purchase of Clorox would not have reduced competition.

Following its success in *P & G,* the Federal Trade Commission sought to extend the potential competition doctrine to reach instances where the acquiring firm admittedly was unlikely to enter the acquired firm's market by internal expansion (i.e., *de novo*). In Bendix Corp. (1970) a diversified manufacturer of automotive components and assemblies sought to buy the third largest producer of auto filters (with over 17 percent of the aftermarket). The FTC found that Bendix (the acquirer) would not have entered the auto filter market *de novo* and therefore was not itself a potential entrant, but it nonetheless barred the acquisition because Bendix would have been a likely entrant into the concentrated filter market by acquiring and expanding a "toehold" firm. Competition within the filter market could have been improved if Bendix had bought a smaller firm and through expansion had competed independently with Fram (the acquired firm) as well as with other filter makers.

Though inventive, the toehold acquisition theory is not airtight. Recall that Section 7 requires a probable substantial lessening of competition. In *Bendix,* the FTC made no

aware that some mergers which lessen competition may also result in economies but it struck the balance in favor of protecting competition."

finding that actual or future competition would lessen; rather, it banned the merger for not *improving* competition as much as another merger might have done. That Congress sought to limit (or sound policy would have limited) conglomerate mergers to those demonstrably improving the competitive structure in the acquired firm's market is doubtful.

So far the Supreme Court has specifically declined to decide whether the toehold theory is consistent with Section 7, see United States v. Falstaff Brewing Corp. (1973); United States v. Marine Bancorporation (1974), although it noted in *Falstaff* that "[t]here are traces of this view [that the toehold theory is consistent with Section 7] in our cases." The Court reserved decision on the validity of the "actual potential competition" theory that, but for the merger, the acquiring firm would have entered a concentrated market (de novo or by acquiring a much smaller firm). However, it did establish two preconditions in *Marine Bancorporation:* (1) the evidence must show that the potential entrant could enter other than by buying the target firm; and, (2) this entry was substantially likely to deconcentrate the target market or produce other procompetitive effects.

Falstaff expanded the concept of "potential competitor" by looking beyond the acquiring firm's actual intent. The district court had dismissed the government's complaint after finding that the acquiring firm had decided not to enter the market except by purchasing a significant rival; because Falstaff was not a potential entrant, the merger was merely a substitution of ownership by the acquired firm. In an opinion reminiscent of *Penn–Olin,* the Supreme Court reversed the decision on the ground that Falstaff still might have been "perceived" by firms in the market to be a potential entrant and consequently might have constrained their pricing practices. The Court remanded the case for consideration of whether Falstaff was so positioned on the market's edge (an "on the fringe potential competitor" who is "waiting in the wings") that it exerted a beneficial influence on it—and therefore that its elimination harmed future competition. As in *Penn–Olin*, however, the Court did not reach the ultimate question of whether Falstaff's elimination as a potential competitor would affect the market significantly.

F. GOVERNMENT MERGER GUIDELINES AND PREMERGER NOTIFICATION

On four occasions since the late 1960s—in 1968, 1982, 1984, and 1992—the federal enforcement agencies have issued non-binding guidelines concerning how they expect to exercise their prosecutorial powers under Section 7 of the Clayton Act. The 1992 Justice Department/FTC Horizontal Merger Guidelines constitute the federal government's current statement of enforcement policy for horizontal transactions, and the 1984 Justice Department Merger Guidelines provide the latest statement of federal enforcement intentions for non-horizontal mergers. Taken together, the 1992 and 1984 guidelines are important for antitrust counseling and adjudication, and their central features are summarized below.

The revision of the federal guidelines in the 1980s was accompanied by a significant retrenchment of federal merger enforcement policy. The Justice Department and the FTC adopted a less restrictive approach for reviewing horizontal mergers and used rebuttable structural presumptions that operated at thresholds well above those endorsed in decisions such as *Von's*. Moreover, the federal agencies employed market definition and market power measurement techniques that generally defined markets more broadly and thereby reduced the likelihood that individual mergers would trigger the structural presumptions. The policy change was even more pronounced for non-horizontal transactions. From 1982 through 1992, the federal agencies issued no complaints against purely vertical or conglomerate transactions.

These developments did not please the National Association of Attorneys General (NAAG). State enforcement officials moved to counteract what they perceived to be the Reagan Administration's unduly permissive enforcement policies. Beyond suing more frequently to challenge mergers under Section 7, the states issued their own merger guidelines in 1987 and made revisions in 1993. Despite substantial convergence between the Justice Department/FTC 1992 guidelines and the NAAG 1993 guidelines, important differences persist. While an important indicator of state prosecutorial action, the NAAG Guidelines have not achieved the precedential force or impact of the federal guidelines.

1. FEDERAL MERGER GUIDELINES

The 1984 Justice Department Guidelines and the 1992 joint federal Guidelines state that the "unifying theme" of federal merger enforcement is that "mergers should not be permitted to create or enhance market power or to facilitate its exercise." For horizontal mergers, the 1992 Guidelines prescribe five steps for identifying competitive hazards:

• Does the merger cause a significant increase in concentration and produce a concentrated market?

• Does the merger appear likely to cause adverse competitive effects?

● Would entry sufficient to frustrate anticompetitive conduct be timely and likely to occur?

● Will the merger generate efficiencies that the parties could not reasonably achieve through other means?

● Is either party likely to fail, and will its assets leave the market if the merger does not occur?

To assess the merger's impact on concentration, the 1992 Guidelines use the market definition and market power measurement methods described in Chapter 4. These methods constitute a major departure from earlier Supreme Court merger precedents. This change is significant, because market definition is the basis for determining market shares and concentration, which remain the starting points for merger analysis. The Guidelines essentially ask: which products or firms are now available to buyers, and where could buyers turn for supplies if relative prices increased by five percent? These alternative suppliers and their production generally are included in the market denominator. By casting a larger net and redrawing market boundaries to cover more products and a greater area, the federal Guidelines tend to yield lower concentration increases than Supreme Court merger decisions of the 1960s.

To quantify concentration effects, the federal Guidelines substituted the Herfindahl–Hirschman Index (the HHI) for 4–firm market share measures of concentration. The HHI is calculated by summing the squares of the market shares of each firm in the market. For example, in a market with ten firms which each account for 10 percent of sales, the HHI is 1000. The square of each firm's share is 100, and the sum of the firms' squares yields 1000. The HHI measures concentration in a way that reflects both the absolute level of concentration and the significance of larger firms within the market. The 1992 Guidelines focus on market shares and concentration data to create a presumption of illegality (if the HHI is above 1800 and it is increased by more than 100 points) or legality (if the HHI is below 1000, or between 1000–1800 and the increase is less than 100). In this calculus, the federal Guidelines ignore trends toward concentration.

The 1992 Guidelines focus on two types of anticompetitive effects in horizontal mergers. One goal is to prevent mergers likely to permit the exercise of market power through coordinated interaction. Consistent with modern theory—generally accepted, but not indisputable—about oligopolistic behavior (see Chapter 7), the concern here is not simply with express collusion, but also with mutually accommodating behavior that falls short of an express exchange of assurances. The 1992 Guidelines consider criteria that indicate whether the post-merger market is conducive to solving the three basic problems that beset efforts by rivals to coordinate their conduct: Can the firms reach consensus on the terms of collective action; can they detect deviations from these terms; and can they punish cheaters? Relevant factors include product homogeneity or heterogeneity, the availability of information about specific transactions or individual firm pricing or output decisions throughout the industry, patterns of common pricing or marketing practices, and the ability of buyers to implement effective counterstrategies.

The second concern in the Guidelines' competitive effects analysis is whether the merger will reduce competition through unilateral conduct, even though the ability of market participants to coordinate their behavior is not enhanced. The clearest example would be a merger that creates substantial market power. A more subtle possibility is reflected in an important innovation in the 1992 Guidelines. Where the market features substantial product differentiation, the merger may have anticompetitive effects if consumers see the products of the merging parties as their first and second choices and other firms are unlikely to reposition their product lines closer in product space to the offerings of the merging parties. The 1992 Guidelines presume that adverse unilateral price effects are most likely to occur when (1) a significant share of sales in the market are accounted for by consumers who regard the merging firms' products as their first and second choices, (2) the market concentration data fall outside the Guidelines' "safe-harbor" areas, and (3) the merging firms have a combined market share of at least 35 percent. Cf. United States v. Gillette Co. (1993) (denying Justice Department's motion to enjoin merger of premium fountain pen producers; declining to find substantial likelihood of competitive harm based on coordinated or unilateral effects).

As described in more detail in Chapter 4, the federal Guidelines emphasize that ease of entry frustrates the creation or exercise of market power. The Guidelines also consider whether otherwise objectionable mergers may be necessary to achieve efficiencies such as scale economies, plant specialization, improved integration of production facilities, and transportation cost reductions. The merging parties bear the burden of proof concerning efficiencies; the federal agencies tend to be skeptical of most efficiency claims and will reject such arguments where the asserted benefits can be attained in other ways.

The 1992 Guidelines provide a limited defense for failing firms and failing divisions of firms. The defense is available if impending failure would cause the assets of one party to leave the market if the merger does not occur. Thus, to establish a *failing firm* defense, the parties must show that the failing firm cannot (1) meet its financial obligations, (2) reorganize in bankruptcy, and (3) find another buyer whose purchase of the firm would pose lesser anticompetitive risks. The parties must further show that (4) without the merger, the failing firm's assets will exit the market. The *failing division* defense requires that the division have a negative cash flow from operations, that the assets will leave the market in the near term if the division is not sold, and there is no other buyer whose purchase of the division would pose fewer competitive hazards.

Like the 1992 Guidelines' treatment of horizontal transactions, the 1984 Justice Department Guidelines backed away from Supreme Court precedents governing non-horizontal mergers. The 1984 Guidelines focus solely upon the "horizontal effect from nonhorizontal mergers" and generally presume that vertical mergers do not threaten competition. The 1984 Guidelines provide that efficiencies will receive "relatively more weight" in the review of vertical transactions than in the consideration of horizontal mergers. The 1984 Guidelines largely abandon the foreclosure theory of *Brown Shoe* and limit scrutiny of vertical mergers to transactions that promise to: increase entry barriers by forcing entrants to enter two markets simultaneously; facilitate collusion by acquiring a buyer who can make it "easier to monitor price[s]" or whose past "disruptive" behavior has impeded operation of a collusive scheme; or enable the merging parties to avoid rate regulation—e.g., when a regulated utility acquires an important input supplier who in the post-merger period can inflate the prices at which it sells to its new parent.

2. STATE MERGER GUIDELINES

In important respects, the 1993 NAAG Guidelines share analytical approaches common to the 1992 federal Guidelines for horizontal mergers. Like the federal Guidelines, for example, the NAAG Guidelines use the HHI to calculate concentration increases and adopt basically the same the concentration-based presumptions. Nonetheless, several noteworthy differences remain. First, the NAAG Guidelines give state officials greater latitude to define narrow markets and thereby increase the range of transactions subject to prosecution. Second, the NAAG Guidelines consider historical trends toward concentration as a criterion bearing upon illegality. Third, the state guidelines treat efficiency claims more skeptically, reducing the possibility that the merger's proponents will overcome a presumption of illegality. Finally, the NAAG Guidelines state that the prevention of wealth transfers from consumers to producers is the chief goal of Section 7 enforcement. Thus, where a merger is likely to increase prices but also generate substantial efficiencies, the NAAG Guidelines would disregard the efficiency effects and prohibit the transaction on the ground that it would raise prices to consumers.

3. PREMERGER NOTIFICATION

The Hart–Scott–Rodino Antitrust Improvements Act of 1976 created a mandatory premerger notification procedure for firms to certain mergers. Adopted as Section 7A of the Clayton Act, 15 U.S.C.A. § 18A, the Hart–Scott–Rodino (HSR) process requires the merging parties to notify the FTC and the Justice Department before completing certain transactions. In general, an HSR premerger filing is required when (a) one of the parties to the transaction has annual net sales (or revenues) or total assets exceeding $100 million and the other party has annual net sales (or revenues) or total assets exceeding $10 million; and (b) the acquisition price or value of the acquired assets or entity exceeds $15 million. Failure to comply with these requirements can result in the rescission of completed transactions and can be punished by a civil penalty of up to $10,000 per day. See ABA Antitrust Section, *Premerger Notification Practice Manual* (2d ed. 1991).

The Hart–Scott–Rodino Act also established mandatory waiting periods during which the parties may not "close" a proposed transaction and begin joint operations. In transactions other than cash tender offers, the initial waiting period is thirty days after the merging parties have made the requisite premerger notification filings with the federal agencies. For cash tender offers, the waiting period is fifteen days after the premerger filings. Before the initial waiting periods expire, the federal agency responsible for reviewing the transaction can request the parties to supply additional information relating to the transaction. These "second requests" often include extensive interrogatories and broad demands for the production of documents. See William Blumenthal, *Market Imperfections and Over–Enforcement in Hart–Scott–Rodino Second Request Negotiations,* 36 Antitrust Bull. 745 (1991). A request for further information can be made once, and the issuance of a second request extends the waiting period for ten days for cash tender offers and for twenty days for all other transactions. These extensions of the waiting period do not begin to run until the merging parties are in "substantial compliance" with the government agency's request for additional information.

If the federal government decides not to challenge a merger before the HSR waiting period expires, a federal agency is highly unlikely to sue at a later date to dissolve the transaction under Section 7. The federal government is not legally barred from bringing such a lawsuit, but the desire of the federal agencies to increase predictability for business planners has made the HSR process the critical period for federal review. However, the decision of a federal agency not to attack a merger during the HSR waiting period does not preclude a lawsuit by a state government or a private entity. To facilitate analysis by the state attorneys general, NAAG has issued a Voluntary Pre–Merger Disclosure Compact under which the merging parties can file a copy of their federal HSR filings and responses to second requests with NAAG for circulation among states that have adopted the Disclosure Compact.

G. MODERN LOWER COURT APPLICATIONS

The case law since the Supreme Court's last word on mergers in 1975 has reflected both academic criticism of the Court's merger jurisprudence of the 1960s and the acceptance of many analytical techniques contained in the federal merger guidelines issued in 1982 and revised in 1984 and 1992. The lower courts generally have retreated from the expansive possibilities of *Brown Shoe* and its progeny; this adjustment has permitted larger transactions to be consummated and has raised the defendants' ability to prevail in litigated disputes. For at least the past decade, Justice Stewart's lament in his *Von's* dissent (see supra p. 385) has ceased to be an accurate predictor of outcomes in government merger cases. See Stephen Calkins, *Developments in Merger Litigation: The Government Doesn't Always Win,* 56 Antitrust L.J. 855 (1988) (reporting that from 1982 through mid–1988 the Justice Department lost all but one of its merger prosecutions that were contested in court).

1. MARKET DEFINITION

Lower court analyses of market definition issues over the past decade have changed significantly compared to approaches that prevailed in the first two decades after *Brown Shoe.* See Gregory J. Werden, *The History of Antitrust Market Delineation,* 76 Marquette L.Rev. 123 (1992). Some tribunals have dispensed with "submarkets" altogether. See Satellite Television & Associated Resources, Inc. v. Continental Cablevision of Va., Inc. (1983); but see Olin Corp. v. FTC (1993) (sustaining FTC's identification of relevant product submarket consisting of dry sanitizing chemicals for cleaning swimming pools). Other courts have continued to recite *Brown Shoe's* "practical indicia," but they generally have done so in a way that reflects concern about using such indicia to delineate contrived narrow markets. See, e.g., Pennsylvania v. Russell Stover Candies, Inc. (1993) (rejecting alleged product market consisting of "branded gift boxed chocolates sold nationally through chain drug stores and mass marketers"). Still other decisions have emphasized considerations that *Brown Shoe* briefly mentioned but largely ignored. For example, courts increasingly focus on supply substitution to expand the product market or attribute larger market shares to firms other than the merging parties. See United States v. Calmar Inc. (1985). These developments have contributed to a general tendency to delineate broader markets, with the result that post-merger market shares more often fall below the requisite thresholds for prima facie illegality.

2. COMPETITIVE EFFECTS IN HORIZONTAL MERGERS

Modern academic commentary and the federal merger guidelines issued since 1980 have exerted their greatest impact on lower court assessments of competitive effects in horizontal merger cases. Although courts recognize that the Supreme Court decisions from the 1960s permit the condemnation of mergers merely by reference to modest concentration increases, most judges have declined to rely on structural criteria alone. See Hospital Corp. of. Am. v. FTC (1986); United States v. Archer–Daniels–Midland Co. (1991). Instead, lower courts have undertaken a more sophisticated, intensive analysis of market structure and firm behavior to determine whether firms could successfully coordinate their behavior in the post-merger period.

Courts have been more willing to permit large mergers in concentrated markets where various economic factors suggest that efforts to exercise market power will fail. See Andrew N. Kleit & Malcolm B. Coate, *Are Judges Leading Economic Theory? Sunk Costs, the Threat of Entry and the Competitive Process,* 60 Southern Econ. J. 103 (1993). Several noteworthy decisions have relied on ease of entry to reject the government's challenge to a merger, despite high market shares or concentration levels. See United States v. Syufy Enters. (1990); United States v. Waste Mgmt., Inc. (1984). Other cases have refused to find liability in concentrated markets where large, sophisticated buyers of the merged entity's output would likely adopt strategies (e.g., threatening to enter its supplier's market) that would deny the market's participants power to raise prices after the merger. See United States v. Baker Hughes, Inc. (1990); United States v. Country Lake Foods, Inc. (1990); see also Mary Lou Steptoe, *The Power–Buyer Defense in Merger Cases,* 61 Antitrust L.J. 493 (1993). Defendants have enjoyed relatively little success in advancing efficiency defenses in court, but several tribunals have recognized that such arguments, if supported by persuasive facts, could rebut a presumption of illegality. See FTC v. University Health, Inc. (1991).

3. COMPETITIVE EFFECTS IN NONHORIZONTAL MERGERS

In examining non-horizontal transactions, lower court decisions since the mid–1970s have reflected skepticism about foreclosure and entry barrier arguments. For example, in Freuhauf Corp. v. FTC (1979), the Second Circuit overturned an FTC ruling that an acquisition foreclosing 5.8 percent of the market for heavy duty truck wheels had violated Section 7. The court held that a realignment of sales patterns and the possible foreclosure at issue did not by themselves warrant a conclusion that competition would suffer, and it emphasized that the FTC had introduced no other evidence of likely anticompetitive effect. In Alberta Gas Chemicals, Ltd. v. E.I. du Pont de Nemours & Co. (1987), the Third Circuit noted that weaknesses in foreclosure theory had led "respected scholars" to "question the anticompetitive effects of vertical mergers." The court proceeded to reject the plaintiff's challenge to a vertical merger of two chemical firms, noting that the transaction might well "result in efficiencies." But see United States v. American Cyanamid Co. (1983) (rejecting district court's approval of modification of vertical merger consent decree).

Recent experience features few instances in which lower courts have been asked to review essentially conglomerate transactions. Decisions since the mid–1970s have not removed doubts that courts are ill-equipped to undertake the complex factual inquiries that the Supreme Court's conglomerate merger opinions seemed to invite—especially to ascertain whether limit-pricing would be profitable and likely or of a reasonable probability of entry by the acquiring firm in the near future. Anomalous results are likely.

Where barriers are high, the acquiring firm (and all others) may be unlikely entrants; where the barriers are low, the market is competitive and the elimination of a potential entrant is irrelevant. Compare Tenneco, Inc. v. FTC (1982) (entry barriers protecting market from competition excluded acquiring company from being a potential entrant) with Yamaha Motor Co. v. FTC (1981) (finding both high entry barriers and that the acquiring firm was a likely entrant) and Mercantile Texas Corp. v. Board of Governors (1981) (acquiring firm deemed a significant future entrant because entry barriers were limited).

H. CONCLUSION

The past twenty years have been a period of extraordinary ferment in antitrust merger policy, and the coming years promise to feature further important adjustments in analysis. The ongoing process of change is likely to be shaped by at least three basic conditions. The first is a persistent tension between the longstanding concern with social and political effects of large mergers and the realization that large corporate consolidations can confer important economic benefits on society. Neither courts nor commentators have devised an administrable theory of enforcement that reconciles these competing forces, yet both concerns arise frequently in connection with specific transactions.

A second condition is a continuing search by scholars to devise a suitable theoretical basis for determining which mergers are likely to have net anticompetitive effects. In the past decade or so, merger analysis has become more attuned to economic realities, yet the structural thresholds that provide the basic framework for modern judicial analysis and government enforcement guidelines are still wanting for a solid foundation in economic theory and evidence. See David T. Scheffman, *Ten Years of Merger Guidelines: A Retrospective, Critique, and Prediction,* 8 Rev. Indus. Org. 173 (1993). Despite increasing recognition that efficiency considerations deserve greater emphasis in evaluating mergers, efforts to formulate methods to account for efficiency arguments—for example, by redefining the burden of proof for the merging parties, or by accepting certain efficiency claims at face value and conducting an ex post assessment of whether such efficiencies have been realized—have proceeded with great difficulty and have yielded largely unsatisfying results.

A third formative condition is the Supreme Court's recent silence on merger issues. The absence of a Supreme Court decision on substantive merger doctrine since 1975 has magnified the role of the government enforcement agencies. Merger proceedings are an important departure from the general tendency of the antitrust system to evaluate conduct after the fact. Mainly as a result of the premerger notification process, most mergers are examined before the fact, with the government acting essentially like a regulatory body. See E. Thomas Sullivan, *The Antitrust Division as a Regulatory Agency: An Enforcement Policy in Transition,* 64 Wash. U.L.Q. 997 (1986). To a degree unequalled in other areas of antitrust, merger policy is governed by guidelines promulgated ex ante by enforcement agencies, and results in proposed transactions depend heavily on the ability of the merging parties and the government to negotiate solutions to perceived competitive problems ("fix it first") without recourse to litigation.

The Supreme Court's modern silence on merger issues also has left the evolution of merger standards in the hands of the lower federal courts. In many instances, these tribunals have endorsed analytical approaches that depart from the letter or spirit of the Supreme Court's merger cases of the 1960s. This raises the question of whether, in a future case, the Court would modify its existing statements of merger principles and accommodate the views of more recent district court and court of appeals decisions.

The decision of the D.C. Circuit in United States v. Baker Hughes, Inc. (1990) offers an intriguing glimpse of what the future may hold. In *Baker Hughes,* the court of appeals rejected the Justice Department's effort to enjoin a merger of two oil drilling equipment producers where the post-merger HHI exceeded 4000. In a major departure from *PNB's* prima facie test, the D.C. Circuit ruled that the defendant's burden of rebutting a case of prima facie illegality varies according to the type of evidence used to make the prima facie case. Where concentration data alone establishes the government's prima facie case, the court stated, the defendant's burden of rebutting the government's case—e.g., by arguing that entry into the market is easy, that powerful buyers can defeat postmerger price increases, or that the merger will create efficiencies—is reduced. The author of *Baker Hughes* (Clarence Thomas) and one other member of the unanimous D.C. Circuit panel (Ruth Ginsburg) are now associate justices of the Supreme Court. If the Supreme Court addresses merger standards in the near future, the more tolerant approach embodied in *Baker Hughes* and other modern lower court merger decisions may well influence the Court's thinking.

CHAPTER X

PATENT AND INTELLECTUAL PROPERTY ISSUES

"The patent system added the fuel of interest to the fire of genius." A. Lincoln.

The efforts of firms to acquire, use, and enforce intellectual property rights—patents, copyrights, trademarks, and trade secrets—sometimes provoke challenges under the antitrust laws. For many years such rights were viewed suspiciously under the antitrust laws.[1] More recently, federal enforcement agencies and the courts have recognized that the intellectual property and antitrust laws are not mutually inconsistent but instead are both directed at the enhancement of consumer welfare. See, e.g., Atari Games Corp. v. Nintendo of Am., Inc. (1990) (observing that the patent and antitrust laws "are actually complementary, as both are aimed at encouraging innovation, industry and competition"). This Chapter reviews the main antitrust issues that arise as businesses seek to obtain and exploit

---

1. This distrust is perhaps best captured by the Justice Department's attack in the 1970s against the "nine no-nos"—patent-related practices it condemned as illegal per se. The Department repudiated this policy in the 1980s, see Charles R. Rule, Jr., *Patent–Antitrust Policy: Looking Back and Ahead*, 59 Antitrust L.J. 729, 732 (1991), but Clinton Administration enforcement officials have announced that the Justice Department is reexamining permissive enforcement policies concerning antitrust and intellectual property adopted during the Reagan Administration. See Anne K. Bingaman, *Antitrust and Innovation in a High Technology Society*, presented on January 10, 1994 and reprinted in Trade Reg.Rep. (CCH) ¶ 50,128, at 48,995.

intellectual property rights. Reflecting the chief trends in modern antitrust litigation, we focus on the adoption and enforcement of patent licenses.

Patents are government sanctioned property rights which grant inventors exclusive rights to their inventions, thus barring others from using the inventions (unless they pay the inventor for the use) for seventeen years. A patent's power resides in the legal right it gives the owner to exclude others from practicing the patent's claims.[2] For many years, this trait led many courts to speak of the "patent monopoly";[3] patents often were viewed as conflicting with the antitrust laws, since the latter endeavor to prevent or destroy the creation of monopoly power. However, this conflict is more illusory than real. The patent's exclusive right for the use of an invention does not necessarily confer monopoly power; substitutes may be readily available or the invention may have little commercial value. More important, a central aim of both the patent and antitrust laws is to promote innovation and to encourage the efficient

2. Copyrights also are statutory grants that confer exclusivity on an author's original expression of ideas. 17 U.S.C.A. § 101 et seq. Unlike a patent, a copyright must exist in a work of authorship. Because courts rely on patent antitrust decisions to analyze antitrust issues associated with copyrights, this Chapter focuses mainly on patent antitrust issues.

3. See, e.g., Zenith Radio Corp. v. Hazeltine Research, Inc. (1969) (patentee holds a "lawful monopoly); United States v. Aluminum Co. of Am. (1945) (patents are "lawful monopolies"). The Court of Appeals for the Federal Circuit, which has jurisdiction over patent appeals, has rejected this terminology:

Nowhere in any statute is a patent described as a monopoly. The patent right is but the right to exclude others, the very definition of "property." That the property right represented by a patent, like other property rights, may be used in a scheme violative of the antitrust laws creates no "conflict" between laws establishing any of those property rights and the antitrust laws.

Schenck v. Norton Corp. (1983).

use of resources. Both seek to increase output—with the ensuing overall effect of lowering prices.[4]

A. AN INTRODUCTION TO PATENTS

Under the broad authority of Article I, Section 8 of the Constitution "[t]o promote the progress of science and useful arts, by securing for limited times to authors and inventors the exclusive right to their respective writings and discoveries," Congress adopted a patent code. This code permits patents to be issued for "any new and useful

4. The patentee receives a monopoly on her invention, but it will not be commercially marketable unless it is an improvement over, or is available at a lower price than, the products for which it is a substitute. This is illustrated in Figure 12:

FIGURE 12: MARKETABLE PATENTS

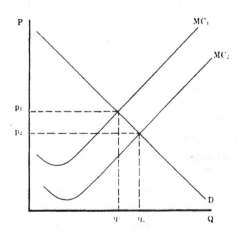

MC_1 is the cost of producing the nonpatented product. In a competitive market that product will be sold at price p_1. The patented product is commercially valuable because it has a lower production cost (MC_2) and can therefore be sold at a lower price (p_2). Because of the exclusivity provided by the patent grant, it will be sold above price p_2 but below the process, machine, manufacture, or composition of matter, or any new and useful improvement thereof" for a term of seventeen years from the date of issue. 35 U.S.C.A. § 101. To meet these requirements, the inventor must show that she is the first person to reduce the invention to practice and that the invention is both nonobvious and useful. See Anderson's–Black Rock, Inc. v. Pavement Salvage Co. (1969); Graham v. John Deere Co. of Kansas City (1966). When a patent expires, the invention can be used by all without restriction. See Brulotte v. Thys Co. (1964) (licensee's obligation to pay royalties ends at the conclusion of the 17–year patent term); Meehan v. PPG Indus. (1986) (patent held to be abused and licensing agreement deemed unlawful per se where royalty payments extended unchanged beyond the life of the patent); see also Harold See & Frank M. Caprio, *The Trouble with Brulotte: The Patent Royalty Term and Patent Monopoly Extension,* 1990 Utah L. Rev. 813.

Applications for patents are made to the Patent Office, which examines them ex parte to insure that the invention is new and nonobvious, that it was not previously developed or was not known to the public for more than a year before the application was filed, that the invention has practical utility, and that it does what it claims to do. See Robert L. Harmon, *Patents and the Federal Circuit* 457–92 (2d ed. 1991); Robert Patrick Merges, *Patent Law and Policy* 30– 32 (1992). Not all applications filed with the Patent Office result in patent grants, and the issuance of a patent does not ensure that the patent will be held valid if subsequently challenged. A patent's validity can be contested in many situations: when the patentee sues for infringement or the infringer seeks a declaratory judgment that the patent is

previous price (of p_1), and a greater quantity (i.e., more than q_1) will be produced.

invalid; when a licensee challenges it (Lear, Inc. v. Adkins (1969)); when the government or private plaintiff in an antitrust suit challenges a patent relied on by the defendant (Walker Process Equip., Inc. v. Food Mach. & Chem. Corp. (1965)); or when the question of validity is otherwise involved in the case (United States v. Glaxo Group Ltd. (1973)).

Patents may be used by the inventor, sold, licensed to others for their use, or not used at all. The mere nonuse of a patent has not yet been held to violate either the patent or the antitrust laws. See Continental Paper Bag Co. v. Eastern Paper Bag Co. (1908); cf. Dawson Chem. Co. v. Rohm & Haas Co. (1980) ("[c]ompulsory licensing is a rarity in our patent system"). A number of recent cases also have rejected antitrust claims based on refusals to license copyrighted materials. See Corsearch, Inc. v. Thomson & Thomson, Inc. (1992); Data General Corp. v. Grumman Sys. Support Corp. (1991).

Licensing is usually done for a fee (called a royalty), with the amount charged frequently based on usage, or in exchange for another's patented technology (cross-licensing). Patent licensing generally expands the use of the invention, increases competition in its use, and disperses the technology, thereby encouraging improvements. On the other hand, licensing has drawbacks, such as encouraging the development of close relations among competitors (thereby possibly facilitating price-fixing), lessening the likelihood of challenges to invalid patents, and reducing incentives to invent more efficient alternatives.

–

The primary rationale for patent grants is to give individuals and firms a financial incentive to invest in research and development that yield inventions. See Stanley M. Besen & Leo J. Raskind, *An Introduction to the Law and Economics of Intellectual Property,* 5 J. Econ. Perspectives 3, 5 (1991). Without some protection for the inventor, others could merely copy her ideas and sell the products thereof at a lower price because they avoided the cost of developing the invention. (The marginal cost of using an invention, once it has been determined how to copy it, is zero.) The patent laws, then, prevent "free riders" from denying the inventor a return on her investment and ingenuity. This is not to say that without such laws there would be no inventions. But it is a premise of the patent laws—largely unverified—that without such protection fewer socially valuable inventions would result.[5] In addition, without statutory protection against unauthorized use, inventors might otherwise seek to keep their inventions secret; one condition of the patent grant is that the patentee disclose how the invention works. By this process the inventor's knowledge is shared and, after 17 years, is available for use by anyone.

In addition to antitrust review, competition issues involving intellectual property also attract scrutiny under the "patent misuse" doctrine. Patent misuse is an equitable remedy (analogous to the tort law doctrine of unclean hands) that allows defendants in an infringement action or

5. Whether the 17–year grant of exclusivity is necessary to maximize invention and efficient resource use is a matter of scholarly dispute. See Louis Kaplow, *The Patent–Antitrust Intersection: A Reappraisal,* 97 Harv. L. Rev. 1813 (1984); George L. Priest, *What Economists Can Tell Lawyers About Intellectual Property: Comment on Cheung,* 8 Res. in L. & Econ. 19 (1986).

a contract action to collect unpaid royalties to claim that the patentee has "misused" her patent grant and therefore is not entitled to the requested relief. Compare Lasercomb Am., Inc. v. Reynolds (1990) (recognizing "copyright misuse" doctrine); Stephen A. Stack, Jr., *Recent and Impending Developments in Copyright and Antitrust*, 61 Antitrust L.J. 331 (1993). Much conduct condemned as patent misuse also violates the antitrust laws by, for example, fixing the price of patented goods on resale or tying the sale of a patented product to the sale of an unpatented product. See Motion Picture Patents Co. v. Universal Film Manufacturing Co. (1917) (tying arrangement in which the patentee required exhibitors to show only its movies on its patented projector constituted patent misuse). In recent years a significant debate has focused on the desirability of maintaining a patent misuse doctrine in addition to antitrust standards of general applicability. Compare Kenneth J. Birchfiel, *Patent Misuse and Antitrust Reform: "Blessed Be the Tie,"* 4 Harv. J.L. & Tech. 1 (1991) (defending patent misuse doctrine) with Mark A. Lemley, *The Economic Irrationality of the Patent Misuse Doctrine,* 78 Calif. L. Rev. 1599 (1990) (patent misuse doctrine seen as needless, duplicative). Until this debate is resolved, both antitrust and patent misuse principles must be considered in analyzing the competitive consequences of intellectual property practices.

B. PRICE, TERRITORIAL, AND USE RESTRICTIONS

Price-fixing among competing sellers (horizontal) and between supplier and retailer (vertical) is, as previously noted, illegal per se. While the application of this rule to horizontal cartel arrangements is generally applauded, it is less clear that it should be as rigidly applied to vertical agreements (see Chapter 8). Debate over the wisdom of the rule of *Dr. Miles* has carried over into the patent licensing area, but with somewhat different results.

A patentee's right to exclude others from making and selling her invention allows her to keep all the business it generates. Like the producer of non-patented goods, she also is entitled to set whatever price she wishes. And in the case of patented products, it can be assumed that she will charge a monopoly price, if the market permits (see Figure 12, supra), to maximize her revenues.

Where the patentee's ability to produce the invention fails to satisfy demand, she may wish to license others to manufacture and sell it. The question then arises whether the patentee may control the price at which her licensee sells the patented product.[6] Despite several efforts to overturn it, the Supreme Court has never abandoned the rule, first announced in E. Bement and Sons v. National Harrow Co. (1902), that a patentee may enforce minimum price clauses in its licensing arrangements. Thus, in *Bement* the Court enjoined one of several competing licensees from selling below the license-prescribed price; since the patentee had the right to prohibit others from using the patent—including the licensee—the Court reasoned that it also had the lesser included right of requiring the licensee to sell the patented article. See also USM Corp. v. SPS Technologies,

---

6. The question here differs from that decided in *Dr. Miles* (which did not involve a patent) in that the patentee has not made and sold the product to the retailer. In an early case, Bauer & Cie v. O'Donnell (1913), the Supreme Court held that RPM agreements relating to patented products were unenforceable. The Court distinguished *Bement* on the ground that it involved licensing, not resale.

Inc. (1982) (upholding price discrimination in royalty schedule of a license agreement).

The Supreme Court relied on a different rationale to reaffirm this rule in United States v. General Elec. Co. (1926). GE had licensed Westinghouse to manufacture and sell lamps under GE's patents. Prices were to be maintained at the same level as GE fixed for its distributors. Upholding the price-fixing condition in GE's licenses, the Court switched its grounds and justified the condition as reasonably adapted to secure for the patentee the pecuniary reward of its patent rights. The Court feared that if GE could not set the price at which Westinghouse sold the lamps, Westinghouse might sell them at a price which would render GE's lamp production and sales unprofitable.

On the other hand, if Westinghouse can make and sell the item much cheaper, it arguably should be encouraged to do so (and, therefore, price-fixing should be prohibited). Yet, if faced with this option, GE might decide not to license Westinghouse to manufacture and sell these lamps. Nor could GE necessarily protect itself by adjusting the royalty. If it overestimated Westinghouse's costs, the royalty rate would be too low; yet if it set the rate too high, it could make the manufacture and sale of lamps by Westinghouse unprofitable.[7] In other words, setting a minimum price may be the most efficient way to protect the patentee, to encourage licensing, and, as the Court said, to assure that GE obtained its monopoly reward.

7. This point is illustrated by the figure on the following page.

There is another possible explanation for the GE license to Westinghouse, however. The two firms may have used the price-fixing license to help form and operate a cartel. If the validity of GE's patent was questionable, GE, rather

FIGURE 13: SETTING THE ROYALTY RATE

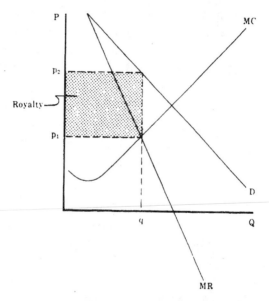

This figure merely repeats the drawing of the monopoly pricing figure (Figure 7, supra). *MC* represents the cost of producing the invention. To obtain her monopoly reward, the patentee sets her price at such a level that her output (the quantity demanded) is at the point where her marginal revenue (*MR*) equals her marginal cost (*MC*). (See Chapter 3 for an explanation of monopoly pricing.) To assure that she obtains this reward when licensing others, the patentee will set a royalty rate that equals the difference between the marginal cost (i.e., competitive price) and the monopoly price—or the difference between p_1 and p_2 on the above figure. The total royalties (reflected by the shaded area) will equal the monopoly profits the patentee would have received had she produced the output herself.

than risk a ruling of invalidity, may have licensed Westinghouse in order to share its market (while still maintaining its monopoly price). If this explains the GE license, as seems likely, the Court's approval of the price-fixing condition is erroneous.

Continuing doubts about the *GE* ruling have caused the Justice Department to attack it repeatedly. Each time the issue came before the Supreme Court, however, the matter was resolved without expressly overruling *GE*—though four justices would have done so in 1948 and perhaps again in the 1960s. See United States v. Line Material Co. (1948); United States v. Huck Mfg. Co. (1964). And the Supreme Court has distinguished the *GE* rule whenever possible. In United States v. Masonite Corp. (1942), the Court ruled that a patentee could not fix the price at which its (former) competitors sold the patented product under a price-limiting license. The Court viewed the arrangement as a classic horizontal price-fixing conspiracy. It distinguished *GE* on the ground that Masonite, unlike GE, did all the manufacturing for the group. Such a distinction seems artificial. In both cases the patentee sought to use independent business entities to distribute the invention at a patentee-fixed price. Yet in one case the arrangement was upheld while in the other it was barred by the Sherman Act.

Then, in *Line Material* (1948), the Court examined a cross-licensing agreement through which separate grantees of a "basic patent" and an "improvement patent" licensed each other in order that each could efficiently exploit both inventions. The cross-license was necessary if the full benefit of these "blocking" inventions were to be made available to the public, since the improvement infringed on the basic patent and therefore could not be made available independently. The cross-license arrangement contained a price limitation, as in *GE,* designed to assure that each patentee received its monopoly reward without a complex royalty arrangement. Nevertheless, the Court distinguished *GE* by arguing that two patentees had combined in *Line Material* and held that such license combinations were illegal per se. But, as one scholar has observed: "A more arbitrary and unprincipled per se rule would be difficult to construct." Ward S. Bowman, Jr., *Patent and Antitrust Law: A Legal and Economic Appraisal* 195 (1973). The patents here were not competing; thus, the price feature could not have served to eliminate noninfringing competition. If *GE* is still the law, then *Line Material* seems illogical. It was, in any case, a victory for accountants.

This decline in the *GE* doctrine has continued. For example, in United States v. New Wrinkle (1952), the Court barred a price restraint in the license of pooled patents assigned to a holding company—even though the patents did not complement each other (as in *Line Material*). If the pooled patents conflicted, as the parties assumed, the price-restricted pool could have had no effect other than in sharing the monopoly reward among claimants. The Court's distinction of *GE* obscured the fact that the license terms could not have contributed to a price cartel beyond the degree allowed a patentee by *GE.* Today the *GE* rule for patent licenses that contain price controls appears limited to cases involving unilateral licensing and a single licensee.[8]

8. In *Copperweld* (1984), a corporation and its wholly-owned subsidiary were deemed incapable of conspiring for Sherman Act Section 1 purposes because they did not represent separate economic interests. A similar analysis conceivably might apply to the relationship between a patent holder and its licensee. See Levi Case Co. v. ATS Prod., Inc. (1992) (patent holder and exclusive licensee could not violate Section 1 because

Antitrust's per se approach to price-restricted patent licenses has not extended to market or territorial allocations. Section 261 of the Patent Code declares that the patentee may assign its exclusive right "to the whole or any specified part of the United States." 35 U.S.C.A. § 261. Courts have upheld patent licenses assigning licensees geographic territories as authorized by Congress. But such restraints are exhausted by the first sale; that is, one who purchases a patented product, even from a restricted licensee, may use or sell it without restraint. Keeler v. Standard Folding–Bed Co. (1895); see Adams v. Burke (1873).

Another type of limited license is that defined as the "field of use," which restricts the use of the patented technology to specified applications. In the leading case of General Talking Pictures Corp. v. Western Elec. Co. (1938), the patentee had divided its licensing of a sound amplification invention into two classes of use: "home" (radio receivers) and "commercial" (e.g., motion picture sound equipment). Each was licensed for manufacture by different companies. In upholding the patentee's claim that a purchaser from its home-restricted licensee had infringed upon the patent through commercial use of the device, the Court implied (though it specifically declined to rule) that the use restriction was lawful. As with price restrictions, however, the Supreme Court has not extended or subsequently reaffirmed this rule. See Automatic Radio Mfg. Co. v. Hazeltine Research, Inc. (1950) (licensing of multiple patents under a single license upheld). Nonetheless, courts often have relied on *General Talking Pictures* to uphold various field-limited licenses. Compare United States v. Studiengesellschaft Kohle (1981) (field of use restriction they were not independent sources of economic power; patent holder, by granting exclusive license, removed itself from the market).

upheld) with Robintech, Inc. v. Chemidus Wavin, Ltd. (1980) (field of use restriction constituted patent misuse).

Only recently has the Court ruled that a tie-in aimed at controlling an unpatented product is permitted. Early cases first held that a tie-in barred an infringement suit. Thus, in Morton Salt Co. v. G.S. Suppiger Co. (1942), the licensor of a patented salt dispensing machine could not condition its use on the lessee's purchase of nonpatented salt tablets from the patentee-licensor. This constituted a misuse of the patent, and the patentee was disqualified from enforcing the patent, even against direct infringers. Two years later the Court extended this doctrine of patent misuse to antitrust law in holding that a contributory infringer could not be sued by a patentee who refused to license a combination invention without purchase of key unpatented components. Mercoid Corp. v. Mid–Continent Inv. Co. (1944); Mercoid Corp. v. Minneapolis–Honeywell Regulator Co. (1944). Subsequently, in 1953, Congress added sections 271(c) and (d) to the Patent Code "for the express purpose of reinstating the doctrine of contributory infringement as it had been developed by decisions prior to Mercoid ..." Aro Mfg. Co. v. Convertible Top Replacement Co. (1964).

More recently, in Dawson Chem. Co. v. Rohm & Haas Co. (1980), the Court ruled that a contributory infringement suit is not barred by the patentee's reliance on a tie-in to control the sale of an unpatented product. The plaintiff (Rohm & Haas) owned a patent on the only proven method of applying a chemical herbicide to crops. The compound itself was unpatented, but it also had no commercial use except as part of the plaintiff's patented process. When the defendant made and sold the compound with instructions detailing its use as a herbicide—knowing that its customers' use of the chemical as instructed would directly infringe the patent—Rohm & Haas charged the defendant with contributory infringement. The defendants had sought a license on the patented process alone from the plaintiff—without buying the chemical—but Rohm & Haas had refused all such requests. The defendant argued, therefore, that the plaintiff illegally had tied the license of its patented process to the purchase of the unpatented product. However, the Court upheld the infringement suit, concluding that sections 271(c) and (d) of the Patent Code had, in effect, overruled the *Mercoid* cases. The decision is also important for its recognition of the property rights created by the patent system (and their need for protection) and its finding that a patentee need not license her invention. It is a further acknowledgment that tying arrangements may serve desirable ends. See also Aronson v. Quick Point Pencil Co. (1979) and Chapter 8.

Where patent licensing arrangements have been challenged as illegal tying agreements under the antitrust laws, litigants often have focused on the requirement of tying doctrine that the seller have sufficient economic power in the market for the tying product to enable it to restrain competition in the market for the tied product. For many years, courts often presumed the existence of market power in the tying product where the tying item was patented or copyrighted. See *IBM* (1936); *International Salt* (1947). More recently, however, the presumption that a patent or copyright confers sufficient market power to establish this element of an antitrust tying case has come under strong attack and has been overturned by statute in the patent misuse context. Compare 35 U.S.C.A. § 271(d)(5) (to establish patent misuse by tying, plaintiff must prove that patent holder had market power in the tied item just as in the case of nonpatented products).

In *Jefferson Parish* (1984), a majority of the Supreme Court stated in dictum that the presumption of market power exists when the tied product is patented or copyrighted: "[I]f the Government has granted the seller [of a product] a patent or similar monopoly over a product, it is fair to presume that the inability to buy the product elsewhere gives the seller market power." In a concurring opinion, Justice O'Connor contended that a patent does not automatically give its owner market power, observing that "a patent holder has no market power in any relevant sense if there are close substitutes for the patented product." Most lower court decisions since *Jefferson Parish* have adopted Justice O'Connor's view and refused to presume market power from the existence of a patent or copyright alone. See Abbott Laboratories v. Brennan (1991); A.I. Root Co. v. Computer/Dynamics, Inc. (1986).

C. SETTLEMENT AND ACCUMULATION

Due to doubts about their validity and coverage, competing patents often are disputed and settlements sought. See Mark Crane & Malcolm R. Pfunder, *Antitrust and Res Judicata Considerations in the Settlement of Patent Litigation*, 62 Antitrust L.J. 151 (1993). In other areas of law, settlement usually is urged as socially preferable to litigation. This position was adopted in Standard Oil Co. (Indiana) v. United States (1931) (*Cracking Case*), where several refining companies held competing patents on a "cracking" process for extracting additional gasoline from crude oil. To avoid further litigation of their claims, four refiners pooled their patents, cross-licensed each other, and agreed to share in some fixed proportion the royalties they received (mainly from others) under the multiple licenses. The government attacked this pooling arrangement for eliminating competition in royalty rates among the patentees. The agreement to divide royalties was alleged to violate Section 1 of the Sherman Act and enable the defendants to maintain royalties at monopoly levels.

Accepting the government's conclusion that the pooled patents were competing, the Court nevertheless upheld the cross-license arrangement and royalty division. It applied a rule of reason test, observing that settlements which exchange patent rights and permit royalty divisions are often necessary if technical advances are not to be blocked by litigation; the interchange of patents on reasonable terms to all manufacturers desiring to participate may promote competition. Moreover, royalties cannot, the Court said, fix or adversely affect prices where the patented cracked gasoline constituted only 26 percent of total gas supplies.

The Court's analysis is not without its critics. Settlements are not always preferable in the patent context. The patent law's aim, according to the *GE* rule, is to reward the inventor. But settlement shares the reward among competing claimants, thus indiscriminately rewarding both subsequent infringers and holders of invalid patents—since litigation would have determined the priorities or possibly overruled all claims. And if none of the patents was valid, a settlement which shared royalties would result in higher prices, for without the settlement prices would have been set at a competitive level. That is, the royalty payments act to raise the marginal cost of the patented products. Nor is it clear from the Court's evidence that these "costs" are less than the social costs of litigation except where "blocking" patents are involved (as in *Line Material*).

Moreover, if, as the Court said, the patents being settled were competing, then the ruling seems questionable for one other reason. The Court's conclusion that the defendants' royalty rates could neither control the supply nor fix the price of cracked gas because their control was limited to one-quarter of available gas supplies is erroneous. A simple diagram shows that the price of gas is determined by the supply of straight run *and* cracked gas combined:

FIGURE 14: SUPPLY OF GASOLINE

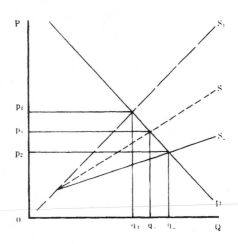

In Figure 14, S_1 is the amount of straight run gas which will be supplied. Quantity q_1 will be made available at price p_1 if the market is competitive. Using the cracking process, additional gas is available (after straight run gas is obtained) as shown by S_2—and quantity q_2 will be supplied at price p_2. If the defendants agree to a shared royalty, the "cost" of cracked gas will rise, as illustrated by the supply curve S_3—and quantity q_3 will be produced at price p_3. Royalty rates cause the cost of gas to rise, thereby reducing supply and raising the price, whether or not the defendants have monopoly power in the total gasoline market.[9] This

9. The Court's economic analysis also erroneously selected total gasoline as the relevant market (and found that the defendants controlled only 26 percent of it). In fact the market was for patents on "cracked" gas—

suggests then that, contrary to the Court's view in the *Cracking Case,* it would pay for the defendants to have conspired to fix royalty rates—and the Court should have examined their conduct more closely.

The Court has been less charitable in applying the rule of reason standard of the *Cracking Case* to other patent settlements. For example, in United States v. Singer Mfg. Co. (1963), a Swiss manufacturer's assignment of its American patent to an American licensee (Singer) in order to facilitate suit against a Japanese infringer and exclude Japanese imports into the U.S., was held to violate Section 1. The Court concluded that it was unreasonable for Singer to combine with another firm to challenge a third person's patent in order to prevent entry into the market.

Patent acquisition activities by a single firm sometimes raise concerns that the patent holder will gain and exercise market power unilaterally. See Richard J. Gilbert & David Newberry, *Preemptive Patenting and the Persistence of Monopoly,* 72 Am. Econ. Rev. 514 (1982). A company's aggregation of patents as a result of internal R & D ordinarily does not violate the antitrust laws. See *Automatic Radio* ("mere accumulation of patents, no matter how many, is not in and of itself illegal"); cf. Xerox Corp. (1975) (settling claims that Xerox violated Section 5 of the FTC Act by creating a patent thicket around its dry paper copying technology to prevent other firms from introducing dry paper copiers). However, the acquisition of patents and other intangible property rights such as copyrights and trademarks may violate the antitrust laws, including Section 7 of the Clayton Act, if the effect is to reduce competition or tend to create a monopoly. See SCM Corp. v. Xerox Corp. (1981); see also Kobe, Inc. v. Dempsey Pump Co.

for which there were no close substitutes. Here the defendants had monopoly power, controlling 100 percent of the market.

(1952) (Section 2 of Sherman Act held violated where defendant engaged in acquisition, nonuse, and enforcement of "every important patent" in the field with intent to exclude rivals).

One way for a patent holder to acquire patents is to condition the grant of a license to its patent on the licensee's promise to "grantback" to the patent holder any improvement patents that it secures, or to license the patent holder to use any patents it develops. In Transparent–Wrap Machine Corp. v. Stokes & Smith Co. (1947), the Supreme Court considered a grantback provision that required the licensee to assign to the licensor all patents for improvements to a patented packaging machine; the agreement gave the licensee a nonexclusive, royalty-free license on the improvements. After noting that grantback clauses could raise antitrust concerns by discouraging the licensee from pursuing new inventions, the Court ruled that grantbacks do not constitute per se violations and should be analyzed with a rule of reason standard. In later cases, relevant factors in applying a rule of reason test to grantback clauses have included whether the grantback is exclusive or nonexclusive and the duration of the grantback arrangement. See Santa Fe–Pomeroy, Inc. v. P & Z Co. (1978) (grantback upheld where arrangement was "limited in time and subject matter ... and therefore had no restrictive or 'chilling' effect on any improvements").

The holder of a lawfully obtained patent typically has no duty to license its patent to other parties. See United States v. Westinghouse Elec. Corp. (1981). In *SCM* the Second Circuit held that "where a patent has been legally acquired, subsequent conduct permissible under the patent laws cannot trigger any liability under the antitrust laws." *SCM*. The Court ruled that Xerox' refusal to license its patents did not constitute a Section 2 violation.

D. ENFORCEMENTS OF PATENTS AS AN ANTITRUST VIOLATION

In Walker Process Equipment, Inc. v. Food Machinery & Chemical Corp. (1965), the Supreme Court held that enforcement of a patent procured through knowing and willful fraud may violate Section 2 of the Sherman Act and expose the patentee to treble damage claims. To establish a Section 2 violation based on the fraudulent procurement of a patent, the moving party must show that (1) the patentee knowingly and willfully misrepresented facts to the Patent Office in obtaining the patent, (2) the patent would not have issued "but for" the patentee's fraud, and (3) the claims of the fraudulently obtained patent, by themselves, give the patentee monopoly power in a relevant market. To satisfy the *Walker Process* fraud element, the moving party must prove the elements of common law fraud: namely, the misrepresentation of a material fact intentionally made to deceive and reasonably relied on by the party to whom the misrepresentation was made. See Cataphote Corp. v. De Soto Chem. Coatings, Inc. (1971)

Closely related to a *Walker Process* claim for fraudulent patent procurement is the initiation of litigation to enforce a patent known to be invalid. See Handgards, Inc. v. Ethicon, Inc. (1979). The specific intent required to find a Section 2 violation is satisfied because the patentee instituted the lawsuit in bad faith—that is, with knowledge of the patent's invalidity. See also CVD, Inc. v. Raytheon Co. (1985) (bad faith assertion of a trade secret may be actionable under Section 2). The other elements of the claim are the same as under *Walker Process*. Because a patentee normally is entitled to rely on the statutory presumption of validity under the patent laws, proof of the patentee's bad faith must be made by clear and convincing evidence.

In Professional Real Estate Investors, Inc. v. Columbia Pictures Indus., Inc. (1993), the Supreme Court considered when an allegedly vexatious lawsuit constitutes sham conduct and is not entitled to antitrust immunity under the *Noerr* doctrine (see Chapter 13). In affirming the dismissal of an antitrust claim based on the filing of an allegedly vexatious copyright infringement action, the Court ruled that filing a lawsuit is sham conduct only if the suit is objectively baseless in that no reasonable litigant realistically could expect to succeed on the merits. In a footnote, the Court said "We need not decide here whether and, if so, to what extent *Noerr* permits the imposition of antitrust liability for a litigant's fraud or other misrepresentations," and cited *Walker Process*. *Professional Real Estate* addressed the effect of lawsuits whose legal *theory* is baseless. By contrast, the bad faith at issue in a *Walker Process* cause of action ordinarily involves misrepresenting *facts* (making false statements in a patent application or attacking the infringement of a patent known to be invalid). Thus, *Professional Real Estate* does not seem to affect the pursuit of a *Walker Process* cause of action.

CHAPTER XI

PRICE DISCRIMINATION AND THE ROBINSON–PATMAN ACT

In introducing the model of perfect competition in Chapter 3, we assumed that the seller offered her product at a uniform price to all buyers. In practice, sellers often upset this simplifying assumption by engaging in price discrimination—charging different prices to different buyers for essentially the same product. We briefly saw one species of this phenomenon in examining tying arrangements in Chapter 8. There we considered how a monopolist might impose a tie-in as one way to segregate buyers according to the intensity of their demand—for example, by using the tied product (e.g., punch cards) to charge, in effect, a higher price to buyers whose demand for the tying product (a tabulating machine) was relatively inelastic.

The possibility that price discrimination imposed by powerful sellers or elicited by powerful buyers might yield or protect monopoly power has been an enduring antitrust concern. Scholars have identified several ways in which price discrimination may reduce consumer welfare. See Richard A. Posner, *The Robinson–Patman Act: Federal Regulation of Price Differences* 10–12 (1976); F.M. Scherer & D. Ross, *Industrial Market Structure and Economic Performance,* at 499–502. Among other effects, systematic price discrimination may entrench dominance by enabling large firms to obtain inputs at prices unavailable to their smaller rivals. Systematic discrimination also may enable a powerful buyer to grow at its competitors' expense without relation to its own or its competitors' efficiency.

Notwithstanding such concerns, the history of efforts to devise and enforce antitrust legislation to address price discrimination is a story of almost unrelieved policy failure. First enacted as Section 2 of the Clayton Act in 1914 and later augmented by the Robinson–Patman Act in 1936, enforcement of antitrust's ban against price discrimination frequently has yielded perverse results by, for example, discouraging oligopolistic sellers from granting selective price concessions that tend to undermine oligopolistic coordination. On the whole, Robinson–Patman Act enforcement has tended to contradict the procompetitive aims of antitrust's other statutes. See Terry Calvani & Gilde Breidenbach, *An Introduction to the Robinson–Patman Act and Its Enforcement by the Government,* 59 Antitrust L.J. 765, 765–66 (1991).

A. THE ORIGIN AND ENFORCEMENT OF SECTION 2 OF THE CLAYTON ACT

As enacted in 1914, Section 2 of the Clayton Act originally sought to forbid local price-cutting by monopolistic suppliers who were trying to exclude competitors from their markets. See ABA Antitrust Section, *Monograph No. 4, The Robinson–Patman Act: Policy and Law,* Vol. I, at 7–8 (1980). Courts initially ruled that Section 2 did not apply to conduct that reduced competition among rival buyers. See National Biscuit Co. v. FTC (1924). Other decisions exempted all quantity discounts whether or not such discounts were justified by differences in the costs of making high volume sales. The Supreme Court eventually concluded that Section 2 covered transactions affecting competition among buyers, see George Van Camp & Sons v. American

Can Co. (1929), but not until chain stores had become important participants in the distribution of consumer goods.

Section 2 of the Clayton Act was amended by the Robinson–Patman Act in 1936 after it became clear that other Depression–Era legislation would not stem the growth of large chain stores and halt the decline of independent merchants. The legislative history of the 1936 amendment displays acute congressional concern for the fate of beleaguered small businesses and a desire to limit price concessions granted powerful buyers, particularly food chain stores. Senator Huey Long captured some of these feelings when he said he "would rather have thieves and gangsters than chain stores in Louisiana." Carl Fulda, *Food Distribution in the United States: The Struggle Between Independents and the Chains,* 99 U. Pa. L. Rev. 1051, 1051 (1951). Representative Wright Patman, the measure's namesake, reflected its populist spirit in his charge that "[t]he bill has the opposition of all cheaters, chislers, bribe takers, bribe givers, and the greedy who seek monopolistic powers which would destroy opportunity." 80 Cong. Rec. 3446 (1936).

The amended Section 2 barred price discrimination unless it was supported by cost savings or was proven necessary to meet a competitor's price offer. Section 2 was enforceable against buyers seeking, as well as sellers offering, "unjustified" price discounts or their equivalents. These steps were unabashedly protectionist, for Congress intended the Robinson–Patman Act to prevent "injury to the competitor victimized by the discrimination, and not injury to competition." Hugh C. Hansen, *Robinson–Patman Law: A Review and Analysis,* 51 Ford. L. Rev. 1113, 1124 (1983). See also Jefferson County Pharmaceutical Ass'n v. Abbott Laboratories (1983) ("Under our interpretation, the Act's benefits would accrue, precisely as intended, to the benefit of small, private retailers.'').

In practice the Act has been the most criticized antitrust statute, both for its complexity and for its tendency to dampen desirable forms of rivalry. See, e.g., Daniel F. Spulber, *Regulation and Markets* 544 (1989) (''Repeal of laws against price discrimination appears to be desirable.''). Although aimed principally at large retailers, it has been applied mainly against small sellers who granted discounts to compete against larger sellers and against firms engaging in vigorous competition. As a result, the Robinson–Patman Act has been attacked for discouraging price competition and promoting price uniformity. Consequently, its significance in antitrust enforcement has faded in recent years. Although the statute was once the basis for many actions by the FTC (to whom the Justice Department ceded prosecutorial jurisdiction), government-initiated lawsuits are exceedingly rare today. In 1966 alone, the FTC issued over 70 complaints and consents. By contrast, from the time that Ronald Reagan's first nominee to FTC (James C. Miller III) took office in October 1981 through the end of the Bush Administration, the FTC filed a single Robinson–Patman Act complaint. Recent litigation under the statute overwhelmingly has involved private suits.

For lawyers and business managers alike, the Robinson–Patman Act is a troublesome tangle of complex, indeterminate language. Although many criticize its form and purpose, the Act cannot be dismissed as unimportant. It influences almost all pricing decisions of every major business in the U.S. Despite inactivity by federal enforcement agencies, the statute does generate private treble damage suits, and small businesses have retained sufficient political power to prevent its repeal.

B. THE STATUTE ANALYZED

The Robinson–Patman Act applies only (1) to sales (2) of commodities (3) of like grade and quality (4) in commerce. Each of these jurisdictional elements must be established, in addition to the substantive criteria of (5) price discrimination and (6) injury to competition—or one of the alternative violations noted below. See Robert M. Klein, *The Robinson–Patman Act: Jurisdictional Aspects and Elements,* 59 Antitrust L.J. 777 (1991). A seller does not violate the Act unless she has sold similar commodities to two different purchasers. While an enforceable contract may substitute for one of the sales, the Act does not apply to offers to sell, leases, agency or consignment arrangements, or to a seller's refusal to deal. One of the sales involved in a price discrimination must cross a state boundary for the "in commerce" requirement to be satisfied. Gulf Oil Corp. v. Copp Paving Co. (1974). In addition, the Act does not apply to sales of services or intangibles such as access to a communications system or advertising since they are not "commodities." See Metro Communications Co. v. Ameritech Mobile Communications (1993); Ambook Enters. v. Time, Inc. (1979); but see City of Kirkwood v. Union Elec. Co. (1982) (electric power deemed to be a commodity for Robinson–Patman purposes). Nor does it cover different prices for goods with physical differences that affect their acceptability to buyers—though giving a brand name to a product (which affects its consumer "acceptability") does not add sufficient "physical difference."

Once the foregoing elements are satisfied, a prima facie violation of Section 2(a) is established by showing that the seller discriminated in her prices with the effect of lessening competition. Any price difference is a price discrimination. See FTC v. Anheuser–Busch, Inc. (1960). However, charging the same price to two customers is never price discrimination under the Act—even though the seller's costs of serving one are much higher than those of serving the other (and therefore charging both customers the identical price constitutes economic price discrimination). Injury to competition includes "primary line" injury to competitors of the seller, "secondary line" injury to competitors of the buyer, and "tertiary line" injury to competitors of the buyer's customers.

While the Act focuses on price discrimination by the seller, other provisions prohibit false brokerage or discriminatory allowances or services that are not made available to competing customers on proportionately equal terms. These complement the price discrimination prohibition by condemning disguised price reductions.[1] Injury to competition need not be shown, and affirmative defenses are limited.[2] In addition, Section 2(f) imposes liability on buyers

---

1. Section 2(c) prohibits a party to a sales transaction from either granting to, or receiving from, the other party a "commission, brokerage, or other compensation, or any allowance or discount in lieu thereof, except for services rendered." Although originally enacted to prohibit disguised rebates, Section 2(c) recently has been interpreted more broadly to reach commercial bribery "tending to undermine the fiduciary relationship between a buyer and its agent, representative, or others intermediary." Harris v. Duty Free Shoppers Ltd. Partnership (1991). Section 2(d) requires that payments by a seller to a buyer for services or facilities used by the buyer in executing a sales transaction be made available on a "proportionately equal" basis to all buyers. Section 2(e) imposes a parallel requirement with respect to furnishing services or facilities to buyers.

2. See FTC v. Simplicity Pattern Co. (1959). The meeting competition defense, discussed below, is available to sellers charged with promotional discrimination, but if the defense is not established, the discriminatory allowance or service is per se unlawful. See Motive Parts Warehouse v. Facet Enters. (1985). The FTC has established guidelines for advertising allowances and other merchandising payments and services to assist businesses seeking to comply with Sections 2(d) and 2(e) of the Act. See A. Roy Lavik, *The 1990 Revision to the FTC Guides for Advertising Allow-*

who "knowingly ... induce or receive a discrimination in price which is prohibited by this Section." This subsection is the other side of the price discrimination (Section 2(a)) coin. For example, in Automatic Canteen Co. v. FTC (1953), the Court ruled that a buyer is not liable under Section 2(f) if the lower price that he "induced" is within one of the seller's defenses such as cost justification or if he reasonably could not know that it was not so protected. See also Kroger Co. v. FTC (1971) (defenses must also fit buyer's perspective).

More recently, in Great Atlantic & Pac. Tea Co. v. FTC (1979) (*A & P*), the Court held that a buyer could not be liable for price discrimination under Section 2(f) where the seller made its offer in a reasonable and good faith effort to meet competition. Seeking to reconcile the Robinson–Patman Act with the competitive aims of the Sherman Act, the Court ruled that a buyer has no affirmative duty to disclose the exact amount by which competing bids undercut the seller with whom she is negotiating. Uncertainty in this circumstance benefits competition, and if it leads to one seller undercutting the other, the buyer should not be "rewarded" with Robinson–Patman Act liability.

Finally, an almost unused part (Section 3) of the Act makes it a criminal offense to discriminate geographically or to sell at "unreasonably low prices" where the purpose of either action is to destroy competition or eliminate a competitor. See United States v. National Dairy Products Corp. (1963) (statute upheld against constitutional challenge of void for vagueness). This rarely-used provision did not amend the Clayton Act. Hence it is not an "antitrust" law under Section 4 of the Clayton Act and is not a subject

ances and Other Merchandising Payments and Services, 59 Antitrust L.J. 871 (1991).

of private treble damage enforcement. See Nashville Milk
Co. v. Carnation Co. (1958).

C. INJURY TO COMPETITION

A review of basic decisions involving the competitive
effects requirement under Section 2(a) is central to understanding most cases involving charges of price discrimination, and it illustrates the Act's limitations and peculiari-
ties.

1. PRIMARY LINE INJURY

Although it has been held that price discrimination which
diverts any sales from a competitor supports the inference
that competition has been injured, the general rule is that
the mere diversion of sales to the discriminating seller from
her competitors is not in itself sufficient to establish an
impairment of primary line competition. Compare Samuel
H. Moss, Inc. v. FTC (1945) with Anheuser–Busch, Inc. v.
FTC (1961). See also Frederick M. Rowe, *Price Discrimination Under the Robinson–Patman Act* 162 (1962) ("To
equate the diversion of business among rival sellers with
injury to competition is to indict the competitive process
itself.") Thus, in contrast to secondary line cases, injury
only to an individual competitor does not establish injury to
competition in a primary line case.

On the other hand, price discrimination will be found to
injure competitors if the purpose or effect of the seller's
selective price cut is to drive rivals out of business. (Uniform price cuts do not violate the Act because they involve
no price difference). The concern is that selective price
discrimination by a powerful seller can eliminate competitors, discipline mavericks, or otherwise entrench the dis-

criminating seller's (or favored buyer's) monopoly power. This scenario will work, however, only if the subsequent monopoly profits exceed the costs of driving out competitors—a result that depends heavily on the existence of high barriers to entry and exit in the affected market. Because such predatory price discrimination seldom will be profitable, it is probable that the price discriminator is not acting with a predatory intent but rather with a desirable (i.e., competitive) purpose—to increase its sales, market share, and profits. Careless or overly vigorous application of Section 2(a) may yield price uniformity and may dampen rather than enhance price competition.

Primary line price discrimination cases generally arise when a national seller charges different prices for the same product in separate geographic areas. The question in such territorial price discrimination cases is whether the seller's price differentiation is competitive and lawful or predatory and unlawful. In Utah Pie Co. v. Continental Baking Co. (1967), the Supreme Court applied a stringent rule against aggressive pricing by national sellers. Utah Pie controlled two-thirds of the market for frozen pies in the Salt Lake City area. Apparently attracted by the high profits being earned in this market, Pet Milk (and two other large companies) entered with its own line of pies priced much lower—below those Pet Milk charged in nearby California and other markets. After its share fell to roughly half of the market, Utah Pie sued for treble damages, charging geographic price discrimination. The Supreme Court emphasized three factors in ruling that Utah Pie's evidence adequately supported a jury finding of probable competitive injury: (1) Pet had engaged in geographic price discrimination at prices "less than its direct cost plus an allocation for overhead" (a formula vaguely suggestive of an average total cost test); (2) Pet's "persistent sales below cost and radical price cuts themselves discriminatory" displayed an intent to injure its rival; and (3) Pet's conduct had produced a declining price structure in the market. The Court's reasoning perversely indicated that a national firm could face treble damage liability if it used price cuts to enter a market controlled by a local dominant firm. See Ward S. Bowman, Jr., *Restraint of Trade by the Supreme Court: The Utah Pie Case,* 77 Yale L.J. 70 (1967).

In Brooke Group Ltd. v. Brown & Williamson Tobacco Corp. (1993), the Supreme Court revisited the issue of primary line discrimination under Section 2(a). As discussed in Chapter 4, *Brooke Group* involved claims by Liggett & Myers that Brown & Williamson (B & W) had sold generic cigarettes below average variable cost in order to subdue Liggett's sales of generics. Even though B & W's market share never exceeded 12 percent during the relevant period, Liggett alleged that B & W's pricing strategy injured competition by reinforcing oligopolistic pricing in the concentrated cigarette industry. Liggett also argued that B & W recouped its investment in below cost sales by arresting the decline in sales of its branded cigarettes.

In rejecting Liggett's predation claims, the Supreme Court began its analysis by addressing the relationship between predation standards under Section 2 of the Sherman Act and Section 2(a) of the Robinson–Patman Act. After noting that the Robinson–Patman Act might offer "additional flexibility" to reach pricing conduct unaffected by the Sherman Act, the Court stated that "the essence of the claim under either statute is the same: A business rival has priced its products in an unfair manner with an object to eliminate or retard competition and thereby gain and exercise control over prices in the relevant market." The Court held that, to prevail on predatory pricing claims under either the Sherman Act or the Robinson–Patman

Act, the plaintiff must show that (1) "the prices complained of are below an appropriate measure of its rival's costs" and (2) the defendant could reasonably expect to recoup its investment in below-cost pricing. Liggett failed to satisfy the second requirement. The Court found that various structural and performance characteristics of the generic cigarette market following the alleged episode of predation (e.g., a rapid expansion of industry output, the divergence of interests among leading cigarette producers) foreclosed the possibility that B & W's pricing strategy would enable it to exercise market power through tacit coordination with other cigarette manufacturers. However, the Court specifically declined to adopt "a per se rule of nonliability" where recoupment is alleged to occur through supracompetitive oligopolistic pricing.

Brooke Group is an important shift in the Court's analysis of primary line predation claims. Adopting a view that had gained currency in the lower courts, *Brooke Group* requires plaintiffs in primary line cases to show that the defendant has a reasonable likelihood of recouping its investment in below-cost sales. See also A.A. Poultry Farms v. Rose Acre Farms (1989) (rejecting primary line claim where ease of entry ensured that defendant could not recoup its investment in localized price discrimination); ITT Continental Baking (1984) (ease of entry precluded recoupment); General Foods Corp. (1984) (market conditions impeded defendant from gaining, or threatening to gain, market power). The Court's emphasis on recoupment repudiates the view expressed in *Utah Pie* and some subsequent lower court decisions that primary line liability can be established simply by showing that the defendant set prices below its costs and displayed a predatory intent to harm a competitor. Compare Henry v. Chloride, Inc. (1987) (requiring plaintiff to show pricing below average total cost, but allowing a violation to be established with proof that defendant had a specific intent to injure a rival). Although the Court did not expressly overrule *Utah Pie,* the reasoning of *Brooke Group* renders the earlier decision virtually meaningless.

2. SECONDARY LINE INJURY

Protection of buyer-level competition was a principal reason for the 1936 amendment of the Clayton Act. Secondary line injury considers the effect of discriminatory prices given one buyer (e.g., chain stores) on their competitors (e.g., small stores) who cannot obtain the favorable price. There must, of course, be competition between the two buyers—between the one buying the commodities at the higher price and the other buying at the lower price. See DeLong Equipment Co. v. Washington Mills Electro Minerals Corp. (1993) (requisite competition found where two distributors located in different areas of the country competed for the same account). Thus different prices can be lawfully charged to customers of different functional classes; wholesale purchasers do not normally compete with retail purchasers. Similarly, customers who do not compete for sales in the same geographic market cannot generally suffer competitive injury. See Adcom, Inc. v. Nokia Corp. (1993).

Once competitive contact exists, however, courts have readily inferred injury from sustained and substantial price differentials among competing customers. Thus, in the leading case of FTC v. Morton Salt Co. (1948), a substantial price differential which could influence resale prices supported a finding of probable adverse effect. Later cases made clear that competitive injury is not established by a price differential so small as to be inconsequential in its influence on sales (and hence on competition), and also that injury occurs only when the differential existed for a sufficient period of time to affect competitors. Cases in which competitive injury from price discrimination has been inferred often have involved longstanding discriminatory pricing between competing customers in markets featuring low profit margins. See, e.g., J.F. Feeser, Inc. v. Serv–A–Portion, Inc. (1991) ("customer loyalty is compromised at two cents a case"); Rose Confections, Inc. v. Ambrosia Chocolate Co. (1987) (defendant's absorption of $309,000 in freight costs over two and one-quarter years).

Morton Salt's inference of injury to competition is rebuttable, even when there is a significant price differential. In Falls City Industries, Inc. v. Vanco Beverage, Inc. (1983), the defendant sought to avoid the *Morton Salt* presumption of competitive injury from a price difference by arguing that its lower prices had not favored large buyers and that it was not a monopolist. The Supreme Court rejected this view, repeating its stand that "injury to competition is established prima facie by proof of substantial price discrimination between competing purchasers over time." This inference can be overcome only by "evidence breaking the causal connection between a price differential and lost sales or profits." [3] The "causal connection" between price differentials and injury to competition can be broken in various ways, including evidence that disfavored purchasers have enjoyed commercial success and that the price differential constituted an introductory discount designed to attract

3. The *Morton Salt* presumption is less significant in private damage actions where the plaintiff must show a violation of the Act and actual injury to competition. See J. Truett Payne Co. v. Chrysler Motors Corp. (1981). The presumption applies only to the first requirement of a showing of violation. Actual injury to competition is unlikely because price competition (i.e., discrimination) usually intensifies rather than diminishes actual market rivalry.

new customers. See Boise Cascade Corp. v. FTC (1988) (disfavored purchasers enjoyed net increase in sales and profits); Motive Parts Warehouse v. Facet Enters. (1985) (differential prices excused as "new customer discount").

D. DEFENSES

Two major statutory defenses to a price discrimination claim involve meeting competition and cost justification. Courts have supplemented these protections with a related, judicially-conceived defense based on "functional availability."

1. "MEETING COMPETITION"

The meeting competition proviso in Section 2(b) makes discriminatory prices lawful when the seller acts "in good faith to meet an equally low price of a competitor." This defense is absolute—regardless of other injury to competitors or competition—and has been explained as "the primary means of reconciling the Robinson–Patman Act with the more general purposes of the antitrust laws of encouraging competition between sellers." *A & P* (1979); see also Robert T. Joseph & Blake T. Harrop, *Proof of the Meeting Competition Defense: Investigation and Verification of Reported Competing Offers*, 62 Antitrust L.J. 127 (1993) (meeting competition defense "may be the most potent device for sellers seeking to minimize Robinson–Patman Act risks"). The test for applying the defense is whether "a reasonable and prudent person ... [would] believe that the granting of a lower price would, in fact, meet the equally low price of a competitor." United States v. United States Gypsum Co. (1978).

In *A & P*, after a seller's bid was rejected by a customer as "not even in the ball park," its second bid was upheld even though lower than that of rivals.[4] The seller was not required to verify the competitive price in proving good faith; it was enough that the seller (1) relied on information from a reliable customer "who had personal knowledge of the competing bid," (2) had tried to investigate by asking the customer for more information, and (3) faced "a credible threat of termination of purchases" if it did not lower its bid.

In *Gypsum* (1978) (see Chapter 6), the Supreme Court held that defendants cannot justify direct, systematic comparison of prices, sales terms, and other services with competitors as being necessary to conform with the meeting competition requirements. All the Robinson–Patman Act requires is "[a] good-faith belief, rather than absolute certainty" that another seller has offered the buyer a lower price. In most circumstances a "commercially reasonable belief" that without a price concession the sale will be lost will be established by documentary evidence of competing quotes, corroborating evidence from other buyers, or buyer threats to stop making purchases. In any case, the meeting competition defense will not serve to insulate price-fixing or its facilitation from attack under the Sherman Act.

Finally, in *Vanco* (1983), the Supreme Court settled a long dispute among the circuits by ruling that a genuine price cut in response to prevailing competition may be made on an area-wide rather than individual customer basis. Relying on congressional intent, marketplace realities, the cost of individual customer assessments, and the need to protect vigorous price competition, the Court expanded the practicality of the defense by recognizing the good faith

4. *A & P* involved a charge of unlawful inducement of price discrimination by a buyer under Section 2(f). Because the buyer's liability derives from the unlawfulness of the seller's conduct, the issue in the case was whether the seller had a valid "meeting competition" defense.

standard as "a flexible and pragmatic concept ... [that allows] the prudent businessman [to] respond ... fairly to what he reasonably believes is a situation of competitive necessity." The seller cannot rely on a competitive price that is "inherently unlawful" or that knowingly undercuts a competitive offer. *Vanco* also established that the meeting competition defense may be available if prices are reduced to attract new customers in response to a competing lower price rather than simply to retain current customers.

Gypsum, A & P, and *Vanco* have expanded the availability and importance of the meeting competition defense. Some lower courts have further extended the application of the defense. In Reserve Supply Corp. v. Owens–Corning Fiberglas Corp. (1992), the Seventh Circuit ruled that a seller can assert the defense even if, in making a good faith bid to meet the competition, she in fact beats the competition. Lower court decisions also have indicated that sellers are likely to establish the defense more readily where they offer contemporaneous evidence documenting that they responded to the possibility of lost sales, as revealed by a customer describing a competing offer. See *Reserve Supply* (1992); cf. Alan's of Atlanta, Inc. v. Minolta Corp. (1990) (rejecting meeting competition defense where defendant failed to offer contemporaneous records identifying the perceived competitive threat and showing how its response was tailored to address that threat).

2. COST JUSTIFICATION

Section 2(a) permits an otherwise unlawful discriminatory price where the differential "makes only due allowance for differences in the cost of manufacture, sale, or delivery, resulting from the differing methods or quantities" in which the goods are sold. Thus, if the difference in two selling prices reflects only a difference in the seller's cost of supplying the different purchasers, regardless of the effect of such price differences upon other sellers or disfavored buyers, the seller's price discrimination is lawful. Cost justification is an affirmative defense, with the burden of proof resting on the defendant; it relates only to price discrimination and cannot rebut charges of promotional discrimination (under Section 2(d) or 2(e)). See David G. Hemminger, *Cost Justification: A Defense with New Applications,* 59 Antitrust L.J. 827 (1991).

In practice, the defense is difficult to establish because of its "rigorous requirements." Texaco, Inc. v. Hasbrouck (1990). To prove cost justification, the seller must group customers in meaningful functional categories with similar buying characteristics. It is critical that members within each group are reasonably similar with respect to the seller's cost of doing business with them. Thus, in United States v. Borden Co. (1962), the Supreme Court rejected a seller's attempt to differentiate between chain and non-chain retail grocery stores whose volumes of purchases were often similar. Later cases have focused on whether, in grouping buyers, the seller has in fact properly matched the supposed cost saving with the price difference and the cost saving factor is one of those identified in the statute.

Complex questions arise concerning the measurement and assignment of costs, particularly in times of exaggerated inflation or deflation and in cost allocations involving multinational firms or companies with multiple product lines. Due to these burdensome accounting obstacles, it is often better to characterize cost differences as a functional discount—i.e., one given to a purchaser based on services it performs in the seller's distribution system. In this context, the issue is whether the discount properly compensates the buyer for its distribution services. *Hasbrouck,* the most recent Supreme Court decision on this subject, left unresolved whether the reasonableness of a functional discount should be determined by the wholesaler's cost of performing the function or by the value of that service to the seller. See Francis H. Dunne, *Functional Discounts Under Hasbrouck and Secondary Line Competitive Injury,* 59 Antitrust L.J. 793 (1991).

3. "FUNCTIONAL AVAILABILITY"

The judicially created defense of functional availability recognizes that there can be no violation of Section 2(a) if the allegedly discriminatory price is practically and functionally available to the complaining customer. See FLM Collision Parts, Inc. v. Ford Motor Co. (1976). Similarly, some courts have held that the availability of comparable products at equivalent prices from other sellers may preclude a finding of price discrimination by negating causal injury. See Hanson v. Pittsburgh Plate Glass Industries, Inc. (1973); but see Fowler Manufacturing Co. v. Gorlick (1969) (availability from another party deemed not to be a defense).

CHAPTER XII

THE ENFORCEMENT AND ADJUDICATION PROCESS

The impact of any statutory command depends on how it is interpreted and enforced. The Sherman Act's chief innovation was to authorize public and private enforcement of prohibitions against restraints of trade derived from the common law (see Chapter 2). The federal antitrust statutes decentralize the power to prosecute violations to a degree unequalled by any other system of federal economic regulation. Enforcement authority is vested in two federal agencies, and the antitrust statutes also give standing to state governments, private firms, and individuals to seek treble damages and injunctions. The antitrust system also delegates broad authority to federal judges, who enjoy considerable discretion to shape litigation outcomes by interpreting key statutory terms.

A. PUBLIC ENFORCEMENT

1. THE FEDERAL ENFORCEMENT AGENCIES

Antitrust is the only area in which two substantial federal government bureaus—the Justice Department's Antitrust Division and the FTC—share enforcement responsibility for an economic regulatory scheme. The Justice Department has authority to enforce the Sherman and Clayton Acts. The Antitrust Division is headed by an Assistant

Attorney General, who is nominated by the President and confirmed by the Senate. The Department exercises its enforcement authority through civil and criminal actions. All of the Justice Department's lawsuits are brought in the federal courts. When it proceeds through civil suits, the Department can obtain equitable relief (e.g., an injunction forbidding specific conduct), or it can collect treble damages when it sues on behalf of the United States as a purchaser of goods and services. Section 4B of the Clayton Act creates a four-year statute of limitations from the time the claim for monetary relief "accrues." No statute of limitations governs suits for injunctive relief, and (unlike private parties) neither the Justice Department nor the FTC are constrained by the equitable doctrine of laches.

The Justice Department and the FTC rely extensively on consent decrees and orders to redress antitrust violations. These measures constitute judicial or agency approval of settlements and are as enforceable as any other court or agency order. As compromises, they are not authoritative and do not necessarily reflect the state of the law. The Antitrust Procedures and Penalties Act of 1974 (also known as the "Tunney Act") requires the Justice Department to give public notice of proposed settlements 60 days before the entry of a consent decree to solicit public comments. The Department also must file a "competitive impact statement" with the court, which may enter the consent decree as a judgment only if it finds that the decree is in the "public interest." 15 U.S.C.A. § 16. FTC consent orders must be published in the Federal Register for sixty days to obtain public comments. 16 C.F.R. § 16 (1993).

The Justice Department alone has authority to enforce the criminal provisions of the federal antitrust laws. The Department is likely to seek criminal sanctions when direct competitors covertly engage in naked output restraints and know of the probable anticompetitive effects of their conduct. Department of Justice, *Antitrust Guidelines for International Operations,* 4 Trade Reg. Rep. (CCH) ¶ 13,109, at § 3.1 (Nov. 10, 1988). The Department must commence its criminal antitrust suits within five years of the offense, 18 U.S.C.A. § 3282; but where an illegal conspiracy is continuing in nature, the limitations period begins to run only from the "last act" in furtherance of the conspiracy. To encourage disclosure of illegal conduct, the Department has adopted a Corporate Leniency Policy which grants amnesty to corporations that report antitrust offenses and cooperate in criminal investigations.

Nearly all Justice Department criminal suits have consisted of Sherman Act Section 1 cases against horizontal restraints such as price-fixing, bid-rigging, market division schemes.[1] In recent years the Department increasingly has pursued multicount indictments that charge defendants with Sherman Act violations and with other substantive offenses that arise from conduct providing the basis for Sherman Act prosecution. Commonly alleged collateral offenses include conspiracy to defraud the government, mail fraud, wire fraud, presenting false claims for payment by the government, and making false statements to government organizations and officials.

Criminal sanctions for antitrust violations have increased substantially in the past decade. The Sherman Act sets a maximum fine of $10 million for corporate defendants, and antitrust felonies also can result in corporate fines equal to twice the company's pecuniary gain or twice the pecuniary loss by victims, whichever is greatest. 18 U.S.C.A. § 3623. Individuals may be punished by fines of up to $350,000 and

1. Section 3 of the Robinson–Patman Act imposes criminal penalties for various violations of the price discrimination law. 15 U.S.C.A. § 13a. Prosecutions under this provision have been exceedingly rare.

by jail sentences as long as three years. Moreover, guidelines promulgated by the U.S. Sentencing Commission have made it more likely that judges will impose substantial fines and prison terms upon entities or individuals convicted of engaging in bid-rigging, price-fixing, or market allocation schemes. The Sentencing Guidelines create minimum fines of $100,000 for convicted corporate antitrust defendants and $20,000 for convicted individuals and call for individuals to serve a minimum of four months in jail, with provisions for probation. *Federal Sentencing Guidelines Manual* § 2R1.1, at 209 (1992). The Guidelines also provide that convicted organizations can be required to make restitution, forfeit assets, and be subject to continuing court supervision. Id. at 357–93.

The FTC shares responsibility with the Justice Department for civil enforcement of the Clayton Act. The agency is headed by five commissioners appointed by the President and confirmed by the Senate. Commissioners serve seven-year terms, and no more than three commissioners may belong to the same political party. Antitrust cases are developed by the agency's Bureau of Competition, with assistance from the Bureau of Economics. The FTC exercises its enforcement authority mainly through administrative adjudication, but the Commission also uses Section 13(b) of the FTC Act to file civil suits in federal district court for injunctive relief to preserve the status quo pending the conclusion of an administrative proceeding. To avoid duplicative investigations and prosecutions, the FTC and Justice Department use a clearance procedure to notify each other before commencing investigations and to decide which agency will handle specific matters.

The FTC has exclusive authority to enforce Section 5 of the FTC Act and its prohibition of unfair methods of competition. Courts have interpreted Section 5 as enabling the FTC to prosecute conduct that violates the letter of the antitrust statutes (including the Sherman Act) and to proscribe behavior that contradicts their spirit. The Commission's remedial authority is limited to issuing equitable decrees such as cease and desist orders. FTC efforts to use Section 5 to attack conduct beyond the reach of the other antitrust laws have yielded few contributions to antitrust jurisprudence. See Ernest Gellhorn, *Regulatory Reform and the Federal Trade Commission's Antitrust Jurisdiction,* 49 Tenn. L. Rev. 471 (1982).

The FTC and the Justice Department use policymaking tools other than bringing cases. Both agencies influence counseling and adjudication by promulgating enforcement guidelines such as the Justice Department/FTC *1992 Horizontal Merger Guidelines.* As a more recent illustration, in response to massive structural change in the Health Care Industry, the Justice Department and FTC in 1993 jointly issued six statements of their enforcement policies concerning such matters as mergers, joint ventures, information sharing, and joint purchasing involving health care providers. See 4 Trade Reg. Rep. (CCH) ¶ 13,150 (Sept. 15, 1993). Each agency also reveals its enforcement intentions through procedures that give business officials guidance about the antitrust consequences of proposed conduct.[2] Both agencies also advise other government bodies such as regulatory commissions and legislative committees about the competitive effects of existing or proposed regulations and statutes.

Although non-adjudication initiatives are important, the chief activity of the Justice Department and FTC is prose-

2. The Antitrust Division issues "business review letters," see 28 C.F.R. § 50.6 (1993), and the FTC issues "advisory opinions," see 16 C.F.R. § 1.1 (1993). These procedures tend to be time-consuming and do not preclude subsequent changes in the government's enforcement posture.

cuting cases. From the end of World War II through the 1970s, federal enforcement policy consisted of a steady campaign by the Justice Department against horizontal output restraints, a substantial number of cases involving distribution practices such as RPM (brought mainly by the FTC), occasional challenges to single-firm behavior, and relatively strict scrutiny of horizontal and vertical mergers. The enforcement mix varied over time—for example, featuring a large number of single-firm and shared monopolization prosecutions from the late 1960s through the late 1970s—but federal enforcement slighted few segments of the entire spectrum of horizontal and vertical substantive prohibitions.

From 1981 through 1988, federal enforcement patterns changed significantly. Building on the intellectual ascent of the Chicago School and on enforcement adjustments begun tentatively in the late 1970s, the Reagan Administration fundamentally redirected the allocation of federal antitrust resources. From 1981–1988, the virtually exclusive concerns of the federal agencies were large horizontal mergers and agreements between direct rivals to curb output. Reagan antitrust officials began three attempted monopolization or monopolization actions—the smallest number of such initiatives that the federal agencies had filed in any eight-year period since 1900. President Reagan's appointees to the Justice Department and the FTC initiated no cases enforcing prohibitions against price or nonprice vertical restraints and filed one case against price discrimination. The Reagan agencies brought no cases against conglomerate or vertical mergers and substantially loosened restrictions against horizontal mergers. See William E. Kovacic, *Federal Antitrust Enforcement in the Reagan Administration: Two Cheers for the Disappearance of the*

Large Firm Defendant in Nonmerger Cases, 12 Res. in L & Econ. 173 (1989). At the same time, the Justice Department and the FTC greatly expanded the proportion of resources dedicated to attacking horizontal output restrictions. During the 1980s, the Justice Department began more grand jury antitrust proceedings than it had pursued in the entire prior history of the Sherman Act.

The Bush Administration largely adhered to the Reagan antitrust agenda, but with some important shifts in emphasis. The Bush enforcement agencies filed four vertical restraints matters, ending a de facto policy of federal neglect. Bush antitrust officials also expressed greater skepticism toward arguments that their Reagan counterparts had accepted in foregoing challenges to horizontal mergers. The federal *1992 Horizontal Merger Guidelines* rely on post-Chicago economics to analyze competitive effects and tighten the requirements that the merging parties must satisfy (for example, concerning ease of entry) to overcome the presumption of illegality based on market shares. Both agencies also initiated somewhat novel horizontal restraints cases dealing with invitations to collude, attempted price-fixing, and facilitating practices to arrest conduct that traditionally has fallen outside Section 1 of the Sherman Act (see Chapter 7).

The Clinton Administration is expanding the Bush Administration's limited redirection of federal enforcement beyond the Reagan antitrust agenda. The Clinton Administration is pursuing four basic adjustments in previous federal enforcement policy: (1) reviewing horizontal mergers more stringently and reviving scrutiny of vertical transactions; (2) accelerating the revitalization of vertical restraints enforcement that Bush antitrust appointees tentatively began;[3] (3) initiating a significant number of single-firm exclusionary practices cases; and (4) extending Bush Administration initiatives to address facilitating practices and invitations to collude that fall short of an agreement to set output levels. Cf. United States v. Airline Tariff Publishing Co. (1993) (consent decree settling challenge to pricing practices of major commercial airlines under Section 1 of the Sherman Act). In each area, the Justice Department and the FTC will draw heavily on post-Chicago economics dealing with game theory, strategic behavior, and information (see Chapter 3).

2. ANTITRUST ENFORCEMENT BY STATE GOVERNMENTS

The Sherman Act was not America's first antitrust experiment. At least 26 states had adopted constitutional or statutory antimonopoly measures. From 1890 until 1920, the states used their antitrust statutes to achieve significant victories. Measured by the number of cases filed and the amount of fines recovered, state enforcement rivaled the Justice Department's early accomplishments in applying the Sherman Act. See James May, *The Role of the*

---

3. Soon after her confirmation as President Clinton's first Assistant Attorney General for Antitrust, Anne Bingaman announced that "[h]enceforth, the Antitrust Division will treat vertical price fixing as *per se* illegal." General Bingaman also rescinded nonprice vertical restraints guidelines that the Reagan Justice Department had issued in 1985 and criticized the 1985 guidelines because they "seem so thoroughly to discount the anti-competitive potential of vertical intrabrand restraints and so easily to assume their efficiency-enhancing potential as to predetermine the conclusion against enforcement action in almost every case." Anne K. Bingaman, *Address to the ABA's Antitrust Section,* reprinted in 65 Antitrust & Trade Reg. Rep. (BNA) 250 (Aug. 12, 1993). See also United States v. Canstar Sports USA, Inc. (1993) (consent order settling first Justice Department RPM prosecution in over 12 years).

States in the First Century of the Sherman Act, 59 Antitrust L.J. 93 (1990).

For the half-century following the end of World War I, state antitrust enforcement lapsed. Resource constraints, doubts about the constitutional reach of the state statutes, and the emergence of sustained federal enforcement stifled state antitrust activity. In 1961, one commentator said that state antitrust statutes "have been so dead that it may be wondered whether it would have been unethical in recent years for lawyers in most states to tell their clients to ignore them." James A. Rahl, *Toward a Worthwhile State Antitrust Policy,* 39 Tex. L. Rev. 753, 753 (1961).

The seeds of a major revival were planted in the 1970s, as over 20 states enacted new antitrust statutes, and federal grants enabled the states to create new, or expand existing, antitrust offices. See Ralph H. Folsom, *State Antitrust Remedies: Lessons from the Laboratories,* 35 Antitrust Bull. 941 (1990). Through the 1970s, the states prosecuted local horizontal output restraints and filed federal antitrust suits on behalf of state and local bodies which had been victimized by bid-rigging. The idea that states might play a major part in merger enforcement was alien to state authorities. In 1974, one state antitrust official observed that the Justice Department "is geared up to handle the larger investigations and actions which the states are [not] now, and probably never will be, able to handle because of the economics of the situation. The types of cases to which I am referring are the monopoly and merger cases.... We have to concentrate on the hard-core violations and leave the complex economic cases ... to the federal government." Michael Zaleski, *Utilization of State Laws in Anti–Trust Prosecutions* (1974), quoted in National Association of Attorneys General, *State Antitrust Laws and Their Enforcement* 45 (Oct. 1974).

In the 1980s, the Reagan Administration simultaneously reduced federal intervention in the market and decentralized political power by emphasizing federalism. As they retrenched federal antitrust enforcement, Reagan officials miscalculated how state attorneys general—many of them hostile to the Reagan agenda—would respond to the federal government's relaxation of antimerger standards and its abandonment of vertical restraints enforcement. To the Reagan Administration's dismay, the states sought to fill the gap by challenging mergers and distribution restraints (such as RPM) that the federal agencies regarded as benign or procompetitive.

State enforcement today proceeds along two paths. One is to apply state antitrust laws. See ABA Antitrust Section, *State Antitrust Practice and Statutes* 44–53 (1990). Most state statutes contain close analogues to Sections 1 and 2 of the Sherman Act, and the courts of many states rely on federal antitrust jurisprudence to construe these provisions. As of January 1994, twelve states had enacted antimerger provisions. State courts have declined to interpret provisions similar to Section 1 of the Sherman Act to serve as merger control measures akin to Section 7 of the Clayton Act. See State ex rel. Van de Kamp v. Texaco, Inc. (1988). State statutes usually allow the state attorney general to file civil or criminal suits and permit private suits for damages and injunctions. In addition to antitrust statutes, over 30 states also have adopted prohibitions on certain "below-cost" sales and allow enforcement through private suits. These statutes generally apply less demanding liability tests than those developed by the federal courts in adjudicating predatory pricing claims under the Sherman Act and the Robinson–Patman Act. See, e.g., American Drugs, Inc. v. Wal–Mart Stores, Inc. (1993) (finding liability under a below-cost pricing provision of the Arkansas Unfair Trade Practices Act).

The second path for state enforcement is to file federal antitrust suits. Private persons injured or threatened with injury by reason of antitrust violations may sue under Sections 4 and 16 of the Clayton Act to obtain damages and injunctive relief, respectively; a state and its political subdivisions (e.g., cities) are "persons" for these purposes. See Chattanooga Foundry & Pipe Works v. City of Atlanta (1906). In Hawaii v. Standard Oil of California (1972), the Supreme Court concluded that Section 4 of the Clayton Act did not entitle states to sue in their sovereign capacity as *parens patriae* to recover damages for injury to their general economies.

Congress tried to overcome this restriction through the Hart–Scott–Rodino Antitrust Improvements Act of 1976, which added Sections 4C through 4H to the Clayton Act. These provisions enabled states to seek treble damages as *parens patriae* for injuries to natural persons within their borders and sought to provide an alternative to class actions where many individuals each had suffered relatively small monetary harm. The Supreme Court severely limited the effect of this reform in Illinois Brick Co. v. Illinois (1977), which held that states could not invoke the *parens patriae* mechanism to sue on behalf of consumers who were not "direct purchasers" of the product affected by anticompetitive conduct. *Illinois Brick's* impact has been partly attenuated by state statutes (called "*Illinois Brick* repealers") that allow indirect purchasers in state antitrust cases to recover damages. In California v. ARC America Corp. (1989), the Supreme Court ruled that the federal antitrust statutes do not preempt state statutes which allow recovery by indirect purchasers.

States face fewer restrictions when they seek injunctive relief under Section 16 of the Clayton Act. A state can obtain injunctive relief as *parens patriae* for actual or threatened harm to its general economy. See *Hawaii* (1972). States also can obtain divestiture to remedy federal antitrust violations, such as illegal mergers. In California v. American Stores Co. (1990), the State of California had sought to obtain divestiture to cure the anticompetitive effects of a merger of two grocery store chains. Before the state's suit, the merging parties had accepted an FTC consent order forcing divestiture of some retail outlets. The state considered the FTC consent order to be inadequate and sued to compel further divestitures. The Supreme Court ruled that Section 16 of the Clayton Act authorized states and other private parties to obtain divestiture to remedy federal antitrust violations, but cautioned that "equitable defenses such as laches ... may protect consummated transactions from belated attacks by private parties when it would not be too late for the [federal] Government to vindicate the public interest."

Since the mid–1980s, state efforts to enforce the federal antitrust statutes sometimes have diverged from Justice Department and FTC case selection preferences. State officials have displayed greater skepticism about the benefits of mergers. Contrary to federal enforcement policy, a number of state merger prosecutions seem designed chiefly to protect employment within the state filing suit. See Pennsylvania v. Russell Stover Candies Co. (1993); Connecticut v. Newell Co. (1992). State enforcement officials also have favored more aggressive efforts to attack distribution practices such as exclusive territories, RPM, and tying.

The tension between these divergent enforcement approaches abated somewhat during the Bush Administration. Bush antitrust officials sought to establish more harmonious relations with the National Association of Attorneys General (NAAG) and its Multistate Antitrust Task Force. The Justice Department and the FTC adopted cooperative programs with NAAG to reduce duplicative requests by federal and state agencies for information from the parties to proposed mergers.

The Clinton Administration seems inclined to move still further toward accommodating state preferences. Nonetheless, an important degree of tension between the two enforcement regimes in their treatment of mergers and distribution practices may persist. The states view the populist perspective and economic structuralism of many pre-*Sylvania* precedents more favorably than their federal counterparts, and merger enforcement by individual states will continue to be motivated by the desire to block transactions that will move jobs out of their jurisdictions. In any event, state officials now see themselves as the equals of the federal agencies and will pursue their own enforcement agendas, regardless of how federal antitrust officials respond.

B. PRIVATE ENFORCEMENT

The Clayton Act authorizes private parties to sue for treble damages (Section 4) and injunctions (Section 16) to remedy federal antitrust violations. Successful private plaintiffs are entitled to recover reasonable attorneys' fees. (There is no fee-shifting for prevailing defendants.) Section 4B of the Clayton Act creates a four-year statute of limitations for private antitrust actions. The limitations period generally runs from the time the plaintiff suffers injury. Zenith Radio Corp. v. Hazeltine Research, Inc. (1971). If the plaintiff alleges concerted anticompetitive behavior, a new cause of action may arise from subsequent acts in furtherance of a challenged conspiracy. Section 5(i) of the Clayton Act provides that the statute of limitations for private suits may be suspended while certain federal government antitrust suits are pending and for one year thereafter. Under Section 5(a), private plaintiffs may use judgments or decrees entered against a defendant in a government antitrust suit as "prima facie evidence against such defendant ... as to all matters respecting which said judgment or decree would be an estoppel as between the parties."

Treble damages and attorneys fees have made the private action an important antitrust enforcement tool. From 1941 until the mid–1960s, the ratio of private to government cases tended to be 6 to 1 or less. From the mid–1960s to the late 1970s, private cases exceeded government filings by 20 to 1. During the 1980s, private filings fell substantially, and the ratio of private to public cases stabilized at roughly 10 to 1. See Steven C. Salop & Lawrence J. White, *Private Antitrust Litigation: An Introduction and Framework,* in Private Antitrust Litigation 4 (Lawrence J. White ed. 1988). Private cases also have spurred the development of doctrines that are crucial to the evolution of antitrust law—see, e.g., *Sylvania.*

Antitrust is one of several federal statutory regimes that give private parties the power to prosecute. The wisdom of using private rights of action to supplement government enforcement is a matter of extensive scholarly debate. Three basic arguments support enforcement by "private attorneys general." First, private enforcement enlists the help of parties closest to information about violations. For example, a commercial buyer of raw materials may best be able to detect suspicious, cartelistic bidding by suppliers. Second, private suits afford a safeguard against lax public enforcement that results from sloth or corruption. Third, a private right of action can increase overall levels of enforcement without expanding public enforcement bureaus.

Despite their potential benefits, private enforcement schemes—including private antitrust enforcement—also can have perverse consequences. Private enforcement can generate substantial numbers of frivolous suits, see Edward D. Cavanaugh, *Detrebling Antitrust Damages: An Idea Whose Time Has Come?,* 61 Tul. L. Rev. 777 (1987), and can enable firms to use the courts to impede efficient behavior by direct rivals or a vertically-related supplier or customer. See Edward A. Snyder & Thomas E. Kauper, *Misuse of the Antitrust Laws: The Competitor Plaintiff,* 90 Mich. L. Rev. (1991). Although private enforcement reduces the need to enlarge public enforcement bodies, private suits can consume substantial social resources in the form of costs incurred to prosecute and defend such cases. See Kenneth G. Elzinga & William C. Wood, *The Costs of the Legal System in Private Antitrust Enforcement,* in Private Antitrust Litigation 107 (Lawrence J. White, ed. 1988).

Perhaps recognizing these adverse possibilities, courts have established limits on the ability of private plaintiffs to obtain relief under the Clayton Act. One group of restrictions, treated immediately below, narrows the set of plaintiffs who may attack antitrust violations. These devices screen claims according to the type of injury alleged (requirements that the plaintiff suffer harm to her business or property and allege antitrust injury) and the plaintiff's proximity to the source of harm (limits on standing and recovery by indirect purchasers). See William H. Page, *Antitrust Damages and Economic Efficiency: An Approach to Antitrust Injury,* 47 U. Chi. L. Rev. 467 (1980). A second group of restrictions increases the evidentiary burden that plaintiffs must satisfy to establish liability. The evidentiary limits apply to public and private antitrust plaintiffs, alike, and are addressed below in connection with the role of the federal courts in the antitrust system.

1. INJURY TO BUSINESS OR PROPERTY

To obtain damages under Section 4 of the Clayton Act, the plaintiff must show that the defendant's conduct harmed her "business or property." The term "business" broadly encompasses "commercial interests or enterprises." See *Hawaii* (1972). "Property" includes any legally-protected property interest. In Reiter v. Sonotone Corp. (1979), the Supreme Court held that consumers who pay more for goods acquired for personal use are injured in their "property" under Section 4. Pleading requirements for injunctive relief under Section 16 of the Clayton Act are less stringent; the plaintiff need only allege "threatened loss or damage" by reason of an antitrust violation.

2. ANTITRUST INJURY

In Brunswick Corp. v. Pueblo Bowl–O–Mat, Inc. (1977), the Supreme Court established the requirement that the private plaintiff in a treble damage action show that its injury resulted from the anticompetitive effects of the defendant's conduct. In *Brunswick,* the owners of several small bowling alleys claimed that a bowling equipment manufacturer (Brunswick) violated Section 7 of the Clayton Act by acquiring bankrupt bowling alleys that competed with the plaintiffs. The plaintiffs argued that, had Brunswick not intervened, the bankrupt firms would have left the market, enabling the plaintiffs to earn higher profits. In rejecting these claims, the Supreme Court emphasized that the asserted injury flowed not from any reduction in competition, but from competition itself. For a unanimous Court,

Justice Marshall stated: "Plaintiffs must prove *antitrust injury*, which is to say injury of the type the antitrust laws were intended to prevent and that flows from that which makes defendants' acts unlawful. The injury should reflect the anticompetitive effect either of the violation or of anticompetitive acts made possible by the violation." See also Cargill, Inc. v. Monfort of Colorado, Inc. (1986) (applying antitrust injury rule to private suits for injunctions under Section 16 of the Clayton Act).

The antitrust injury requirement is an imposing obstacle for private antitrust plaintiffs. See Roger D. Blair & Jeffrey L. Harrison, *Rethinking Antitrust Injury,* 42 Vand. L. Rev. 1539 (1989). Among other effects, the injury requirement has attenuated the impact of nominally severe liability rules. For example, in *Arco* (1990) (see Chapter 8), the Court reaffirmed that maximum RPM is illegal per se, but it found no antitrust injury where the defendant had set the maximum price at a non-predatory level. In effect, the Court applied a rule of reason standard to determine whether the plaintiff was entitled to relief for conduct denominated illegal per se. The antitrust injury requirement allows courts to mitigate the impact of liability standards perceived as excessively harsh, or of the automatic trebling of damages, or both.

3. STANDING

Standing focuses on the plaintiff's proximity to the alleged harm. See William H. Page, *The Scope of Liability for Antitrust Violations,* 37 Stan. L. Rev. 1445 (1985). In Blue Shield of Virginia v. McCready (1982), the Supreme Court held that Section 4 of the Clayton Act gave standing to a health insurance policyholder (McCready) to sue her insurance company for allegedly conspiring with physicians to refuse to deal with a psychologist whose services the plaintiff wanted the insurer to reimburse. The Court observed that "Congress did not intend to allow every person tangentially affected by an antitrust violation" to maintain a treble damage action. To determine standing, it is necessary to examine "the physical and economic nexus between the alleged violation and the harm to the plaintiff." The Court rejected the defendants' argument that, because the concerted refusal to deal targeted the psychologists, McCready's injury was "too 'fortuitous' 'incidental' ... and 'remote'" to confer standing. Instead, McCready was "within the area of the economy ... endangered by the breakdown of competitive conditions, resulting from Blue Shield's selective refusal to reimburse."

The Supreme Court tightened standing requirements the next year in Associated General Contractors, Inc. v. California State Council of Carpenters (1983). There the Court ruled that a union lacked standing to sue an association of construction contractors and its members for allegedly forcing third parties not to do business with union contractors and subcontactors. The Court concluded that the union was not a "person" under Section 4 because it was neither a consumer nor a competitor in the market in which the challenged restraint affected competition. *Associated General* directed lower courts to analyze standing in light of five factors: (1) the causal connection between the antitrust violation and injury to the plaintiff, and whether the injury was intended; (2) the nature of the injury, including whether the plaintiff is a consumer or competitor in the relevant market; (3) the directness of the injury and whether claimed damages are too speculative; (4) the potential for duplicative recovery and whether apportioning damages would be too complex; and (5) the existence of more direct victims.

4. DIRECT PURCHASERS

Two concerns in the *Associated General* factors are the court's ability to identify damages flowing from the defendant's conduct and to apportion them to victims. These criteria relate to a distinct requirement that considers the plaintiff's proximity to the defendant in the distribution chain through which the defendant's goods or services reach end users. In *Illinois Brick* (1977), the Supreme Court ruled that the Clayton Act does not contemplate damage suits for illegal overcharges where the plaintiff does not purchase the product directly from one of the conspirators. Indirect purchasers ordinarily cannot recover damages under Section 4 by arguing that the direct purchasers "passed on" the overcharges to them. The Court feared that permitting indirect purchasers to sue would create intolerable administrative difficulties as courts sought to trace the amount and locus of harm throughout the distribution chain and to apportion damages to each claimant.[4] Uncertainty about the amount of overcharge owing to each plaintiff might "reduce the incentive to sue," and the complexity of tracing and apportionment could lead to duplicative recoveries, thus overdeterring various business practices.

Illinois Brick established a strong presumption that the Clayton Act's remedial goals are best advanced by allowing direct purchasers to disgorge all overcharges rather than apportioning damages to indirect purchasers. This presumption is not absolute. *Illinois Brick* indicated that indirect purchasers might be allowed to recover: (1) where

4. In Hanover Shoe, Inc. v. United Shoe Mach. Co. (1968), the Supreme Court barred defendants in treble damage suits from avoiding damage liability by arguing that the plaintiff-direct purchaser had passed all price-fixing overcharges on to subsequent purchasers.

fixed quantity, pre-existing cost-plus contracts enable the direct purchaser to pass on overcharges while being "insulated from any decrease in its sales ... because its customer is committed to buying a fixed quantity regardless of price"; or (2) where the customer owns or controls the direct purchaser. However, these exceptions have proven extremely difficult to establish in practice. See Kansas v. Utilicorp United, Inc. (1990).

C. FEDERAL JUDICIARY

The federal antitrust system gives federal judges considerable discretion to interpret the antitrust statutes (see Chapter 2). Judges exercise this discretion in three principal ways. First, they play a pivotal role in defining liability standards. Antitrust liability standards have changed over time, often in response to new economic learning and to shifting views about antitrust's goals. The adoption of price-cost relationships and recoupment tests to evaluate predatory pricing claims (see Chapter 4) and the movement from per se condemnation to rule of reason treatment for nonprice vertical restraints (see Chapter 8) are but two noteworthy examples of judicial modifications of liability rules.

Second, judges have defined which "persons" qualify to press claims for relief under the Clayton Act. The requirements that the plaintiff establish injury to her business or property, antitrust injury, standing, and directness are largely the product of judicial construction. Some screening doctrines are long-lived and, like substantive liability tests, have changed over time. See John F. Hart, *Standing Doctrine in Antitrust Damage Suits, 1890–1975: Statutory Exegesis, Innovation, and the Influence of Doctrinal History,* 59 Tenn. L. Rev. 191 (1992). Others, such as *Brunswick's* antitrust injury requirement, are recent creations. All bear the judiciary's deep imprint.

The third major source of judicial influence is the courts' ability to define evidentiary requirements that plaintiffs must satisfy to establish liability. The conservatism of Supreme Court antitrust jurisprudence since *Sylvania* often has taken the form of imposing formidable evidentiary requirements on plaintiffs. See William H. Page, *The Chicago School and the Evolution of Antitrust: Characterization, Antitrust Injury, and Evidentiary Sufficiency,* 75 Va. L. Rev. 1221, 1278–89 (1989). Several developments underscore this phenomenon. One involves the plurality requirement in Section 1 of the Sherman Act. *Copperweld* (1984) emphasized the basic distinction between unilateral and concerted action, and Supreme Court decisions in *Monsanto* (1984) and *Matsushita* (1986) have curbed the ability of plaintiffs to use ambiguous circumstantial proof to reach the jury. The Court also has undermined the *Dr. Miles* per se rule against RPM by holding in *Sharp* (1988) that plaintiffs must prove an agreement to set specific price levels.

Another illustration is the Court's suggestion in *Matsushita* (1986) that claims lacking economic plausibility are vulnerable to summary judgment. In *Matsushita,* the Court said that "if the factual context renders [plaintiffs'] claim implausible—if the claim is one that simply makes no economic sense—[plaintiffs] must come forward with more persuasive evidence to support their claim than would otherwise be necessary." Many lower court decisions saw this observation as a mandate to weed out claims that lacked a coherent economic theory. See Susan S. DeSanti & William E. Kovacic, *Matsushita: Its Construction and Application by the Lower Courts,* 59 Antitrust L.J. 609, 635–53 (1991). However, in *Kodak* (1992), the Court retreated from its position in *Matsushita*. In upholding a reversal of summary judgment against the plaintiff's tying and monopolization claims, the Court said "the requirement in *Matsushita* that the plaintiffs' claim make economic sense did not introduce a special burden on plaintiffs facing summary judgment in antitrust cases." The Court portrayed *Matsushita* as merely articulating the same "reasonable inference" standard that courts apply in all cases in evaluating arguments of the party opposing a summary judgment motion. In finding that the plaintiff had made an economically plausible claim, the *Kodak* Court relied on post-Chicago economic literature whose outlook varies sharply from the views of scholars cited favorably in *Matsushita*.

Judges do not consider issues of standing/injury, substantive liability standards, evidentiary requirements, and, ultimately, remedies in isolation. These considerations are closely interrelated, as the court can adjust its treatment of any single factor to compensate for the perceived inadequacies of another factor in the antitrust calculus. Judges can neutralize expansive liability rules by imposing antitrust injury requirements that effectively preclude damage recoveries by private plaintiffs or by defining evidentiary standards in ways that ensure that violations of nominally draconian conduct standards rarely will be proven.

Modern antitrust jurisprudence highlights connections that link issues of standing/injury, liability rules, evidentiary tests, and remedies. See Stephen Calkins, *Equilibrating Tendencies in the Antitrust System, with Special Attention to Summary Judgment and to Motions to Dismiss*, in Private Antitrust Litigation 185, 194–95 (Lawrence J. White ed. 1988). In *Monsanto* the Supreme Court feared that an insufficiently rigorous evidentiary test for distinguishing unilateral from concerted action would expose firms to treble damage claims for benign or procompetitive conduct.

In *Arco* the Court appears to have reconciled its evident doubts about per se condemnation for maximum RPM by endorsing an antitrust injury test that few private treble damage plaintiffs can satisfy. The Court's repeated refusal to abandon a per se ban against minimum RPM might result from a concern that repudiating *Dr. Miles* would elicit congressional backlash, and from confidence that the evidentiary tests in *Monsanto* and *Sharp* have placed only the clumsiest RPM schemes beyond the reach of potential plaintiffs. In these and other cases, federal judges have played the crucial role in orchestrating these factors and determining their net effect on business behavior.

D. CONCLUSION

To assess the antitrust significance of an episode of business conduct, one must ask a series of interrelated questions about the enforcement process. See Joe Sims, *Agreements Among Competitors*, 58 Antitrust L.J. 433, 439–41 (1989). Who is likely to challenge the behavior in question? For example, is there a risk of criminal enforcement by the Justice Department, or might the FTC use Section 5 of the FTC Act to reach behavior not condemned by the Sherman or Clayton Acts? Suppose the federal agencies decline to attack a merger. Will a state attorney general intervene—perhaps by invoking the Warren Court's expansive horizontal merger jurisprudence? If a competitor or customer sues, can she satisfy the threshold requirements of harm to business or property, standing, antitrust injury, and directness? Can the plaintiff bear evidentiary burdens essential to establishing liability, or are there evidentiary ambiguities or analytical weaknesses (e.g., economic implausibility) that may warrant summary judgment? Finally, what are the preferences of the judges who will hear the dispute? Judges control the gates—governing threshold standing/injury requirements, liability standards, and evidentiary tests—through which successful claimants must pass. Judges have considerable discretion to determine how freely each gate will open, and knowing what animates their choices can be crucial in predicting antitrust litigation outcomes. See W. Kovacic, *Reagan's Judicial Appointees and Antitrust in the 1990s,* 51–53.

CHAPTER XIII

LIMITS ON THE SCOPE OF THE ANTITRUST SYSTEM

The operation of the American antitrust system is not unbounded. Congress, state governments and their political subdivisions, and foreign nations have adopted numerous policies that displace free markets and frequently collide with the antitrust system. Moreover, by statute and case law, the jurisdiction of the antitrust statutes does not reach all commercial activity. This Chapter considers how jurisdictional restrictions and competition-suppressing actions by government institutions confine the application of the U.S. antitrust laws.

A. JURISDICTIONAL RESTRICTIONS

The geographic context and impact of commercial activity that is claimed to restrict competition raise threshold questions about the jurisdictional scope of the U.S. antitrust laws. The federal antitrust laws are grounded in the constitutional power of Congress to regulate interstate or foreign trade or commerce. The Sherman Act applies only to agreements or conduct "in restraint of trade or commerce among the several States, or with foreign nations." The Sherman Act reaches restraints which are "in" interstate commerce or which have a substantial "effect" on such commerce. See Mandeville Island Farms, Inc. v. American Crystal Sugar Co. (1948).

The Clayton Act (as amended by the Robinson–Patman Act) has a narrower jurisdictional scope and applies only to persons operating "in" interstate commerce. See Gulf Oil Corp. v. Copp Paving, Inc. (1974). An important exception is the Clayton Act's antimerger provision (Section 7), which applies to transactions satisfying the weaker "effect" test that governs Sherman Act matters. The FTC's jurisdiction under Section 5 of the FTC Act is comparable to that of the Sherman Act.

1.   INTERSTATE COMMERCE REQUIREMENT

The Sherman Act's interstate commerce requirement is easily satisfied today. See Andrew I. Gavil, *Reconstructing the Jurisdictional Foundation of Antitrust Federalism,* 61 Geo. Wash. L. Rev. 658 (1993). This jurisdictional element can be established by showing that the challenged conduct directly interfered with the flow of goods in commerce (the "in commerce" test), or that it substantially affected interstate commerce (the "effect on commerce" test). See McLain v. Real Estate Board of New Orleans, Inc. (1980) (holding that real estate brokerage has an appreciable effect on interstate commerce in residential financing and title insurance).

Under the "effect on commerce" test, the Sherman Act reaches a wide range of decidedly local behavior. In Summit Health, Ltd. v. Pinhas (1991), the Supreme Court held that the Sherman Act applied to claims that a Los Angeles hospital and its medical staff had conspired to exclude a single opthalmologist. The Court emphasized that if the alleged conspiracy succeeded, the plaintiff's exclusion would have curtailed opthalmology services in Los Angeles, which attracted out-of-state patients and generated revenues from out-of-state sources. Compare United States v. ORS, Inc.

(1993) (affirming dismissal of Sherman Act indictment for failure to allege facts showing a nexus between the defendants' market allocation scheme and interstate commerce). The small residuum of commerce that remains purely intrastate after *Pinhas* ordinarily is subject to challenge under state antitrust laws (see Chapter 12).

2. FOREIGN JURISDICTIONAL BARRIERS

With increasing frequency, antitrust disputes involve the extraterritorial reach of the U.S. antitrust statutes. See ABA Antitrust Section, *Antitrust Law Developments* 855–915 (3d ed. 1992). The Sherman Act applies to conduct that restraints trade or commerce "among the several States, or with foreign nations." Cases interpreting this limitation have concluded that the antitrust laws ordinarily do not apply to conduct by U.S. companies or foreign firms outside the United States where such conduct neither affects consumers or markets in the United States nor restricts export opportunities for U.S. firms. See McGlinchy v. Shell Chemical Co. (1988); see also Hartford Fire Ins. Co. v. California (1993) ("it is well established by now that the Sherman Act applies to foreign conduct that was meant to produce and did in fact produce some substantial effect in the United States").

In the Foreign Trade Antitrust Improvements Act of 1982 (FTAIA), Congress excluded from the jurisdiction of the U.S. antitrust laws conduct "involving trade or commerce (other than import trade or import commerce) with foreign nations unless (1) such conduct has a direct, substantial and reasonably foreseeable effect (A) on [domestic or import commerce], or (B) on export trade or export commerce ... of a person engaged in such commerce in the United States." 15 U.S.C.A. § 6a. Claimants who base jurisdiction on subclause (B) must show that the conduct involves "injury to export business in the United States." Thus, the FTAIA essentially immunizes American firms from attack under the U.S. antitrust laws for activity in foreign commerce where the only injured parties are foreign firms or foreign consumers.

Taken together, the FTAIA and judicial interpretations of the Sherman Act's extraterritorial reach allow courts to apply the U.S. antitrust laws to conduct arising in three basic situations: (1) where foreign firms take actions within the United States and in doing so affect the U.S. economy; (2) where foreign firms take actions outside the United States and those actions affect the U.S. economy; and (3) where American firms take actions outside the United States that affect the U.S. economy. To apply the U.S. antitrust laws extraterritorially, the plaintiff also must establish personal jurisdiction over the defendant and, in many instances, obtain discovery abroad.

Several judge-made doctrines have further limited the application of the U.S. antitrust statutes to transnational business activity. Since the mid–1970s, American courts have used the doctrine of *comity* in determining whether to apply the antitrust laws extraterritorially where doing so might damage relations between the United States and foreign governments. Where the law of the defendant's home country conflicts with the U.S. antitrust laws, courts will balance foreign interests against U.S. interests in deciding whether to exercise jurisdiction. See Mannington Mills, Inc. v. Congoleum Corp. (1979); Timberlane Lumber Co. v. Bank of America (1976).

In Hartford Fire Ins. Co. v. California (1993), the Supreme Court considered whether principles of international comity should preclude the exercise of jurisdiction over

British reinsurance companies which were alleged to have conspired with American insurance companies to limit certain forms of insurance coverage. After noting that Congress in the FTAIA had expressed no view about whether an American court should decline to exercise Sherman Act jurisdiction on comity grounds, the Court stated that American courts should refrain from exercising jurisdiction only where American law and foreign law truly conflict. The British reinsurance firms argued that such a conflict existed because their activities were legal under British law. Stating that "[n]o conflict exists 'where a person subject to regulation by two states can comply with the laws of both,'" the Court ruled that a conflict would exist only if the British law compelled the behavior in question. Without a conflict, there was "no need to address other considerations that might inform a decision to refrain from the exercise of jurisdiction on grounds of international comity."

A second limit on extraterritoriality is the *act of state* doctrine, which bars U.S. courts from considering the validity of sovereign acts by foreign governments where such acts occur in the foreign state. In W.S. Kirkpatrick & Co. v. Environmental Tectonics Corp. (1990), the Supreme Court refused to ban the application of the Robinson–Patman Act to the alleged payment of bribes to government officials in Nigeria to obtain a government contract. The Court ruled that act of state issues "only arise when a court must decide—that is, when the outcome of the case turns upon—the effect of official action by a foreign sovereign." The doctrine tolerates the application of the U.S. antitrust laws where judicial inquiry "involves only the 'motivation' for, rather than the 'validity' of, a foreign sovereign act." Here the act of state doctrine did not apply because the plaintiff did not challenge the validity of the contract issued by the Nigerian Government, but only questioned the motive (a possible bribe) for the agreement. Immunity under the act of state doctrine may be lost when the sovereign's acts are purely commercial in nature. See Alfred Dunhill of London v. Republic of Cuba (1976).

A third, related limit involves acts by foreign sovereigns. The Foreign Sovereign Immunities Act, 28 U.S.C.A. § 1602, immunizes foreign governments from suits challenging the acts of the sovereign. The Foreign Sovereign Immunities Act withholds immunity when the sovereign's acts constitute "commercial activity" carried on in the United States or undertaken abroad with a direct effect in the U.S. See Saudi Arabia v. Nelson (1993); Republic of Argentina v. Weltover, Inc. (1992). Courts also will not impose antitrust liability where conduct that otherwise would constitute an antitrust violation results from compulsion by a foreign government. See Interamerican Ref. Corp. v. Texaco Maracaibo, Inc. (1970).

Efforts to apply the U.S. antitrust laws to foreign firms have created tensions between the United States and its trading partners. Foreign governments have reacted warily to efforts by U.S. plaintiffs to obtain treble damages from foreign firms and to obtain expansive discovery overseas. Some nations have adopted laws that restrict discovery within their borders, limit the enforcement of U.S. judgments, or entitle firms to sue in the country's courts to "claw-back" from the plaintiff two-thirds of any treble damage judgment paid in the U.S.

At the same time, American policymakers have complained that foreign firms—sometimes acting with the encouragement of their governments—collude to impede American exporters from selling abroad. In 1992 the Justice Department announced that it would enforce U.S. antitrust laws against "conduct occurring overseas that restrains United States exports, whether or not there is direct harm to U.S. consumers." U.S. Department of Justice, *Statement of Enforcement Policy Regarding Anticompetitive Conduct that Restricts U.S. Exports,* reprinted in 62 Antitrust & Trade Reg. Rep. (BNA) 483 (Apr. 9, 1992). The 1992 policy statement reversed the position taken in the Justice Department's 1988 *Antitrust Enforcement Guidelines for International Operations.* There the Department had said it would not challenge foreign cartels unless there was direct competitive harm to U.S. consumers. While such policies are seldom tested in court, their validity (and application) are debated. For example, a foreign cartel to raise prices in a foreign country would seem to increase opportunities for U.S. exporters. On the other hand, a boycott refusing to deal with U.S. exporters could injure such exporters.

Congress has provided limited antitrust dispensations for export-related collaboration by U.S. competitors. The Export Trading Company Act of 1982 (ETCA) allows U.S. exporters to obtain a Certificate of Review from the Secretary of Commerce that immunizes export-related cooperation which neither substantially reduces competition in the U.S. nor substantially restrains exports by a U.S. competitor. 15 U.S.C.A. §§ 4001–4021. The Certificate shields the holder from all criminal and treble damage liability for conduct described in the Certificate while the Certificate is in effect. The ETCA's standards basically codify requirements established by the Webb–Pomerene Export Trade Act of 1918, which also confers limited antitrust immunity for the joint marketing activities of export associations. 15 U.S.C.A. §§ 61–65. Unlike the Webb–Pomerene Act, the ETCA applies to the export of services, including the licensing of intellectual property rights.

Fears about possible conflicts arising from the application of national antitrust laws to international commerce have led the United States to form bilateral cooperation agreements with the Commission of the European Communities and with various individual countries, including Australia, Canada, and Germany. These measures generally require each participant to inform other participants when it initiates an antitrust investigation that is likely to affect the other participants' laws, policies, or national interests. See Diane P. Wood, *The Impossible Dream: Real International Antitrust,* in Europe and American In 1992 and Beyond: Common Problems ... Common Solutions? 277, 293–97 (University of Chicago Legal Forum 1992). Such arrangements also provide a framework for coordinating the investigation of mergers that may be subject to review under the antitrust laws of several nations. In recent years, American antitrust officials also have encouraged foreign countries (most notably, Japan) to use their own antitrust laws to attack conduct in their domestic markets that restricts export opportunities for U.S. firms. See Abbott B. Lipsky, Jr., *Current Developments in Japanese Competition Law: Antimonopoly Act Enforcement Guidelines Resulting from the Structural Impediments Initiative,* 60 Antitrust L.J. 279 (1991).

B. THE EFFECT OF GOVERNMENT INTERVENTION

Antitrust is only one of many forms of government intervention in the economy. In some cases, regulation attempts to cure genuine market failures by, for example, controlling natural monopolies. In many other instances, however, regulation reflects successful rent-seeking by private economic interests and generally reduces consumer welfare by restricting output. Compared to individual firms, whose private agreements to curb output often are difficult to enforce, government bodies have superior tools—such as criminal sanctions—for punishing deviations from output-restricting controls.

This poses a serious dilemma for the antitrust system. On one hand, firms know that government controls can encumber rivals more effectively than private trade restraints. Manipulating the machinery of government—for example, by filing a meritless lawsuit or persuading a zoning board to pass ordinances that bar new entry—can impede entry without the expense of exclusionary strategies such as below-cost pricing. See Steven C. Salop & David T. Scheffman, *Raising Rivals' Costs*, 73 Am. Econ. Rev. 267 (1983). On the other hand, First Amendment guarantees of free speech and petitioning contemplate few limits on the ability of individual citizens or companies to urge public officials to adopt favored policies, including measures that reduce competition. In addition, federalism gives a substantial economic policymaking role to state governments— at least for activities occurring largely within their own boundaries.

The overlap of the federal antitrust laws with competition-suppressing statutes and regulations has required the development of principles to reconcile conflicting approaches for organizing the economy. These principles have emerged mainly in antitrust litigation that attacks: (a) private efforts to elicit government intervention, (b) government agencies for imposing regulations that curb rivalry, or (c) anticompetitive conduct of private actors who purport to act with government approval.

1. FEDERAL REGULATION AND EXEMPTIONS

a. *Basic Framework of Exemptions*

Antitrust exemptions that result from federal intervention in the market arise in two basic ways. The first is where Congress expressly declares that the antitrust laws do not apply, or apply only in a modified form, to specific conduct. Express statutory exemptions of varying scope exist for a number of industries, including agriculture, communications, energy, financial services, and insurance. See ABA Antitrust Section, *Antitrust Law Developments,* at 1024–1166. In a second (and small) set of cases, immunity arises by implication. Where Congress establishes a pervasive regulatory scheme that the application of the antitrust laws would disrupt, courts sometimes hold that the activity of regulated firms is impliedly immune. See Gordon v. New York Stock Exchange (1975). However, regulatory complexity alone does not create immunity. The Supreme Court has warned that "[r]epeals of the antitrust laws by implication from a regulatory statute are strongly disfavored, and have only been found in cases of plain repugnancy between the antitrust and regulatory provisions." *Philadelphia National Bank* (1963); see also National Gerimedical Hospital & Gerontology Center v. Blue Cross (1981).

The power to exempt conduct from antitrust attack resides with Congress—not individual federal officials. Without authority from Congress, federal officials have no power to exempt conduct from the antitrust laws. See Otter Tail Power Co. v. United States (1973). Firms usually cannot avoid antitrust liability by arguing that federal officials endorsed conduct that otherwise violated the antitrust laws unless the federal officials had actual authority to immunize the behavior. See *Socony* (1940); cf. Office of Personnel

Management v. Richmond (1990) (officials lacking actual authority generally cannot bind the government). However, the defendant's reasonable, good faith reliance on the approval of a federal official arguably should weigh against a finding of criminal intent in an antitrust case and should count in favor of applying a rule of reason (rather than a per se test) in a civil action.

Private plaintiffs sometimes have argued that cooperation between agencies of the federal government or combinations by federal officials and private actors constituted antitrust violations. Courts consistently have refused to apply the antitrust statutes to the acts of federal agencies or individual federal officials acting within their official capacity. See Rex Systems v. Holiday (1987).

Extensive federal regulation may have antitrust significance even if it does not create immunity. If a federal agency has substantial regulatory authority in a specific area, antitrust courts sometimes have ruled that the agency has *primary jurisdiction* over the dispute and have stayed a decision until the agency considers the matter. See Ricci v. Chicago Mercantile Exchange (1973). This permits the court to have the benefit of the agency's expert analysis without refusing the plaintiff recourse to the antitrust laws. The decision as to whether referral to a regulatory agency is appropriate is left to the discretion of the district court. See Lower Lake Erie Iron Ore Antitrust Litigation (1993). Whatever the agency's views, the antitrust court remains responsible for deciding whether the conduct violates the antitrust laws.

Regulation also can limit the remedies available in an antitrust case. The Supreme Court has held that treble damages are unavailable for private shippers who challenge, on antitrust grounds, the reasonableness of rates submitted to and approved by the ICC. See Keogh v. Chicago & Northwestern Railway (1922). Despite some misgivings, the Supreme Court recently endorsed the vitality of the "filed rate" doctrine, stating that *Keogh* does not create general antitrust immunity but only bars the recovery of treble damages in actions involving ICC-approved rates. Square D Company v. Niagara Frontier Tariff Bureau (1986). Compare Maislin Indus., U.S., Inc. v. Primary Steel, Inc. (1990) (confirming vitality of filed rate doctrine in non-antitrust dispute).

Finally, extensive federal regulation that fails to provide immunity nonetheless can alter the application of antitrust rules. Some cases recognize a regulatory justification defense to antitrust liability. In Phonetele, Inc. v. AT&T Co. (1981), Judge (now Justice) Anthony Kennedy wrote that "[i]f a defendant can establish that, at the time the various anticompetitive acts alleged here were taken, it had a reasonable basis to conclude that its actions were necessitated by concrete factual imperatives recognized as legitimate by the regulatory authority, then its actions did not violate the antitrust laws." See also MCI Communications Corp. v. AT&T Co. (1983). Other tribunals have relied on extensive government rate regulation to reject antitrust claims against public utilities. See Town of Concord v. Boston Edison Co. (1990) (emphasizing public utility regulation of wholesale and retail rates in rejecting price squeeze allegations under Section 2 of the Sherman Act). These decisions are important, because the deregulation of industries once subject to complete regulation of rates, service, and entry (e.g., airlines and telecommunications) has increased the number of antitrust disputes that arise where antitrust and other federal regulatory regimes intersect.

b. Specific Illustration: Organized Labor

Among the most important antitrust exemptions are those granted to labor unions and collective bargaining agreements. The Clayton Act sought to exempt unions from the antitrust laws, and this position was fortified by the Norris–LaGuardia Act of 1932. See Daniel J. Gifford, Redefining the Antitrust Labor Exemption, 72 Minn.L.Rev. 1379 (1988). Unions seek to improve the wages, hours, and working conditions of workers largely by monopolizing the supply of labor and policing concerted refusals to deal. See Robert H. Lande & Richard O. Zerbe, Jr., *Reducing Unions' Monopoly Power: Costs and Benefits*, 28 J. L. & Econ. 297 (1985). Without an exemption, antitrust would threaten the existence of unions. In Apex Hosiery Co. v. Leader (1940), the Supreme Court held that union monopolization of the labor supply does not violate the antitrust laws. One year later, in United States v. Hutcheson (1941), the Court held that union actions are exempt from antitrust scrutiny as long as the union "acts in its self interest and does not combine with non-labor groups" to accomplish its ends.

Unions ordinarily achieve their ends through collective bargaining agreements with employers. In Allen Bradley Co. v. International Bd. of Elec. Workers (1945), the Supreme Court declined to exempt a union bargaining agreement with electrical contractors to use only union-made equipment where the agreement was part of a larger scheme of bid-rigging and concerted refusals to deal by firms. Thus, a union's actions generally were not exempt when they facilitated a conspiracy among business officials. However, the precise limits of the collective bargaining exemption remained ill-defined. Compare Amalgamated Meat Cutters v. Jewel Tea Co. (1965) (upholding agreement between meat cutters' union and supermarket to set hours at which meat can be sold) with United Mine Workers v.

Pennington (1965) (Sherman Act may be violated by a showing of exclusionary intent where bargaining agreement obliges union to impose wage rate on firms not signatory to the agreement).

In Connell Construction Co. v. Plumbers & Steamfitters Local No. 100 (1975), the Supreme Court synthesized its earlier cases and declared that the labor exemption has two distinct branches. The first is a "statutory" exemption that protects only unilateral union activity and does not shield collective bargaining. The second is a "nonstatutory" exemption, which is a judicial effort to accommodate congressional policies favoring, respectively, collective bargaining and free competition in business markets. The nonstatutory exemption immunizes bargaining agreements that seek to remove wages, hours, and working conditions from competition, but does not protect agreements which restrain competition in business markets and which have anticompetitive effects not following "naturally from the elimination of competition over wages and working conditions."

In cases since *Connell,* courts generally have focused on four issues to determine whether the antitrust laws apply to union activities: (1) whether an employer-employee relationship exists and the union is acting as a representative of labor; (2) whether a union has combined with a nonlabor group; (3) whether the union is acting in its self-interest; and (4) whether the union's methods for serving its self-interest are more restrictive than reasonably necessary to achieve its goals.

In H.A. Artists Assocs. v. Actors' Equity Ass'n (1981), the Supreme Court upheld a system that required union actors to deal only with "franchised" agents as necessary to defend the union's wage structure and as designed to promote the union's self-interest. However, the Court struck down an agreement on the fees to be charged for the franchises as unnecessary to regulate the agents. In In re Detroit Auto Dealers Ass'n (1992), the Sixth Circuit ruled that the non-statutory exemption did not immunize an agreement among automobile dealers to restrict their hours of operation. The court emphasized that the restrictions did not result from a bona fide collective bargaining agreement, but instead arose from the dealers' efforts to avoid unionization by sales personnel over the issue of hours of operation. See also Powell v. National Football League (1989) (nonstatutory exemption applies beyond expiration of collective bargaining agreement and impasse in negotiations between sports league owners and their players).

2. STATE REGULATION

a. *State Action Immunity*

Since Parker v. Brown (1943), the Supreme Court has provided antitrust immunity for state officials and private economic entities who act pursuant to "state action" that limits competition. See Einer R. Elhauge, *The Scope of Antitrust Process,* 104 Harv. L. Rev. 668 (1991). *Parker* involved a California prorationing mechanism that permitted private growers and packers to cartelize the raisin industry subject to limited oversight by the state's agriculture agency. Despite the pivotal regulatory role of private producers in establishing and approving production quotas, the Supreme Court said that "it is the state ... which adopts the program and which enforces it with penal sanctions, in the execution of a governmental policy." Given this level of state involvement, the Court concluded that federalism precluded the application of the antitrust laws. See also City of Columbia v. Omni Outdoor Advertising, Inc. (1991).

The Supreme Court largely left the elaboration of *Parker* to the lower courts until 1975, when Goldfarb v. Virginia State Bar (1975) signaled the Court's willingness to narrow *Parker's* broad scope. In *Goldfarb* the Court withheld immunity for minimum fee schedules set by a county bar association and for enforcement of the schedules in disciplinary proceedings by the state bar. The Court termed this conduct "essentially a private anticompetitive activity," as neither Virginia's laws nor the rules of its Supreme Court required the minimum fees.

The Court provided the current framework for state action analysis in California Retail Liquor Dealers Association v. Midcal Aluminum, Inc. (1980), which articulated a two-pronged standard for *Parker* immunity: the alleged restraint on competition must be "one clearly articulated and affirmatively expressed as state policy," and the policy must be "actively supervised" by the state. In *Midcal,* an alleged system of RPM for wholesale wine sales rested on a clearly articulated state policy, but the state failed to exercise the requisite supervision over the process by which private parties recommended wholesale price levels.

Midcal's clear articulation requirement asks whether the state has clearly chosen to displace competition. In Southern Motor Carriers Rate Conference, Inc. v. United States (1985), the Supreme Court ruled that "a state policy that expressly *permits,* but does not compel, anticompetitive behavior may be 'clearly articulated' within the meaning of *Midcal.*" Thus, it is enough that the state policy merely authorizes (but does not command) departures from competition.

Midcal's active supervision element seeks to ensure that immunity "will shelter only the particular anticompetitive acts of private parties that, in the judgment of the State, actually further state regulatory policies." Patrick v. Burget (1988). In *Patrick,* the Court found that Oregon had exercised insufficient oversight of a peer review mechanism by which physicians determined whether to grant a rival doctor hospital privileges. For state oversight to constitute active supervision, state officials must "have and exercise power to review particular anticompetitive acts of private parties and disapprove those that fail to accord with state policy." Such scrutiny serves to ensure that states do not simply repeal fundamental elements of national competition policy without installing alternative, operational public oversight machinery. See William H. Page & John E. Lopatka, *State Regulation in the Shadow of Antitrust: FTC v. Ticor Title Insurance Co.,* 3 Supreme Ct.Econ.Rev. 189 (1993).

The Supreme Court revisited the active supervision issue in FTC v. Ticor Title Insurance Co. (1992), where it withheld immunity from title insurance companies that jointly set fees for title searches and examinations through rate bureaus subject to state regulation. The defendants' proposed rates took effect unless state regulators exercised a "negative option" to veto the rates. The Supreme Court said that the active supervision test requires an inquiry into "whether the State has exercised sufficient independent judgment and control so that the details of the rates or prices have been established as a product of deliberate state intervention, not simply by agreement among private parties." Several features of the regulatory oversight process belied the existence of adequate "independent judgment and control." In two states, the regulators examined rate filings for "mathematical accuracy" alone or left filings "unchecked altogether." In other states, the regulators failed to press private rate bureaus to comply with requests for information.

Ticor sought to define when nominal state oversight might fall short of active supervision. The Court said an "infrequent lapse of state supervision" might not eliminate immunity; oversight tools such as "sampling techniques or a specified rate of return" might provide the requisite "comprehensive supervision without complete control." Moreover, the Court said *Ticor* "should be read in light of the gravity of the antitrust offense [horizontal price-fixing], the involvement of private actors throughout, and the clear absence of state supervision." Despite these attempts at limitation, *Ticor* may pose difficult challenges for firms attempting to predict the effect of state oversight. Courts increasingly may be called upon not only to examine the structure and operation of regulatory procedures, but also to assess their efficacy. One can ask whether this evaluative task (akin to serving as a super-public service commission) suits the capabilities of the federal courts.

Other recent cases have explored the impact on state action immunity of affirmative misconduct by public officials. In City of Columbia v. Omni Outdoor Advertising, Inc. (1991), the Supreme Court ruled that there is no "conspiracy exception" to state action immunity where government officials form corrupt agreements with private economic actors. In *Omni* the plaintiff billboard operator claimed that a competing billboard company and various government officials had conspired to enact a zoning ordinance to prevent the plaintiff from constructing new billboards in Columbia, South Carolina. The Court refused the plaintiff's invitation to withhold immunity where the challenged government actions were not in the "public interest." Such a standard would be "impractical" because "[f]ew governmental actions are immune from the charge that they are 'not in the public interest' or in some sense 'corrupt.'"

b. *Local Governments and Other Political Subdivisions*

The decisions of political subdivisions such as cities, counties, and townships are not entitled to the same immunity from antitrust prosecution as the decisions of the state itself. See City of Lafayette v. Louisiana Power & Light Co. (1978). State action immunity based on the acts of a political subdivision exists only if the subdivision is acting pursuant to a mandate from the state itself. See Hertz Corp. v. City of New York (1993) (exercise of city's home-rule authority deemed not to immunize city law that barred rental car firms from imposing certain fees). In Town of Hallie v. City of Eau Claire (1985), the Supreme Court considered how the *Midcal* test applies to anticompetitive conduct by political subdivisions. *Hallie* involved a city's refusal to provide sewage treatment services to neighboring unincorporated townships unless landowners in those areas agreed to have their properties annexed. *Midcal's* clear articulation standard was met if "it was clear that anticompetitive effects logically would result from this broad authority to regulate." The defendant city's behavior was "a foreseeable result of empowering the City to refuse to serve unannexed areas." See also *Omni* (zoning regulation satisfied *Hallie's* "foreseeable result" test because "[t]he very purpose of zoning regulation is to displace unfettered business freedom in a manner that regularly has the effect of preventing normal acts of competition").

Hallie also held that states need not supervise their subdivisions' exercise of authority for state action immunity to apply: "Once it is clear that state authorization exists, there is no need to require the State to supervise actively the municipality's execution of what is a properly delegated function." Recent lower court decisions have concluded that *Hallie* obviates the need for states to actively supervise state agencies to create immunity. See Benton, Benton & Benton v. Louisiana Public Facilities Authority (1990).

The application of the antitrust laws to local governments in *Lafayette* and Community Communications, Inc. v. City of Boulder (1982) (Colorado's home rule statute held not to immunize Boulder from antitrust liability for its regulation of cable television) raised fears that cities might suffer massive treble damage liability. Through the Local Government Antitrust Act of 1984 (LGAA), 15 U.S.C.A. §§ 34–36, Congress barred antitrust damage suits against local governments and against private parties acting under their direction. The LGAA permits suits for equitable relief under Section 16 of the Clayton Act and allows the recovery of attorneys fees for plaintiffs who substantially prevail in such suits.

c. Preemption

State regulation must withstand scrutiny under the Supremacy Clause of the Constitution, which preempts state laws that are inconsistent with federal legislation. The preemption inquiry in antitrust cases has focused on whether state regulation clashes so substantially with the federal antitrust statutes that the two regimes cannot coexist. Preemption occurs only in cases of acute conflict and is a weak check on state regulation that displaces competition.

In Rice v. Norman Williams Co. (1982), the Supreme Court refused to enjoin enforcement of a California statute that allowed liquor importers to buy liquor outside California only if the liquor was consigned to a licensed importer. The Court held that preemption would occur only if the statute "necessarily constitutes a violation of the antitrust laws in all cases, or if it places irresistible pressure on a private party to violate the antitrust laws in order to comply with the [state] statute." The Court indicated that a facial inconsistency would exist only if conduct compelled by the state law is illegal per se—a condition found lacking in *Rice*. See also Fisher v. City of Berkeley (1986) (municipal rent control ordinance held not to be facially preempted by Section 1 of the Sherman Act; ordinance did not necessarily violate Section 1 "in all cases," mainly because the city unilaterally imposed the rent control ordinance and the concerted action needed under Section 1 was lacking).

3. PETITIONING

Antitrust cases that involve exemptions or state action defenses often pose claims based on private efforts to solicit government action that reduces competition. See Einer R. Elhauge, *Making Sense of Antitrust Petitioning Immunity,* 80 Cal.L.Rev. 1177 (1992). Guided mainly by First Amendment concerns, antitrust doctrine treats petitioning activity permissively and relies largely on other public policies to protect the integrity of the policymaking process. See *Omni* (1991). Thus, criminal laws seek to stop bribery, and other anti-corruption, lobbying, and campaign finance laws—along with public discussion and publicity—serve to insure that official actions reflect the public interest.

Petitioning analysis is grounded in three Supreme Court decisions issued in the 1960s and early 1970s. In Eastern R.R. Presidents Conference v. Noerr Motor Freight, Inc. (1961), the Court immunized joint efforts by 24 railroads and an association of railroad presidents to obtain legislative and executive action unfavorable to competing trucking firms. The Court emphasized that condemning the railroads' lobbying campaign "would impute to the Sherman Act a purpose to regulate, not business activity, but political activity, a purpose which would have no basis whatever in the legislative history of that Act." A finding of Sherman

Act liability also "would raise important constitutional questions" concerning the right to petition under the First Amendment. The Court cautioned that immunity might be withheld when petitioning activity "ostensibly directed toward influencing governmental action, is a mere sham to cover ... an attempt to interfere directly" with a rival's business relationships. In United Mine Workers v. Pennington (1965), the Court extended the principle of *Noerr* to efforts to influence government administrative processes.

Building on *Noerr's* admonition about "sham" conduct, the Court retreated somewhat from a broad definition of petitioning immunity in the third case of the trilogy, California Motor Transport Co. v. Trucking Unlimited (1972). There the Court sustained a complaint that a combination of the 19 largest trucking firms in California violated the Sherman Act when they opposed all applications (regardless of merit) by smaller truckers before federal and state agencies and in the courts. The Court ruled that the First Amendment does not protect sham conduct and suggested that the Sherman Act reaches misrepresentation or other unethical conduct more readily when used to subvert adjudicative processes, which are less able to protect themselves and where other constitutional values (i.e., due process) are implicated. Accord Otter Tail Power Co. v. United States (1973). With understatement, the Court said the boundary between legitimate petitioning and sham behavior might prove to be "a difficult line to discern and draw."

Subsequent cases have focused on defining the appropriate targets of petitioning activity and describing the contours of the sham exception. In Allied Tube & Conduit Corp. v. Indian Head, Inc. (1988), the Supreme Court examined collective attempts by a producer of steel conduit and independent sales agents to recruit persons to join a private trade association that set performance standards (which often were adopted by cities in their fire codes) for electrical products. The recruitment effort included packing the trade association's meeting with the steel company's employees for the sole purpose of voting against a rival's product (plastic conduit) without regard to the product's merits. Observing that *Noerr* immunity "depends ... on the source, context, and nature of the anticompetitive restraint at issue," the Court refused to immunize efforts to shape the standard-setting activities of a private trade association. The Court added that *Noerr* immunity might apply if the defendants' conduct, though directed at a private body, was mainly "political" rather than "commercial."

In FTC v. Superior Court Trial Lawyers' Association (1990), the Supreme Court withheld petitioning immunity from attorneys who collectively refused to represent indigent criminal defendants unless the District of Columbia government raised the fees for such work. After the D.C. City Council increased the fees, the FTC challenged the lawyers' actions as an illegal group boycott. In refusing to find *Noerr* immunity, the Supreme Court emphasized that the restraint of trade was not the intended consequence of public action (as it had been in *Noerr*) but instead was the means by which the lawyers had attempted to gain favorable legislation. Thus, the source of the higher fees was a private refusal to deal, not a government decision. The Court also ruled that the boycott's "expressive component"—i.e., to publicize the plight of indigent criminal defendants—did not preclude using a per se test.

In *Omni* (1991) the Supreme Court conferred state action protection on a zoning measure and immunized, under *Noerr,* the defendant's efforts to persuade the city to adopt the ordinance. Sham conduct "involves a defendant whose activities are 'not genuinely aimed at procuring favorable government action.' " By contrast, the *Omni* defendant clearly wished to exclude the plaintiff, but "it sought to do so not through the very process of lobbying, or of causing the city council to consider zoning measures, but rather through the ultimate *product* of that lobbying and consideration, viz., the zoning ordinances." Thus, the Court limited the sham exception to "a context in which the conspirators' participation in the governmental process was itself claimed to be a 'sham,' employed as a means of imposing cost and delay." The Court also refused to withhold immunity on the ground that government officials had conspired with a private party to stifle competition.

In many petitioning cases, the filing of vexatious litigation is alleged to be sham conduct. In Professional Real Estate Investors, Inc. v. Columbia Pictures Indus., Inc. (1993), the Supreme Court considered whether the defendant's action in bringing a single copyright infringement suit was sham conduct and thus supported restraint of trade and monopolization claims under the Sherman Act. To constitute sham conduct, *Columbia Pictures* ruled that the allegedly vexatious litigation must satisfy two tests: first, the lawsuit must be objectively baseless to the extent that no reasonable litigant could realistically expect to succeed on the merits. The plaintiff must meet this requirement to reach the second element of the test, which considers whether the vexatious suit conceals "an attempt to interfere directly" with a rival's business relationships through the process of government deliberation rather than by the outcome of that deliberation. Because the plaintiff had failed to disprove the legal viability of the challenged copyright infringement suit, summary judgment for the defendant was appropriate.

CHAPTER XIV

THE CHANGING BALANCE
IN ANTITRUST

The American antitrust experience has featured a fundamental tension between two views of the marketplace. One perspective regards markets as fragile, prone to distortion by private firms, and readily correctable through public intervention. The willingness to intervene often reflects confidence in antitrust's ability to achieve social and political goals beyond efficiency. The second view regards business rivalry as generally robust, doubts the efficacy of public efforts to cure imperfections, and emphasizes the relative ability of market processes to erode privately imposed competitive restraints or privately acquired market power. The second view disavows the use of antitrust to pursue non-efficiency aims and prescribes nonintervention unless behavior clearly harms efficiency.

When the previous edition of this text appeared in 1986, the latter view seemed ascendant. In the courts, such a trend was evident in decisions that treated vertical contractual restraints more permissively, imposed tougher evidentiary and standing requirements on plaintiffs, and emphasized reasonableness tests to examine behavior with plausible efficiency rationales. The Supreme Court punctuated this progression in 1986 in *Matsushita,* which doubted the dangers of predatory pricing and invited lower courts to weed out claims that lacked economic rationality. Even pro-plaintiffs' decisions such as *Aspen Skiing* (1985) focused on efficiency effects and relied prominently on Chicago School commentary such as Robert Bork's *Antitrust Paradox*.

As the courts moved rightward, so did federal enforcement policy. By 1986, the Justice Department and the FTC had embraced a nearly singleminded focus on prosecuting large horizontal mergers and horizontal output restrictions. New federal guidelines dealing with mergers and non-price vertical restraints departed dramatically from analytical techniques that the Supreme Court had endorsed in the 1960s. Budget cuts at both federal agencies—a decrease of about 50 percent in professional personnel from 1981 to 1988—ensured that federal enforcers would have resources to do little more than prosecute mergers and horizontal restraints. And the state attorneys general had moved only tentatively to fill gaps in traditional enforcement patterns created by the retrenchment of federal enforcement activity.

The future direction of antitrust appears less certain today than it did in 1986. Some recent Supreme Court decisions—e.g., *Kodak*—have downplayed Chicago School principles and have displayed a receptivity to post-Chicago economic analysis. State governments have brought vertical restraints and merger cases that the Reagan Administration and, to a lesser extent, the Bush Administration declined to pursue. And Bill Clinton gained the presidency on a platform that criticized Reagan/Bush economic regulatory policies, including antitrust enforcement.

Three institutional variables will determine how far the antitrust pendulum swings to the left of its mid–1980s equilibrium. The first is how the Clinton Administration changes public enforcement policy. The Clinton Justice Department and FTC are pursuing significant adjustments to the policies of Bush Administration antitrust officials, who adopted a more activist approach than their Reagan predecessors.   The Clinton officials are exerting greater efforts to prosecute vertical restraints (such as RPM), single-firm exclusionary conduct, vertical mergers, and horizontal mergers.   The federal agencies are relying more extensively on non-efficiency concerns (e.g., wealth transfer effects) and on post-Chicago economic learning dealing with game theory, strategic behavior, and information.

Despite these adjustments, most federal enforcement resources will remain focused on the prosecution of large horizontal mergers and horizontal output restrictions such as price-fixing.   This is partly a function of resources; budget constraints promise to foreclose a major expansion of the federal enforcement agencies, leaving relatively few personnel to address matters reaching beyond the Reagan agenda.   Experimentation with new enforcement approaches will focus heavily on horizontal conduct such as attempted price-fixing and price-signaling.   Moreover, the Clinton Administration's concern with the competitiveness of American industry is producing some loosening of existing antitrust controls, such as more tolerant treatment of cooperative ventures involving direct rivals (such as health care providers) and a more permissive approach to horizontal mergers in industries beset with substantial overcapacity (such as the defense sector).

Whatever their actual policy choices, the Justice Department and the FTC alone will not determine the course of public enforcement.   An important issue for the 1990s is how the federal agencies will respond to the emergence of state antitrust agencies as independent sources of antitrust policymaking.   Unless the federal agencies completely endorse the states' favored agenda of expansive vertical restraints and merger enforcement—an unlikely development, even as the Clinton Administration broadens federal enforcement horizons—state enforcement will diverge from federal preferences in a number of instances. In state merger enforcement, for example, where the decision to prosecute often seems motivated by local employment concerns, states are likely to continue to bring lawsuits that the federal agencies disfavor.

The possibilities for a lasting divergence between federal and state merger policies raise broader questions about how the American antitrust laws are enforced. No other scheme of economic regulation in the United States decentralizes prosecutorial authority so extensively, with standing granted to two federal agencies, 50 state attorneys general, and countless private companies and individuals. This splintering of decision making—indeed, policymaking—activity not only is difficult to justify in terms of antitrust's substantive merit, but in areas such as merger enforcement it has become a serious obstacle to devising sensible competition policies. A reassessment of the enforcement system usefully could begin with a reevaluation of the structure of public enforcement of the federal antitrust laws. Given the urgency to reduce federal expenditures and improve the efficiency of public administration, a fresh review of the respective antitrust roles of the Justice Department and the FTC is an appropriate place to start. See Ernest Gellhorn, Charles A. James, Jr., Richard W. Pogue & Joe Sims, *Has Antitrust Outgrown Dual Enforcement?*, 35 Antitrust Bull. 695 (1990).

The second institutional determinant of change will be the Congress. In the coming years, two types of antitrust-related measures are likely to command serious congressional attention. The first is a group of proposals to repudiate *Monsanto* and *Sharp* by easing the burden of proof that plaintiffs in RPM cases must bear to establish the existence of an agreement to set price levels. The second consists of bills to reduce the antitrust exposure of firms which cooperate with rivals to develop and produce new products. Congress recently has extended the protections of the National Cooperative Research Act of 1984 to include joint production ventures, and additional measures for specific industry groups may be forthcoming.

The joint venture measures and proposals to override *Monsanto* and *Sharp* display a troubling inconsistency in congressional antitrust attitudes. A central rationale for relaxing restrictions on collaboration by direct rivals is to enhance efficiency by enabling firms to appropriate the gains from inventive activity. Transaction cost economics underpins this analysis by explaining how such cooperation can frustrate free-riding by firms that do not directly contribute to product development efforts. At the same time, the *Monsanto/Sharp* repealers seek to reinforce the *Dr. Miles* rule of per se illegality for RPM—a standard that ignores transaction cost considerations that can make RPM an efficiency-enhancing strategy in many situations. Legislation that entrenches unqualified condemnation for RPM would contradict contemporary mainstream economic understanding of vertical restraints and undermine the attainment of the competitiveness objectives that appear to animate congressional efforts to facilitate certain horizontal contractual agreements.

A third institutional determinant of change is the federal courts. Next to persuading Congress to amend the antitrust statutes, a president's best means for durably adjusting antitrust policy is to select judges who share the president's vision of competition policy. Elections alter public enforcement policy, scholars propose new rationales for antitrust intervention, and private litigants propose novel theories of liability, but life-tenured judges control the gate through which most doctrinal innovations must pass.

Through 1992, Ronald Reagan and George Bush appointed two-thirds of the nation's federal judges, including five members of the Supreme Court. In the greatest retooling of the federal courts since Franklin Roosevelt's presidency, the Reagan and Bush Administrations sought to transform the judiciary's ideology by selecting individuals who, among other views, doubted the efficacy of government intervention in the market. The power to shape the courts was an enormous prize in the 1992 presidential election, and President Clinton has a major opportunity to place his own ideological stamp on the federal courts. By filling vacancies he inherited from his predecessor and filling positions created by retirements, President Clinton could appoint as much as 40 percent of the federal bench by the end of 1996.

In contemplating new appointments, President Clinton faces a judiciary whose antitrust views often reflect Chicago School thinking. This is largely a function of Reagan/Bush appointments, including prominent law and economics scholars such as Robert Bork, Pasco Bowman, Frank Easterbrook, Douglas Ginsburg, Alex Kozinski, Antonin Scalia, Stephen Williams, and Ralph Winter. In voting in antitrust cases, Reagan and Bush appointees generally have adhered more closely to a Chicago School agenda than judges appointed by President Carter. See W. Kovacic, *Reagan's Judicial Appointees and Antitrust in the 1990s,* at 82–114. Their presence on the federal bench will operate as an important constraint on the efforts of Clinton Administration antitrust officials to expand the frontiers of public enforcement.

Commentators often attribute the retrenchment of antitrust doctrine since the mid–1970s to the appointment of conservative judges, but the Chicago-oriented retrenchment in antitrust would not have been so strong or widespread without the support of many judges not ordinarily associated with hostility to government intervention. Consider the antitrust votes of two of the Supreme Court's more liberal members in the post-World War II era—William Brennan and Thurgood Marshall. From 1977 onward, these jurists were instrumental in imposing severe restrictions on private antitrust plaintiffs. Justice Marshall introduced the "antitrust injury" requirement in his *Brunswick* opinion, and Justice Brennan's opinions in *Cargill* and *Arco* significantly extended the application of this doctrine. Marshall voted with the Court majority in *Monsanto, Matsushita, Cargill, Sharp,* and *Arco* ; Brennan likewise endorsed the results in *Monsanto* and *Sharp.* Modern, judicially-led efforts to curtail the private antitrust suit could not have been so broad and effective if liberals on the Supreme Court and in the lower courts had not given their support.

The crucial significance of judicial appointments is evident in President Clinton's choice of a successor to replace Justice Byron White, who retired from the Court in 1993. Justice White left a mixed antitrust legacy. He authored some of the best and the worst of the Court's antitrust opinions over the past thirty years. Both sets of opinions help define the challenges facing the courts in determining antitrust's future path.

In the debit category, Justice White wrote *Utah Pie* and *Albrecht.* Few decisions have attracted more scorn, yet the Court has never overruled them. Instead, they belong to antitrust's "mothball fleet"—a flotilla of dormant cases whose logic or impact the Court has severely undercut, but whose holdings the Court has not overruled. See Richard M. Steuer, *Monsanto and the Mothball Fleet of Antitrust,* 30 Antitrust Bull. 1 (1985). The ideological preferences of

President Clinton's appointees will play an important part in determining whether the judiciary eventually scraps the mothball fleet, leaves it moored harmlessly in port, or allows it to sail again on behalf of antitrust plaintiffs.

Criticism of *Utah Pie* and *Albrecht* is offset by praise for Justice White's opinions in *BMI* and *Indiana Federation of Dentists*. The latter opinions recognize that classification schemes which fail to account properly for market phenomena harmfully distort doctrine and analysis. Justice White scorned formalistic labels that misapprehend the market effect of various business practices. In doing so, he spurred a much needed reassessment of the relationship between per se condemnation and rule of reason analysis. Despite Justice White's substantial contributions, one of antitrust's greatest needs today remains the clarification of the content of reasonableness standards and of the role of per se tests within the coverage of the rule of reason enunciated by Chief Justice Edward White in *Standard Oil (N.J.)* in 1911.

Through his appointments, President Clinton can deeply influence future judicial efforts to grapple with the per se/rule of reason dichotomy and similarly difficult analytical challenges. His first appointee to the Supreme Court, Justice Ruth Ginsburg, and the process that led to her selection provide an interesting glimpse of where the mainstream of judicial analysis is today and where the future path of doctrine is likely to lead. Justice Ginsburg was one of several court of appeals judges—others included Stephen Breyer, Amalya Kearse, and Jon Newman—who were appointees of President Carter and were candidates for President Clinton's first nomination to the Court.

A striking characteristic of the judges named above is that each has compiled a conservative voting record in antitrust cases. See William E. Kovacic, *Judicial Appointments and the Future of Antitrust Policy,* 7 Antitrust 8

(Spring 1993). As a member of the D.C. Circuit, Justice Ginsburg joined Robert Bork's opinion in *Rothery* (1986) and Clarence Thomas's opinion in *Baker Hughes* (1990), both of which have strongly pro-defendant implications. *Baker Hughes* in particular looms as a major obstacle to government efforts to adopt more stringent horizontal merger policies—both for its analysis and its suggestion of how Justices Ginsburg and Thomas might vote on merger cases before the Supreme Court.

Critics of cases such as *Rothery* and *Baker Hughes* often dismiss such decisions as the product of conservative "court-packing" that enabled Reagan appointees such as Bork and Bush nominees such as Thomas to embed a permissive, pro-business philosophy in the law. This critique understates the extent to which Chicago School antitrust views about antitrust are widely held among federal judges, including many of Jimmy Carter's appointees. Nor can this pattern be dismissed as the clever manipulation of naive jurists. Stephen Breyer, Ruth Ginsburg, Amalya Kearse, and Jon Newman are formidable analysts and are unlikely to succumb to intellectual slight of hand by advocates who promote permissive antitrust standards.

Justice Ginsburg's appointment to the Court is both a tacit recognition that antitrust ideas once deemed extreme have become mainstream judicial views, and an indirect acknowledgment that the conservative course of much antitrust doctrine and analysis since the late 1970s involved more than brute force applications of ideology by Reagan and Bush judges. In the near and medium terms, widespread acceptance of Chicago School views throughout the federal judiciary will impede efforts by public enforcement agencies and private plaintiffs to persuade courts to endorse an expansion of existing liability standards or a weakening of prevailing evidentiary and injury requirements.

APPENDIX

SHERMAN ACT [1]

§ 1. Every contract, combination in the form of trust or otherwise, or conspiracy, in restraint of trade or commerce among the several States, or with foreign nations, is declared to be illegal. Every person who shall make any contract or engage in any combination or conspiracy hereby declared to be illegal shall be deemed guilty of a felony, and, on conviction thereof, shall be punished by fine not exceeding $10,000,000 if a corporation, or, if any other person, $350,000, or by imprisonment not exceeding three years, or by both said punishments, in the discretion of the court. [15 U.S.C.A. § 1]

§ 2. Every person who shall monopolize, or attempt to monopolize, or combine or conspire with any other person or persons, to monopolize any part of the trade or commerce among the several States, or with foreign nations, shall be deemed guilty of a felony, and, on conviction thereof, shall be punished by fine not exceeding $10,000,000 if a corporation, or, if any other person, $350,000, or by imprisonment not exceeding three years, or by both said punishments, in the discretion of the court. [15 U.S.C.A. § 2]

1. 26 Stat. 209 (1890), as amended, 15 U.S.C.A. §§ 1–7. Only selected sections are reprinted.

CLAYTON ACT [2]

§ 2. (a) It shall be unlawful for any person engaged in commerce, in the course of such commerce, either directly or indirectly, to discriminate in price between different purchasers of commodities of like grade and quality, where either or any of the purchases involved in such discrimination are in commerce, where such commodities are sold for use, consumption, or resale within the United States or any Territory thereof or the District of Columbia or any insular possession or other place under the jurisdiction of the United States, and where the effect of such discrimination may be substantially to lessen competition or tend to create a monopoly in any line of commerce, or to injure, destroy, or prevent competition with any person who either grants or knowingly receives the benefit of such discrimination, or with customers of either of them: *Provided,* That nothing herein contained shall prevent differentials which make only due allowance for differences in the cost of manufacture, sale, or delivery resulting from the differing methods or quantities in which such commodities are to such purchasers sold or delivered ... *And provided further,* That nothing herein contained shall prevent price changes from time to time where in response to changing conditions affecting the market for or the marketability of the goods concerned, such as but not limited to actual or imminent deterioration of perishable goods, obsolescence of seasonal goods, distress sales under court process, or sales in good faith in discontinuance of business in the goods concerned. [15 U.S.C.A. § 13(a)]

(b) ... nothing herein contained shall prevent a seller rebutting the prima facie case thus made by showing that

2. 38 Stat. 730 (1914), as amended, 15 U.S.C.A. §§ 12–27. Only selected sections are reprinted.

his lower price or the furnishing of services or facilities to any purchaser or purchasers was made in good faith to meet an equally low price of a competitor, or the services or facilities furnished by a competitor. [15 U.S.C.A. § 13(b)]

(c) It shall be unlawful for any person engaged in commerce, in the course of such commerce, to pay or grant, or to receive or accept, anything of value as a commission, brokerage, or other compensation, or any allowance or discount in lieu thereof, except for services rendered in connection with the sale or purchase of goods, wares, or merchandise, either to the other party to such transaction or to an agent, representative, or other intermediary therein where such intermediary is acting in fact for or in behalf, or is subject to the direct or indirect control, of any party to such transaction other than the person by whom such compensation is so granted or paid. [15 U.S.C.A. § 13(c)]

(d) It shall be unlawful for any person engaged in commerce to pay or contract for the payment of anything of value to or for the benefit of a customer of such person in the course of such commerce as compensation or in consideration for any services or facilities furnished by or through such customer in connection with the processing, handling, sale, or offering for sale of any products or commodities manufactured, sold, or offered for sale by such person, unless such payment or consideration is available on proportionally equal terms to all other customers competing in the distribution of such products or commodities. [15 U.S.C.A. § 13(d)]

(e) It shall be unlawful for any person to discriminate in favor of one purchaser against another purchaser or purchasers of a commodity bought for resale, with or without processing, by contracting to furnish or furnishing, or by contributing to the furnishing of, any services or facilities connected with the processing, handling, sale, or offering for sale of such commodity so purchased upon terms not accorded to all purchasers on proportionally equal terms. [15 U.S.C.A. § 13(e)]

(f) It shall be unlawful for any person engaged in commerce, in the course of such commerce, knowingly to induce or receive a discrimination in price which is prohibited by this section. [15 U.S.C.A. § 13(f)]

§ 3. It shall be unlawful for any person engaged in commerce, in the course of such commerce, to lease or make a sale or contract for sale of goods, wares, merchandise, machinery, supplies, or other commodities, whether patented or unpatented, for use, consumption, or resale within the United States or any Territory thereof or the District of Columbia or any insular possession or other place under the jurisdiction of the United States, or fix a price charged therefor, or discount from, or rebate upon, such price, on the condition, agreement, or understanding that the lessee or purchaser thereof shall not use or deal in the goods, wares, merchandise, machinery, supplies, or other commodities of a competitor or competitors of the lessor or seller, where the effect of such lease, sale, or contract for sale or such condition, agreement, or understanding may be to substantially lessen competition or tend to create a monopoly in any line of commerce. [15 U.S.C.A. § 14]

§ 7. No person engaged in commerce or in any activity affecting commerce shall acquire, directly or indirectly, the whole or any part of the stock or other share capital and no person subject to the jurisdiction of the Federal Trade Commission shall acquire the whole or any part of the assets of another person engaged also in commerce or in any activity affecting commerce, where in any line of commerce or in any activity affecting commerce in any section of the country, the effect of such acquisition may be substantially to lessen competition, or to tend to create a monopoly....   [15 U.S.C.A. § 18]

FEDERAL TRADE COMMISSION ACT [3]

3.   38 Stat. 717 (1914), as amended, 15 U.S.C.A. §§ 41–58.   Only one provision is reprinted.

INDEX

References are to Pages

511

References are to Pages

†